D1713790

# THE THEOLOGY OF HULDRYCH ZWINGLI

# THE THEOLOGY OF

# HULDRYCH ZWINGLI

❧

W. P. STEPHENS

*Clarendon Press* · *Oxford*
1986

Oxford University Press, Walton Street, Oxford OX2 6DP
Oxford New York Toronto
Delhi Bombay Calcutta Madras Karachi
Kuala Lumpur Singapore Hong Kong Tokyo
Nairobi Dar es Salaam Cape Town
Melbourne Auckland
and associated companies in
Beirut Berlin Ibadan Nicosia

Oxford is a trade mark of Oxford University Press

Published in the United States
by Oxford University Press, New York

British Library Cataloguing in Publication Data
Stephens, W. P.
The Theology of Huldrych Zwingli.
1. Zwingli, Ulrich—Contributions in doctrinal
theology    2. Theology, Doctrinal—History—
16th century
I. Title
230'.092'4    BR345
ISBN 0-19-826677-4

Library of Congress Cataloging in Publication Data
Stephens, W. P. (W. Peter)
The theology of Huldrych Zwingli.
Bibliography: p.
Includes index.
1. Zwingli, Ulrich, 1484–1531.    I. Title.
BR345.S74  1985    230'.42'0924    85-13822
ISBN 0-19-826677-4

Set by Joshua Associates Limited, Oxford
Printed and bound in Great Britain by
Biddles Ltd, Guildford and King's Lynn

*To my Brother and Sisters*

# Preface

THIS book grew out of the Fernley Hartley Lecture, given at the Methodist Conference in Nottingham in 1972. Many factors have delayed its completion, but others have helped it on its way, in particular a year's research fellowship at The Queen's College, Birmingham.

My indebtedness to others began with a period of research on Zwingli in Zurich in 1958, which brought me into contact with an earlier generation of Zwingli scholars in Oskar Farner, whom I met only a week before his death, and Fritz Blanke. Since then I have been grateful to several scholars in Switzerland for their help in obtaining books and articles not available in England: Professor Fritz Büsser, Professor Rudolf Pfister, and Dr Peter Stotz in Zurich, Professor Gottfried W. Locher in Berne, and Professor H. Wayne Pipkin and Herr Christoph Weichert in Rüschlikon. On my visits to Switzerland I have benefited greatly from the hospitality and facilities of the Institut für Schweizerische Reformationsgeschichte in Zurich and the Baptist Theological Seminary in Rüschlikon. I should like to express my thanks to the British Academy for a grant towards this work and to the Emil Brunner Stiftung for a grant towards publication. I owe an especial debt to Mrs Sheila Howard for her work in reading and typing the manuscript.

*The Queen's College*
*Birmingham*
*Easter Day 1984*

PETER STEPHENS

# Contents

CONTENTS

# Abbreviations

| | |
|---|---|
| ARG | *Archiv für Reformationsgeschichte* (Berlin, 1903– ) |
| BW | *Martin Bucers Deutsche Schriften* (Gütersloh and Paris, 1960– ) |
| CR | *Corpus Reformatorum* (Brunswick, 1834–1900) |
| DTC | *Dictionnaire de Théologie catholique* (15 vols., Paris, 1930–50) |
| LCC | The Library of Christian Classics (26 vols., London, 1953–70) |
| MQR | *Mennonite Quarterly Review* (Goshen, Indiana, 1927– ) |
| PL | *Patrologiae cursus completus accurante J. P. Migne* (Series Latina) (221 vols., Paris, 1857–79) |
| S | *Huldreich Zwingli's Werks*, Erste vollständige Ausgabe durch Melchior Schuler und Joh. Schulthess (8 vols., Zurich, 1828–42) |
| WA | *D. Martin Luthers Werke*, Kritische Gesamtausgabe (Weimar, 1883– ) |
| Z | *Huldreich Zwinglis Sämtliche Werke* (Berlin, Leipzig, Zurich, 1905– ) |
| ZKG | *Zeitschrift für Kirchengeschichte* (Gotha, 1877– ) |
| ZWA | *Zwingliana. Beiträge zur Geschichte Zwinglis, der Reformation und des Protestantismus in der Schweiz* (Zurich, 1897– ) |

# Note on Zwingli's Works

THE works are cited, where possible, from the modern critical edition. So far fourteen volumes have been published, volume VI in three parts. These are volumes 88–101 of the Corpus Reformatorum. They are referred to by the letter *Z*, followed by the number of the volume (from I to XIV)—with volume VI also by the number of the part of the volume (i to iii)—and then by the number of the page and the line. Where Zwingli's works have not been published in this edition they are usually cited from the nineteenth-century edition of Schuler and Schulthess. They are referred to by the letter *S*, followed by the number of the volume (I to VIII)—with volumes II and VI also by the number of the part of the volume (i, ii, or iii)— and then by the number of the page and the line.

Some works have been published in a modern popular edition *Zwingli Hauptschriften* (Zurich, 1940–63). Volumes 1–4, 7, 9–11 have been published. In this edition the Latin works have been translated into German. In 1957 Oskar Farner published in Zurich two volumes of translated selections from Zwingli's sermons, *Aus Zwinglis Predigten zu Jesaja und Jeremia* and *Aus Zwinglis Predigten zu Matthäus, Markus and Johannes*.

Five volumes of English translations have appeared, three of which have recently been reprinted: S. M. Jackson, *The Selected Works of Huldreich Zwingli* (Philadelphia, 1901, repr. 1972), *The Latin Works and the Correspondence of Huldreich Zwingli*, Vol. I: 1510–1522 (New York, 1912); W. J. Hinke, *The Latin Works of Huldreich Zwingli*, Vol. II (Philadelphia, 1922, repr. as *Zwingli on Providence and Other Essays*, Durham, NC, 1983); C. N. Heller, *The Latin Works of Huldreich Zwingli*, Vol. III (Philadelphia, 1929, repr. as *Commentary on True and False Religion*, Durham, NC, 1981); G. W. Bromiley, *Zwingli and Bullinger* (Library of Christian Classics, XXIV) (London, 1953). These are referred to as *Selected Works*, *Works* I, *Works* II, *Works* III, LCC XXIV, followed by the page from which a quotation is made. At the end of S. M. Jackson's biography of Zwingli (*Huldreich Zwingli*, New York, 1901) there are translations of two of Zwingli's writings. These are referred to as Jackson, followed by the page from which the quotation is made. Where an alternative translation is available, its reference is given in brackets after the reference to the translation which has been used. Changes of spelling and capital letters have been made to give consistency; otherwise changes have been made only where the meaning has been obscured.

Details of the editions and translations, and of the books and articles on Zwingli, can be found in G. Finsler, *Zwingli-Bibliographie* (Zurich, 1897), H. W. Pipkin, *A Zwingli Bibliography* (Pittsburgh, 1972), and U. Gäbler, *Huldrych Zwingli im 20. Jahrhundert* (Zurich, 1975). For the period since the two recent bibliographies, an annual list of books and articles is published in *Zwingliana*.

# Introduction

ZWINGLI's part in the reformation has been overshadowed, and the study of his theology limited, in comparison with that of Luther and Calvin, to whom two great communions of the church look back as spiritual fathers. The quincentenary of Zwingli's birth offers a challenge to present him afresh, not in the light of Luther or Calvin, but in his own light.

A study of Zwingli almost inevitably leads to comparisons between him and Luther, but always with the risk of distorting the presentation of Zwingli. Luther appears as the key to the reformation, the norm by which all other reformers and all other expressions of the reformation are judged. But Zwingli was not Luther, nor a variant of Luther. He was a reformer in his own right. He became a reformer independently of Luther, and formulated his theology largely in independence of Luther's theology. Both men wrestled with the same scriptures; and both had an overwhelming sense of the grace of God in Christ. But they were different, and so were the ways by which they came to a reformation faith and in which they expressed it. This study of Zwingli relates him to Luther at many points, but its fundamental concern is to let Zwingli's theology stand in its own context and in its own right.

Zwingli study in the twentieth century has been stimulated by the modern critical edition of his works (alas, still incomplete), of which the first volume appeared in 1905,[1] and the journal *Zwingliana*, of which the first number was published in 1897.[2] The interest in Zwingli has not been limited to Switzerland, but has owed most to Swiss scholars, for whom Zwingli is part of their heritage. Three notable exceptions have been Samuel Macauley Jackson, Walter Köhler, and Jacques Pollet, OP. It is to Jackson that the English-speaking world owes the publication of a range of Zwingli's works in translation.[3]

---

[1] *Huldreich Zwinglis Sämtliche Werke* (Berlin, Leipzig, Zurich, 1905– ).

[2] *Zwingliana. Beiträge zur Geschichte Zwinglis, der Reformation und des Protestantismus in der Schweiz* (Zurich, 1897– ).

[3] See the Note on Zwingli's Works, p. xiii above. Other works, including some for which S. M. Jackson arranged the translation, will shortly be published by Pickwick Press (Allison Park, Pennsylvania) in their Pittsburgh Theological Monographs New Series as *Selected Writings of Huldrych Zwingli*, Vols 12 and 13: *The Defense of the Reformed Faith*, ed. E. J. Furcha, and *In Search of True Religion: Reformation, Pastoral and Eucharistic Writings*, ed. H. W. Pipkin. These, unlike earlier translations, will include the page references of the critical edition of Zwingli, and will make available for the first time in English a number of his most important works.

In Britain Zwingli has suffered from relative neglect. There have been valuable articles by G. W. Bromiley in *Zwingli and Bullinger*,[4] Gordon Rupp in *The New Cambridge Modern History*,[5] and Basil Hall in *A History of Christian Doctrine*,[6] but no major studies have appeared in over half a century apart from the late G. R. Potter's biography in 1976.[7] Yet Zwingli's importance for the English reformation and in particular for the eucharist has long been recognized.[8] Indeed the word 'Zwinglian' is most often used to characterize a particular understanding of the eucharist.

The changing image of Zwingli's life and thought derives in large measure from the methods and presuppositions of his interpreters. The books of Guggisberg and Büsser, the articles of Köhler and Locher, Büsser and Gäbler, testify to an extraordinary variety of interpretations both in successive periods and even within the same period.[9] Zwingli is in turn reformer or rationalist, humanist or spiritualist, politician or preacher.

The historical and theological presuppositions of the writer have played their part in interpretation. They have often led to an interpretation that has stressed Zwingli's dependence on, or independence of, Luther, or the influence on him of scholasticism or Erasmian humanism. Sometimes the method used has been more important than the presuppositions, particularly in the selection of Zwingli's writings. Works that cite these writings at random, without any reference to the time in which they were written and the situation for which they were written, tend to ignore variation or development in his theology and the way in which what Zwingli wrote was formulated in terms of the positions he

[4] G. W. Bromiley, *Zwingli and Bullinger* (The Library of Christian Classics XXIV) (London, 1953).

[5] E. G. Rupp, 'The Swiss Reformers and the Sects. The Reformation in Zürich, Strassburg and Geneva', *The New Cambridge Modern History*, Vol. II, *The Reformation 1520-1559*, ed. G. R. Elton, pp. 96-119 (Cambridge, 1968).

[6] B. Hall, 'Ulrich Zwingli', *A History of Christian Doctrine*, ed. H. Cunliffe-Jones with B. Drewery pp. 351-70 (Edinburgh, 1978).

[7] G. R. Potter, *Zwingli* (Cambridge, 1976).

[8] See P. N. Brooks, *Thomas Cranmer's Doctrine of the Eucharist* (London, 1965). For the earlier debate between Dix and Timms, see G. B. Timms, 'Dixit Cranmer', *Church Quarterly Review*, 143 (1947) 217-34; 144 (1947) 33-51, and G. Dix, 'Dixit Cranmer et non Timuit', ibid. 145 (1947) 145-76; 146 (1948) 44-60; and C. C. Richardson, *Zwingli and Cranmer on the Eucharist* (Evanston, 1949).

[9] K. Guggisberg, *Das Zwinglibild des Protestantismus im Wandel der Zeiten* (Leipzig, 1934); F. Büsser, *Das katholische Zwinglibild* (Zurich, 1968); W. Köhler, 'Die neuere Zwingli-Forschung', *Theologische Rundschau*, NF 4 (1932), 329-69; G. W. Locher, 'Die Wandlung des Zwingli-Bildes in der neueren Forschung', *ZWA* 11 (1963) 560-85 (trans. in *Zwingli's Thought* (Leiden, 1981), pp. 42-71); F. Büsser, 'Das Zwingli-Bild von Emil Egli bis Fritz Blanke', *Neue Zürcher Zeitung*, 3 Jan. 1969, No. 4; U. Gäbler, *Huldrych Zwingli in 20. Jahrhundert* (Zurich, 1975).

was opposing. Moreover works that draw largely on one or two writings give a particular colour to their presentation of his theology. This is especially true with a writing such as *The Providence of God*. Taken in isolation from earlier writings, it can make a given doctrine, such as the doctrine of God, seem much less biblical than it is; taken as a key by which to interpret his other writings it can make his whole theology seem more humanist than it is.[10]

This presentation of Zwingli's theology is an attempt to see Zwingli in his own terms, but also in the context of his life and times. All his writings have been used, and in most chapters or sections they have been drawn on in historical order. Where Zwingli's views, for example, on the sacraments, the church, and the state developed, or are thought to have developed, they are presented in terms of particular periods.

In chapter 1 Zwingli's writings are placed in the context of his life and ministry and related to the conflicts, events, and institutions with which he was involved—conflicts with catholics, radicals, and Lutherans, events such as the disputations, the reform of worship, and the Diet of Augsburg, and institutions such as the mercenary system and the prophecy (*Prophezei*). His writings are seen in terms of some of the factors that moulded his thinking (his native patriotism, his study of the schoolmen, his humanist delight both in the literature of Greece and Rome and in the bible and the fathers) and some of the political realities which were the inescapable setting of his ministry (the powers of the city council, the opposition of the catholic cantons, the need for alliances).

The context of a man's writings does not account for them, but it helps to illuminate them. The context both of European thought (whether in late medieval scholasticism or in that renewal of biblical, classical, and patristic learning characteristic of Erasmian humanism) and of European piety (whether in the outwardness of much religious observance or the inwardness of movements like the Modern Devotion) must be set alongside the context of Swiss life and society (the encroachment of the civil powers on the jurisdiction of the ecclesiastical powers and the robust patriotism which opposed foreign alliances). The context of theological conflict (the issues raised by catholics, radicals, and Lutherans) must be set alongside the context both of practical reform, whether in liturgical practice or social and moral laws, and of the serious and scholarly

[10] See, e.g., E. Zeller, *Das theologische System Zwinglis* (Tübingen, 1853). *The Providence of God* can be seen as anti-humanist, if humanism is regarded, as it is by Rich and others, as anthropocentric rather than theocentric (C. Gestrich, *Zwingli als Theologe, Glaube and Geist beim Zürcher Reformator* (Zurich, 1967), p. 123).

grappling with the scriptures (with the endeavour to discover their meaning for all time as well as for Zwingli's own time).

There are, however, problems in the use of Zwingli's writings. The modern critical edition is not yet complete. The edition of important marginal comments in his books, which are an indispensable source for any discussion of the early development of his thought, is not complete and the reliability of some of what has been published so far has been called in question. The commentaries on the new testament and some of the sermons and later writings are still not available in a critical edition. This limits the use that can be made of these commentaries and sermons, and they are most often used in this work only to support what has been said on the basis of other writings. Moreover as the modern critical edition of Zwingli is not widely available, and as the other editions and translations of his works are not well known, there is frequent quotation from, and summary of, what he wrote.

At any time a study of Zwingli's theology would be provisional, but a study today is doubly provisional, for in many areas no monographs have been written and in some important areas scholarly opinion is deeply divided. Until more work has been done on Zwingli's marginal notes and on the use he made of others (in particular the classics, the fathers, the schoolmen, and Erasmus), important insights into his theology will be missing.[11]

---

[11] Books and articles dealing with Zwingli's theology as a whole, or in some particular way, are indicated in the Bibliography by an asterisk.

# 1. The Context of Zwingli's Theology

ZWINGLI was born on 1 January 1484, within weeks of Luther who was born on 10 November 1483. He lived and developed, however, in a very different political, cultural, and theological world from that of Luther. The differences were evident in his upbringing and education, but also in the kind of ministry he exercised as a parish priest and army chaplain rather than as a monk and a professor.

When he began his ministry in Zurich on 1 January 1519, he had already experienced the major influences which were to shape the form, and in some senses the content, of his theology. In his upbringing, in his education, both at school in Berne and at university in Vienna and Basle, and in his time as a priest in Glarus and Einsiedeln, there is evidence of the patriotism, scholasticism, and humanism, as well as of the study of the fathers, that were to be manifest in his later theology. Under the influence of Erasmian humanism his preaching had become strongly biblical and christocentric, and he began to preach systematically through the new testament. Yet it was not till 1522 that his writings manifested fully a reformation theology, with a clear sense of the liberating grace of God in Christ. However, apart from his letters and three poems, few of Zwingli's writings from before 1522 survive, and therefore the theology with which we are engaged is a theology expounded in the nine years from 1522 to 1531, in the setting both of his pioneering ministry in Zurich and his wider ministry in Switzerland and southern Germany.[1]

The reformation in Zurich, heralded by the breaking of the Lenten fast in 1522, was inaugurated with disputations in 1523 and carried further by the abolition of images in 1524 and of the mass in 1525. In 1525 the reform of worship, the passing of social and moral legislation, and the institution of the prophecy marked its consolidation. From 1523, however, Zwingli faced opposition not only from conservatives, but also from radicals—in 1525 they held their first rebaptism. In the same period his differences with Luther emerged, although direct conflict did not take place till 1527. Outside Zurich the Zwinglian reformation experienced defeat at the Baden disputation in 1526 and victory at the Berne disputation in 1528. To safeguard the proclamation of the gospel, alliances were made

[1] For some of the emphases in Zwingli's ministry and their relevance today, see W. P. Stephens, 'Zwingli's Reforming Ministry', *Expository Times* 93 (1981) 6–10.

with reformed cities and attempted with others, but in 1529 the vital attempt at reconciliation with Luther in Marburg failed. Then suddenly two years later, when he was only forty-seven, Zwingli was killed defending the faith on the field of battle.[2]

## Scholasticism

One of the most serious gaps in Zwingli research is the lack of a study of the influence of scholasticism on his thought. It seems clear that his studies at Basle (1502–6) acquainted him with the *via antiqua* and the *via moderna*, although the former almost certainly predominated, given the role of Thomas Wyttenbach in his time at Basle. Moreover Zwingli's library is evidence of his reading of Aquinas and Duns Scotus.[3] It is in keeping with the place of the *via antiqua* that he is spoken of as being an Aristotelian in a letter of 1511.[4]

The lasting impression of scholasticism can be seen later in writings as diverse as *The Providence of God* and the eucharistic works.[5] Zwingli's position on the eucharist, over against Luther's, was a realist one, with, for example, an insistence on the reality of the body and its being in one place. Such a position is consistent with Zwingli's being in the tradition of the *via antiqua*. Pollet, however, argues for associating Zwingli with the *via moderna*, regarding the whole of Zwingli's theological system as Occamist.[6]

[2] The main biographical studies of Zwingli are by R. Staehelin, S. M. Jackson, O. Farner, W. Köhler, *Huldrych Zwingli* (Leipzig, 1943), J. Rilliet, M. Haas, G. R. Potter, G. W. Locher, *Die Zwinglische Reformation im Rahmen der europäisehen Kirchengeschichte* (Göttingen, 1979). See Bibliography.

[3] W. Köhler, *Huldrych Zwinglis Bibliothek* (Zurich, 1921), pp. 10–11, 26. Köhler also points to the many marginal notes in Scotus's commentary on *The Sentences* and the absence of any indication of influence from the *via moderna*, unless it is seen as beginning with Scotus (*Zwingli*, p. 22). Zwingli is regarded as Scotist rather than Thomist by J. F. G. Goeters (see his 'Zwinglis Werdegang als Erasmianer', in M. Greschat and J. F. G. Goeters, *Reformation und Humanismus. Robert Stupperich zum 65. Geburtstag* (Witten, 1969) pp. 257–61).

[4] Z VII 14.1–15.6. Cf. Z V 492.20–2.

[5] Büsser draws attention to evidence of Thomism in his understanding of secondary causes and in the primacy of the intellect. (Z VI iii 83, n. 10 and 220, n. 7.) Locher holds that the Thomistic stress on the simplicity of God may be directed against Luther's Occamist distinction between the hidden and the revealed God. (*Zwingli's Thought*, p. 171.) Evidence of Scotism may be seen in the voluntarism which characterizes elements in his theology, such as law and providence, and perhaps in the strong contrast between the creator and the creature. Köhler points to the agreement between Zwingli's christology and that of Scotus (*Zwingli und Luther, Ihr Streit über das Abendmahl nach seinen politischen und religiösen Beziehungen*. I *Die religiöse und politische Entwicklung bis zum Marburger Religionsgespräch 1529* (Leipzig, 1924), pp. 661–2; Z VI ii 150.11–15). There was also Scotus's stress on the eucharist as a commemoration of the sacrifice of Christ. See F. Clark, *Eucharistic Sacrifice and the Reformation* (London, 1960), pp. 323–41.

[6] J. V. Pollet summarizes some of the main issues in 'Zwingli' *Dictionnaire de Théologie catholique*, XV (Paris, 1950) 3745–749. In part he follows Oskar Farner, *Huldrych Zwingli*, I (Zurich, 1943), 213–29. Köhler (*Zwingli*, pp. 21–7) stresses the unified and rational approach which binds

Although Zwingli's writings show more evidence of Scotist and Thomist thought, yet the question of scholastic influence is not capable of simple resolution, in part because Zwingli was not a follower of one way or the other. He drew freely on a variety of writers. Moreover some elements characteristic of Zwingli's thought may be seen to have different antecedents, as the fact that outward things cannot affect the spirit may be ascribed to a Scotist or to a humanist approach. The same problem arises with the terms used by Zwingli in his discussion of God. Locher has argued that the terms are to be interpreted in the light of scholasticism rather than of humanism, although Zwingli's use of them is more biblical than that of the schoolmen.[7] The evidence of scholastic influence needs of course to be set in the context both of Zwingli's explicit attacks on scholasticism and of his use of scholastic arguments where possible to support his case.[8]

## Patriotism

An important element in Zwingli's theology was his patriotism. This was a factor in his life from the beginning, strengthened rather than weakened by his humanism, for the circle of Swiss humanists to which he later belonged was marked by patriotism.[9]

In his early ministry his love of his country and his desire for its liberty found expression in the dispute about mercenaries. The Swiss had gained a reputation as soldiers fighting for foreign powers, including the pope, and therefore were much sought after as mercenaries. The mercenary system

together Zwingli and Aquinas and points to the way Zwingli and Luther draw on different scholastic traditions in the eucharistic controversy. H. A. Oberman's discussion considers other effects of the different scholastic traditions, including the attitude to images (*Masters of the Reformation* (Cambridge, 1981), pp. 284–95). Several writers suggest nominalist influence in Zwingli's eucharistic doctrine. See, e.g., Richardson, *Zwingli and Cranmer*, pp. 8–10, Rupp, 'Reformation' p. 98, and E. Seeberg, 'Der Gegensatz zwischen Zwingli, Schwenckfeld und Luther', *Reinhold-Seeberg-Festschrift*, I *Zur Theorie des Christentums* (Leipzig, 1929), pp. 55–6.

[7] Köhler, *Zwingli*, p. 26, and Locher, *Zwingli's Thought*, p. 58. Von Muralt points out that many of the terms Zwingli used, such as *summum bonum* and *entelechia*, could have come from scholasticism or from his humanist reading. (Z VI i 446–7.) A similar point is made by A. E. Burckhardt about the origin of Zwingli's teaching on natural law. (*Das Geistproblem bei Huldrych Zwingli* (Leipzig, 1932), p. 102.)

[8] e.g. Z I 377.27–378.8; IV 119.6–8; V 590.12–17; VI ii 804.3–18; IX 537.12–15. The schoolmen are attacked, often by name, from beginning to end, as is the nature of scholastic thought. In his earliest reformation writing Zwingli says, 'After that they come with Thomas Aquinas, as though one single mendicant monk had power to prescribe laws for all Christian folk.' (Z I 109.2–4; *Works* I 88.)

[9] Z V 250.8–11. On Swiss humanism, see Locher, *Zwingli's Thought*, pp. 154, 236–8, and *Die Zwinglische Reformation*, pp. 51–4. Cf. also K. Maeder, *Die Via Media in der Schweizerischen Reformation* (Zurich, 1970), esp. pp. 10–117.

brought considerable profit to those who organized it and to those who fought under it, but at the cost of life and liberty. Zwingli attacked the system and the alliances with foreign powers, and his earliest extant writing, *The Ox*, in 1510, manifested his patriotism precisely in the context of mercenary warfare.[10] In it the ox stands for the Swiss, the cats are the agents of foreign powers seeking to hire the Swiss, the lion is the emperor, the leopard the French, and the herdsman the pope. (Only an alliance with the pope is approved.) The dog stands for the clergy and it shows how even at this stage, in a poem that is patriotic rather than religious, Zwingli saw the role of the priest in something like prophetic terms.

His opposition to the mercenary system was sharpened by experience of war at first hand. He may have gone as chaplain in 1512. If he did, *The Account* was a first-hand account of engagements between the French and the Swiss, and not simply a report of what others said.[11] He certainly went in 1513 and 1515 and on the second of these occasions witnessed the disastrous battle at Marignano in September 1515, in which thousands of Swiss soldiers died. These experiences made him even more aware of the devastation of war and the profound moral and social cost to his own people. The poem, *The Labyrinth*, probably written in 1516, again used an allegory about animals to attack the mercenary system.[12] In this poem, unlike the earlier one, his patriotism is set in a christological context, for he has begun to be influenced by Erasmian humanism, which gives his patriotism an explicitly religious dimension. There is moreover a challenge to princes in it which shows something of the prophetic understanding of ministry that was to characterize Zwingli.[13]

Thus from the start Zwingli's ministry and theology were set in a framework that was social and political, indeed national and international, and not simply individual and personal. It was moreover his opposition to mercenary service, and in particular the French alliance, that caused him to leave Glarus for Einsiedeln in 1516.[14] It was also a factor later in his invitation to Zurich, for there was opposition to this in Zurich long before his arrival there.

---

[10] Z I 10–22. The poem, like all his early writings, is an expression of Zwingli's humanist studies in Glarus.

[11] Z I 30–7.          [12] Z I 53–60.          [13] Z I 59.197–60.232.

[14] Z VII 54.11–13, 55.8–11. Patriotism is a vital and constant element in Zwingli's theology, 'dann all min leeren, hertz und gmuot reicht alles zuo uffenthalt einer Eydgnoschafft, dass die nach harkummen unserer vordren, ir selbs, nit frömder herren achtende, in fryden und früntschafft mit einander leben und blyben möcht.' (Z III 484.13–17.)

## Humanism and Erasmus

We know little for certain of the influence of humanism on Zwingli at school and university. He went to the university of Vienna in 1498 and to the university of Basle in 1502. It may be that in Vienna he had contact with Celtis and Italian humanism. Probably at the end of his time in Basle he became acquainted with the humanist circle there, which included Beatus Rhenanus, Glarean, and Conrad Pellican, men with whom he corresponded in the following years. It was, however, the period at Glarus, to which he went as a priest in 1506, that was most notable for his humanist studies.[15]

He read eagerly and widely. His library testifies to his passionate interest in classical antiquity and his avid reading of literature of all kinds, whether poetry, history, geography, or philosophy.[16] The world of Greece and Rome was always part of Zwingli's world. It was never an independent source for his theology, but it was part of his inheritance. For Zwingli, as for Erasmus and Augustine, truth could be found there, but only if it cohered with Christ. It was natural for him later, as it was not for Luther, to quote classical writers in theological discussion.

The humanist zeal in Zwingli was not directed simply to classical literature. He states explicitly that his learning Greek in 1513 was in order to study sacred letters.[17] It was in this period that he met Erasmus and began an intensive reading of his works. Erasmus was to be in many ways the most important influence in his development as a reformer. The meeting with him was in 1515 or 1516, and it is significant that from 1516 Erasmus used of him, as he had used of Erasmus, the title 'philosopher and theologian'. Zwingli was of course already a theologian in the scholastic sense, but now he was a theologian in a humanist or Erasmian sense. He saw Erasmus as the one who had freed the scriptures from scholasticism.[18]

[15] The first extant letter to him from Glarean in 1510 speaks of Zwingli as 'vir humanissime'. (Z VII 1.1.) Farner (II 109) comments on the entirely humanist character of his correspondence at this stage, with no indication of his work as a priest.

Schmidt-Clausing has argued strongly for the importance of Surgant. See, e.g., 'Johann Ulrich Surgant, ein Wegweiser des jungen Zwingli', ZWA II (1961) 287–320. After commenting on Surgant's influence, Pollet speaks of the influence of Basle on Zwingli: 'C'est de là, à notre jugement, que sont issues les grandes intuitions qui devaient prendre forme sur un théâtre voisin: à Zurich.' (Chronique de théologie historique. Seizième siècle (suite et fin). Réforme suisse', Revue des sciences religieuses, 37 (1963) 37.)

[16] See Additional Note, pp. 49–50 below.

[17] Z VII 22.10–12. He later commended the learning of Greek for the sake of reading the new testament. (Z II 542.24–543.16; V 437.4–438.3.)

[18] Z VII 36.14–19. So important was the freeing from scholasticism that he omits Erasmus's references to Aquinas in his marginal notes on Romans. See W. Köhler, 'Die Randglossen Zwinglis zum Römerbrief in seiner Abschrift der paulinischen Briefe 1516/17', Forschungen zur

The encounter with Erasmus and his writings was important for the method as well as for the content of Zwingli's theology. The return to the sources, in particular the Greek new testament, the study of the fathers, and the use of the historical, critical approach were of permanent significance for Zwingli—and they were part of his debt to Erasmus. But there was also the biblical and christocentric character of Erasmus's religious writings, which was to have a lasting influence on Zwingli's theology. The immediate impact can be seen in *The Labyrinth*, when compared with the earlier poem, *The Ox*, in 1510 or the account of the Italian campaign in 1512. Both poems are patriotic, but in *The Labyrinth* in 1516 there is a clearly biblical and christological reference, with an Erasmian concern for peace and a hostility to war, though Zwingli was never a pacifist. 'In us there is no love of God ... The world is so full of deceit that we have no more the image of Christ than the heathen ... Whoever commits crime and murder is considered a bold man. Did Christ teach us that? "Greater love hath no man than this, that a man lay down his life for his friends. [John 15: 13]" ... Tell me what have we of Christians more than the name?'[19]

Zwingli's comments on Erasmus through the years were fundamentally appreciative, in particular the reference in 1523 to the poem of Erasmus, through which eight or nine years before he had come to see that we need no mediator except Christ, and the statement in 1527 that some had understood the gospel more clearly than Luther or he. Yet his appreciation was not without criticism, both theological and personal. He noticed that, despite his poem on Christ, Erasmus had songs dedicated to the saints, and he sensed that Erasmus had the weakness of an Eli rather than the strength of an Elijah.[20] For his part Erasmus was critical of Zwingli's *Archeteles* and in a way of *A Commentary*.[21] Already, however, Zwingli's fundamental disagreement with Erasmus on free will was evident in *An Exposition of the Articles* in 1523 and *A Commentary* in 1525, yet that does not seem to have affected his ultimate esteem for Erasmus and what he had done.[22]

*Kirchengeschichte und zur christlichen Kunst. Johannes Ficker als Festgabe zum 70. Geburtstag dargebracht* (Leipzig, 1931), p. 93. Zwingli had twenty-three works of Erasmus in his library, and ten others were known to him. See the catalogue of his library in Köhler, *Zwinglis Bibliothek*, pp. 14–16.

[19] Z I 59.197–60.224; *Works* I 54.
[20] Z II 217.5–218.8; V 717.1–718.1; 815.18–818.3; I 440.16–441.5; VII 250.11–15. In a letter to Beatus Rhenanus on 22 Feb. 1519 Zwingli wrote of Erasmus's *Ratio seu compendium verae theologiae*, 'hoc vero mihi ita, ut non meminerim tam parvo libello tantam alicubi frugem invenisse'. (Z VII 139.17–18.)
[21] Z VII 582.1–9; VIII 333.27–334.8.
[22] Z II 180.26–29; III 657.36–662.2, 842.1–845.32; IV 498.39–41.

This points to the ambiguity in Zwingli's relation to Erasmus. Whereas Luther and Erasmus sensed the sharp difference between their positions, Zwingli, for all his differences with Erasmus, sensed his kinship or continuity with him and others like him.[23] Underlying this issue are the questions as to when Zwingli became a reformer and how far as a reformer he was also Erasmian. The matter is complicated by the different ways in which Erasmus, as well as Zwingli, is interpreted and by the definition of the term 'reformer'. (Erasmus is most often interpreted in opposition to Luther, for example in terms of the discussion of free will, and the term 'reformer' is frequently used to describe a fundamentally Lutheran understanding of the gospel.[24]) There can be little doubt of the affinity between Zwingli and Erasmus in many points before 1522, whether or not Erasmus is seen as anthropocentric rather than theocentric, rational rather than existential.[25] Of greater importance is the question how far Zwingli's theology from 1522 is humanist or Erasmian.

[23] In March 1522 Zwingli was concerned to prevent a quarrel between Erasmus and Luther and saw them both as committed to the Christian cause. (Z VII 496.11–497.23.) Myconius, in a letter to Zwingli in March 1522, could not credit rumours of differences between Erasmus and Luther. (Z VII 502.2–13.) By contrast Luther saw the distance between himself and Erasmus as early as 1516, and Erasmus was also aware of it. On 31 Aug. 1523 Erasmus wrote to Zwingli, 'Lutherus proponit quedam enigmata in spetie absurda: omnium opera sanctorum esse peccata, que indigna ignoscuntur dei misericordia; liberum arbitrium esse nomen inane; sola fide iustificari hominem; opera nihil ad rem facere.' (Z VIII 114.9–13.) Zwingli wrote in 1527 as though Erasmus was a pioneer in the preaching of the gospel. (Z V 712.25–713.2, 717.1–718.1, 721.5–722.3.)

Although Zwingli, like Luther, sees himself as breaking with the schoolmen, Erasmus sees the issues that are discussed, such as free will or the mass as a sacrifice, as the very ones debated by the schoolmen. Cf. his letter to Hutten in September 1523 (see H. A. Oberman, *Forerunners of the Reformation* (London, 1967), pp. 37–8).

[24] See, e.g., W. Köhler, 'Zwingli als Theologe', *Ulrich Zwingli. Zum Gedächtnis der Zürcher Reformation, 1519–1919* (Zurich, 1919), pp. 47–50. Scholars' understanding of Zwingli often depends on their understanding of Luther and Erasmus. H. A. Enno van Gelder, for example, in his portrayal of two fundamentally different reformations in the sixteenth century, represented by Erasmus and Luther, places Zwingli with Erasmus (*The Two Reformations in the Sixteenth Century* (The Hague, 1961)).

[25] A. Rich (*Die Anfänge der Theologie Huldrych Zwinglis* (Zurich, 1949)), sees Erasmus as anthropocentric, rational, and ethical, and Zwingli's theology until 1521 as being in that fundamentally humanist framework (pp. 9–72). He does, however, allow that some of Erasmus's expressions are close to a reformation faith (e.g., pp. 34–5 and 41) and also some of Zwingli's before 1521 (p. 69). Cf. J. M. Usteri, *Zwingli und Erasmus* (Zurich, 1885), p. 28. E. W. Kohls argues for an existential view of Erasmus and contests the contrast made by some between Erasmus's and Zwingli's understanding of Christ and scripture. See 'Erasmus und die werdende evangelische Bewegung des 16. Jahrhunderts', *Scrinium Erasmianum* Vol. 1, ed. J. Coppens (Leiden, 1969), pp. 208–14. Christine Christ points to the importance of understanding Erasmus from a later writing such as the *Ratio* (1518) rather than an earlier writing such as *The Enchiridion* (1503), arguing, for example, that the later Erasmus values the natural sense of scripture and frequently uses the term 'gospel' as 'good news' ('Das Schriftverständnis von Zwingli und Erasmus im Jahre 1522', *ZWA* XVI (1983) 111–25). Joachim Rogge argues for Zwingli's dependence on Erasmus in several

Köhler's consistent view of Zwingli is that his theology is a blending of Christian and classical elements, a merging of Lutheran and Erasmian streams. He points to Zwingli's use of humanist terms and his drawing on non-Christian writers, but even more to certain Erasmian or humanist elements in his theology, in particular his understanding of God, the relation of word and Spirit, the place of Christ revealed, for example, by the salvation of non-Christians, and the view of man both in the opposition of flesh and spirit and in the denial of original guilt. The Erasmian world is seen as the rational and the reasonable, the Lutheran as the irrational and the supernatural, not to say miraculous. For Köhler *The Education of Youth* shows a classical view of education, *A Commentary* a theocentric rather than a christocentric theology, *The Providence of God* a Greek rather than a biblical view of God and man, and *An Exposition of the Faith* a Ciceronian rather than a Christian heaven.[26]

There is more force in Köhler's case than has often been allowed. The kinship, or affinity, with Erasmus is more than a matter of Zwingli's thought being dressed in humanist clothes, as it has been described.[27] However, the writings of Blanke, Locher, Pfister, Rich, and others have offered an important corrective to Köhler. Blanke and Locher have shown that what has been ascribed to humanist influence may simply be part of Zwingli's scholastic heritage, in particular in his understanding of God, and moreover that seemingly humanist words or phrases have often been given a Christian twist. Pfister has argued that Zwingli's view of sin and the salvation of non-Christians are set in a biblical and christological framework.[28]

areas, notably original sin, predestination, cosmology, and the sacraments ('Die Initia Zwinglis und Luthers. Eine Einführung in die Probleme', *Luther-Jahrbuch*, 30 (1963), p. 110). See also the discussion in W. H. Neuser, *Die reformatorische Wende bei Zwingli* (Neukirchen, 1977), esp. pp. 90–9.

In the variety of interpretations of Erasmus, J. B. Payne sees his views of salvation and the sacraments as nominalist rather than Thomist, in contrast with Kohls. He also speaks of Erasmus' sacramental theology as in the Franciscan tradition, in particular as represented in Scotism and Occamism. See *Erasmus. His Theology of the Sacraments* (Richmond, 1969), pp. 22, 98, 228–9.

[26] W. Köhler, 'Zwingli als Theologe', pp. 45–70, 'Die neuere Zwingli-Forschung', pp. 366–8, and *Zwingli*, pp. 79–80, 264–6. Köhler refers to words such as *deus optimus maximus*, the use of classical rhetorical terms, and the particular place of writers like Seneca. Locher, although accepting that Zwingli takes over a Platonist anthropology and Stoic ethics, presents a different interpretation of these writings from that of Köhler. See, e.g., *Die Zwinglische Reformation*, pp. 126–7, 503–4. Leonard von Muralt points to similarity and contrast with Erasmus in 'Zwinglis dogmatisches Sondergut', *ZWA* V (1932) 332–9.

[27] F. Blanke, 'Zu Zwinglis Entwicklung', *Kirchenblatt für die reformierte Schweiz*, 86 (1930), 199.

[28] G. W. Locher, *Die Theologie Huldrych Zwinglis im Lichte seiner Christologie* (Zurich, 1952), R. Pfister, *Das Problem der Erbsünde bei Zwingli* (Leipzig, 1939), and *Die Seligkeit erwählter Heiden bei Zwingli* (Zurich, 1952). Locher discusses the relation of Zwingli and Erasmus in 'Zwingli and Erasmus', *ZWA* 13 (1969) 37–61.

A comparison of a single writing such as *The Enchiridion* with Zwingli's works shows an affinity between the two, whether or not Zwingli is dependent on Erasmus. It also shows some of the discontinuity as well as the continuity between them. Zwingli himself attributed to a poem of Erasmus his faith that we need no mediator except Christ and that no one except Christ can mediate between God and us. He contrasted this with seeking help in the creature, which is idolatry.[29] This is a central element in Zwingli's theology which he related in some sense to Erasmus, although it is not characteristic of *The Enchiridion*. In the first rule faith is spoken of as the sole door to Christ, and in the eleventh we are to flee to Christ, distrustful of our strength; yet the Christ portrayed by Erasmus is essentially the teacher and the example. The preface and the fourth rule speak of Christ in terms of his teaching (indeed he is identified with it), while the sixth speaks of him as our sole example. However, the emphasis there is not a simply moral one, but it is set in the context of our common redemption and our common membership of the body of Christ. (There is an underlying concern for the living of the Christian life, expressed in the fourth rule in a concern for loving rather than for learning or rather for a learning that leads to loving, something which can be paralleled in the prayer used in Zwingli's prophecy.) Although the stress on Christ in Zwingli, at least after 1522, is more evangelical than in Erasmus, there is a continuing sense of him as teacher and example, with a corresponding emphasis on living the Christian life.

Zwingli's letter to Erasmus after their first meeting shows that he saw Erasmus as having freed the scriptures from scholasticism. Erasmus helped Zwingli to a new understanding of the bible. In the second section on the weapons of Christian warfare *The Enchiridion* makes the familiar Zwinglian contrast between man as a liar and God as true; and in the first rule he relates what he has to say about Christ to scripture, on which we are to rely, as there is nothing in it that does not pertain to our salvation. This stress on scripture taken in isolation seems Zwinglian, but it lacks the sense of the living power of scripture characteristic of writings such as *The Clarity and Certainty of the Word of God*. A greater contrast is to be found in the section on the weapons of Christian warfare with Erasmus's attack on the literal sense of scripture, his insistence on the allegorical sense, in which the spiritual meaning is hidden, and his preference for interpreters who depart from the literal sense.[30] In this context he could speak of the

[29] Z II 217.5–218.8.

[30] Payne (pp. 45, 50–5) argues that the later Erasmus qualified his earlier approval of the fathers' allegorizing (in particular Origen's) and himself sought a compromise between an

value both of Homer and Virgil if they are treated allegorically and of Platonist philosophers. They are, however, to be related to Christ and 'biblicized' or shaped according to the biblical tradition. In the fifth rule Erasmus's emphasis on the allegorical meaning, in a primarily moral sense, leads him to develop the use of pagan writers, and to prefer them when interpreted allegorically to the old testament books of Kings and Judges if interpreted literally. He also points to the value of such writers in understanding scripture, and appeals to Christ's, Paul's, and Origen's use of allegory. Allegory is related to John 6: 63 and to the view of man as body and soul.

There is some kinship with Erasmus here, but the differences are more notable. Zwingli affirms the literal sense of scripture, and, though he also allows the mystical sense, it is (much more than in Erasmus) given a typological rather than an allegorical meaning. The old testament is much more consistently interpreted in terms of Christ. Zwingli also makes a certain use of non-Christian writers in the interpretation of scripture, for example in the use of rhetorical figures of speech; but for him this is a limited tool.[31]

Erasmus quotes freely and frequently from pagan writers and values them as moral teachers. He has a preference for the Platonists among the philosophers. He supports his use of them in the section on the weapons of Christian warfare by reference to the fathers, in particular Basil, Augustine, Jerome, and Cyprian, and to Moses' not despising the advice of his father-in-law, Jethro. Truth wherever it is found is Christ's. In the sixth rule he testifies to the fine moral lives of many pagans. In all this there is a strong similarity to Zwingli, especially in a work such as The Providence of God, but the total context in which Zwingli uses non-Christian writers is different and their subservience to the biblical revelation is clear. He quotes Plato approvingly, but also critically. He can speak of Seneca as almost a theologian. He refers to the Stoics as close to Christian doctrine. He uses pagan examples in preaching and commends the

over-literal and an over-spiritual interpretation of scripture. He also points to the christological element in his exegesis.

[31] In *Preface to Pindar* he indicates the value, albeit limited, of Pindar: 'quod mea quidem sententia nullus Graecorum autorum sic videtur prodesse ad sacrarum literarum intellectum atque hic noster, praesertim si abstrusissimas Hebraeorum cantilenas ac hymnos, quales Psalmi sunt Jobi carmina . . .'. (Z IV 871.9–15). In part our distance from antiquity hinders our proper understanding of the Hebrew poets, but a poet like Pindar can help us. (Z IV 872.8–873.13.) 'Vale, candide lector, detque deus optimus maximus, ut gentili poeta magistro discas veritatem cum apud Hebraeos intelligere, tum apud omnes gentes amoenissime exponere.' (Z IV 873.17–19.) With Augustine and Origen he can regard pagan writers as believing God to be one, even where they speak of gods. (Z IV 870.8–871.7.)

study of pagan writers, but the main course is the word of the Lord.[32] He defends the use of such writers in terms of Moses' accepting Jethro's advice and Paul's example in Acts. He makes it quite clear, however, that they have no authority in themselves. He deliberately quotes them, conscious that some will object, on the basis that all truth is from God, who is the cause of all things. He affirms and quotes from writers such as Plato and Seneca because they drew from that source.[33] In this of course the influence of Augustine must be set alongside that of Erasmus.

A central element in *The Enchiridion* is the characterizing of man in terms of soul and body and the contrast that is made in him between inward and outward.[34] This opposition affects the whole understanding of the Christian faith and not only the understanding of man. It is developed in three sections: the outward and inward man, the diversity of passions, the inward and outward man and the two parts of man in holy scripture. The mind is set over against the passions of the body in an exposition drawn from Plato, which is used to interpret Paul on the flesh and the Spirit. He points to Origen's treatment of man in his commentary on Romans. This Platonic view of man is present in Zwingli, and is especially evident in *The Providence of God*, but at many points it is subordinate to the Pauline contrast of the flesh and the Spirit. It does, however, have important implications for Zwingli's understanding of word and sacraments, as it does for Erasmus. This emerges in Erasmus's use of John 6: 63, 'The Spirit gives life, the flesh is of no avail.'

This sentence is used in a contrast between outward and inward in scripture and in the fifth rule in relation to outward actions and in particular to the sacraments. The concern is with the inward, not the outward; hence, for example, the necessity for eating and drinking in a spiritual way. Erasmus draws on John 16: 7 and 2 Corinthians 5: 16.

Surely the flesh of Christ stood in the way, and hence it is that he says, 'If I go not, the Paraclete will not come to you; it is expedient for you that I go.' When the corporeal presence of Christ is useless to salvation, should we then dare to establish perfect piety in any corporeal thing? Paul had seen Christ in the flesh. What do you consider greater than this? Yet he contemns it, saying, 'And if we have known Christ according to the flesh, but now we know him so no longer.'

---

[32] Z VI iii 108.11–13; XIII 60.3–6, 101.36; VIII 677–8. Cf. Z III 580.4–7.

[33] Z XIII 382.24–383.11; III 646.27–34; VI iii 106.5–107.1, 110.12–24.

[34] 'The starting point for Erasmus' sacramental thought, as indeed for his whole theology, is the Platonic conception of the contrast between flesh and spirit, which is grounded in the nature of the world and the nature of man.' (Payne, p. 35.) Payne allows that Erasmus also has at points a more Pauline understanding of man (pp. 39–41).

Wherefore did he not know? Because he had made progress toward the better graces of the Spirit.[35]

There are differences here between Erasmus and Zwingli, whose interpretation of John 6: 63 is often clearly in terms of the Holy Spirit, but here and in the rest of the fifth rule there is a great area of common ground between them. There is the emphasis on the inward rather than the outward; the need of children in Christ for what is outward, so that for the sake of them others should not scorn what is outward; the stress on God's desiring inward worship, a worship in spirit and truth, because he is Spirit; the sense that outward religion is Judaism; and the relation between worship and living in love, with the accent on moral, not ritual, acts. There is also the use, even if sometimes differently, of texts such as John 4: 23; 6: 63; 16: 7; and 2 Corinthians 5: 16.

The indebtedness to Erasmus in the eucharist, of which Zwingli spoke to Melanchthon at Marburg, may be understood in terms of Jud's presentation of Erasmus's eucharistic thought in April 1526. Jud ascribed a symbolic view to Erasmus, citing Erasmus's use of the word 'symbol' and drawing attention to the use of John 6 in *The Enchiridion*, with the repudiation of fleshly eating and the stress on spiritual eating. There is in Zwingli and Erasmus a contrast between inward and outward with the emphasis on the inward, or not relying on the sacrament, with the important thing being to eat and drink spiritually. There is in both of them the underlying stress on God as Spirit; and with the view that like affects like, in the relations of God and man, there is a questioning of the role of material things. There are a number of other points of contact between them. Usteri points to Erasmus's concept of sacrament as an oath, to circumcision as not bringing righteousness but as being a pledge, to the eucharist as a memorial, covenant, and fellowship meal. But the relationship between the two depends in part on how each of them is interpreted. On that there is no agreement.[36]

---

[35] LCC XIV 339. Erasmus's comment on John 6: 63 is revealing and contrasts with Zwingli's use of it. 'To me it would have been religion to say that the expression "It profits nothing" was true enough of future events; yet for the present the flesh profits somewhat, but the spirit much more fully. Now the Truth said, "Profits nothing" . . . The body cannot subsist without the spirit; the spirit needs nothing from the body.' (LCC XIV 335.)

[36] J. M. Usteri, *Zwingli und Erasmus*, pp. 28–31. For somewhat different interpretations of Erasmus, see G. Krodel, 'Die Abendmahlslehre des Erasmus von Rotterdam und seine Stellung am Anfang des Abendmahlsstreites der Reformation' (Diss. Erlangen, 1955), and J. B. Payne, *Erasmus. His Theology of the Sacraments*. Payne holds (pp. 222–3) that Erasmus did not specifically apply the understanding of sacrament as an oath to the eucharist. On the basis of Krodel, Kohls argues against a direct line from Erasmus to Zwingli or Oecolampadius ('Erasmus und die werdende evangelische Bewegung', pp. 214–15).

The influence of Erasmus on Zwingli's theology after 1522 is to be seen in the effects of the fundamental turning to Christ and to scripture, but also in some of the shared assumptions (in particular a stress on God as Spirit and a Platonic view of man as body and soul) and common concerns (in particular the concern for an inward rather than an outward piety). Beyond this there is a delight in the ancient non-Christian writers, whom Zwingli drew on freely and naturally. (Zwingli's humanism is evident to the end, as his composing the music for a production of Aristophanes in Greek in 1531 shows.) The larger place they occupy in a work such as *The Providence of God* is probably related to those for whom he was writing, just as he could use canon law in support of his case in other contexts, but the use of them is nevertheless not alien to him nor simply a reflection of those for whom he was writing.[37] At the same time his theology is essentially biblical. This is clearer in *A Commentary* than in *The Providence of God*, although the latter must be set in the context of all his writings, and its strong attack on free will should be noted. *A Commentary*, which opens with a Ciceronian definition of religion, nevertheless begins its discussion of man in terms of Adam and its discussion of religion with the question, 'Adam, where art thou?' The fundamental thrust of Zwingli's theology here as elsewhere is theocentric and evangelical, which goes beyond the dominant thrust of Erasmus's theology.[38]

## The Fathers

In the years before going to Zurich Zwingli engaged in a detailed study of the fathers. Among the books he took to Einsiedeln from Glarus in 1516 were annotated copies of Augustine, Cyril of Alexandria, Gregory of Nazianzus, Gregory of Nyssa, Jerome, and Origen. It was not, however, till his time in Zurich that Augustine was to have a pre-eminent place. Earlier Jerome and Origen played a more important part, as they did for Erasmus.[39]

[37] Zwingli uses classical writers more often in certain writings, including his exegetical writings, where, like many other humanist elements, they appear in the lecture intended for the learned, rather than in the sermon intended for the people. Walter Meyer points to the contrast between Leo Jud's humanist formulation in the introduction to chapter 4, 'Christus semper a terrenis et corporalibus rebus ad coelestia et spiritualia abducit', and the christological one, 'Christus will mit diesen Gleichnissen nichts anderes, als dem Volk zeigen, wie Gott dem menschlichen Geschlecht den Heiland verheissen hat als ein Licht und eine Speise der Seelen'. See 'Die Entstehung von Huldrych Zwinglis neutestamentlichen Kommentaren und Predigtnachschriften', *ZWA* 14 (1976) 290.

[38] Religion originated 'when God called runaway man back to him, when otherwise he would have been a deserter forever'. (Z III 667.30–2; *Works* III 90.)

[39] Farner II 119–24, 238–41. In the Pauline letters Ambrose (i.e. Ambrosiaster) is quoted more often than Jerome and Origen. The order and the omissions in his letter to Beatus Rhenanus in

Before 1522 the evidence for the role of the fathers in Zwingli's theology is mostly in the marginal notes in his editions of their writings and his copy of Paul's letters in Greek. Unfortunately the critical edition of the marginal notes is incomplete and few studies have been made of them.[40] It is not possible to say with certainty how much the fathers contributed to Zwingli's development as a reformer or how far they influenced his theology. However, by his own testimony Augustine had a part in his development, and elements and emphases in Zwingli's theology can undoubtedly be found in his marginal notes as well as in his later use of the fathers.[41] Although Zwingli spoke more positively of the Greek than of the Latin fathers, he was also critical of them.[42]

In his study of the marginal notes on Romans Köhler points to the overwhelming, but independent, use of Origen by Zwingli. There are signs in the notes of later emphases in Zwingli's theology: the relation of justification to the living of the Christian life, sin as something done against conscience, and the confident nature of faith. However, whereas Origen was important for the understanding of sin, Ambrose was important for the understanding of grace and faith, although the marginal notes from him seem to fall mainly in the Zurich period.[43] The marginal notes on Galatians show a difference between the earlier and the later periods. In the earlier period Jerome was the father most quoted, whereas in the relatively small number of later notes it was Augustine. Rich argues that

June 1520 should be noted: 'nam, ut plane scias, homo nihil quam sacras literas tractat et super his Origenes, Cyprianos, Chrysostomos, Hieronymos, Ambrosios, cęteros . . .'. (Z VII 324.23–5.) For statistical information about Zwingli's use of the fathers, see A. Schindler, *Zwingli und die Kirchenväter* (Zurich, 1984), pp. 15–20, 91–7.

[40] Apart from Köhler's writings the main study is J. M. Usteri, 'Initia Zwinglii', *Theologische Studien und Kritiken*, 58 (1885), 607–72; 59 (1886) 95–159. Arthur Rich draws on the marginal notes in *Die Anfänge der Theologie Huldrych Zwinglis*.

[41] Z V 713.2–714.2. Farner (II 135) raises the question whether the fathers led to a study of the bible or the study of the bible led to a study of the fathers, in order to understand the bible better. Zwingli himself commended the study of the fathers when in Einsiedeln, but his reading of them was never uncritical, especially in relation to scripture. See, e.g., Z II 145.5–21 and Usteri, 'Initia', p. 106. 'Welches wort inn treffenlich hat geirret, das ich inn hiess Hieronimum lesen, und zeigt aber daby an, er wurde wenig mer gelten. Was do ze mal min meinung, das ich anhuob empfinden, wie Hieronymus und ander, wiewol sy die geschrifft vil wäger ze handen nomend weder die Sophisten, tatend sy doch der gschrifft gwalt an.' (Z II 145.12–17.) For the affinity between Zwingli's view of man and of the image of God and that of Gregory of Nyssa, see Usteri, op. cit., pp. 633–4.

[42] Z II 534.1–5, 595.1–7. Erasmus also preferred the Greek fathers.

[43] Köhler, 'Die Randglossen', pp. 93–100; Z XII 16.21–22, 17.15–16 (cf. Z V 371.3–6), 35.20–2. In Zwingli's reference in Rom. 3: 28 to Origen's statement 'Indulgentia non futurorum, sed pręteritorum criminum datur' Köhler sees the link Zwingli makes between justification and ethics and a sign of his future unease at the way Luther's view of justification was misunderstood.

Zwingli's earlier interest in Augustine was in his sacramental teaching and the ethical side of his teaching on grace, whereas later there was a more theocentric understanding of Augustine with grace in the centre. Köhler by contrast points to Zwingli's grasp of the gospel in Einsiedeln, although it is in Zurich that Augustine becomes dominant, replacing Jerome and Origen in importance.[44]

Zwingli's well-annotated editions of Jerome manifest his careful study of him in Einsiedeln, although his comments show that he became increasingly critical of him. However, he made particular use of Jerome's grammatical and historical exegesis, with its geographical, historical, and other details, and of his tropological interpretation. Jerome's ethical and ascetic views were noted, and Zwingli also drew on particular places, such as Jerome's comment on Titus 1 that bishops and presbyters were not originally distinguished.[45]

Erasmus's enthusiasm for Origen was related to his pre-eminence in the mystical interpretation of scripture, and from Zwingli's marginal notes this seems to have appealed to him. Many passages that Zwingli underlined or commented on cohere with his later views, for example in the opening of the kingdom of heaven by the preaching of the gospel, although that does not necessarily mean that he was dependent on Origen for those views. In Origen's *Homilies* Zwingli marked passages that gave a spiritual or symbolic understanding of the bread and wine. He noted Origen's discussion of predestination and particularly the ethical elements in his writings. In all this it is primarily Origen as an exegete rather than as a speculative theologian who appealed to him.[46]

The Neoplatonism which was an important element in the Greek fathers was likewise important in Augustine's theology and his influence on Zwingli. Augustine was also a decisive factor in Zwingli's development as a reformer. Köhler asserted sixty years ago that one could construct Zwingli's whole theology from the marginal notes in the nine volumes of Augustine that Zwingli had in his library. Rich, following a suggestion of Köhler's concerning Zwingli's notes on the psalms, offers an exposition of Zwingli's early theology on the basis of these notes. They show the

---

[44] Rich, *Die Anfänge*, pp. 124–31. Köhler (Zwingli, pp. 68–74) sees an understanding of the grace of God in Augustine in Einsiedeln. The reference to Augustine's tractates in Z V 713.2–714.2 implies that Zwingli studied them in Einsiedeln. W. H. Neuser recognizes the importance of Augustine in Zwingli's development, but also refers to the vital role of Luther (*Die reformatorische Wende*, pp. 96–9, 125–47, 151–3).

[45] Usteri, 'Initia', pp. 103–9.

[46] Usteri, 'Initia', pp. 109–15. The mystical use is also a particular feature of Cyril of Alexandria (ibid., p. 98).

strongly theocentric character of that theology, the understanding of the gospel as the grace of God which justifies the sinner and as the mercy of God which places an obligation on the justified sinner. In this the grace of God is seen as effecting knowledge of sin, leading to repentance, and awakening faith. The Christian life is a life of faith, and with God (or Christ) present with us through faith we fear nothing. It is by virtue of faith that the believer is righteous. Christ indeed has made our offences his, so that he may make his righteousness ours. Faith, however, leads to a new life, for the righteous may be said to be those who direct their heart according to the will of God. They meditate day and night in God's law. Those who are in the law act according to the law. Some of the characteristic Zwinglian emphases on grace and faith and on living a life in accordance with God's will are clearly present in the quotations he draws from Augustine.[47]

Zwingli was obviously struck by Augustine's sacramental teaching, especially his tractates on John. The tractates are heavily annotated, with references to 'believe and you have eaten', to the eucharist as a sacrament of piety, a sign of unity, and a bond of charity, and to the flesh as of no avail. The comment that John is speaking only of spiritual eating in chapter 6 is struck out and Augustine is said to speak there of bodily eating. The statement that the body of the Lord, in which he rose, can be only in one place is noted, and also that man according to his body is in one place, whereas God fills all things.[48] Augustine's tractates on John 6 show how close Zwingli is to him at many points. There is the distinction of the pith and the husk or letter in scripture; the use of allegory (indeed Augustine is rather more given to it than Zwingli); the understanding of God's righteousness as the righteousness he bestows on us; the strong sense of the sovereignty of God who acts inwardly in drawing men while we act outwardly with our planting and watering; the difference between the sacrament and the virtue of the sacrament, between eating inwardly in the heart and eating outwardly with the teeth, between the signs and what they signify; the assertion that the person who does not dwell in Christ

---

[47] See Köhler, *Zwinglis Bibliothek*, p. 29, and Rich, *Die Anfänge*, pp. 130-8. The way in which Zwingli strengthens the theocentric emphasis at one point in Augustine shows something of his independence in relation to him as well as the strongly theocentric character of his own theology. He changes Augustine's *mundaverint* into *mundaverit* in 'Deus meus immaculata est via eius, deus enim non venit in homines, nisi mundaverit viam fidei, qua veniat ad eos, quia immaculata est eius vita.' (Z XII 336.21-3.)

[48] Z XII 144.20-1, 34-5, 144.39-145.1, 6-7, 23-5, 30-1. 'Cibus et potus corporis Christi est societas corporis et membrorum suorum in ecclesia sancta.' (Z XII 144.37-8.) On the cover he notes 'accedit verbum ad elementum et fit sacramentum' (153.8-9). Note also the reference to baptism in the sixth tractate, 'baptismum non habeas foris sed intus'. (Z XII 140.13-14.)

does not eat his flesh (spiritually) and that his grace is not consumed by the biting of the teeth; the emphasis on the distinction of Christ's natures and the unity of his person; and the need to believe in order to understand. These four tractates show the striking affinity at many points between Zwingli and Augustine.

Throughout his writings Zwingli remained critical of the fathers, even of Augustine. He nevertheless used them freely and appealed to them in support of his teaching on many issues, most notably in the debate on the eucharist.[49] In his later writings he often appealed to them in support of views formed independently of them. However, in the crucial period before Zurich, and to some extent in the first two or three years there they were his companions while his theology was being formed. Even though they were not read uncritically, they were a factor in its formation, especially in his use and understanding of scripture, and, with Augustine in particular, in the deepening of his understanding of the gospel and in the Neoplatonic cast of his thought.

*Becoming a Reformer*

There is no agreement about when or how Zwingli became a reformer. Some place the date as early as 1515 or 1516, others as late as 1521 or 1522. Some see the decisive influence in Erasmus, others in Luther or Augustine.[50] The matter is complicated by the nature of the evidence available to us and the lack of explicit contemporary evidence. The only contemporary evidence is in the marginal notes Zwingli made in his books. These are only partly published and the accuracy of some of what

---

[49] e.g. *S* VI i 569.19-23. Yet one can note the appeal to them in 1531. 'Das aber weder keiser noch bapst könne gesagen, ir verkerind gottes wort in einen missverstand und werdind damit verfuert, so berueffindt ir uch uomb üwren verstand des götlichen wortes halb, es betreffe nüw oder alt testament an, uff den sinn, den die propheten, apostel und aller eltisten lerer der christlichen kirchen, die der apostel zyten aller nächst gelebt und gelert, gehalten habind.' (*Z* XI 587.25-30.) The development in the use of the fathers may be seen in comparing *The Letter to Matthew Alber*, which refers to Tertullian and Augustine, with *A Commentary*, which adds Origen, Hilary, and Jerome. (*Z* III 346.2-347.12, 809.6-815.38.) As the controversy developed, the range of reference was extended. In this Zwingli also drew on the work of Oecolampadius. In one account of the Marburg colloquy Melanchthon allowed that Augustine seemed to favour Zwingli's view, though he regarded the rest of the fathers as favouring Luther's view. (*S* IV 174.37-9.)

Gottfried Hoffmann offers a study of the use of the patristic argument by Oecolampadius, Zwingli, Luther, and Melanchthon. See his 'Sententiae Patrum—Das patristische Argument in der Abendmahlskontroverse zwischen Oekolampad, Zwingli, Luther und Melanchthon' (Diss. Heidelberg, 1971).

[50] For discussion of some of the more recent studies and the issues involved, see Gäbler, *Zwingli*, pp. 39-60, and Locher, *Die Zwinglische Reformation*, pp. 65-82, 115-22. Particularly notable are A. Rich, *Die Anfänge* and W. H. Neuser, *Die reformatorische Wende*. For a chronological outline, see Locher, ibid., pp. 117-20 and Neuser, ibid., pp. 38-9, 77-84.

has been published has been called in question.[51] They are, however, only indirect evidence and their significance is sometimes ambiguous. They show what Zwingli noted in and from others, not necessarily what he learnt from them. The only first-hand direct evidence is that of Zwingli in passages that he wrote between 1521 and 1527. These show some inconsistency in dates, though that is probably not important, and they may be coloured both by hindsight and by Zwingli's concern to emphasize his independence of Luther. However, they do offer a coherent view and one which in its fundamental standpoint is confirmed by other passages in Zwingli. They concern both the preaching of the gospel of Christ and the authority of scripture.

Zwingli's references to the crucial developments in his past were written in a letter to Haller in 1521, in *Archeteles* and *The Clarity and Certainty of the Word of God* in 1522, in *An Exposition of the Articles* in 1523, and in *A Friendly Exegesis* in 1527.[52] Zwingli held that he had begun to preach the gospel in 1516.[53] In this he asserted vigorously his independence of Luther. He stated that he had begun to preach the gospel two years before people in his area had heard of Luther. There are a number of reasons why Zwingli should want to assert his independence, in particular the danger of being identified with a heretic. Nevertheless most recent study has confirmed this independence. Zwingli seems to have read Luther hastily, to have looked to him for the confirmation of his own views, and to have admired him primarily for the boldness of his stand against the pope.[54] The kind of criticism of Luther that he advanced in his later testimonies could well have been typical of his earlier reaction: that

[51] See Gäbler, *Zwingli*, pp. 39–41, 51–5, and Schindler, pp. 18–19, 31–2, 98–103. The classic examinations are those of J. M. Usteri in *Initia Zwinglii* and W. Köhler in Z XII and elsewhere.

[52] Z VII 484.10–485.5; I 256.13–18, 259.28–261.38, 379.18–32; II 144.32–150.25 (article 18), 217.5–218.8 (article 20), 225.19–227.7 (article 21); V 712.24–724.24, 815.18–818.3.

[53] Z VII 484.10–485.5; I 256.13–18; II 144.32–145.4. In *The Clarity and Certainty of the Word of God* (1522) he wrote of beginning to rely altogether on scripture seven or eight years before; in *An Exposition of the Articles* (1523) of reading Erasmus's poem eight or nine years before; and in *A Friendly Exegesis* (1527) of being helped by certain people twelve years before. (Z I 379.21–25; II 217.8–13; V 721.7–722.1.)

[54] On various grounds Farner, and to some extent Köhler (in their later writings), as well as Rich, recognize Zwingli's independence. Reasons for this are to be found in the recognition of Augustine's place in Zwingli's development, the way he read Luther, the absence of marginal notes in his Luther books, his appearing to see Luther as supporting a reforming, rather than a reformation, position, and his admiration of Luther as the one who had the courage to act against the pope like a David against Goliath. See Köhler, *Zwingli*, pp. 60–81, Farner, II 310–47, Rich, *Die Anfänge*, pp. 79–94. Zwingli's references to Luther are in the exposition of article 18 and in *A Friendly Exegesis*.

Neuser (*Die reformatorische Wende*) regards Zwingli as in some ways dependent on Luther, pointing in particular to his use of Luther's *Babylonian Captivity of the Church* (see esp. pp. 33–4,

Luther was not thorough enough in cleansing religion from reliance on externals rather than on Christ.

In *A Friendly Exegesis* Zwingli asked why he should not acknowledge his debt to Luther in the gospel if he had been indebted to him. Then he invoked God as witness that he had learned the gospel from John, Augustine's tractates on John, and Paul's epistles which he had copied out in Greek, and that he had committed his summary of the gospel to writing. After this he referred to others, presumably Wyttenbach and Erasmus, who had understood the matter of the gospel more clearly than Luther or himself. He claimed that Wyttenbach had taught him that the death of Christ alone was the price for the forgiveness of sins, and he contrasted this with the way Luther seemed to attribute something to absolution and with the place Luther gave to the keys, purgatory, and the intercession of the saints. For him all this makes it in effect impossible that he could have learned the gospel from Luther.[55] Wyttenbach and Erasmus are also mentioned in *An Exposition of the Articles*. The brief reference to Wyttenbach is to his disputation in Basle, probably in 1515, in which he showed indulgences to be a deceit.[56] The reference to Erasmus is to a poem about Jesus which Zwingli said he had read eight or nine years before and from which he had derived his faith that we need no mediator except Christ and that no one except Christ can mediate between God and us. In the poem Christ lamented that people did not seek all their good in him, although he is the fount of all good, a saviour of men. Zwingli contrasted with this the seeking of help in the

---

37, 96–8, 144–7, 152–3): 'Seine apologetische Darstellungsweise, die seine Unabhängigkeit von Luther beweisen soll, führt ihn zu einer Überwertung der geistigen Neuorientierung, die er in den Jahren 1514 bis 1516 erlebte.' (p. 59.)

[55] Z V 712.9–724.24. 'Euangelii autem rationem si abs te didicissem, cur non faterer? Sed ingenue ostendam, ut haec res habeat. Fuerunt multi atque excellentes viri, qui, antequam Luteri nomen esset tam celebre, viderunt, unde penderet religio, longe aliis preceptoribus, quam tu potes, docti. Nam de me ipso coram deo testor, euangelii vim atque summam cum Joannis Augustinique tractatuum lectione didici, tum diligenti Grecanicarum Pauli epistolarum, quas hisce manibus ante undecim annos exscripsi . . .'. (Z V 712.24–714.1.)

Locher and Neuser see the reference to John, Augustine, and Paul as applying to 1520-1. For Neuser these are Zwingli's reformation teachers, because they taught divine election and sovereignty. (op. cit., pp. 70–1, 126–7.) Neuser makes a sharp distinction in Zwingli between religion and gospel (op. cit., pp. 65–70), but the distinction, with the implications, does not suit Zwingli's varied use of the terms. Gäbler suggests that in the reference to Augustine's tractates (in Z V 712.24–715.1) Zwingli may refer to having learnt 'dass Geistiges nicht durch Körperliches erfasst oder vermittelt werden könne und dass zwischen Schöpfer und Geschöpf ein unüberbrückbarer Abstand bestehe'. See 'Huldrych Zwinglis "reformatorische Wende"', ZKG 89 (1978) 128.

[56] Z II 145.28–146.4. See R. Staehelin *Huldreich Zwingli. Sein Leben und Wirken nach den Quellen dargestellt* (Basle, 1895 and 1897) I 40.

creature, which is idolatry. (Yet Zwingli points out that he noticed the inconsistency of Erasmus who also had songs dedicated to the saints.)[57]

It is important to recognize that in his ministry Zwingli saw the fundamental difference between him and his opponents as between trusting in Christ and his atoning death and trusting in anything created. For him therefore the fundamental turning came (through Wyttenbach and Erasmus) with his coming to this conviction. The Pauline understanding of sin and grace was almost certainly not present at that stage, but this does not mean that Zwingli's position was simply, as it has been described, anthropocentric rather than theocentric, rational rather than existential.[58] There is nevertheless a significant deepening of Zwingli's grasp of the gospel, which takes it beyond Erasmus, before the publication of his first reformation writings in 1522.

The period in which Zwingli says that he began to preach the gospel is the period in which he turned to scripture. For him the turning to scripture was a turning from man's word to God's word. The vital role of scripture in Zwingli's theology and of its authority as God's word over against man's word, as well as the role of the Spirit in interpreting scripture, have their origin and much of their content in the turning to scripture which he himself ascribes to 1515 or 1516. His continued insistence on scripture as the decisive criterion in his debate with catholics, though not only with them, shows that this is for Zwingli a fundamental and indispensable mark of the church. To accept scripture is moreover to accept the gospel, for the one involves or contains the other, to which it testifies. The two may be logically distinguishable, but they are not theologically separable. That, at least in part, is why Zwingli could see his own turning to the bible as fundamental. It was at the same time a turning to Christ for salvation, for both are a turning to God and not to man.

Zwingli's testimonies to his turning to scripture were written several years after the event, and were almost certainly shaped by the situation for,

---

[57] Z II 217.5–218.8. The poem is entitled 'Expostulatio Jesu cum homine'.
[58] In his valuable study Rich tends, like many other writers, to make the difference between an Erasmian and a reformation position sharper than many at the time perceived it to be. For many of the reformers, though not for Luther, there was continuity rather than discontinuity between Erasmus and the reformation. (Rich suggests certain points of continuity and discontinuity between Zwingli as a reformer and Erasmus (*Die Anfänge*, pp. 151–64)). For Zwingli it was Luther's action rather than his teaching that distinguished Luther. A sense of the continuity between Erasmus and Luther was still present in Bucer in 1542 in *De vera ecclesiarum*, in which he wrote of Erasmus as showing that salvation comes from faith in Christ not from ceremonies. He regarded both Erasmus and Luther as raised up by God, and he recognized, beside scripture, both their part and that of the fathers in his learning what true religion was. See W. Friedensburg, 'Martin Bucer, Von der Wiedervereinigung der Kirchen (1542)', *ARG* 31 (1934) 161–9.

and out of, which he wrote. Yet one can hardly doubt the freedom that Zwingli experienced in turning to scripture and his sense that that was the fundamental point of departure in his life. The appeal to scripture was not simply an appeal to the most ancient documents, it was an appeal to the source of thöse documents in God. In *The Clarity and Certainty of the Word of God* (1522) he spoke of having begun seven or eight years before to rely wholly on scripture, of learning the teaching of God from his own plain word, and of seeking understanding from God rather than from commentaries and expositors. It was a case of being taught by God and not by man.[59] This passage is similar to one in *Archeteles* which may refer to the same experience in which under God Zwingli came to trust in God's word alone for the attaining of salvation, and in which he saw Christ, the light in which things become clear, as the touchstone of all teaching. Although Zwingli does not clarify what he means by this, he does imply a christological criterion as well as a scriptural one.[60] Whether or not this was as completely a reformation experience as Locher holds, it was nevertheless decisive for Zwingli.[61] It needs also to be borne in mind that Zwingli saw continuity between his understanding of scripture and the gospel in 1522 and 1523 and what he held in his early years in Zurich, and not only between it and what he held in Einsiedeln or the end of his time in Glarus.[62]

There were probably many factors in the change that took place in 1515–16: not only the learning of Greek, the disputation of Wyttenbach, the reading of Erasmus's poem, the meeting with Erasmus, the intensive study of his works, and the copying out of Paul's letters in Greek, but also perhaps experiences such as the disastrous defeat of the Swiss which he witnessed at Marignano in September 1515 and his own sexual lapse, a

---

[59] Z I 379.18–32.

[60] Z I 259.28–261.38. He refers to having laboured for six years with the talent entrusted to him by God, insisting that the teaching is not his, but God's. Later he states that the people of Zurich are so well versed in the gospel that they will not listen to other teachings, and then, demonstrating the indissoluble link between scripture and the gospel, he points out that the council had forbidden people to preach anything not drawn from the scriptures. (Of course the word 'gospel' could be used here as equivalent to Christ's teaching: Z I 256.13–18, 257.23–9.) In his reference in *An Exposition of the Articles* to preaching the gospel in 1516 he spoke of expounding the reading at mass from the bible alone, but he also mentioned his initial reliance on the fathers. (Z II 144.32–145.6.)

[61] Locher, *Zwingli's Thought*, pp. 156–66, and *Die Zwinglische Reformation*, p. 71. It is not clear how far at this stage Zwingli stressed the natural sense of scripture against the spiritual sense favoured by Erasmus (Z I 375.10–14), nor how far he interpreted scripture by scripture (Z II 144.32–145.6), something he may have learned from Lefèvre d'Étaples. (Z XII 282.23–5.) See also Rich, *Die Anfänge*, p. 53, n. 28.

[62] Z I 88.10–89.2; II 14.11–14.

lapse which he admitted when he was appointed to the Great Minster in Zurich. Yet, important as the change in 1515-16 was, there seems no doubt that Zwingli came to a profounder grasp of the gospel and of scripture in his first years in Zurich. His study of John, Augustine, and Paul, his suffering from the plague, the example of Luther at Leipzig, and perhaps his sense of failure as a person and a minister, are all elements in this, however their individual significance and their relationship with each other are interpreted. It is impossible to determine which element was of decisive importance, in part because of the lack of direct evidence, in part because they contributed in different ways. In theological formation, however, it must be the study of John, Paul, and Augustine that was vital, whatever may have been important in Zwingli's personal experience. However, the role of Augustine should not be stressed to the detriment of John and Paul. Although there were many influences on Zwingli in reading the bible, the creative impact of the bible itself must not be underestimated.

Zwingli's awareness of the grace of God and of the righteousness of God which comes through faith becomes evident in the marginal notes. It was probably in part the fruit of his reading of Augustine. Here Köhler ascribes a more formative role to the study of Augustine in Zwingli's development than does Rich and he sees the process as beginning in Einsiedeln. Rich allows that there are in the earlier Zwingli marginal notes that may imply a reformation understanding of the gospel, but regards Zwingli as holding them intellectually rather than existentially.[63] The distinction can be a proper one, but as in the case of John Wesley's grasp of the gospel two centuries later, the distinction is more strictly relevant to a study of Zwingli's life than to a study of his theology.

Luther's stand against the pope at the Leipzig disputation in 1519 played a part in Zwingli's development. It made a profound impression on him, so that years later he praised Luther's courage in being the one who acted, like a David against Goliath, like a Hercules, unlike Erasmus and others.[64] This was the moment at which word became deed—clearly a moment of liberation for Zwingli. He claimed in 1525 that he had asserted

---

[63] Köhler, Zwingli, pp. 68-74: 'Zwingli ist an Augustin zum Reformator herangereift' (p. 70). Rich, Die Anfänge, pp. 124-45, in particular p. 128, n. 19. Schindler (pp. 21-41) recognizes the importance of Augustine for Zwingli, but questions the weight that has been placed on Augustine as influencing Zwingli in his development as a reformer. He sees Luther, however, as less important in that development.

Zwingli's strongly theocentric theology is present in the marginal notes, e.g. in Z XII 336.21-3. Köhler ('Die Randglossen', p. 106) alludes to the anthropocentric character of the earlier marginal notes on Romans.

[64] Z V 721.5-723.3. See also the revealing comments in Z V 815.18-818.3.

from scripture both in Einsiedeln and in Zurich that the whole papacy was poorly based, and that three people, still alive, had often heard him say so.[65] Yet neither Zwingli nor Erasmus took the decisive step, despite the fact that Zwingli's opposition to the pope, though differently expressed from Luther's was also ultimately christological.[66] However, the impact of Luther's boldness in Leipzig succeeded, rather than preceded, the initial theological impact of Augustine and the study of John and Paul. The study of Augustine moreover continued through the early years in Zurich and was vital after the Leipzig disputation, as he prepared lectures on Psalms and Romans.[67]

Zwingli suffered from the plague in 1519. It is hard to assess the role of that experience in his development, for we do not know exactly when he wrote the poem based on his illness, nor how far it was based on other models.[68] The poem does not explicitly express a Pauline sense of the grace of God in Christ, but it does, as nothing before, show an overwhelming sense of the power and mercy of God, a total surrender to his will, and a confident acceptance of his purpose, whether in life or death. It helps to explain both Zwingli's own unshakable conviction that he is an instrument in the hand of God and his yielding of himself utterly to God's purpose in reforming the life of his people.

A further factor in his development is the awareness of God's forgiving love to which Zwingli testified in *An Exposition of the Articles*.[69] We do not know when he wrestled with the words, 'Forgive us our trespasses, as we forgive those that trespass against us'. However, out of his agonized wrestling with words that seemed to make God's forgiveness conditional on his own forgiveness, Zwingli came to see his utter dependence on God's grace, and surrendered himself wholly to that grace.

[65] Z IV 59.5–60.2. Capito wrote later to Bullinger that while Zwingli had been in Einsiedeln they had spoken of the necessity of overthrowing the pope. See J. W. Baum, *Capito und Butzer, Strassburgs Reformatoren* (Elberfeld, 1860), p. 29.

[66] Z VII 250.11–19. He did not surrender his papal pension until 1520. This action may favour the importance attached to that year in Zwingli's development as a reformer. Cf. J. V. Pollet, *Huldrych Zwingli et la réforme en Suisse d'après les recherches récentes* (Paris, 1963), p. 19, n. 4.

[67] Pollet rightly stresses the importance of Luther's example, but in doing so somewhat undervalues the role of Augustine. (*DTC* 3759–61.) Following Usteri, Köhler (*Zwingli*, p. 68) points out that Zwingli's handwriting in the marginal notes changes twice, first in the period of Erasmus's influence and then in July 1519, the time of the Leipzig disputation.

[68] Z I 67–69. See, e.g., the discussion in Farner, II 347–76 and Rich, *Die Anfänge*, pp. 104–19. Farner points to the interpretation of Zwingli's illness and his death (had that occurred) as the judgement of God on his ministry. That would have given added significance to the illness and the recovery. Zwingli's sense of being an instrument in the hands of God, like the pot in the hands of the potter (Rom. 9: 20–4), is evident in a letter to Myconius on 24 July 1520. (Z VII 344.13–17.)

[69] Z II 225.19–227.7. Neuser sees this as a vital stage in Zwingli's breakthrough (*Die reformatorische Wende*, pp. 139–44).

The apparent failure of his successful ministry in Zurich, to which a letter of 24 July 1520 testifies, may have been a further stage in Zwingli's emergence as a reformer.[70] It may be that the opposition he experienced led him to a profounder sense of the inadequacy of human endeavour against the forces of evil and a surer sense that the battle is God's. Rich sees this as the occasion of Zwingli's breaking free in effect from Erasmus.[71]

In the light of Luther, we contrast Erasmus and the reformation and stress the importance of the years in (rather than before) Zurich for Zwingli's development as a reformer.[72] For Zwingli, however, Erasmus was not contrasted with the reformation and he saw the period before Zurich as decisive. It was indeed decisive, even though not complete. The theocentric character of his theology, albeit undeveloped, was present at that point in the turning from man's word to God's word and from the creature to Christ and his atoning death. There was a deepening or maturing in his grasp of scripture and of the gospel, both in Einsiedeln and in Zurich. In this Augustine was probably the stimulus, as Wyttenbach and Erasmus had been in the earlier period. They stimulated him in his study of scripture, although at no point was any of them an unchallenged authority—nor should they be regarded as ultimately more influential than scripture itself. A variety of experiences prepared Zwingli inwardly to grasp more deeply the overwhelming grace of God in the gospel and the living word of God in scripture, but the interpreters along the way were above all Erasmus and Augustine. Zwingli saw the work as God's work. That view is in keeping with his theology, as no doubt his theology was in keeping with his experience.

## The Inauguration of the Reformation

Zwingli's ministry in Zurich began on his thirty-fifth birthday on 1 January 1519. He announced that the next day he would begin a continuous exposition of St Matthew.[73] He did this, not on the basis of human

---

[70] Z VII 341-5.

[71] Rich, Die Anfänge, pp. 96-104.

[72] Apart from the theological problem as to what is involved in being a reformer, there is the historical problem of Zwingli's theology at different stages. His own writings before 1522 were mostly letters and often give only indirect evidence. The letters of others could also have misunderstood him in humanist terms, just as he is thought to have misunderstood Luther. Moreover some see essentially reformation features where others do not. Thus Farner (II 199) sees Zwingli as on the way to his final discovery, though not yet there, in The Labyrinth, pointing to: 'die satanische Unheimlichkeit des Bösen und die absolute Hilfe in der Unterwerfung unter den rettenden Jesus Christus allein'.

[73] Zwingli had determined to do this before coming to Zurich, well aware that it was a departure from church practice. (Z VII 106.3-4.)

interpreters but according to the scriptures themselves.[74] For him the preaching was in the end not his work, but God's.[75]

Zwingli's dozen years in Zurich were remarkable for the central place given to the exposition and proclamation of the word. He preached regularly—not only in the Great Minster, but also on Fridays, market day, in the Minster of our Lady. In the latter he offered a continuous exposition of the psalms, in the former he began by expounding St Matthew and Acts and then in 1521-2 he continued with some of the epistles. Eventually he preached from most of the bible, old testament as well as new.[76] The preaching was practical and topical. It grappled not only with obviously religious issues, but also with social and political issues.[77]

The centrality of preaching went with the centrality of scripture, which was the decisive criterion for Zwingli and the basis for his reforming ministry. It was this that led to the mandate issued by the council in 1520 that preaching should be in accordance with scripture, a mandate renewed in effect after the first disputation.[78] Zwingli's appeal to scripture was therefore a matter of civil as well as theological importance, although the former was derived from, and dependent on, the latter.

Zwingli was three years in Zurich before publishing his first manifestly reformation writings in 1522. It was a period in which he became an increasingly influential and controversial figure through his preaching. Among other things his preaching attacked indulgences and the veneration of the saints and it was in areas like this that he welcomed the writings of Luther. He started reading Luther in Zurich, having become interested in him at the end of his time in Einsiedeln. Luther featured constantly in his correspondence and he looked to him for support on issues such as the invocation of the saints. He encouraged the sale of Luther's writings to convince others of his views. His preaching and Luther's writing were in effect a twofold weapon. Indeed on occasion he was thought to be the

[74] Z II 144.32-145.7, 21-5, 707.31-708.9.

[75] 'This is the seed I have sown. Matthew, Luke, Paul, and Peter have watered it, and God has given it splendid increase . . .'. (Z I 285.25-7; *Works* I 239.)

[76] The most complete account of Zwingli as a preacher is in Farner, III 29-187. The probable order of the books on which he preached is given on pp. 42-3 and shows the transition, in 1525, from the new testament to the old. The importance of the old testament after 1525 is undoubted, but should not be exaggerated. Pollet (*Zwingli*, pp. 30-1) speaks of Zwingli's conversion to the old testament, with its fatal consequences for his thought and action. However, Zwingli continued to expound the new testament and preach regularly from it. See Meyer, 'Die Entstehung', pp. 314-29.

[77] A conflict arose from Zwingli's challenging tithes in terms of divine law in 1520. See his letter to Myconius on 16 Feb. 1520. (Z VII 272.12-17.) Farner (II 128-9) suggests a greater stress on political issues in the second half of his ministry.

[78] See, e.g., Farner, II 206-17.

author of something Luther had written.[79] In July 1519 at the Leipzig disputation Luther challenged among other things the divine right of the papacy. This was a crucial moment for Zwingli, who hailed Luther as a new Elijah,[80] and sometime in the following year he himself took the decisive step of renouncing his papal pension.

Between August 1519 and February 1520 a quarter of the inhabitants of Zurich died of the plague. Zwingli suffered from it and came close to death. Out of this experience came his poem on the plague, with its utter surrender to the will of God. In the midst of the changes brought by these new events there was also continuity with his past. His correspondence attests the strong literary and political interests of a Swiss humanist, as the marginal notes do his grasp of Augustine and his deepening understanding of the gospel. In 1520 he expounded Romans and Psalms, and for the second of these began again the study of Hebrew.

Then in 1522 came the breaking of the Lenten fast. It is this that provoked Zwingli's sermon on 23 March which was published in expanded form on 16 April with the title *Choice and Liberty Respecting Food*.[81] The breaking of the fast, which Zwingli witnessed, but significantly did not share, was in effect a breakthrough in the reformation of Zurich. Yet Zwingli did not see what he had to say as something fundamentally new in his ministry, for he began by referring to the fact that the people had been responding eagerly to the gospel he had been preaching for over three years. In the sermon the note of Christian liberty, so characteristic of Luther, was sounded, but it was sounded in a context of church law and ceremonial which was typically Zwinglian. The sermon was a challenge to the authority of the church in the light of scripture, an appeal to the word of God against the word or ordinance of men. (This challenge and this appeal are manifest in the writings that follow.) There was also, characteristically for Zwingli, an appeal to the evidence of Swiss history.

In the debate that followed Zwingli showed clearly how his understanding of the church was bound up with Christ and faith in Christ. To the appeal of the official representatives of the Bishop of Constance in early April 'to stay with and in the church, for outside it no one can be saved', Zwingli averred that the foundation of the church is Christ, that all who believe and confess him will be saved, adding that they believed themselves to be in that church, outside which no one will be saved.[82]

[79] Z II 146.9–14.
[80] Z VII 222.11–12. Cf. Z II 147.14–20; V 721.5–723.3.
[81] ZI 88–136. It may be compared with Luther's *Concerning Christian Liberty*.
[82] Z I 152.5–22.

*A Solemn Exhortation* in May, addressed to Schwyz, again concerned a practical matter: freedom from the control by foreign powers that came through the raising of mercenary soldiers.[83] This time, however, the issue was not an individual one, but a national one. The admonition was written, said Zwingli, 'from fear of God and love of an honourable confederation'.[84] The appeal to scripture is of a different kind here. It is an appeal to God's purpose for mankind in creation and redemption and a pointing to God's judgement on his people now, just as on the people of Israel then. The greatest danger from mercenary service was not the moral corruption or political subjugation to which it led, but the fact that it placed the whole people under the wrath of God. Unless the people repented they would perish.[85] This solemn exhortation shows that Zwingli's challenge was to the whole life of the people and not just to its religious life, and to civil leaders, not just ecclesiastical ones. Moreover God's wrath was seen in national and not just individual terms.

Two other matters to provoke responses from Zwingli at this time were the celibacy of the priesthood and the intercession of the saints. They were not of course new issues. *The Petition*, written to their bishop by Zwingli and other ministers in July 1522, concerned the first of these. It requests permission to marry. In its attack on celibacy it is a challenge to the authority of the church in the light of scripture, and an appeal to the word of God against the word or ordinance of man.[86] It is a demand for Christian liberty in the sense of scriptural liberty. Zwingli's characteristic use of a range of scriptural testimonies is both an argument from scripture and an interpretation of scripture by scripture. The writing was concerned not only with marriage, but also with the preaching of the gospel, to which—as he pointed out—Christ had appointed the bishop as well.[87]

The second issue, the intercession of the saints, was the subject of the first of Zwingli's debates in July. It was with Franz Lambert, a Franciscan from Avignon. Zwingli persuaded him on the basis of scripture to call on God and not the saints. The other debate was on the authority of scripture and was held with members of the orders in Zurich, which were opposed to the reformation. After it the council made clear its support for

---

[83] Z I 165–88.
[84] Z I 167.1–2.
[85] Z I 175.5–16, 185.19–188.11.
[86] Z I 197–209. In *A Friendly Request* on 13 July Zwingli addressed a similar statement in German to the federation, requesting that the preaching of the gospel should not be hindered and urging the propriety of clerical marriage. (Z I 214–48.) He had already married, but not publicly.
[87] Z I 200.16–21.

preaching from scripture rather than from the schoolmen.[88] It also passed a decree which permitted Zwingli to preach in the Dominican convent at Oetenbach.

The sermon he preached there, *The Clarity and Certainty of the Word of God*, was published on 6 September.[89] The certainty or power of the word brings to pass what it announces. The clarity of the word is its bringing to people its own enlightenment and certainty. The sermon deals with the authority and interpretation of scripture, but with a characteristically Zwinglian emphasis on the Spirit as well as the word, together with his typical contrast between God's word and man's word. The view of man in the image of God with which the sermon begins shows something of Zwingli's humanism and Augustinianism. Another sermon, on Mary, was probably provoked by rumours about Zwingli's views on Mary. *A Sermon on the Virgin Mary* was published on 17 September. It manifests a high regard for Mary, but relates her to Christ, affirming that the greatest honour we can do to her is to honour Christ.[90]

The vital place both of preaching and of the council was expressed a few weeks later, when on 10 November Zwingli resigned from his position at the Great Minster in order to give himself more to the proclamation of the word. The council authorized this change by which in effect the priest became the preacher.

The breaking of the fast produced responses from the Bishop of Constance to the council and chapter. To the second of these, addressed to the chapter on 24 May,[91] Zwingli replied in August with *Archeteles*.[92] It was the longest of his early writings and in its sixty-nine sections it dealt with the bishop's exhortation point by point. This had accused him of holding novel and heretical views and of destroying the unity of the church.[93] He

---

[88] Z I 257–8, n. 3. Here Zwingli stressed that he, and not the monks, had pastoral responsibility for Zurich: 'ich bin in diser statt Zürich bischof und pfarrer und mir ist die seelsorg bevolen; ich han darum geschworen und die münch nit . . .'. This concern is an important element in his reforming ministry. Oberman regards 21 July 1522 (rather than 29 Jan. 1523) as the first disputation, 'when a committee of the lesser council passed the ordinance stipulating scripturally based preaching by both parties in the emerging Reformation' (*Masters of the Reformation*, p. 236).

[89] Z I 338–84.          [90] Z I 391–428.          [91] Z I 263.24–270.8.

[92] Z I 256–327. Erasmus wrote briefly and critically to Zwingli on 8 September after reading part of *Archeteles*. (Z VII 582.)

[93] Zwingli is concerned through his teaching from the new testament to restore what he calls 'the ancient unity of the church of Christ'. (Z I 284.34–5.) He attacks the view that there can be no gospel without the church's unity. The gospel can be preached along with a split in the church, as in the time of Arianism in the early church. As then, the church does not need the pope in its midst in order to preach the gospel. (Z I 292.16–293.3.) The rock on which the church is built is not Peter, but Christ. (Z I 295.8–26.)

defended himself by an appeal to Christ and scripture over against human teaching and invention. God is true, man is a liar. It is Christ and scripture, and not the pope, that distinguish the true church. Far from the church's confirming scripture, it is by scripture that the decisions of councils of the church are to be judged. Zwingli's sense of the urgency of the decision facing them is expressed in his call to escape the wrath of God, which will descend on the German peoples as it did on Sodom and Gomorrah.

Running through all these writings in 1522 was the appeal to scripture against all human teaching, in particular against the authority of the church. This issue came to a head in the first disputation in January 1523, summoned by the council because of the dissension that had arisen. The basis for judgement was to be scripture and the disputation was to be in German and not, like an academic disputation, in Latin. At the end it was judged that Zwingli's preaching was scriptural and that all the priests should preach in accordance with scripture.[94] This important initiative in reform on the part of council was in keeping with its mandate of 1520.

However the disputation may have been intended by others, Zwingli saw it as an opportunity to expound and defend the faith.[95] He did this by presenting in sixty-seven articles what he claimed he had already preached on the basis of the scriptures which are inspired by God.[96] From the start the articles made two fundamental contrasts: between the authority of scripture and that of the church and between Christ and anything or anyone else as the way of salvation. Indeed the central place of Christ emerges more clearly and prominently here than in any of Zwingli's earlier writings. Moreover what is said in the first twenty-three articles about the church, the ministry, the intercession of the saints, good works, and clerical property is related quite specifically to Christ, as are some of the later articles about government and the remission of sins.[97] In the last article Zwingli named other issues, including interest and tithes, that he was willing to discuss.[98] There is an obvious contrast between the sixty-seven articles and Luther's ninety-five theses, for Zwingli's do not elaborate a

[94] Z I 470.14–471.7.
[95] For a discussion of the disputation and its purpose, see Oberman, *Masters of the Reformation*, pp. 187–239. An account is given in Z I 479–569.
[96] Z I 458.3–8. The first three articles state: '1. All who say that the gospel is invalid without the confirmation of the church err and slander God. 2. The sum and substance (*summa*) of the gospel is that our Lord Jesus Christ, the true Son of God, has made known to us the will of his heavenly Father, and has with his innocence redeemed us from death and reconciled us to God. 3. Hence Christ is the only way to salvation for all who ever were, are and shall be.' (Z I 458.11–17; *Selected Works* III.)
[97] Z I 458.11–461.2, 462.14–18, 463.8–9, 28–30, 464.9–11.
[98] Z I 465.14–16.

single issue, but cover a whole programme of reform, the concern being social and political as well as ecclesiastical and personal.

Although the disputation was no real debate, yet it made clear the role of scripture and that of the Spirit as the interpreter of scripture. Zwingli saw the assembly as a council of the church. The scriptures were the criterion for decision, with scholars present who could determine the accuracy of biblical quotation and Christians taught by the Spirit who could decide which party had used scripture properly.[99] Here and in the central place of Christ lay the fundamental challenge to the church. The disputation shows also that Zwingli's view of the church was not of the few, as that of the radicals was to be, but of the whole people renewed; moreover his view of the church included the city council. At the same time the church is defined over against Rome in terms of Christ and faith in Christ, not in terms of the hierarchy.

*An Exposition of the Articles* was published in July 1523.[100] It is the most substantial treatment of his theology in German, to be compared with *A Commentary*, published in March 1525 in Latin, which was his one major systematic work. Some of his characteristic emphases are evident: Christ in his atoning death as the substance of the gospel, the sin of man and his salvation by the mercy of God through faith in Christ, the life of love that flows from faith, the authority of God's word over against man's, the Spirit active along with the word, the sovereignty of God, the church defined in terms of Christ and the Spirit, the Lord's supper as a memorial of the death of Christ, the civil authority with its power of the sword as ordained by God, the duty to oppose that authority if it does not follow the rule of Christ. Some doctrines, such as sin, election, and the eucharist, were to be developed or reformulated in response to new situations, but all are here in some form. Moreover some of the emphases that were later to mark him off from Luther are also present, not least, but not only, in the eucharist.

## A More Radical Reformation

While Zwingli was writing this work there were those seeking a reformation at once more rapid and more radical. Some were pastors, others laymen.[101] Among the issues involved were tithes and the paying of interest, practices not supported by the new testament. Later issues were images, baptism, and the eucharist.

---

[99] Z I 499.2–12.    [100] Z II 14–457.

[101] There was continuity between those who broke the Lenten fast and those calling for more radical change in the summer of 1522 and later. Both social and religious issues were involved, although the two areas overlapped. The radicals were joined in the summer of 1522 by Manz and

The radicals sought a society in conformity with the new testament and in particular with the Sermon on the Mount. A delegation from several parishes met the council on 22 June and among other things raised the question of tithes. Two days later Zwingli preached his sermon on *Divine and Human Righteousness*.[102] It was published in July and was the first of his writings against the radicals. (He was concerned not only for the effects of the radicals on the reformation in Zurich, but also for the repercussions outside, as the dedication to Berne shows.) In it he elaborated the distinction and the relation between divine righteousness, which is inward, and human righteousness, which is outward and which, though weak, is commanded by God. It is because we are sinners and fall short of divine righteousness that we need human righteousness, and that means government. Government, which is ordained by God, must be obeyed, but it is not autonomous; it also must obey God. In the light of this Zwingli argued for respecting property and paying interest and tithes while the government still required them.

In the summer the stress among many for a more radical reformation focused attention on other matters held to be unscriptural, especially the mass and images. Reform was begun in worship. In August baptism was celebrated in German instead of Latin and later in the month Zwingli produced *The Canon of the Mass*, with its criticisms and proposals.[103] Some of the proposals were relatively conservative, as he did not reject eucharistic vestments, and for the sake of the weak he retained the sign of the cross and the traditional singing. He was criticized for not being biblical enough, and his defence in *An Apology for the Canon of the Mass*[104] shows his

Grebel, and later by Hubmaier. Not only were they from Zwingli's supporters, but they shared in many ways a common theological heritage and common social concerns. Only gradually did the question of baptism dominate the dispute.

For an account of the beginnings of the anabaptists in Zurich, see e.g. J. F. G. Goeters, 'Die Vorgeschichte des Täufertums in Zürich', in *Studien zur Geschichte und Theologie der Reformation. Festschrift für Ernst Bizer*, ed. L. Abramowski and J. F. G. Goeters (Neukirchen, 1969) pp. 239–81.

[102] Z II 471–525. Gestrich (p. 176, n. 208.) argues from the parallels between this and Luther's *Von weltlicher Obrigkeit* that Zwingli is dependent on Luther. For a comparison with Aquinas and Luther, see H. Schmid, *Zwinglis Lehre von der göttlichen und menschlichen Gerechtigkeit* (Zurich, 1959), pp. 27–45. Rich sees a relationship between Erasmus's thinking and Zwingli's doctrine of divine and human righteousness. (*Die Anfänge*, p. 41, n. 82.)

[103] Z II 556–608. Zwingli criticized the mass as a sacrifice, but left freedom of choice in many outward matters.

[104] Z II 620–5. For example, he attacks the biblicist idea that one should have only the Lord's prayer. (623.1–14.) At the second disputation Zwingli had changed his view on vestments. But even though he now saw them as a hindrance to true worship, he did not seek to abolish them at once because that would cause an uproar. People must first be taught. (Z II 788.31–789.16.) His fundamental concern is the futherance of the gospel. (Z II 794.6–7.)

rejection of the biblicist position. It was, however, the denunciation of images both in sermons and in writings, together with the violent destruction of images, that led in October to the second disputation, attended by 900 persons.[105] The council wanted images and the mass to be examined in the light of scripture. There was never any doubt that the assembly would hold the mass and images to be unscriptural. However, some of the differences that emerged between Zwingli and the radicals were important, both their objection to details in the celebration of the mass, such as the use of unleavened bread, and their objection that the judgement at the disputation was in the hands of the council.[106] A more literalist approach to the bible and a rejection of the role of the council are two matters which continued to distinguish the radicals from Zwingli. On this occasion, however, it was Schmid's more cautious view that prevailed rather than Zwingli's or the radicals', but Zwingli accepted that it was for the council to determine when the changes agreed should take place. The council decided to introduce no change in the mass or images but, following Schmid's view that people should be adequately taught first, resolved on the publication of a short introduction which would further the preaching of the gospel. Zwingli published A Short Christian Introduction in the middle of November.[107] It is in effect the first official reformation statement of the church in Zurich.

On the third morning of the disputation Zwingli preached a sermon on The Shepherd, which was published in the following March.[108] Like so much of his writing it makes use of contrast, in this case between the true and false shepherd. The true shepherd is the reformed pastor, described as preaching the word of God fearlessly to high and low. The picture is based on Christ and the apostles as much as on the prophets, although it is the prophetic role of the preacher that especially characterizes Zwingli's view and practice of the ministry. Zwingli contrasts the reformed pastor with the unreformed priest, for his primary battle is still with the conservatives rather than with the radicals.

The third disputation in January 1524 was a quite different occasion, with a small select group. Behind it was an attempt by the conservatives to

---

[105] An account is given in Z II 671–803. Jud was among those who denounced images. Goeters relates the attacks on images to the effect of Carlstadt rather than Zwingli ('Die Vorgeschichte', pp. 260–1).

[106] Z II 789.27–790.21, 792.18–27. In response to Simon Stumpf's charge that he was leaving judgement to the council, Zwingli made it clear that no one, including the council, was to pass judgement on the word of God. The assembly is to learn what scripture says about the mass and to advise how to act without disturbance. (Z II 784.10–26.)

[107] Z II 628–63.                                                   [108] Z III 5–68.

undermine the reformation. It failed, but it showed that conservative opposition, both lay and clerical, remained an important factor for the council and for the reformers. The reformers wanted to press ahead with reform in the light of the second disputation, which itself showed the demands to conform the outward and liturgical life of the church more closely to the word of God. In *A Proposal Concerning Images and the Mass*, in May, Zwingli was prepared for delay in the abolition of images until preaching had won people from them, but he wanted to end the sacrificial character of the mass.[109] The commission appointed by the council was divided; nevertheless on 15 June the council decided to do away with pictures and statues in response to the word of God. In a brief fortnight they were removed from the churches. Yet still no action was taken over the mass, which was not replaced by the Lord's supper until the Easter of the following year.[110]

The mass was a theme of increasing controversy. It was probably in the summer of 1524 that Zwingli read Hoen's letter, which presented a more radical approach to the eucharist, with its interpretation of 'is' as 'represents' in the words 'This is my body'.[111] This led Zwingli to develop his symbolic understanding of the eucharist both in major letters to Matthew Alber[112] and Strasburg[113] in November and December 1524 and in *A Commentary*[114] and *The Eucharist*[115] in March and August of the following year. The emphasis in the growing eucharistic controversy moved at this point from the sacrifice of the mass, which was still the uppermost concern in *A Reply to Emser*[116] in August 1524, to the presence of Christ.

[109] Z III 115–18. Zwingli was not precipitate in action. He sought the right moment, but he was concerned to teach and persuade before taking action at all. 'Therefore, good Christians, do not try to push ahead too quickly: for to press on regardless of the weak is the mark not of a strong but of a restless spirit which cannot wait until the poor sheep can catch up behind.' (Z IV 255.9–13; LCC XXIV 158.) Cf. Z II 655.5–8. 'Let us, then, I beg, preach Christian piety with solicitude and purity, and let us not be prematurely troubled as to the abolition of the mass or the casting out of the images, but let us labour to restore to their Creator the hearts that are given over to this world.' (Z V 395.19–22; *Works* II 31.)

[110] See *The Action or Practice of the Lord's Supper*. (Z IV 13–24.)

[111] Zwingli published Hoen's letter in 1525 with a postscript of his own. (Z IV 512–19.) W. H. Neuser regards this as a decisive moment: 'Der Brief des Honius stellt neben der reformatorischen Wende 1520–21 die wichtigste Zäsur in der Theologie Zwinglis dar.' ('Zwinglis Abendmahlsbrief an Thomas Wyttenbach (1523)' *Wegen en gestalten in het gereformeerd protestantisme* (Amsterdam, 1976), pp. 45–6.)

[112] Z III 335–54.

[113] Z VIII 275.23–277.13.

[114] Z III 773.25–820.17.

[115] Z IV 458–504.

[116] Z III 241–87. *A Reply to Emser* is more concerned with the church, the intercession of the saints, and merit, than with the eucharist. The presence of Christ was already an important issue in the letter to Wyttenbach in June 1523. (Z VIII 84–9.)

One effect of the council's long delay in abolishing the mass was an increase in the opposition of the radicals which had been expressed after the second disputation. The radicals were diverse in their concerns, some more social and political, some more religious. There was strong hostility to interest and tithes, and to the role of the council in the reformation of the church, but there was also the desire for a pure congregation, with the exercise of discipline within it in accordance with Matthew 18. It was this separateness that Zwingli most strongly criticized and that was in many ways the dividing point between him and them. The issue of baptism was related to this.

Zwingli's dispute with the radicals was to centre in the issue of baptism, but initially the more obviously social and political issues of tithes, interest, the use of the oath, and obedience to civil authority were prominent. They are evident in *Those Who Give Cause for Tumult*, which he wrote at the end of December 1524.[117] He recognized the abuse of tithes, but argued that they were an obligation people had to meet. He used the command not to steal to defend personal property against the radicals' attack on private ownership. He criticized the extremists for their lack of love, their inconsistency, and their opposition to government.

The issue of baptism began to be important in the summer and autumn of 1524, although as early as February a number of people had refused to have their children baptized. In the autumn Manz and Grebel were in touch with Müntzer and welcomed his criticism of infant baptism. Zwingli's first important writing on the issue was his letter to Strasburg in December 1524,[118] which contains the heart of his position. There were abortive conversations between some of the radicals and Zwingli, along with other ministers, in December 1524. Then a statement was published, probably by Manz, showing that infant baptism was unbiblical and demanding a biblical defence from Zwingli. The council summoned both groups to a disputation on 17 January 1525 and afterwards insisted on the baptism of infants within eight days, on pain of banishment. Various measures were taken against the radicals, but on 21 January Grebel baptized Blaurock, who then baptized fifteen others. A day or two later he presided at the Lord's supper in a house in Zollikon. Despite official action the movement spread in other cantons and beyond. Further meetings or disputations on baptism between the reformers and the radicals in March and November produced no change. On 7 March 1526 the council declared that anyone rebaptizing a person would be put to death by drowning. On 5 January 1527 Felix Manz was the first to suffer that penalty.

[117] Z III 374–469.        [118] Z VIII 261–78.

The discussion was related to Zwingli's view of sacraments, which in part the radicals shared, so that Zwingli sought carefully to distinguish his position from theirs in *A Commentary* in March 1525.[119] After the rebaptisms in 1525 he had to face the additional issue of rebaptism, although it never occupied a large space in his writing. He tackled it in *Baptism, Rebaptism, and Infant Baptism* in May 1525.[120] For Zwingli the radicals' insistence on believers' baptism called in question salvation through Christ alone, as in their different ways catholic and Lutheran views did. Their emphasis on the new testament caused him to formulate anew his understanding of the relation of the two testaments. The debate on baptism continued in two major works, *A Reply to Hubmaier* in November 1525[121] and *A Refutation* in July 1527,[122] and was an important factor in developing Zwingli's doctrine of election. The last substantial discussion of baptism was in 1530 with Schwenckfeld in *Questions Concerning the Sacrament of Baptism*.[123]

The way the radicals moved from place to place, entering parishes on their own authority, caused Zwingli to expound and defend his own understanding of a duly ordered ministry. *The Ministry*[124] in June 1525 distinguished the reformed pastor from the itinerant preacher, as *The Shepherd* had distinguished him from the unreformed priest. Indeed there is a sense in which the prophecy which was established in the same month precisely expressed the Zwinglian view of the ministry over against catholic and radical. At the heart of the prophecy was the study of the bible in the original languages, Hebrew and Greek. This required the most rigorous linguistic study, itself part of the work of the Spirit, who gives the gift of tongues and who is the true interpreter of his own word. A preacher versed in the scripture would be free from the errors of those who relied on human teaching, whether they appealed as catholics to the teaching of the church or as radicals to the Spirit, who was their spirit rather than the Holy Spirit. The reformed preacher would equally be free from that misinterpretation of the text that comes from not understanding the principles of interpretation. The prophecy was notable, not only for its education of the ministry, but for the translations and the flow of commentaries it produced between 1525 and 1531.[125]

---

[119] Z III 757.7–762.3. The section on baptism is 763.6–773.24.

[120] Z IV 206–337.                                           [121] Z IV 585–641.

[122] Z VI i 21–196. In the course of debate a range of theological issues emerged, such as free will, the sleep of the soul, and the salvation of all. (Z VI i 109.14–17, 188.9–194.13.)

[123] S III 563–88.                                           [124] Z IV 382–433.

[125] For the old testament, see Z XIII–XIV; for the new testament, see S VI i–VI ii. Some of the

The name 'the prophecy' came from 1 Corinthians 14 and Zwingli's understanding of prophecy there. Every morning, except Sundays and Fridays, at seven in the summer and at eight in the winter, the preachers and students met in the cathedral choir. After the opening prayer, the old testament text was read in Latin from the Vulgate. Then it was read in Hebrew and expounded in Latin; after that it was read in Greek from the Septuagint and expounded in Latin. Finally what had been done in Latin, the language of the educated, was expounded in German, the language of the people. The leaders changed in the course of time and increasingly it was Zwingli who preached in the final part, which was attended by the general public. The participants were free to speak and ask questions.

The debate with the anabaptists led directly or indirectly to development in a number of important areas in Zwingli's theology: the nature of the church and ministry, the role of government, the use and interpretation of scripture, the understanding of covenant, and election.

### Consolidation, Expansion, and Protection

The year 1525 saw the consolidation of the reformation in Zurich. Legislation concerning baptism on the one hand and the celebration of the Lord's supper instead of the mass on the other demonstrate the reformed character of the church over against the radical or catholic one. The institution of the prophecy in June was vital to the education of a reformed ministry and manifested the centrality of the word in a reformed church. The calling of a synod in 1528 gave a complementary form of oversight. There was also the enactment of the Poor Law in January 1525 and of marriage laws in May 1525. Legislation for the social and political life of the people was as important for Zwingli as legislation for its liturgical life, as the whole life of the community was under the sovereign rule of God. This developed through the years, culminating in the great moral mandate of May 1530. All this shows the crucial part of the council. Its role in church affairs was not new, but was a development of the increasing powers it had gathered to itself before the reformation. For Zwingli the

principles of biblical translation and interpretation are discussed in *Preface to the Prophets* in 1529. (Z VI ii 289–312.)

J. V. Pollet's comment that in the prophecy Zwingli was closer to the *Schwärmer* than to the humanists is surprising. (See 'Recherches sur Zwingli à propos d'ouvrages récentes', *Revue des sciences religieuses*, 28 (1954) 172–3.) The linguistic basis of the prophecy was a challenge to anabaptists. Hubmaier was critical of Zwingli's stress on the importance of the biblical languages and his use of them in controversy. He argued in July 1525 that languages were being used to obscure scripture rather than to build up the church, and that we should have to wait on those with knowledge of languages, as we had waited in the past on popes and councils: 'Das hiesse aber auf ein news papazare, darvon uns gott wölle behueten.' (Z IV 601, n. 8.)

council was indispensable on practical grounds, given the opposition of the bishop, but its role also cohered with his understanding of the role of government in the bible. It was both to permit the word of God to be preached and to rule in accordance with it. What Zwingli sought inside Zurich he sought outside it as well. The fundamental concern in his dealings with the rest of Switzerland and in his search for alliances is freedom for the word of God to be preached and for the ordering of life in response to the word.

His missionary concern expressed itself in March 1525 in the dedication of the main systematic exposition of his theology to the King of France. In its form at least, *A Commentary* seems intended to please French humanists.[126] Its structure and style and, to some extent, its approach show the philosopher and humanist. It begins with the doctrines of God and man rather than with Christ and the gospel, but its inward point of departure is the biblical revelation. It treats the gospel before the law and shows the different understanding of the law from Luther that was already evident in Zwingli's letter to Strasburg some months before.[127] It elaborates his understanding of the sacraments and marks his position off from that of catholic, Lutheran, and radical alike. It discusses government and proper Christian involvement in it. Its fundamental contrast is between true and false religion which it expresses in a fundamentally Zwinglian way. 'It is false religion or piety when trust is put in any other than God. They, then, who trust in any created thing whatsoever are not truly pious.'[128]

The reformation in Zurich was from the first bound up with the rest of Switzerland, both in the desire of Zwingli and others that the word of God should be preached in the other cantons and in the opposition it faced in them. The opposition expressed itself as early as May 1522 and intensified in the following months. In April 1524 the catholic cantons, Lucerne, Zug, Uri, Schwyz, and Unterwalden, met at Beckenried and formed themselves into a league.[129] They failed in their endeavour to get Zurich expelled from the confederation, but their growing strength manifested itself in the successful disputation at Baden in May 1526. It was part of the attempt to

[126] *Z* III 628–911. August Baur sees *A Commentary* as the scholarly and systematic conclusion to the development of Zwingli's anti-Roman teaching (*Zwinglis Theologie. Ihr Werden und ihr System* (Halle, 1885 and 1889), I 461.)

[127] *Z* VIII 263.18–265.24.

[128] *Z* III 674.21–23; *Works* III 97–8.

[129] The growing isolation in April 1524 led Zwingli to write *A True and Earnest Exhortation to the Confederation* with its attack on the mercenary system, its love of his people and their liberty, its appeal for the preaching of the word of God which alone can make things right. (*Z* III 103–13.)

unite the catholic forces of the cantons, the papacy, and the empire against Zwingli and the reformation in Switzerland.

Zwingli's response was theological and political. By his speaking and writing he engaged in a theological battle with his catholic opponents, both in Zurich and outside. The issues were most frequently matters like the gospel, the church, mass, images, the intercession of the saints, and purgatory, questions which had been debated from the beginning. Writings such as *A Reply to Emser* in August 1524,[130] *An Answer to Valentin Compar* in April 1524,[131] and *The Eucharist*, which was a response to Joachim am Grüt in August 1525,[132] must be seen in this context. Zwingli did not take part in the disputation at Baden, but he commented on the theses that concerned the mass, the intercession of the saints, images, and purgatory. Fundamental in the debate, however, was the question of the authority of scripture or that of the church, as Zwingli had made clear earlier in *A Reply to Eck*.[133]

Zwingli sought equally by his speaking and writing to win a response from others to the word of God. There were letters, such as those to Esslingen in 1526,[134] writings dedicated to particular people or places, and there was supremely the disputation in Berne in January 1528, which was vital for the progress of the reformation in Switzerland. The issue of the eucharist, though the dominant one for Zwingli at Berne, was not the only important issue in *The Berne Notes and Speeches* and *The Berne Sermons*.[135] The first sermon, which expounds the creed, is one of Zwingli's few systematic presentations of his theology, yet even it shows the centrality of the eucharist in the debate by giving it almost half of its space.

Zwingli's concern that the word of God should be freely preached led to political action also. It is not that his confidence in the word of God diminished, for that is present in his later, as in his earlier, writings. It is rather his sense that the free preaching of the word of God is bound up with the security of those places where it is already preached and the

---

[130] Z III 241–87.        [131] Z IV 48–159.        [132] Z IV 458–504.

[133] 'Dann es nit hilfft, den gemeinen tant ynwerffen: Man verstat das gotzwort nitt glych; darumb muoss man ein richter darüber han. Denn also stuende das gotzwort an des menschlichen verstands urteil. Sunder das gotzwort sol dich und mich und alle menschen urteilen.' (Z III 309.9–13.)

[134] Z V 275–85, 419–26. Locher writes of the first letter, 'Im ersten Sendschreiben wird wie in kaum einer anderen Schrift das ganze reformatorische Programm aus dem "solus Christus" und der Einmaligkeit und Alleingültigkeit seines Opfers abgeleitet; damit entfallen die Ablässe, die Heiligenverehrung, das Verdienst der Werke, die Messe, das Fegfeuer, die Bilder, die Beichte.' (*Die Zwinglische Reformation*, p. 188.)

[135] Z VI i 243–432, 450–98. Zwingli, for whom the Spirit is important, comments in only two lines on 'I believe in the Holy Spirit'. (Z VI i 488.14–15.)

opening up of those places where it is not. It is in this context that his *Plan for a Campaign*, probably produced in 1526, is to be understood.[136] Zwingli's plan for a campaign shows his detailed military knowledge and his political and diplomatic interest, but the fundamental matter is its relation to his theology, clear in the opening words, with their concern for the glory of God and the gospel of Christ.[137]

From 1527 alliances were entered into with cities such as Constance, Berne, Basle, and Strasburg.[138] Then from the Marburg colloquy in 1529 there was an intensified effort to establish alliances with Lutheran powers as well, in face of the growing catholic opposition, manifest at Speyer in 1529 and Augsburg in 1530. Philip of Hesse was the leader in this, but the concern for alliances fitted Zwingli's view of what was needed, and shows how different his theology and practice were from Luther's. He was prepared for alliances with other powers as well, if they would serve the proclamation of the word of God. Alliances meant a willingness that the sword should defend the preaching of the word and this became evident in 1529 and again in 1531. In 1529 peace was concluded between Zurich and the catholic cantons without the decisive battle which would have been in Zurich's favour. In 1531 it was the catholic cantons that gained the advantage, and Zwingli himself was killed in the battle. Yet, as the conditions of peace in 1529 show, Zwingli's concern was first, but not only, for the free preaching of the word of God.[139]

The importance of an alliance is one of the factors in the eucharistic debate with Luther and the many works it produced and it is an element in other of Zwingli's later writings. *Isaiah* published in 1529[140] and *Jeremiah* published in 1531[141] were dedicated in the one case to the cities

[136] Z III 551–83. It was thought to date from the period between July 1524 and 4 Jan. 1525 (Z III 539–49), but is now generally held to come from the beginning of 1526. See Oskar Vasella, 'Ulrich Zwingli and Michael Gaismair, der Tiroler Bauernführer', *Zeitschrift für Schweizerische Geschichte* 24 (1944) 388–413.

[137] 'In gottes namen! Amen. Disen radtschlag hatt der autor betracht zuo eer gottes und zuo guotem dem euangelio Christi, damit frävel und unrechts nit überhand neme gotsvorcht und unschuld vertrucke.' (Z III 551.1–5.)

[138] A typical statement in 1527: 'Erstlich dient er zuo der er gottes und ufnung sines heligen wortes.' (Z VI i 200.4.)

[139] Z VI ii 460.3–461.8. Zwingli's later vision of what Zurich and Berne could do together went beyond this. (S II iii 101–7.) Von Muralt refers with approval to the comment of Schuler and Schulthess (S II iii 77) on the draft for the five cantons: 'Diese Zuschrift giebt einen wichtigen Grund zu dem Urtheil, dass Zwingli nur, wenn alle Versuche, Bund und Frieden mit den V Orten zu erhalten, fruchtlos wären und alle Bande brechen müssten, einen neuen Bund zu bilden billigte, der die religiöse mit der politischen Freyheit gegen die V Orte, den Kaiser und andere katholische Feinde sichere.' (Z VI iii 301.)

[140] Z XIV 5–410.

[141] Z XIV 417–679.

of the Civic Union and in the other to Strasburg, and both prefaces deal with the relationship of church and state. This was an issue also in the letter to Ambrosius Blarer in May 1528.[142] Zwingli's response to the diet at Augsburg was *An Account of the Faith*.[143] This summary of his faith was both an account and a confession of his faith. In support of it he appealed to scripture and to the Spirit.[144] He presented this symbolically in twelve articles. The work is bold in its statements and in its concluding address to the emperor and princes, concerned rather to confess the faith than to compromise it in the search for unity. Thus his understanding of the eucharist, with its differences from the catholic and Lutheran position, is clearly delineated. Yet Zwingli was capable of a milder approach in which differences are less sharply presented, as *The Letter to the Princes of Germany* shows.[145] In response to Bucer he expounded his views more positively[146] and significantly addressed this defence of the reformation in Zurich not to the emperor, but to the German princes.

His last major work, *An Exposition of the Faith*, sprang from his hopes for the reformation in France.[147] He was seeking an alliance with France and this declaration of his faith must be set in that context. Its humanist colouring almost certainly reflects Zwingli's concern to persuade the French court where humanism was influential. But the humanism is also a genuine element in Zwingli's theology, although it is in the end controlled by his grasp of the biblical revelation. As in *An Account of the Faith*, the credal form of the writing implies that Zwingli holds the true faith of the church. His concern for the safety of the reformation meant that in both works he dissociated himself from the anabaptists. In both he referred to the question of government and, since it was the most divisive issue, he dealt at some length with the eucharist.

---

[142] Z IX 451–467. The letter marks Zwingli's position off from Luther's with its reference to Christ's kingdom as outward. (454.13–17.)

[143] Z VI ii 790–817. W. Köhler points out that there is only one use of condemn (*damnare*) compared with many in the Augsburg Confession. He also sees in Zwingli a disciple of the renaissance in his reference to painting and sculpture as gifts of God in Z VI ii 813.3–6 (see 'Zwinglis Glaubensbekenntnis', *ZWA* 5 (1931) 251, 255).

[144] Z VI ii 792.6–10, 815.17–23.

[145] Z VI iii 249–91.

[146] Z XI 82–9.

[147] S IV 44–78. The original title was *Professio Fidei* rather than *Fidei Expositio*. '"Professio" ist ein juristischer Terminus technicus und bezeichnet eine öffentliche, verbindliche Deklaration. . . . Zwingli . . . wollte für die Städte des Christlichen Burgrechts sprechen und das Recht ihrer Reformation gegen Verleumdungen verteidigen.' (G. W. Locher, 'Zu Zwinglis "Professio fidei". Beobachtungen und Erwägungen zur Pariser Reinschrift der sogenannten Fidei Expositio', *ZWA* 12 (1968) 691–2.)

*Zwingli and Luther*

The relationship of Zwingli to Luther will remain one of the fascinations of Zwinglian research, but the issue is confused when Zwingli is measured by Luther as a criterion of what it is to be a reformer. Both came independently to a fundamentally common grasp of the faith, but within the fundamental unity there is real diversity.

Some of the differences between them could be expected from differences in their background, although the one does not necessarily lead to the other. Their different scholastic education is one factor that could naturally lead them to different presuppositions in theology and Zwingli's Erasmian heritage could do the same.[148] Their different experience of the priesthood (Zwingli as a parish priest and army chaplain, Luther as a monk) could naturally provoke Zwingli to a theology more concerned with society as a whole and Luther to one more concerned with the individual.[149] The different political and social contexts of their ministry, with Zwingli needing the support of a council and not simply that of one man, could naturally stimulate him to have a different understanding of ministry and to engage in it in a different way.[150]

It seems clear that Zwingli did not come to his grasp of the gospel through Luther's teaching, nor was there any period when his teaching was identical with that of Luther. It was rather Luther's example in standing against the pope that was of immeasurable importance for Zwingli in becoming a reformer. He most probably read Luther to confirm himself in views he already held, and he did not, when he read him first, grasp the more distinctive elements in Luther's writings.[151] Yet while asserting his independence of Luther in the gospel, Zwingli expressed both his high regard for him and his difference from him. This is evident as early as 1523 in the sixty-seven articles and his later exposition of them. In expounding

---

[148] Oberman (*Masters of the Reformation*, pp. 284–95) argues for differences in terms of the two ways. Köhler (*Zwingli*, p. 80) sees Zwingli as blending the classical and the Christian, and his Erasmian heritage as keeping him independent of Luther. One does not need to hold that view to recognize the formative influence of Erasmus on Zwingli.

[149] The difference between them as persons and as priests should not be exaggerated, as it sometimes is. See, e.g., J. Rogge, *Die Initia Zwinglis und Luthers*, pp. 112–14. Zwingli experienced *Anfechtung* as well as Luther (Z II 225.19–227.7), though Locher points to their different view of it (*Die Zwinglische Reformation*, p. 116, n. 227).

[150] Apart from the differences between Switzerland (and Zurich in particular) and Saxony, there was the difference in the threat that faced the two reformations.

[151] See, e.g., Rich, *Die Anfänge*, pp. 79–95. He argues that Zwingli criticized indulgences, the veneration of the saints, papal power, tithes, and celibacy independently of Luther, and that he read the works of Luther which confirmed these views. His interest in Luther then waned until he moved from a reforming to a reformation position.

the eighteenth article he states that there has been no one to equal Luther for a thousand years as a warrior of God and a wrestler with scripture, and that no one else leads so many to God through preaching. The work, however, is God's work, while the unity in Luther's teaching and his comes from the fact that the Spirit of God is one.[152]

Yet here and elsewhere there is evidence of differences, some of which Zwingli hints at, in particular in their understanding of the eucharist and the law. Zwingli uses the term 'testament' like Luther, but prefers the term 'memorial'. Unlike Luther he speaks of the law as gospel and criticizes those who speak of the law as causing despair and hatred of God.[153] His emphasis on the Christian life as doing good, his way of relating the Spirit and the word, and his understanding of idolatry, all distinguish him from Luther, where the stress or combination or concept would be different.[154] Zwingli's complaint was not that Luther went too far, but that he did not go far enough, whether in penance, in the term 'sacrament', or in prayers for the dead.[155] This complaint was repeated four years later in the midst of the eucharistic controversy. In *A Friendly Exegesis* he appealed to what he had said in *An Exposition of the Articles* about the keys, purgatory, and the intercession of the saints, to which Luther was alleged to cling in all his books. For Zwingli these doctrines or practices conflicted with salvation which is through faith in Christ. If Luther had dealt with these and had removed images, as well as not eating the body of Christ bodily in bread, then he would 'not only have cleansed the Augean stables, but would have carried heaven itself'.[156] For Zwingli the underlying issue is the same as the one formulated in articles 50 to 52: ascribing to the creature what belongs to God, seeking forgiveness other than through the death of Christ. This has implications for the use of all outward things in the Christian life, including word and sacrament.

[152] Z II 147.14–22, 149.36–150.7. Blanke offers some points of comparison between Zwingli and Luther in 'Zwinglis Beitrag zur reformatorischen Botschaft', *ZWA* 5 (1931) 262–75.

[153] Z II 144.17–26, 150.16–25, 231.33–233.15.

[154] Z II 149.19–22, 111.7–11. Ascribing salvation not to God or to Christ, but to the creature, is idolatry. The role of idolatry and the contrast between God and everything or everyone created is evident in articles 50 to 52. (Z I 463.29–464.5.) Some implications of this emerge in an exchange with Faber at the first disputation. (Z I 527.24–8.)

[155] Z II 148.3–149.7.

[156] Z V 712.9–724.24. He also points out that he stopped calling the eucharist a memorial because of Luther. Zwingli does not do justice here to what Luther wrote, but at least one ground of the difference between them emerges. It should also be remembered that Zwingli praises Luther as well as criticizes him in this passage. In particular his comment on Luther's teaching the hostility of flesh and Spirit should be noted. It implies a sense of affinity with Luther at a point where he is often thought to be nearer Erasmus.

The differences between Zwingli and Luther were focused in the eucharist, though other differences emerged, for instance in original sin, where Zwingli seemed to Luther to err in the direction of free will. Luther was reacting to the section on original sin in *Baptism, Rebaptism, and Infant Baptism* published in May 1525, which in part provoked Zwingli's *Original Sin* in August of the following year.[157] Other differences also became clearer. Zwingli's view of the law and his speaking of gospel and law rather than law and gospel were evident in December 1524 in the letter to Strasburg.[158] His understanding of the relation of church and state was from the beginning unlike that of Luther, which was expounded in the doctrine of the two rules. The difference was pointedly expressed in the letter to Ambrosius Blarer in May 1528 in his insistence that the kingdom of Christ is outward.[159] Even more of the differences manifested themselves in the eucharistic controversy, in particular in the understanding of Christ, man, and faith.

There are hints of eucharistic divergence in 1523, but it was not till he received the letter from Hoen, probably in the summer of 1524, that Zwingli expressed an explicitly symbolic view of the eucharist. The controversy was confused both by the failure of Zwingli and Luther to understand the fundamental concern of the other and by Luther's seeing Zwingli from the start in terms of Carlstadt. The associating of Luther with the catholic position helped to widen the breach and prevent an understanding and accommodation between them. Most of Zwingli's eucharistic writings grew out of this controversy, although initially it was not conducted directly with Luther. After the letter to Alber in November 1524 and before he engaged directly with Luther there were four important statements of Zwingli's view in relation to a Lutheran one: *A Reply to Bugenhagen's Letter*,[160] *The Lord's Supper*,[161] *A Reply to the Letters of Billican and Rhegius*,[162] and *An Answer to Strauss's Book*.[163] They spread from the end of 1525 to the beginning of 1527 and reflect the engagement of many on both sides of the debate, which had repercussions far beyond Zurich and Wittenberg.[164] In them Zwingli began to raise the christological basis of his case and the principles of biblical interpretation involved. It is these,

---

[157] See the discussion of sin in chapter 6.　　　　[158] Z VIII 263.18–265.24.
[159] Z IX 452.15–454.17.　　　　　　　　　　　　　[160] Z IV 558–76.
[161] Z IV 789–862. This also concerned views other than Luther's which were important then and later.
[162] Z IV 893–941.
[163] Z V 464–547.
[164] On Zwingli's side the most notable participants were Bucer and Oecolampadius, although their eucharistic theology was not identical with his.

together with the role of faith, that are crucial in the four major works addressed directly to Luther in 1527 and 1528: *A Friendly Exegesis*,[165] *A Friendly Answer*,[166] *Zwingli's Christian Reply*,[167] and *Two Replies to Luther's Book*.[168] In the conflict there emerge important differences of emphasis in their understanding of Christ. Zwingli stressed the divinity, Luther more the humanity, Zwingli the distinction between the natures, Luther the sharing of properties.[169]

The desire and the need for unity led to the Marburg colloquy. Despite its unhappy end, it produced substantial agreement in fifteen articles, although ambiguity enabled both sides to interpret them differently.[170] The fourteen articles on the trinity, Christ, original sin, redemption through faith alone in Christ, faith as the gift of God and as our righteousness before God, the outward word, baptism, good works, confession, government, tradition, and infant baptism, were accepted. Although some of the articles might sound Lutheran, they had Zwinglian phrases in them or were capable of a Zwinglian interpretation. Thus, although in the sixth article faith comes when we hear the gospel, it is referred to as a gift of the Spirit, who gives it where he wills, and although in the eighth article the Spirit ordinarily does not give faith without the word's going before, nevertheless he gives it where and in whom he wills, and, as Zwingli later pointed out, it is not the word that gives faith, but the Spirit.[171] The fifteenth article on the eucharist marks agreement in five points, with the one point of disagreement put into a subordinate clause. This article was also interpreted by Zwingli to sustain his position.[172]

The colloquy did not bring unity, but it effectively ended the bitter conflict, even though the mediating efforts of Bucer were to bear real fruit only after Zwingli's death. Zwingli's views did not change, but the controversy with Luther was not the primary setting of his major works after Marburg. Even *The Providence of God*, an extended version of the sermon which Zwingli preached at Marburg, is not to be understood in that setting.[173] His later writings, however, continue to show characteristic

---

[165] Z V 562–758.         [166] Z V 771–94.         [167] Z V 805–977.

[168] Z VI ii 22–248. It is Luther who caused Zwingli to go back to Aquinas and Scotus in the eucharistic debate. (Z VI ii 198.18–199.20; IX 537.13–15.)

[169] Locher argues that the christological difference underlies the other differences in Zwingli's and Luther's theology. (*Die evangelische Stellung der Reformatoren zum öffentlichen Leben* (Zurich, 1950), pp. 19–20.)

[170] Z VI ii 521–3.

[171] Z VI ii 521.30–522.3, 12–17. The vital place of faith is crucial for Zwingli, as his later comments show. (Z VI ii 550.1–4, 9–10, 16–18.)

[172] Z VI ii 551.1–21. For Zwingli, though not for Luther, the differences between them were not ultimately grounds for disunity.         [173] Z VI iii 64–230.

differences from Luther, whether in the statement on the eucharist or in the absence of an article on justification by faith in *An Account of Faith* or in the including of non-Christians in heaven in *An Exposition of the Faith*.[174]

## ADDITIONAL NOTE

The library that Zwingli took to Einsiedeln included annotated copies of Aristotle, Cicero, Demosthenes, Homer, Josephus, Juvenal, Livy, Pliny, and Plutarch, besides the fathers and other theological works. (Farner, II 114-24.) At the end of his time at Einsiedeln he wrote, 'versare diurna non cessat Gręcorum Latinorumque et philosophos et theologos ...'. (Z VII iii 31-2.) Zwingli's position was in some ways akin to that of Erasmus in the second chapter of *The Enchiridion*. 'Nor would I, for my part, disapprove your taking your preliminary training for military service in the writings of the pagan poets and philosophers ... Nor ought you to despise pagan authors, for they too are often good moral teachers.' (LCC XIV 304.) It is difficult to assess the influence of the Florentine Platonists. Pollet argues for their influence and sees it in the philosophical side of Zwingli's teaching, in his understanding of God and of man, his universalism, and his emphasis on John's gospel (*Huldrych Zwingli et la reforme en Suisse d'après les recherches récentes* (Paris, 1963) pp. 44-53). Zwingli undoubtedly read both Picos della Mirandola with care and there are copious marginal notes in his edition of John, as well as notes in his volumes of John Francis, including *Liber de providentia dei contra philosophastros*. (The first letter to Zwingli in 1510 includes a reference to Pico: Z VII 4.6-7.) Yet there is almost no reference to them in Zwingli. On the possible influence of both Picos, see Köhler, *Zwinglis Bibliothek*, pp. 11-12; Farner, I 236-8, II 121-2, 135-7; Pollet, *DTC* 3753; and Z VI ii 150, n. 10 and VI iii 50 , 116, notes 2 and 3.

Zwingli's library, as it developed, included some 300 to 350 books and manuscripts. Its similarity to Bucer's library shows a common humanist background. Beside the Greek and Latin classics, there were commentators on them, such as Lefèvre d'Étaples on Aristotle and Xenophon. Zwingli had editions of Ambrose, Athanasius, Augustine, Basil, Chrysostom, Cyprian, Eusebius, Jerome, Origen, and various works of Cyril, Gregory of Nazianzus, Gregory of Nyssa, Hilary of Poitiers, Irenaeus, John of Damascus, and Lactantius, as well as Anselm, Aquinas, Peter Lombard, Nicholas of Lyra, and Scotus. The largest number of books were those by Erasmus and Luther, the significant difference between them being that Erasmus's were heavily annotated and Luther's were not, implying a different use

[174] 'Von der Rechtfertigungslehre, Luthers Herzstück, sagte Zwingli nichts. Verleugnet war sie darum nicht, aber sie passte nicht in den Rahmen, sie schaute vom Menschen aus, Zwingli von Gott aus—ein Unterschied lutherischer und reformierter Religionsbetrachtung auch sonst.' (Köhler, *Zwingli*, p. 223.) For discussions of Zwingli's theology in relation to Luther's, see e.g. ibid., pp. 262-76; Farner, IV 72-5; and G. W. Locher, 'Grundzüge der Theologie Huldrych Zwinglis im Vergleich mit derjenigen Martin Luthers und Johannes Calvins', ZWA XII (1967) 470-509, 545-95, and *Zwingli's Thought*, pp. 142-232.

made of each. There were several works of Bucer and Oecolampadius and some
of other reformers such as Melanchthon, most notably—for their possible influence—his *Loci communes* and *De duplici magistratu themata*. The radical reformers
were well represented (Martin Cellarius, Denck, Hubmaier, Hätzer, and
Schwenckfeld) as well as opponents such as Eck and Faber.

# 2. *The Bible*

THE bible is central in Zwingli's works as a reformer and crucial in the development of his theology.[1] He indeed saw his turning to it as the starting-point and his use of it as the basis of his reforming ministry. In *An Exposition of the Articles*, when rebutting those who rejected the teaching of Christ by calling it Lutheran, he affirmed his independence of Luther in terms of his preaching from the bible alone.[2]

For Zwingli to turn to the bible was to turn from man to God, for the bible is God's word. The appeal to the bible was a constant element in his writings, but it comes with especial freshness and vigour in early writings such as *Archeteles* and *The Clarity and Certainty of the Word of God*. It is rooted in the conviction that man is a liar and that only God is the truth (Ps. 116: 11, Rom. 3: 4), a conviction to which Zwingli returned repeatedly in a variety of contexts.[3] The scriptures, as God's word, bring light where there is merely human light or the darkness of error.[4] Zwingli testified to this out of his own experience.

No matter who a man may be, if he teaches you in accordance with his own thought and mind his teaching is false. But if he teaches you in accordance with the word of God, it is not he that teaches you, but God who teaches him. For as Paul says, who are we but ministers of Christ and dispensers or stewards of the mysteries of God? Again, I know for certain that God teaches me, because I have experienced the fact of it: and to prevent misunderstanding this is what I mean when I say that I know for certain that God teaches me. When I was younger, I gave myself overmuch to human teaching, like others of my day, and when about seven or eight years ago I undertook to devote myself entirely to the scriptures I was always prevented by philosophy and theology. But eventually I came to the point where led by scripture and the word of God I saw the need to set aside all

---

[1] The main studies are E. Nagel, *Zwingli's Stellung zur Schrift* (Leipzig, 1896) and E. Künzli, 'Zwingli als Ausleger von Genesis und Exodus' (Diss. Zurich, 1951).

[2] *Z* II 144.17–147.27. Cf. *Z* I 379.18–380.1. The introduction to the sixty-seven articles asserts their basis in scripture, which is affirmed as the sole criterion for judging Zwingli and the articles. (*Z* I 458.3–10.)

[3] *Z* I 151.10–11, 375.27–31; II 23.25–32, 74.20–76.4; VIII 288.20–5; IX 64.2–5, 111.6–7; *S* VI i 268.22–3, 648.33–4, 760.36–41. (In some passages Christ or the Spirit is spoken of as the truth. Indeed within the trinity truth is ascribed in particular to the Spirit: *Z* VI iii 77.13–15.) The use of the biblical contrast is of course not unique to him, but can be found in friend (Bucer) and foe (Hubmaier). (*Z* IV 642.) Zwingli moves naturally in a passage from speaking of God or Christ as true, to speaking of scripture as true. (*Z* II 74.20–75.13.)   [4] *Z* I 91.1–6, 365.32–3.

these things and to learn the doctrine of God direct from his own word. Then I began to ask God for light and the scriptures became far clearer to me—even though I read nothing else—than if I had studied many commentators and expositors. Note that that is always a sure sign of God's leading, for I could never have reached that point by my own feeble understanding. You may see then that my interpretation does not derive from the over-estimation of myself, but the subjection.[5]

### Scripture—Councils and Popes, Fathers and Doctors

The appeal to scripture was made initially against catholic opponents, with their appeal to the church—whether to councils, fathers, doctors, or popes. The catholics appealed to them to settle any issue in dispute, but for Zwingli such authorities were all human and liable to err; indeed had erred.[6] Moreover some councils were in conflict in their judgements and had to be tested by scripture, and especially by Christ as the touchstone.[7] But Zwingli's opposition to the pope and councils was not merely that giving heed to them subjects God's word to man's word, but that it means surrendering God's word and giving power to those who oppose it. 'To cry for councils is nothing but to cry for the word of God to be imprisoned again and imprisoned in the power of the swaggering bishops.'[8]

The fathers and doctors of the church were less immediately dangerous than councils and popes, for councils and popes were a present reality or possibility. Nevertheless an appeal to them allowed man to determine the issue rather than God. Of course the fathers sometimes disagreed among themselves, which left open the question as to which one was right,[9] but that was not the fundamental question, for Zwingli could regard them all as wrong on the matter of baptism.[10] What was fundamental was that the word of man is always subject to the word of God, so that 'the fathers must yield to the word of God and not the word of God to the fathers',[11] for the

---

[5] Z I 379.14–380.1; LCC XXIV 90–1.

[6] Z I 375.22–7, 537.9–19. F. Schmidt-Clausing discusses Zwingli's attitude to councils in 'Zwinglis Stellung zum Konzil', ZWA II (1962) 479–98.

[7] Z I 302.35–303.10. Cf. Z II 25.30–26.10.

[8] Z II 449.17–19. Cf. Z III 77.18–78.2, 448.17–18.

[9] Z I 515.1–6.

[10] Z IV 216.14–25.

[11] Z III 50.5–9. Zwingli appeals to canon law as being on his side. Cf. Z I 260.19–26. F. Schmidt-Clausing contrasts Zwingli's and Luther's use of canon law with the words, 'Luther hat's verbrannt, Zwingli hat's benutzt' ('Das Corpus Juris Canonici als reformatorisches Mittel Zwinglis', ZKG 80 (1969) 21). In debate with Eck Zwingli draws on a quotation from canon law affirming the authority of God's word over against man's word. Later, in The Lord's Supper, he quotes from canon law a sentence from Ambrose supporting the term 'signify'. (Z III 310.6–311.1; IV 853.13–25.) An early example of appeal to canon law is in Z I 181.15–19.

scripture is master, teacher, and guide, not the fathers.[12] In this context he
attacked the statement of Augustine, 'I should not believe the gospel
unless the church had approved the gospel', arguing that otherwise 'he
would never have believed if he had heard that the gospel was preached
before it had been written down. For no man had then stamped it with
approval, much less any general council'.[13]

Zwingli's insistence on the word of God rather than the word of man did
not prevent him from using the councils, the fathers, and even the much
despised schoolmen in arguing his case.[14] He cited the councils and fathers
and even canon law against his catholic opponents, claiming that they
pointed to scripture. Unlike Erasmus, he gave them no kind of independent
authority and used them in his early writings, simply in order to debate with
his opponents on their own ground and fight them with their own
weapons.[15] Yet Zwingli was also concerned to show that the views he held
were not his alone, but were supported by the fathers, and the same applies
to his interpretation of certain biblical passages. This was a matter of considerable importance when the eucharistic controversy broke out, but it is
evident in his earlier writings also.[16] In the discussion of the sacraments he
draws—with Oecolampadius—on a range of patristic testimony, above all
Augustine,[17] but never with any sense that it added to the force of scripture.

After citing a series of patristic texts in *A Commentary*, he stated
explicitly the reason for using the fathers:

I have quoted these things from the weightiest of the fathers, not because I wish to
support by human authority a thing plain in itself and confirmed by the word of

God, but that it might become manifest to the feebler brethren that I am not the first to put forth this view, and that it does not lack very strong support.[18]

In *An Answer to Valentin Compar* he proclaimed that he was not against the doctors of the church, as long as they conformed to God's word, and he gave examples of where they did. They are not to be despised, but to be read, although with care.[19] On occasion, however, he seemed to regard the agreement of the fathers as having a slightly more independent role. When writing to Berchtold Haller in 1526, he said that he did not deny a certain view because of the exposition of all the doctors, and as none of them interpreted the passage as being about the immortality of the soul he would leave the matter free.[20] Ultimately, however, the fathers were used primarily to win those for whom they were important, so that Zwingli's reference to them at the end of *An Exposition of the Faith* is characteristic.

For we teach not a single jot which we have not learned from the sacred scriptures. Nor do we make a single assertion for which we have not the authority of the first doctors of the church—prophets, apostles, bishops, evangelists and expositors—those ancient fathers who draw most purely from the fountain head.[21]

Zwingli dismissed non-biblical writers with scorn,[22] but he also saw them on occasion as useful, not least in his biblical commentaries.[23] He referred to Aristotle in his earliest reformation writing, stating that he must offer a heathen argument for those who were better read in Aristotle than in Paul or the gospels.[24] In *A Commentary* he referred to Paul's citing of a pagan writer in Acts 17: 28:

We see here in passing how the apostle quotes from profane writers, not by any means using them as authorities, but, when the heavenly Spirit has willed to say anything through their mouths, showing where we may find this, so that we may not have to dig over all their filth in the search for one or two pearls.[25]

---

[18] Z III 816.1–4; *Works* III 247–8. Cf. Z IV 571.9–11; VI ii 131.18–20. He could even claim in a response to Faber: 'I have not learnt a single thing without the basis of biblical writing, also without the agreement of the most ancient teachers . . .'. (Z V 56.7–9.) He held that with the two natures of Christ Luther spoke in a new way, contrary to the fathers and the schoolmen as well as to scripture. (Z V 943.11–14.) By contrast, in reply to Luther's *Bekenntnis*, he pointed out that the fathers, along with faith and scripture, are on his side. (Z VI ii 247.28–30.) Bucer in a letter to Zwingli supported the use of expressions by reference to their use by the fathers whom he and Zwingli saw as witnesses of their view. (Z XI 298.4–6.)

[19] Z IV 78.10–82.7.                                          [20] Z VIII 761.5–7, 26–9.
[21] S IV 67.4–8; LCC XXIV 278 (*Works* II 274).                [22] Z I 126.8–11.
[23] Z XIII 266.3–5; S VI ii 252.2–5.
[24] Z I 98.3–6. He offers a similar justification in *A Commentary*: 'I have brought in these things from the heathen in order that, if possible, even those who are devoted to philosophy may receive eyes with which to see what man is.' (Z III 664.23–5; *Works* III 86.)
[25] Z III 646.30–4; *Works* III 66.

Likewise he regarded the example of Jethro in the old testament as in some sense a biblical precedent for a positive use of Gentiles. 'Let us receive from them anything good or true that they have said and turn it to the glory of our God, and from the spoil of the Egyptians let us adorn the temple of the true God.'[26] It was self-evident to Zwingli, quoting Augustine, that 'all truth is of God'. When therefore a pagan writer spoke the truth it was really God who spoke rather than he.[27] Zwingli was ready to draw on 'divine and human letters . . . for even . . . secular erudition is of God'.[28]

His use of pagan writers in *The Providence of God* is more problematic, for he seems almost to use the bible in support of a position built up by philosophical argument. He defended his approach in part by conceding the attack.

This opinion, treated rather philosophically, as it has been (although why call that philosophical which is sacred and according to religion, except that some people do not hesitate to make the truth odious, attributing it to the philosophers and not noting that the truth, wherever found and by whomever brought out is from the Holy Spirit), this opinion, I say, I will support first by an example and then by scripture.[29]

Although there is no comparison with this kind of philosophical argument in *An Exposition of the Faith*, yet it does show Zwingli's conscious adjusting of his presentation to the reader as well as his fundamentally biblical standpoint. 'But leaving these matters, which I have introduced only to meet the requirements of such philosophical reflection as may happen to engage you, O King, I will now turn to the unassailable testimonies of scripture.'[30]

## The Inspiration, Canon, and Authority of Scripture

The bible is God's word because it was spoken by God and because he speaks through it. That God or the Spirit is the author of scripture was

[26] Z XIII 382.19–383.11. Cf. *S* VI i 243.41–4. *Preface to Pindar* shows how non-biblical writers can be used in understanding the bible and how they can be interpreted in its light. Following Augustine and Origen, Zwingli argues that though the philosophers and poets seem to speak of many gods they were well aware that God must be one. So Pindar is held to believe in God as one, although he refers to gods in the plural, just as the Hebrews do who use the plural *elohim* of God. (Z IV 870.8–871.15.) At the end of his preface Zwingli writes, 'Vale, candide lector, detque deus optimus maximus, ut gentili poeta magistro discas veritatem cum apud Hebraeos intelligere, tum apud omnes gentes amoenissime exponere.' (Z IV 873.17–19.)

[27] Z XIII 153.6–8; *S* VI i 314.20–6. The view is not limited to Augustine. In Jerome he underlined the words, 'A quocunque enim verum dicitur, illo donante dicitur, qui est ipsa veritas.' (Z XII 312.22–3.)

[28] *S* VI i 376.2–7.

[29] Z VI iii 94.5–11; *Works* II 144.

[30] *S* IV 52.16–18; LCC XXIV 256 (*Works* II 250).

taken for granted and needed no proof. Zwingli referred quite naturally both to the Spirit speaking in Paul and to Paul, who had the Spirit of God, giving a command.[31]

It is because the scriptures come from the dictation of the Spirit that everything must yield to them.[32] Zwingli asserts, 'The doctrine of God is never formed more clearly than when it is done by God himself and in the words of God.'[33] (The words that Paul speaks are in the end not Paul's but God's, and for this reason Paul is to be heard.[34]) Moreover, since the scriptures derive from the Spirit, who is the Spirit of concord, they are bound to be in agreement with each other.[35]

Zwingli's view of inspiration is not mechanical, although occasionally a somewhat mechanical expression is used.[36] As in Erasmus and the fathers, God is held to accommodate himself to human ways of speech.[37] However, human authorship is also evident, for Zwingli wrote of Mark's making a summary of Matthew and in his commentaries he noted the differences in the gospels, even the inconsistencies; but these did not trouble him, as faith does not depend on such things.[38] In general, however, differences were regarded as only apparent; they were reconciled, on the assumption that the true author is the Spirit, who does not contradict himself.

Zwingli did not accept the apocryphal books as canonical, although they had their uses,[39] nor—with Luther—the Revelation of St John the Divine. Following Jerome, he did not think that it was held as canonical in the early church and regarded it as lacking the heart and spirit of John.[40]

---

[31] Z I 205.25-8, 207.21-2.

[32] Z I 260.21-3. When Zwingli was challenged at Berne over the Pauline authorship of Hebrews, he argued in favour of it, but did not regard authorship as the important issue. (Z VI i 402.1-5, 22-33.)

[33] Z I 378.17-18; LCC XXIV 89-90.

[34] Z XIII 153.4-6.

[35] Z V 735.21-3. Cf. Z IV 841.18-22.

[36] S IV 46.25-7.

[37] Z V 729.25-730.4. Cf. Payne, p. 50.

[38] S VI i 254.41-5, 503.41-2, 615.43-616.5; S VI ii 70.37-8. Zwingli could allow error in questions concerning people and times, but not in the essential matter: 'Tametsi enim in persona et tempore nonnunquam, in re tamen nunquam errarunt sanctissimi viri.' (Z XIII 41.31-2.)

[39] Z II 203.9-22; VI i 402.7-17; XI 599.2-7. Christians take over the old testament from the Jews and keep to its canonical books, which do not include Baruch, just as those becoming Christians today would receive from us the new testament in its present form. (Z II 203.3-22.) When he attacks purgatory, he dismisses any use of Maccabees to support the doctrine, as it is not part of 'the true holy scriptures'. (Z II 414.3-8, 419.22-420.11.)

[40] Z II 208.33-209.5; VI i 395.21-4. Although Zwingli stresses certain parts of scripture, e.g. calling John the noblest part of the new testament, he does not, like Luther, have a canon within the canon. His appeal is rather to the whole of scripture.

The apocryphal gospels were rejected, not by bishops, but by ordinary Christians who saw that they did not conform with God's word.[41]

It is precisely the fact that the scriptures are God's word and not man's that gives them their authority. They are not, however, merely a word spoken in the past, for the Spirit breathes through them.[42] They are living and powerful to do God's will and not simply the source of divine teaching. As they are God's word and not man's, all matters of faith are to be settled by them and Zwingli appealed to them against his opponents and even against himself.[43] Their indisputable place is demonstrated by the way copies of the bible in Hebrew, Greek, and Latin were brought into the first disputation and laid open before the assembly. They, and not the council nor the people, were to be the judges.[44] Later, in debate with the anabaptists, Zwingli insisted on the study of the biblical languages, so that the bible could be properly understood.[45]

Frequently throughout his writings Zwingli, like others of his day, offered to be corrected or to be better taught by the bible.[46] He was, however, content to be in a minority, as Christ and the apostles were, indeed a minority of one, if he spoke with scripture and not against it.[47]

His appeal to scripture was not a denial of his view that God had spoken elsewhere. In a work such as *A Commentary*, where he was particularly open to non-biblical writings, he directed attention to scripture with the affirmation, 'But we, to whom God himself has spoken through his Son and through the Holy Spirit, are to seek these things not from those who were puffed up with human wisdom, and consequently corrupted what they received pure, but from the divine oracles.'[48] Here, as on some other occasions, Zwingli saw the bible christologically, although that is not his characteristic emphasis in referring to it. In *Archeteles* Christ is referred to as the touchstone, whereas in *St Matthew* the touchstone is the word of

[41] Z IV 73.30–74.12
[42] Z I 311.27–31.
[43] Z I 324.26–32; II 725.10–14; III 775.11–17.
[44] Z I 497.26–498.6. Cf. Z III 317.13–28. In debate Zwingli appeals on occasion to the Greek or Hebrew text against the translation used by an opponent, as in Z II 751.9–20.
[45] Z IV 417.23–419.6. Zwingli challenged the anabaptists for appealing to the Spirit and rejecting the need to know the languages in which the scriptures were written.
[46] Z I 133.10–134.2; II 457.7–11; III 758.8–12; VI ii 815.17–23.
[47] Z I 375.14–21, 380.34–381.4; VIII 146.19–23. Pollet (*DTC* 3778) misunderstands Zwingli here. His willingness to have the whole world against him in a literal exposition of the words of institution is in the context of his own wider appeal to scripture and the Christian faith—a confidence that they are on his side. There is no change here in the later Zwingli. (Z IV 910.24–913.2.) Cf. Z III 33.12–14, 790.7–21, and IV 73.7–11. He admits his own mistakes and changes in interpretation of particular texts. (Z III 734.18–22.)
[48] Z III 643.24–27; *Works* III 62.

God. Christ is seen as allowing himself to be tested by the scriptures—and the implication is drawn that whatever is less than Christ should subject itself to the same testing.[49]

From the beginning of his reforming ministry Zwingli presented the scriptures as our 'master, teacher, and guide'.[50] He recognized the danger that we come to them seeking confirmation of our own opinions, so that they become our pupil rather than our teacher,[51] and that we want someone to act as judge when there is a disputed interpretation or an obscure passage. But that is to seek to be master of scripture and not to let it be master.[52] The scripture or the Spirit speaking in scripture is its own judge.[53]

### The Use and Interpretation of Scripture

In works such as *Choice and Liberty respecting Foods* and *An Exposition of the Articles* Zwingli seems content to quote a passage or passages of scripture, and to regard that as settling the point at issue. Thus, after quoting nine passages he concluded, 'These announcements seem to me to be enough to prove that it is proper for a Christian to eat all foods.'[54] Moreover the absence of a prohibition in scripture meant that God had left the matter free, especially as no one may add to or subtract from God's word.[55] Clear testimonies of scripture were decisive in his earlier writings, but also in his later ones.[56]

Yet Zwingli was aware from the start that the simple presence or absence of something in scripture was not decisive. Moreover simple quotation from scripture was not enough, for both sides in the debate quoted scripture.[57] Thus in one of his earlier works, *The Clarity and*

---

[49] Z I 260.39–261.15; S VI i 386.29–38. 'For he is indeed the heretic who tests the sacred writings not by the light of Christ, but by his own.' (Z I 283.19–20.) In *Archeteles* there is also a reference to testing everything by the touchstone of the gospel and by the fire of Paul. (Z I 319.6–7.) In *An Exposition of the Articles* the criterion for Christian teaching is explicitly christological. (Z II 25.20–26.19.) The word of God can mean Christ or scripture and therefore both can be seen as the criterion: 'dann ab dem einigen waren gotteswort, das sich inn dem herren Jesu Christo, warem sun gottes, sichtbarlich und aller eigentlichest ussgetrukt hat yetzt zuo den letsten zyten, unnd vor dem im alten testament (doch ringer) in vilen vätteren und propheten'. (Z III 13.8–12.)

[50] Z I 307.1–4.

[51] Z VIII 146.27–34. He does not allow an appeal to experience when it conflicts with scripture, as when Emser appeals to the way people have invoked the aid of St Nicholas in storms at sea. Apart from pointing out that Castor and Pollux have rescued many more from shipwreck and therefore ought to be invoked rather than Nicholas, he points to scripture which states that our help comes from God alone. (Z III 273.1–276.17.)

[52] Z II 62.24–8.          [53] Z I 558.2–5, 561.7–30. Cf. Z IV 757.19–20.

[54] Z I 98.3–4; Jackson 413 (*Works* I 79).          [55] Z I 106.28–107.2, 134.7–12.

[56] Z II 169.9–12, 425.21–426.4. Cf. Z XIII 325.13–14; VI i 399.2–7; S VI i 386.35–6.

[57] Z I 566.2–567.6.

*Certainty of the Word of God*, he recognized in a measure his opponents' case. 'I know that you will reply that you have worked through the scriptures and discovered texts which support your opinion.'[58] This situation led Zwingli to assert one of his fundamental principles: the necessity of the Spirit in understanding and using scripture. The development of this principle enabled him to continue the simple quotation of scriptural testimony in his support and to challenge his opponents when they did the same.[59]

The appeal to the sole authority of scripture as God's word (over against the fathers, councils, popes, and doctors of the church, who express only man's word) raised acutely the problem of how to understand, use, and interpret scripture. Zwingli developed his views initially in debate with his catholic opponents, though certain elements emerged more clearly in debate with anabaptists and Lutherans. In the course of the various controversies he adduced a whole series of rules for interpretation, most of them being developments or applications of positions present at the beginning. There was development, though little change, in the decade covered by his major works.

The principles that guide Zwingli's interpretation derive primarily from his humanist education and his reformed understanding of the bible and the Christian faith. Fundamental, however, is the sense that scripture is from the Spirit and can be understood only where the Spirit gives understanding. This is developed in a variety of ways in the course of controversy, but it is revealing to see what is present up to the first disputation in January 1523.

## The Spirit and the Word

The Spirit plays an important role in Zwingli's theology, as is apparent in the understanding of scripture. The order of Spirit and Word, though not invariable in Zwingli, is there from the start in controversy with catholic opponents. They misunderstand scripture because they go to it to find support for their own views, whereas the right approach is:

Before I say anything or listen to the teaching of man, I will first consult the mind of the Spirit of God (Psalm 85): 'I will hear what God the Lord will speak.' Then you should reverently ask God for his grace, that he may give you his mind and Spirit, so that you will not lay hold of your own opinion but of his. And have a firm trust that he will teach you a right understanding, for all wisdom is of God the Lord. And then go to the written word of the gospel. ... You must be

---

[58] Z I 376.15–17; LCC XXIV 88.
[59] Z III 844.25–30, 848.8–27; V 780.18–781.20.

*theodidacti*, that is, taught of God, not men: that is what the Truth itself said (John 6), and it cannot lie.[60]

It is not that the Spirit is enough without scripture, nor that it is by the Spirit that the scripture is tested; it is rather that the Spirit is indispensable for the understanding of scripture and must be sought before we turn to it. In *Archeteles* Zwingli challenges the view that judgement about the meaning of scripture belongs to one or two people. It belongs to all those who believe in Christ and who therefore possess his Spirit. For with the Spirit ordinary people will understand scripture in accordance with the mind of God in the plainest way.[61] It is not that God's word is not clear, but that we are not open and receptive to it.[62]

The stress on the Spirit could have led to a diminished stress on the importance of scholarship in the understanding of scripture. However, the fact that the bible was present in the first disputation in Hebrew, Greek, and Latin, is evidence that Zwingli assumed that there was need for languages and therefore a task for the scholar, and he did in fact mention the presence of scholars before that of the assembly of Christians taught by the Spirit. In the disputation Zwingli appealed to the scripture's expounding itself through the Spirit or the Spirit himself deciding from the scripture.[63] In a reference to the conflict with Arius Zwingli argued for the scriptures as interpreting themselves, since they are inwardly consistent. In all this the Spirit and the scriptures are conjoined, not opposed.[64] Even those passages that stress in an almost Lutheran way that the word brings its own clarity, remain distinctively Zwinglian, with reference to understanding coming from 'the light and Spirit of God, illuminating and inspiring the words . . .'.[65] The word has its power and clarity because of God and the clarity may be alongside, or even before, the word.

---

[60] Z I 377.7–21; LCC XXIV 88–9. Cf. Z II 22.19–24.

[61] Z I 321.35–322.3. Characteristically for the reformers, 1 Cor. 2: 15 is cited in this context. (Z I 279.18–21.) In *An Exposition of the Articles* Zwingli states that it is the Spirit who is needed for the interpretation of scripture and not man (whether the pope, councils, or the fathers); who is a liar. (Z II 51.7–19.)                                                                                          [62] Z I 359.13–360.9.

[63] Z I 557.30–558.5. In the discussion of two passages concerning Christ's presence he said, 'The scripture speaks evidently of the corporal presence or bodily attendance of Christ and declares that Christ died, was buried, arose on the third day, and having ascended to the heavens sits on the right of his Father.' (Z I 558.27–559.2; *Selected Works* 103.) Here some argue that the creed, as a summary of scripture, is used in interpretation, as well as later in Zwingli, though in his later writings where faith is used as a criterion, it is essentially not the creed, but Christian faith itself.

[64] Z I 561.18–23. Spirit and flesh are opposed, although there is an earlier reference to the contrast between scripture as the letter that kills and scripture as the Spirit who gives life. (Z I 311.27–31, 306.7–8.)

[65] '. . . sunder des liechts und geists gottes, der in sinen worten also erlüchtet und atmet'. (Z I

This concurrent or prevenient clarity of the word found outward representation at the birth of Christ when the glory of the Lord shone round about the shepherds, and then the angel began to speak with them (Luke 2) and the shepherds believed the words of the angel and found all things as he had said.[66]

The tests that conclude *The Clarity and Certainty of the Word of God* throw light on some of Zwingli's later principles of interpretation, especially the glory of God and the good of the neighbour. They follow a reference to the necessity of being versed in scripture.[67]

The Holy Spirit continued to be vital in the understanding and interpreting of scripture in the later Zwingli, for without the Spirit one is guided by the flesh or human reason and is blind.[68] He gives his varied gifts to men and none should despise or envy the gift of interpretation given to another. In that context Zwingli made his contribution and offered it to the judgement of the church, recognizing that 'the sacred scripture is an immense and unfathomable sea' which no one has worthily measured.[69] The later Zwingli had less confidence than in *Archeteles* that the Spirit would lead to the same interpretation, but still it is the Holy Spirit in the church that can judge between interpretations. At the Berne disputation Treger pointed to differences between Luther, Zwingli, and others, and asked where the Spirit was through whom they boasted that they understood scripture.[70] The stress on the Spirit did not, however, lead to any sense that the scriptures are other than indispensable, for without them we should come again under the anti-Christian papacy.[71] The Spirit is not a substitute for them.

---

365.17–18; LCC XXIV 78.) However, reference is not always made to the Spirit. 'Das wort gottes, sobald es anschynet die verstentnus des menschen, erlüchtet es sy, das sy es verstat, bekennet und gwüss würt.' (Z I 361.31–2.) The contrast is between God and man. God grants illumination and understanding of the word, whereas human reason disbelieves and rejects the word. Cf. Z I 365.14–21. Understanding does not come from human teachers, but from God. We have to be taught by the Father or drawn by the Spirit. (Z I 365.36–366.4; 366.26–367.5.) It is not, as has been alleged, that the individual decides on the bible, instead of its authenticating itself, but rather that the Spirit enlightens the believer to discern which words are his and what they mean.

[66] Z I 362.5–10; LCC XXIV 75.

[67] Z I 383.1–6, 28–32, 384.15–16.

[68] S VI i 316.45–6; Z IV 56.7–16, 57.1–7.

[69] Z VI ii 291.7–294.6; S VI ii 255.45–256.16. Cf. 'submit our judgements to the holy scriptures, and the church deciding according to them by the Spirit'. (Z VI ii 815.21–23; Jackson 481 (*Works* II 58).)

[70] Z VI i 263.1–264.3. It was Bucer who offered an immediate reply.

[71] Z V 264.5–16, 265.24–266.14. The Zurich letter to Eck referred to God's word and the Spirit of God as judges. (Z IV 757.19–20.)

## The Spirit and the Letter

In Zwingli the contrast of spirit and letter is in part the Erasmian one between the letter and the sense or meaning of something and in part the contrast between the letter and the Holy Spirit. However, the two overlap. First, we consider passages where the reference is primarily to Spirit and letter in 2 Corinthians 3: 6.[72]

In *Choice and Liberty Respecting Food* there is a Lutheran colour to his view that the letter of the law in the new testament as well as in the old kills, but that it is given to us by Christ that we may take refuge in him.[73] The reference in *Archeteles* to scripture not as the letter that kills, but as the Spirit who gives life,[74] was developed in a letter to Martin Bucer in 1524. 'Who is taught by scripture? How many thousands of men have had scripture and not believed; therefore indeed faith is not from the letter nor from the elements, for it does not spring from the sense but it is from the Spirit inwardly teaching, exhilarating and making alive.'[75] The reference here to 'letter' in contrast to the Spirit seems negative. They are opposed to each other, although in the following sentences Zwingli speaks positively about scripture in comparison with images. Yet the contrast or opposition of Spirit and letter is in a sense only apparent, as the Spirit is the author of scripture and so the Spirit agrees in all things with scripture and scripture with the Spirit.

Discussing Mary's virginity, in exposition of Isaiah 7: 14, Zwingli defends her perpetual virginity by reference not to the church's authority, but to scripture. If therefore something is of the Spirit, then the letter must agree, even if those who are devoid of the Spirit do not discern it from the letter.[76] In this context the letter is dead unless we have the Spirit, a meaning that is explicit elsewhere. In the exposition of Luke 16: 16 Zwingli was concerned to show that the Spirit reconciles apparently contradictory passages of scripture. For the bare letter is not to be considered. The letter kills, but the Spirit gives life. Therefore we must compare the passages in the Spirit.

However, the word 'spirit' is used ambiguously by Zwingli and slips at various points between two of three possible meanings: the Spirit, the mind illuminated by the Spirit, and the meaning of the word or words

---

[72] See Additional Note 1, pp. 77–8.

[73] *Z* I 103.32–104.25.

[74] *Z* I 306.7–8.

[75] *Z* VIII 194.19–22. In his letter Bucer referred to the same text, though in the more positive form: even the scripture is the letter that kills, unless the Spirit teaches inwardly. (*Z* VIII 176.36–177.3.)

[76] *Z* XIV 181.10–18.

(which may themselves be referred to as letter). He affirms that God alone gives understanding, but that we ought not to scorn the letter, for it is the key by which the human mind penetrates to the spirit (meaning). The letter in fact does not kill, but anyone who relies on the letter without penetrating to the spirit kills himself. There follows an analogy (used also in *A Friendly Answer*) of a horse and reins, in which the reins do not draw without the horse, nor the horse without the reins, but both are joined. The reins keep the horse on the track. Without the letter of scripture people would say what they wanted. Scripture therefore is the rule and reins, in accordance with which everything is directed. The Spirit of truth, that is, the faithful mind illuminated by the Spirit of God, takes hold of the letter and controls it. The letter does not compel the spirit or sense, but the Spirit explains and illuminates the letter. How often does it happen in all languages, says Zwingli, that someone understands the words without grasping the sense. He then gives the example of the word 'law'.[77]

There are other places where it is stressed that the words of Christ are spirit and not letter; therefore one should not stick to the bare letter, but the letter is to be expounded by the Spirit (or spirit).[78] In a comment on Matthew 19: 6 Zwingli refers to sticking to the letter and neglecting other laws when the same Spirit dictates. Here the letter misleads if one ignores the Spirit lying behind those, and also other, words.[79] The point is made more clearly in the extended exposition of Luke 3: 14. Zwingli relates Christ's command to turn the other cheek to his not doing this before the high priest and concludes that the words must have a different meaning from what the bare words have at first sight. Words of scripture that seem to be repugnant to each other are to be reconciled by faith and the Spirit. For the Spirit of faith is not in disagreement with himself.[80]

The distinction between spirit and letter as one between the words and their real meaning, so frequent in Erasmus, is also alluded to in *Archeteles*, the contrast being between the word and the sense.[81] In the old testament commentaries the contrast between flesh or letter or shell on the one hand and spirit or spiritual understanding or kernel on the other is between the

[77] S VI i 679.4–681.2. Zwingli uses the analogy of the horse and its ropes and harness in *A Friendly Exegesis* where the primary emphasis is on scripture rather than the Spirit, indeed on scripture as a criterion by which to judge appeals to the Spirit. (At the same time he can give priority to the Spirit, or the believer imbued by the Spirit.) In the eucharistic controversy with Luther he has in the previous section urged Luther to collate passages of scripture, because there is no contradiction in scripture. (Z V 733.29–735.2.)

[78] S VI i 369.27–30.
[79] S VI i 345.6–8.
[80] S VI i 564.30–565.23.
[81] Z I 294.20–4.

surface meaning and the deeper hidden meaning.[82] In the new testament
commentaries the concern is for the sense or meaning of passages, which
the bare letter may not disclose by itself.[83] Attention must be given to the
sense, not the letter, and it is necessary therefore to interpret the letter
according to the sense and not the sense according to the letter.[84] In this
way other passages may throw light on the words concerned,[85] and the
analogy of faith and the rule of the Spirit (or spirit) should be used in interpretation.[86]

## Context and Comparison

Zwingli uses a number of principles of interpretation in common with his
contemporaries, in particular setting disputed passages in their context
and comparing passages of scripture, together with the analogy of faith
and the traditional fourfold use of scripture. All these modify a simply
literalist interpretation of a passage, but, more important for Zwingli, they
are part of what it means to let the Spirit (or scripture), rather than men,
interpret scripture.

Attention to the immediate context is a prerequisite in understanding a
passage,[87] and that includes the purpose that lies behind say a parable of
Christ.[88] In the eucharistic controversy Zwingli stressed that 'This is my
body' must be seen in the light of the words that immediately follow, such
as 'Do this in remembrance of me' or 'which is given for you'.[89]

The comparing of passages of scripture in effect sets them in a wider
context. This is necessary with obscure passages, although Zwingli points

[82] Z XIII 132.15–17, 191.23–7, 209.8–12, 233.1–4, 280.23–32. 'Ecce, quam infantilia et puerilia
scribit spiritus sanctus in divinis literis, si carnem ac putamen tantum respicimus, magna vero et
admiranda, si mente ad spiritum penetramus.' (132.15–17.) 'In historiis veteris testamenti, si
quando carnalia et quae in speciem mala sunt, scribuntur, non solum litera historiae, sed spiritus
et significatio spectanda sunt.' (191.23–5.) This deeper meaning emerges with the use of typology
and allegory.

[83] S VI i 564.30–565.23, 640.13–16. Cf. the contrast of letter and sense made against those who
miss the point of a passage by literalism. In this context Zwingli refers to the letter as killing. (Z
IV 130.9–24.) Ignorance of the biblical languages can also lead to an interpretation that has no
basis in the original text. Against the anabaptists Zwingli appeals to the true understanding of the
letter against those who appeal mistakenly to the Spirit, but whose spirit is not the Holy Spirit.
(Z IV 419.3–6, 420.25–421.18.)

[84] S VI i 216.12–17, 366.4–9, 635.9–11.

[85] S VI i 564.38–41.

[86] S VI i 487.18–22. Cf. S VI i 216.28–9, 564.38–40.

[87] There is an example of this in 1520. (Z VII 290.15–16.) Cf. Z II 255.15–25, 752.17–21, and S
VI ii 267.36–8.

In interpretation Erasmus stressed 'not only what is said but also by whom, to whom, with
what words, at what time, on what occasion, what precedes, and what follows'. Cf. Payne, p. 45.

[88] Z III 862.17–26.

[89] Z VIII 456.1–16; V 850.11–28, 904.16–24.

out that they are obscure to us, but were not to those who wrote or heard them.[90] Comparison can be made (and that includes the reconciliation of apparently contradictory passages) because the Spirit, and therefore the scripture, is everywhere consistent.[91] Such a comparison is supported by reference to Christ's command to search the scripture (John 5: 39) and to read Moses and the prophets.[92] Comparison is a constant element in his writing, both in the commentaries and elsewhere, and features especially at points of controversy, not least the eucharistic controversy.[93] It is used interestingly when he tries to determine which accounts in the various gospels are parallel, so that one can establish the meaning of a word or passage in one gospel from something parallel in another, as for example in the discussion of the keys.[94]

Another form of comparison is that of analogy, which Zwingli discusses in *A Friendly Exegesis*, although he uses it earlier. There can be analogies of similar and dissimilar things. The analogies Zwingli used most persistently were between the passover and the eucharist, circumcision and baptism. Thus, as circumcision was given to infants, so should baptism be given to them.[95] By contrast he asserts against Luther and others that certain things are not analogous, as for example 'The word became flesh' and 'This is my body'.[96] The same principle can be used where the same word has to be interpreted metaphorically in two passages—one may throw light on the other. Zwingli applied this analogy to a word such as 'stone' standing for Christ and to sayings such as 'This is the passover' and 'This is the body of Christ'.[97]

The comparison of passages of scripture includes the reconciliation of apparently conflicting passages, although he does not do this at the same length and with the same detail as Bucer in his commentary on Romans. This happens with passages that concern such diverse issues as divorce,[98]

[90] Z V 853.26-8; S VI i 665.30-5; VI ii 69.9-11. There are passages which Zwingli finds obscure, for which he offers only a tentative exegesis. (S VI ii 204.46-7.)

[91] Z I 561.18-22; V 735.21-3; S VI i 221.16-17. Zwingli compares this with the exposition of civil laws in terms of each other. (Z V 12.10-16.)

[92] Z III 309.12-310.1.

[93] Z I 558.25-559.11; IV 250.32-251.10; VI ii 31.23-32.18; S VI i 312.35-42. Locher writes, after referring to Zwingli's understanding of covenant: 'unter allen Reformatoren ist Zwingli derjenige, der am wenigsten an einzelnen biblischen Texten haftet, sondern in den grossen Linien der von der Bibel skizzierten Geschichte Gottes mit den Menschen lebt' ('Geist und Gemeinschaft—Theologie in öffentlicher Verantwortung', *Reformierte Kirchenzeitung*, 110 (1969) 8).

[94] Z II 381.16-388.13; III 723.21-741.2; S VI i 507.14-41.

[95] Z V 733.6-24; VI i 110.27-111.3.

[96] Z V 732.34-733.1.

[97] Z V 881.22-882.16. This kind of analogy is associated here with the analogy of faith.

[98] Z VIII 137.5-138.9.

the permission or prohibition of a staff,[99] Arius on Christ,[100] faith in Paul and James,[101] and the conflict between using the sword and forgiving.[102]

In the course of making such comparisons, other criteria are also developed, especially the role of faith or the analogy of faith, sometimes combined with love or the Spirit, and the place of God's glory.

## Faith

Faith (in the sense especially of faith in God or in Christ rather than in ourselves) is necessary for understanding and interpreting scripture, and Zwingli opposed it to reason. In *The Clarity and Certainty of the Word of God* this opposition is seen in the context of Abraham's knowing that the command to slay Isaac was the word of God, even though the command was seemingly in conflict with the promise God had made to him. 'His reason (*gedanck*) could not accept the command, but faith withstood reason (Rom. 4) saying: The one who promised and gave thy son at the first can raise him up again from the dead, or he can use some other means to give to the world the saviour promised through him.'[103] This same example is taken up in *A Commentary* to show that only those with faith can hold together apparently contradictory passages of scripture.[104] Faith moreover is combined with love, so that where reason would say that we should erect a statue to God's honour, faith and love would contradict reason and say that the money should be spent on the poor.[105]

Faith and reason are not always seen in opposition, for Zwingli used the term 'reason' ambiguously. This is particularly the case in the eucharistic controversy where in *An Answer to Strauss's Book* he states that he is not arguing on the basis of human reason ('the reason of the flesh'), but rather on the basis of the reason of the inward man (or believer) as in Romans 7.[106] It is faith that is indispensable in understanding God's word—the faith

---

[99] Z III 37.18–23.

[100] Z V 854.2–23.

[101] Z XIII 152.3–12.

[102] S VI i 564.30–565.16.

[103] Z I 363.8–13; LCC XXIV 76. Following reason, as Saul did in disobeying God, is idolatry. 'There is no doubt that if someone holds something to be good on the basis of his reason and does not learn what is right and good from God and his word, he sets up an idol in himself, namely his own reason and opinion.' (Z III 29.28–31.)

[104] Z III 706.8–13.

[105] Z III 900.15–18.

[106] Z V 502.12–15. Cf. Z VI ii 37.18–38.5. In a similar approach earlier, with an attack on a literal interpretation of the words 'This is my body', he insisted that he was referring to God's word and not to human understanding. (Z IV 809.13–810.7.) There does, however, seem a positive use of human reason a few pages later, where he wrote that they not only speak against all reason (in which they are worse than the sophists) but also against God's word. (Z V 509.18–21.)

of which Isaiah spoke in 'If you do not believe, you will not understand', the same faith which is needed to judge the words of those teaching (in 1 Cor. 14: 29).[107]

Faith, or the analogy of faith (the second term is not used till later), is a constant and vital criterion in the eucharistic controversy, but is not limited to it. In 1523 in *The Canon of Mass* he opposes the intercession of the saints on the grounds that the scriptures do not teach it, that it is repugnant to true faith, and that it repudiates God's offer of mercy in Christ—the faith is a faith in God in whom we place our hope for all things. A similar point is made in a letter to Bucer in June 1524 and in December 1524 in *Those Who Give Cause For Tumult*. True faith knows that it comes from God, not from images. However Zwingli adds the further criterion, which is in fact fundamentally the same, that where there are two contradictory words from scripture then the one that ascribes glory to God is to be accepted.[108]

In the Strasburg letter six months later the context is the eucharist and that remains the chief context.[109] Thus in *A Commentary* he speaks of faith as determining the meaning of a passage. Faith that there is only one way to heaven and that Christ is the only pledge of salvation means that you cannot attribute the attaining of salvation to sensible things.[110] The criterion of faith (or the rule or analogy of faith) continued to be used in a variety of contexts, such as the discussion of grace and works[111] and of purgatory,[112] and in the commentaries as a guideline where passages were interpreted allegorically,[113] in the reconciling of apparently contradictory passages,[114] in attributing remission of sins to God or to the apostles,[115] in showing 'baptize' to mean 'teach',[116] and in interpreting praise.[117] Faith and scripture are often closely linked. The unbeliever finds many things in the bible unbelievable, as for example the virgin birth, but the believer does not since he cannot but believe the clear word of scripture.[118]

In *A Friendly Exegesis* Zwingli attacks Luther for not using the principles he has himself advocated, in particular faith.[119] Zwingli refers to the principle in a variety of ways: the rule of faith and the simple knowledge

---

[107] Z V 886.9–13. Here Zwingli is translating Isa. 7: 9 as the Septuagint and the Vulgate do. He does also translate it more correctly, using the Hebrew. (Z XIV 180.6–22.) It is a view of faith present in Augustine, e.g. in Tractate 29 on John 7: 14–18.

[108] Z II 575.22–578.5; VIII 194.35–195.7; III 408.3–32.          [109] Z VIII 276.1–16.

[110] Z III 785.1–8. Cf. 798.1–23.          [111] Z III 790.29–791.8.

[112] Z V 774.9–26.          [113] Z XIII 310.32–7.

[114] Z XIII 425.3–11.          [115] S VI ii 230.11–17.

[116] S VI i 487.15–22.          [117] S VI i 640.11–16.

[118] Z IV 492.27–33.          [119] Z V 648.7–15.

of faith,[120] scripture and the articles of faith, and the apostolic letters or the analogy of faith. Against Luther's refusal to depart from the literal sense of the words, Zwingli refers to Isaiah's word, 'If you do not believe, you will not understand' and quotes Luther as saying that a word is to be taken in the natural sense unless faith admonishes otherwise. 'Faith therefore is the teacher and interpreter of the words.' Scripture is to be interpreted by faith. Zwingli argues that Luther would have to reject the literal interpretation of Matthew 16, for the words are absurd and repugnant to scripture. However, Zwingli was not thinking of what is absurd to men, but of what is absurd to faith and scripture—and faith sees that it has no need of bodily food.[121] Faith must determine where something in the bible is not literal, but a trope.[122]

*A Friendly Answer* refers to the need to use faith and the written word in judging someone's teaching—scripture being rightly understood according to faith, and faith being tested by scripture. If you seek to move something, you need both the animal and the harness. The animal stands for living faith and the harness for scripture. When the church makes a judgement it uses both, and neither by itself accomplishes anything. This is developed by considering Matthew 5: 25-6, a passage which the pope used in support of purgatory. Faith, however, will not tolerate purgatory, for it asks what Christ died for if we must pay for our sins. Faith and scripture must therefore be held together, and Zwingli cites Christ's own appeal to scripture and his willingness to be judged by it. He draws on scripture and on faith in support of understanding the words of institution tropically and not literally.[123]

Zwingli gives two examples of faith's role. First, Christ says, 'Whoever believes in me has eternal life' and 'Whoever comes to me [meaning: believes in me] will not hunger and whoever believes in me will never thirst.' From this Zwingli argues that faith senses that God assures us inwardly with his Spirit and that outward things, which come into us from outside, in no way help towards justification. Outward things are done away with by Christ, and the description of faith in Hebrews 11 is against bodily eating. In short, true faith believes in Christ's divinity and acknowledges his death to be our life. It knows nothing of bodily eating, which does not profit us, for God promised nothing to bodily eating and also did not institute it. Second, the word says, 'He ascended into heaven, sits at the right hand of God the Father Almighty, from whence he will come to judge . . .' Christ is bodily ascended and so cannot be here. Moreover, after the resurrection he was not in two places at once and the angel at the tomb said: 'He is not here'. After this Zwingli draws on the role of scripture to show that it will not tolerate the bodily eating of Christ's flesh and blood; referring to passages such as John 6: 63 and John 16: 28.[124]

In *Zwingli's Christian Reply* faith is seen in terms of trust in Jesus Christ, the true Son of God (with a reference to Romans 10: 8–9 and to Christ's life, suffering and death, and resurrection) and the word 'scripture' is applied to precise texts (John 6: 63; Matt. 26: 64; Mark 16: 19; John 16: 28; 17: 11) and to the immediate context of the disputed words, 'This is my body'. This context shows that, if the words are taken literally, we would have to eat the body which was given for us and as it was given for us (on the cross), while 1 Corinthians 11: 25–6 makes it clear that 'this' refers not to eating flesh and blood, but to the signs of bread and wine or the feast as a memorial of the body.[125]

A more detailed exposition occurs in *Two Replies to Luther's Book*. Faith, it is held, teaches us not to take the words of institution literally—faith understood as trust in God alone. Such living faith, by which we know ourselves children of God, does not come from, consist in, or receive strength from any creature. It does not even come from the bodily presence of Christ. A discussion of Hebrews 11: 1 stresses the distinction between faith as mere assent and faith as trust in God for salvation. (Nor is faith believing the body of Christ to be eaten bodily in the bread, or else Abraham could not have been saved.) Moreover the reference in Hebrews 11 to invisible and visible makes a clear distinction between God and creatures. Faith is not in the creature; indeed it is in Christ as God and not as man, a view supported by John 12: 44. Hence bodily eating does not

---

[124] Z V 773.16–789.27 The analogy of faith may refer on occasion to the creed. (Z VI i 362, n. 14.) However, even where there are quotations from the creed the phrase itself need not refer to it. (Z V 788.10–13.)

[125] Z V 903.22–907.8. In his comment on Luke 4: 1, where he speaks of the analogy of faith and the usage of scripture, Zwingli seems to mean by faith the fact that faith comes from the Spirit (or from God) and not from outward things and that it is faith that makes him present; and by the usage of scripture he means the way in which the bible sometimes ascribes to us what properly belongs to God. (S VI i 569.1–28.)

remove sins. We no longer know Christ after the flesh, but our faith is in God bodily crucified, not bodily eaten. After this Zwingli argues on the basis of scripture against a literal interpretation of 'This is my body', arguing that Luther ignores everything that is contrary to his view, as if it were not God's word.[126]

Faith is one of the dominant criteria in Zwingli's interpretation, but it is rarely isolated and frequently associated with God's glory or love, as well as with the Spirit and scripture. The need of the Spirit and of true faith and love in reading the bible is expressed in the prayer at the end of the preface to the translation of the prophets.[127]

The law of love is the only law that binds a Christian.[128] Therefore it helps in interpreting the bible. When the question about whom one may marry was raised (in relation to the discussion in Leviticus 18) Zwingli stated clearly, 'it is better to be pious than subtle, to be kindled with Christian love than with subtlety and contentiousness'.[129] In the matter of remarriage the judgement was similar: that one should act according to God's word out of love.[130]

Love is to be our teacher,[131] just as elsewhere faith is said to be our teacher. Indeed faith and love are so intimately related that they can be used almost synonymously[132] and in the commentaries are joined together as a criterion. They are the surest teacher,[133] and in the matter of war we should abstain 'unless the Lord commands, that is unless faith and love dictate'.[134]

Love is also associated with a principle which is appealed to more often: God's honour or glory. Taking from God his honour and giving it to anything else is for Zwingli the true idolatry.[135] This is a central element in Zwingli's theology and naturally plays a part in his interpretation of the bible, especially in his controversy with Rome[136] but also in that with anabaptists.[137] From the beginning it is often linked with love, as it was by Jud in the second disputation.[138] They are joined because they summarize the

---

[126] Z VI ii 206.16–211.25.                              [127] Z VI ii 312.3–8.
[128] Z I 135.12–15.                                        [129] Z VIII 269.4–5.
[130] Z VIII 298.16–17. In the context of oaths, cf. Z VI i 145.30–146.11.
[131] Z V 873.33.
[132] Z V 900.15–21.                     [133] Z XIII 219.18–19; S VI i 228.20–1.
[134] Z XIII 376.20–1. Zwingli rejects a literalist approach, whether used by catholic or anabaptist. Love is the decisive criterion, because we live under grace and not under law. (Z IX 465.13–20, 467.10–12.)
[135] Z II 391.9–11.
[136] Z III 280.1–21, 408.20–32; S VI i 321.30–3.
[137] Z VI i 26.2–12.
[138] Z II 695.19–23. It is also naturally associated with the analogy of faith. S VI ii 230.12–14.

two commands on which all the law and the prophets depend;[139] and they help, for example, a true understanding and use of the sabbath.[140] Sometimes it is not the love of the neighbour, but the salvation of the neighbour or of the church that is in view. They are what the interpreter should be seeking,[141] for rightly understood the scriptures serve God's glory and our salvation.[142]

## The Old Testament

The old testament played an important part in the debate with the anabaptists in the understanding of both baptism and the magistracy. (Zwingli appealed to circumcision against the anabaptists and to the passover against catholics and Lutherans.) The conviction that the old covenant and the new were fundamentally one enabled him to use the old testament with a somewhat different emphasis in these controversies and in his later writings. The stress is less on the contrast, more on the continuity, between them. However, the change must not be exaggerated. There was a contrast of old and new testaments in his later as well as in his earlier writings, just as there was a positive use of the old testament in both earlier and later ones.

A text of central importance in Zwingli's use of the old testament is 1 Corinthians 10: 11, 'Everything happened to them as a symbol, but they were written for our instruction'. When it is used in *A Solemn Exhortation*, where Zwingli is critical of warfare, it interprets the wars of the Jews as symbolizing the warfare we should wage against vice and unbelief.[143] This moralizing of scripture is characteristic of Zwingli. But he does not here, or in *Choice and Liberty Respecting Food*, allow that symbolical events did not happen, showing in this a stress on historicity which marks all his old testament exegesis.[144]

The frequent use of the old testament in the early writings and the pattern of using quotations from it before those of the new do not indicate any theological priority for it. His desire is 'always to be guided by the scriptures of the new and old testament',[145] the order he continued to

---

[139] Z V 822.4-11. Cf. Z II 482.12-31.

[140] Z IV 128.14-129.30; S VI ii 224.17-36. Following the words of Christ in Mark 2: 25-8, Zwingli shows great freedom in regard to the sabbath, although observance of the sabbath is God's law and not man's. (Z I 99.18-102.25.)

[141] S VI i 720.39-41; VI ii 256.5-8.

[142] S VI i 216.12-14.

[143] Z I 177.21-178.4. Cf. Z XIII 421.32. The importance of the text increased when Zwingli stressed the unity of the two testaments rather than the diversity. Cf. S VI ii 161.35-162.10.

[144] Z I 92.30-93.6.

[145] Z I 133.13-14.

use,[146] although mandates and letters of the council used the reverse order.[147] The old testament is to be read in the light of the new, indeed in the light of Christ, and not Christ and the new testament in the light of the old. This is the view Zwingli enunciated in rejecting the use of arguments from the old testament that the eucharist is a sacrifice. Such a method is a turning from the light to the shadow. For him you could find in the old testament only what is expressed in Christ, and until then it is not clear. Thus no one would have known that the serpent pointed to Christ on the cross until Christ came. Therefore to argue from the old testament to the new is like saying that what an astrologer predicted had happened, even though it had not, because he had said it would happen.[148]

However, the old testament came to be of increasing importance, especially, though not only, against the anabaptists. They challenged Zwingli's use of it, while he saw them as rejecting it altogether and therefore rejecting God, who is God of both old and new testaments.[149] In his defence of infant baptism he emphasized that Christ and the apostles appealed to the old testament. In John 5: 39 Christ said, 'Search the scriptures, in which you think you have eternal life, and they bear witness of me'.[150] Paul moreover wrote, 'Everything that was written was written for our instruction' (Rom. 15: 4) and 'Everything happened to them as a symbol (bedütnus), but was written for our sake' (1 Cor. 10: 11). Zwingli concluded, 'If they are written for our sake, we should in no way despise them.' We should go to them not just over baptism, but over other outward matters, for where—to give two examples—do we learn in the new testament about restitution or the decrees of marriage,[151] and what other scriptures did the apostles have recourse to in their decisions but those to which Christ went, the law and the prophets? The apostles would therefore have acted against scripture, if they had denied baptism to infants.[152] The old testament is still, however,

---

[146] e.g. in the controversy over baptism. (Z IV 325.18-21; VI i 29.3-4.) Cf. Z X 153.20-1. The order is curiously reversed by Köhler in the introduction to *A Friendly Letter* (Z V 3) despite Zwingli's order in Z V 12.3-5. The exception in Z VI i 62.15-19 is understandable in the context.

[147] Z II 628.18-20, 679.10-11; IV 656.18-20.

[148] Z III 187.1-6, 193.18-195.15. Yet Zwingli could speak of the old testament as making Christ or the new testament more believable, in particular where it offers a type of what happens in Christ. (Z XIII 143.2-8, 147.36-148.3.)

[149] Z VI i 56.13-59.2, 62.15-19. The anabaptist attitude to the old testament caused Zwingli on occasion to argue primarily from the new. (Z IX 463.27-464.1.)

[150] This text was used earlier against his catholic opponents to show that Christ pointed to the biblical testimony as decisive, and not to men judging the bible. (Z II 23.5-16; III 309.18-310.1.) With them he also spoke of Christ's drawing his attacks against the Jews from the old testament. (Z III 672.22-5.)

[151] Z IV 325.17-326.17. Cf. 639.12-31.

[152] Z IX 110.2-17. Cf. VI i 110.16-111.3, 187.11-19.

interpreted in the light of the new, in particular by the double command to love on which Christ said that the law and the prophets depend.[153]

## The Natural, Moral, and Mystical Sense

Zwingli's commentaries come from the prophecy and show signs both of the scholarly examination of the text and of the exposition and preaching that followed. However his attitude to the traditional fourfold use of scripture is also evident before that in scattered references in his writing.

His fundamental concern was with the natural sense.[154] This led to a thorough exploration of the text, using the Septuagint and the Vulgate for the old testament, as well as the Hebrew. Zwingli regarded Hebrew as important for understanding the new testament also, as its writers were Hebrew. Alongside a grasp of the language was a grasp of the figures of speech used.[155] Certain of them, such as alloiosis, catachresis, and synecdoche, were drawn on frequently in debate with his opponents, and several were dealt with at some length in his writings.[156] A knowledge of these was indispensable for an understanding of the natural sense. In addition there was the comparison of various passages of scripture.[157] In all this Zwingli drew freely on the learning of colleagues such as Jud, Megander, and Pellican, the writings of friends such as Bucer and Oecolampadius, the commentaries of the fathers (especially Augustine, Jerome, and Origen), and the tradition of exegesis that preceded him.

A stress on the natural sense was not new, for it marks fathers such as Jerome, a medieval scholar such as Nicholas of Lyra, and a contemporary

[153] Z V 822.2–8. Cf. Z IX 464.4–31.

[154] Z I 375.10–14; III 112.29–33. The natural sense was in reality the spiritual sense. It is the sense of the Spirit who is the author of scripture, rather than the sense that comes from human reason. (Z III 205.25–206.12.)

'Darum ergibt sich als erstes Moment der Hermeneutik die Forderung, den *natürlichen Sinn*, den sensus literalis unter Berücksichtigung aller Tropen, Figuren, Schematismen und Idiotismen der Sprache herauszuarbeiten. Damit ist erst der Grund für die weitere Arbeit gelegt. Denn die Schrift will nicht nur erzählen, Geschehnisse berichten und damit die Vergangenheit nicht verloren gehen lassen, sondern sie will auch jedes Geschlecht mahnen, belehren und erziehen. Daraus ergibt sich für Zwingli eine zweite Aufgabe der Exegese: sie hat die *Beispiele* (exempla), den traditionellen sensus moralis aufzuzeigen, damit Ähnliches in uns gepflanzt oder unterdrückt werde. Als dritte Aufgabe der Exegese wird schliesslich die Forderung genannt, den Zusammenhang einer Stelle oder Perikope mit Christus aufzuzeigen. Es handelt sich hiebei um die Herausarbeitung des *mystischen Schriftsinnes*.' (Künzli, 'Zwingli als Ausleger', p. 47.)

[155] Z V 729.25–730.6, 731.1–732.11. A list can be found in Z XIII 837–54. Künzli (op.cit., p. 57) points to seventy rhetorical terms in *Genesis* and *Exodus* and to 200 in *Isaiah* (Z XIV 884).

[156] The terms are not always used in controversial theological contexts, e.g. S VI ii 105.41–3 and Z XIV 129.29–31. Alloiosis is used primarily, but not exclusively, in the christological and eucharistic debate with Luther, while synecdoche is used frequently, but not only, in the baptismal debate with anabaptists.

[157] Z V 730.6–31, 732.12–733.28.

such as Luther. Nevertheless it is fundamental in Zwingli and has a clear priority for him. To arrive at it he uses his various principles of interpretation including figures of speech, for the literal is not always the true sense.[158]

However, the natural sense is not the only one. There is also the moral sense, although Zwingli does not use this term. As Künzli notes, it is simply the application to the hearer or reader of the natural sense (or indeed of the mystical sense).[159] Zwingli had a strong conviction that the bible was written for our sake. He used texts such as 1 Corinthians 10:11 to prove this for the old testament, but he held it equally of the new.[160] The prayer used at the beginning of the prophecy expressed his concern for the transformation of one's life as well as the illumination of one's mind.[161] There was a constant concern that the hearer or reader should learn from what happened, this being the reason why things were written. Indeed there is nothing in the bible that does not teach, admonish, or console.[162] This moral purpose was furthered particularly by the use of examples, as Megander and Jud pointed out in reference to Zwingli at the end of Genesis.[163] The commentaries are full of such examples, often mentioned quite explicitly,[164] and this is a feature of the way the bible is used outside

[158] Z IV 799.18–800.26.The detailed etymological, linguistic, historical, and geographical concerns are common to Zwingli and Jerome. Künzli argues for the influence of Nicholas of Lyra on Zwingli in his setting the verses or chapters of the old testament in context, and for Zwingli's superiority here. 'Seine Zusammenfassungen des Inhalts einzelner Kapitel sind weit prägnanter, auf das Wesentliche gerichtet und—stärker als bei Nicolaus—nicht nur an der Geschichte, sondern an der *Heilsgeschichte* orientiert.' ('Zwingli als Ausleger' p. 91; cf. p. 71.) In grammatical matters Zwingli was dependent on Reuchlin.

[159] In a comment on Z XIII 209.8–12. (Künzli, op. cit., p. 100.) He does, however, recognize that in some forms the mystical and moral sense are close to each other ('Quellenproblem und mystischer Schriftsinn in Zwinglis Genesis- und Exoduskommentar', *ZWA* 9 (1951) 263). Cf. Z XIII 295.1–3.

[160] Cf. Z I 421.12–423.9. L. W. Spitz speaks of many of the reformers having the moralizing and spiritualizing tendencies characteristic of German humanism. (*The Religious Renaissance of the German Humanists* (Cambridge, Mass., 1963), p. 292.)

[161] '. . . aperi et illumina mentes nostras, ut oracula tua pure et sancte intelligamus et in illud, quod recte intellexerimus, transformemur, quo maiestati tuae nulla ex parte displiceamus . . .'. (Z IV 365.3–5.) Cf. Z XIII 294.26–295.1 and the prayer before the sermon with its petition that we may live according to the divine will. (Z IV 686.16–19.)

Schmidt-Clausing affirms that Zwingli's stress on the Spirit is particularly evident in the prayer at the opening of the prophecy and in his baptismal prayer, arguing especially, though not altogether convincingly, in terms of the association of light and the Spirit ('Das Prophezeigebet', ZWA 12 (1964) 10–34, 'Die liturgietheologische Arbeit Zwinglis am Sintflutgebet des Taufformulars', ZWA 13 (1972–3) 516–43, 591–615).

[162] Z XIII 126.17–20 and 157.25–35.

[163] '. . . simul ex hystoria ad mores ac pietatem exempla eruens'. (Z XIII 287.29.) Cf. 'Id enim in sacris literis unice spectandum et observandum est, ut exempla recte vivendi ex eis petamus.' (Z XIII 288.14–16.)          [164] Z XIII 266.3–7, 319.36–320.1, 343.23–9.

the commentaries. The biblical account is also constantly related to specific people and situations in the church and community of Zwingli's day, not least to those he sees as opponents of God's word: papists, anabaptists, and tyrants.[165]

Besides the natural and moral sense there was also what was traditionally known as the mystical sense.[166] Zwingli does not clearly distinguish different kinds of mystical sense (such as the allegorical and the anagogical), nor does he sharply distinguish the various terms (such as allegory, type, figure, anagoge) from each other. Nevertheless this sense is a central feature of his use of the old testament and is present in the new.

*Preface to the Prophets* ends with the need for the Christian reader to bear in mind Paul's words in 1 Corinthians 10: 6 and 11, that everything happened in the old testament symbolically and symbolizes something to us, and that it was written for our sake.[167] This conviction underlay Zwingli's reading of the old testament in the light of Christ. The divine providence always prefigures something in external events; and what was prefigured was accomplished and fulfilled in Christ.[168] It needs to be emphasized that Zwingli insisted on the historicity of the events which had a symbolical meaning (and one might say the historicity of the events they symbolize). The approach is not a Platonizing one, as Pollet alleges, but a historical and christological one, modelled in some ways on Paul's approach in Galatians 4 and 2 Corinthians 8. To read the old testament literally, as if, for example, the promises of the prophets have to do only with an earthly Israel or an earthly Jerusalem is to read it in a fleshly way, as the Jews do, who do not allow an allegorical or symbolical sense.[169]

Before the period of the commentaries Zwingli enunciated certain principles for interpreting the old testament, in particular that one must argue back from Christ who is its fulfilment. Only what can be seen in

---

[165] e.g. Z XIII 298.27–299.10.

[166] Cf. XIII 294.11–18. Augustine distinguished between the literal and figurative senses of scripture in terms of faith and love. 'Whatever there is in the word of God that cannot, when taken literally, be referred either to purity of life or soundness of doctrine is to be classified as figurative.' *On Christian Doctrine*, III 10.14 (*PL* XXXIV, col. 71).

[167] Z VI ii 311.24–35. Cf. XIII 157.25–35.

[168] Z XIII 299.31–2 and S VI i 208.13–24. Cf. Z VI ii 297.4–14.

[169] Z VI ii 305.28–308.14. In his commentaries Zwingli constantly points beneath the surface in his exposition of the text, but always in terms of what is clear elsewhere in scripture. Thus the jar containing the manna in Exodus 16 is the humanity of Christ, in which is the divinity which is the bread of life, for Christ is food for the soul according to his divinity. (Z XIII 374.24–7.) The two feet of Jacob in Genesis 32 stand for the desires of the flesh and of the Spirit. He is accursed who is lame in both feet, that is, who desires at the same time to please God and the flesh. He is happy who is lame in one foot, the flesh, so that he rests only on the Spirit and trusts in him alone. (Z XIII 213.8–12.)

him may be read into the old testament person or event. Allegory can be used, but it is no more than a condiment is to a meal. It is nothing by itself, but for the believer it can give a pleasant taste to something which has its basis in scripture.[170] There is also the appeal to faith or the analogy of faith; and in the commentaries reference is often made to this in the mystical or symbolical approach.

Many writers have criticized Zwingli's considerable use of allegory. Künzli, by contrast, stresses Zwingli's use of typology and his relatively small use of allegory.[171] The difference lies in large part in the understanding of the term 'allegory'. Künzli uses it in a narrow sense for places where the exposition excludes, or does not strictly arise from, the natural sense, or where Zwingli's exegesis is less christological and is marked by an element of uncertainty. Künzli's central concern here is broadly right, but his case needs to be modified in important respects.[172] (Indeed it would be entirely proper, though misleading, to deal with the mystical sense of scripture under the heading of allegory, for Zwingli uses that term broadly in *Preface to the Prophets* in opposition to a merely literal and fleshly understanding.[173]) His stress on typology in this context does make clear the strongly christological nature of the mystical sense.[174] This is expressed most clearly in the varied types of Christ, such as Noah, Isaac, Joseph, and Moses.

A notable example is that of Abraham and Isaac in Genesis 22, which expresses God's so loving the world that he did not spare his own Son, but gave him to die for us. The story, in which Abraham represents God and Isaac is the type of Christ, shows many features of Zwingli's use of typology. It shows similarity: the three days correspond with Christ's resurrection on the third day, the ass with Christ's ass on entering Jerusalem, the wood borne by Isaac with the cross borne by Christ, and so on. Equally it shows dissimilarity: two boys compared with three disciples, showing the truth to be superior to the shadow, and Isaac's not dying, while Christ did

---

[170] Z III 193.18–195.15; II 398.17–400. 6. See Additional Note 2, p. 78.

[171] See, e.g., *DTC* 3768 and E. Künzli, 'Quellenproblem', pp. 253–307.

[172] See Additional Note 3, pp. 78–9.

[173] Z VI ii 305.28–308.14.

[174] What is said of types applies broadly to anagoge. Type and related terms are used mostly in *Genesis* and *Exodus* and anagoge mostly in the other old testament commentaries, while both type and anagoge are used in the new testament commentaries. Clear examples of anagoge are given in Z VI ii 310.1–311.23, after references to those who see only the surface meaning in the text. Anagoge is described as a kind (*species*) of allegory in Z XIV 584.11–12. In the new testament the type or foreshadowings may refer to Zwingli's day; thus the citizen of the far country who sent the younger son into his field to feed swine adumbrates the pope. (*S* VI i 672.27–9.) Faith teaches what things are to be understood typologically. (Z XIII 280.29–32.)

die, for if Isaac had been like Christ in all things he would have been the truth and not the figure.[175]

Typology is immensely varied. Not only are various people types of Christ, but they can also be types of the church and they can be the one and then the other in rapid succession. Thus in Genesis 22 Isaac is a type of Christ, whereas Abraham represents God; but in the following chapter Abraham becomes a type of the faithful, as Isaac does four chapters later, before becoming (four chapters after that, where Jacob returns to him) in effect the figure of the Father to whom Christ his Son ascends.[176] Things can also be types or figures—of Christ, the church, evil powers, and the last things.

With many of the examples of figures, types, and allegories, there seems a certain arbitrariness, something which the principle of dissimilarity assists; and there are perhaps hints that Zwingli was not altogether convinced about some examples.[177] Moreover the assertion that Christ is figured as the alpha and omega in Genesis 11 by Noah's being the last in the old generation and the first in the new (for there were ten generations from Adam to Noah and ten from Noah to Abraham) and also in Exodus 12 by the lamb's being slain in the first month of the year, does arouse the suspicion that almost anything in the old testament can mean almost anything in the new.[178]

## ADDITIONAL NOTES

1. When Zwingli commented on 2 Cor. 3: 6 in *II Corinthians* he contrasted the letter that kills (in a command such as 'Do not covet') and Christ who makes believers alive through his Spirit in the heart. The letter kills until the Spirit has been given. Here Zwingli sees the contrast between Paul's ministry and that of Moses. (*S* VI ii 194.37-195.12.) He appears to be influenced by the discussion in Augustine's *On the Spirit and the Letter*, quoted in *St Matthew* (*S* VI i 242.17-32). Augustine sees the fundamental distinction of letter and spirit in 2 Cor. 3: 6 not as between the literal and the figurative or spiritual meaning of a passage, but as

[175] Z XIII 147.36-148.32. Those who want more are referred to Origen and others. Künzli has shown something of Zwingli's dependence on, and independence of, Origen. In particular Zwingli is more christological in interpretation and gives greater stress to the natural sense ('Quellenproblem', pp. 285-7, 299-302). There is at many points a kinship with Erasmus and Origen in Zwingli's mystical use of scripture. Zwingli can however criticize Origen's not treating a passage as historical. (Z IX 458.4-13.)
[176] Z XIII 157.16-18, 176.8-9, 202.18-20.
[177] e.g. seeing the coat of many colours as typifying the variety of virtues in a Christian. (Z XIII 227.12-13.) Zwingli recognizes that there can be more than one allegorical sense in a passage. (Z XIII 310.36-7.)
[178] Z XIII 66.1-8, 347.7-10.

between the letter and the Holy Spirit, although he allows that there are many passages, as in the Song of Songs, where we must look for the spiritual, not the literal, meaning. As an example of the letter that kills he quotes the command not to covet. It is to be taken literally and not figuratively; yet taken literally it kills, because without the Holy Spirit who gives life we cannot keep it.

2. In *An Exposition of the Articles* Zwingli rejects the use of allegory in the raising of Lazarus to prove something not otherwise firmly based in scripture. It is in this way that Paul uses the story of Leah and Rachel in Galatians 4, and that is like the use of condiments in a meal which make the food tastier. If auricular confession were explicitly commanded by God, then the story of Lazarus could be used allegorically to make the point in a pleasing way. (*Z* II 398.17–400.6.) At Berne Zwingli disputed Buchstab's use of Solomon and his mother to support the intercession of the saints. He declared of anagoge that it should be used only where something is expressed in clear words of scripture. It must be a decoration rather than the foundation of an argument. (*Z* VI i 404.2–9.)

In their preface to *Exodus* Jud and Megander write: 'Quis nam tandem erit modus allegoriarum aut quae scripturae autoritas, si cuivis liceat quodvis fingere? Scimus eas nonnunquam veluti condimenta posse adhiberi, et ea lege, ne, quod principalis cibus et res est, obliteretur. Sunt enim multi, qui, nisi allegorice omnia intelligant, intellexisse sibi nihil videantur; cum vobis id unice sit atque inter prima expediendum, ut linguarum peritia atque illarum ipsarum tropis, figuris, schematismis, idiotismis, naturalem sensum ornemus, secundo loco exemplum sic pectoribus inseramus, ut simile quiddam in nobis aut pampinet aut prematur. Postremo et haec negligenda minime ducimus, quae in hunc usum vel dicta sunt vel facta, ut, quae Christus postmodum aliquando gesturus erat, adumbrarent. Tropologiae, allegoriae, anagogae legem non habent, nisi ut modus cum analogia servetur.' (*Z* XIII 294.7–20.)

3. Künzli has rightly stressed important elements in Zwingli's exegesis of scripture: the fundamental emphasis on the natural sense and the historicity of the events described, the centrality of the christological dimension in the mystical sense, and the intention to use the old testament in the way Paul does. But other factors need to be noted.

1. Künzli's definition of allegory does not correspond with Zwingli's definition or use of the term, either in *Genesis* and *Exodus* or in his other writings.

2. There is a wide use of allegory in Zwingli. In *Ezekiel* he actually refers to everything from ch. 40 to ch. 47 as being allegory. (*Z* XIV 739.23–4.) Allegory involves an understanding of a word or a passage that is symbolical or figurative rather than literal. See, e.g., *Z* III 698.39–699.7, 841.28–30 and XIV 148.6–149.23.

3. In *Genesis* and *Exodus* Künzli separates typology from allegory, although he slightly qualifies this separation, essentially taking as allegory only passages where the word is explicitly used. Yet even then he consciously uses some of these passages in the section on typology. (*Z* XIII 164.31–

165.2, 368.24–26, 398.24–26 in 'Quellenproblem', pp. 271 and 273.) Moreover, in that section, he uses words such as 'figure', 'shadow', and 'signify', whereas they could equally well be included under allegory. Indeed Zwingli himself uses 'figure' and 'signify' and even 'type' in the context of allegory. (Z XIII 137.1–32, 194.7–15, 209.11–12, 400.31–37.)

4. Zwingli's critical words about allegory (and those of Jud and Megander in *Exodus*) seem to be directed against using it unnecessarily (e.g. when the natural sense is sufficient) or incorrectly (e.g. according to one's pleasure and not according to the rule or analogy of faith). (Z III 860.16–22; VI ii 305.6–27; XIII 14.23–15.8, 310.22–3, 361.27–35, 373.2–4; XIV 150.38–152.32; S VI i 240.8–12, 261.16–19; cf. Z XIII 294.7–20.)

5. A christological interpretation can go with the explicit use of allegory. (Z XIV 217.14–15.)

6. There is an explicit use of allegory in the new testament as well as the old testament commentaries, with events, sayings, and parables being allegorized. (S VI i 303.38–47, 333.15–17, 476.42–5.) Allegory in the new testament is on occasion also explicitly christological.

# 3. God

THE centre of Zwingli's theology is God—not God as opposed to Christ, but as opposed to all that is not God. His whole concern is to bring men back to this centre. In *A Commentary* he expresses the character of true and false religion in this way:

> True religion, or piety, is that which clings to the one and only God . . . True piety demands, therefore, that one should hang upon the lips of the Lord and not hear or accept the word of any but the bridegroom. . . . It is false religion and piety when trust is put in any other than God. They, then, who trust in any created thing whatsoever are not truly pious. They are impious who embrace the word of man as God's.[1]

Zwingli's challenge is to a religion and theology where the centrality of God has been lost. In religion this means placing one's trust in the creature rather than the creator; in theology it means placing one's trust in human tradition and teaching rather than in God's word. This double challenge is characteristic of Zwingli's writings from beginning to end.

To affirm that the centre of Zwingli's theology is God is not in itself to deny the central role of Christ and the Holy Spirit. In *A Commentary* he states, 'Some, when we teach vigorously that all our confidence is to be placed in God our Father, spring up with the impudent suggestion that we must be guarded against; for in all our teaching, they say, our aim is that we may do away with Christ . . .'. For Zwingli, however, when you speak of Father, Son, or Holy Spirit 'you speak of one and understand all three'.[2]

[1] Z III 669.17–25, 674.21–4; *Works* III 92, 97–8. Cf. Z II 192.29–33. In the fifty-first article such alien trust is described as idolatry. Trusting in the saints as a means of approaching God implies a false view of God as a tyrant rather than the true view of him as the most loving Father. (Z II 577.3–23.) In both *An Account of the Faith* and *An Exposition of the Faith* the first article deals with God, as do the Apostles' and Nicene Creed. In *An Exposition of the Faith* faith in the one creator is then contrasted with faith in the creature, such as the saints or the sacraments. (S IV 45.1–46.1, 46.48–47.6.)

[2] Z II 675.3–15; *Works* III 98. Cf. Z IV 262.6–7; V 293.1–2. Of course references to Christ in this context are to him as God, not as man. See, e.g., Z VIII 792.8–793.4. In many cases Zwingli moves naturally in a text which refers to God to speaking of the Son or the Spirit. (Z II 65.19–26.) The doctrine of the trinity as such does not have a dominant or creative role in Zwingli's theology. The stress lies on the unity of the godhead, as is natural when the stress is on the divinity of Christ. For a discussion of the trinity, see Locher, *Die Theologie Zwinglis*, pp. 99–133.

In the first article of *An Account of the Faith* Zwingli affirms that his teaching on the trinity is in accordance with the creeds. (Z VI ii 792.11–17.)

The fundamental importance of the doctrine of God is apparent in the systematic expositions of his theology. In *A Commentary*, as in *An Account of the Faith* and *An Exposition of the Faith*, which are modelled on the creed, he begins with the doctrine of God. Each in its own way affirms the place of God as opposed to all that is not God. God is creator. In him alone we should put our trust, not in anything that is created.[3] God orders all things and his purpose does not depend on the occasion of any creature.[4] The faithful 'believe in one only true and omnipotent God and have faith in him only'.[5] Yet it is in his more systematic presentations of the faith that Zwingli is judged by some to be as much a philosopher as a theologian, as much dependent on non-biblical sources as biblical. Certainly his two most sustained expositions of the doctrine of God show his strongly philosophical cast of mind.

Writers who give prominence to *The Providence of God* present a view of Zwingli's theology that is philosophical rather than biblical. This, however, distorts the picture, as it sees the work in isolation from his other works, and ignores the fact that the God who is being presented in it is ultimately the God of the biblical revelation.[6] This is more evident when it is seen in relation to *A Commentary* and *An Exposition of the Faith*, which are in some ways comparable works.

## The Knowledge of God

*A Commentary* begins with a discussion of the knowledge of God. Zwingli makes the traditional distinction between knowledge of God's existence and knowledge of his nature. He allows that most people have been aware of God's existence, yet only few of those who recognized him as one God worshipped him as they ought. However, the knowledge of God is not inherent in man. At the beginning of the exposition Zwingli quotes Paul's words, 'The knowledge of God is manifest among them, for God has manifested it to them' (Rom. 1: 19), stressing the fact that it is God who has

---

[3] *S* IV 45.26–8.

[4] *Z* VI ii 794.31–795.1.

[5] *Z* III 642.12–14; *Works* III 60. Cf. the Berne sermon which expounds the Apostles' Creed. (*Z* VI i 452.19–453.7.)

[6] Pfister points out that the neuter *numen* is used more than the masculine *deus* in *The Providence of God*, but that the former is nevertheless defined from the latter. See *Z* VI iii 88.2. Cf. 'scio numen istud summum, quod deus meus est' in *An Account of the Faith*. (*Z* VI ii 794.31.) Moreover he attributes the Neoplatonist terms in Zwingli to Augustine and the schoolmen (Pfister, *Die Seligkeit*, p. 17). Locher argues that in his use of scholastic terms such as *summum bonum* Zwingli goes beyond the scholastic use in a biblical way ('Grundzüge', pp. 497–501, *Zwingli's Thought*, pp. 168–72). However, the stress in *The Providence of God* is different from that in most other writings where the emphasis is on God's revelation and he is portrayed, e.g., as Father, as in *Z* I 216.9–15.

manifested the knowledge. What some attribute to nature or to intellect comes from God, who works all things in everyone.[7] Indeed Zwingli goes on to speak of the faith believers have in God, saying, 'It is of God alone . . . that you believe that God exists and that you have faith in him.'[8]

So far is Zwingli from allowing that there is any knowledge of God natural to man, that he states that we do not of ourselves have any more knowledge of what God is than a beetle has of what man is. If some of the heathen have said what is true, it must have come from God, who has sown some seeds of knowledge of himself among them, though sparingly and obscurely. Christians, however, are not to seek their knowledge of God other than in his revelation in Christ, for, as Zwingli puts it, we 'to whom God has spoken through his Son and through the Holy Spirit' should seek our knowledge from God himself and therefore from scripture.[9] The insistence that knowledge of God does not come from any human endowment is a feature of Zwingli's theology from beginning to end. The initiative is always with God, as it was historically in his dealings with Adam. Zwingli denies 'that one who was so bent upon running away and hiding that he could scarcely be dragged out would have returned if the Lord had not followed him up in his flight'. Rather 'religion took its rise when God called runaway man back to him, when otherwise he would have been a deserter for ever'.[10] It is not from human reason, but from God's revelation of himself, that man's knowledge of God comes. Characteristically Zwingli ascribes this action to the Spirit of God.[11]

[7] Z III 640.28–641.18. Cf. Z I 215.9–216.15, which speaks of God's making himself known to all, but which then focuses that in the history of the old testament and in Christ. A knowledge of God is referred to among the Gentiles in the bible, as well as among those outside it. (Z VI ii 300.21–301.8; XIII 301.11–15, 378.3–9.) When, according to Paul, the Gentiles, who do not have the law, do by nature what the law requires (Rom. 2: 14), then Paul approaches the Gentile use of the term 'nature'; but he does not think that knowledge of God or the law comes from human reason. Zwingli follows Augustine in interpreting nature in terms of God, and thus in seeing Seneca and Cicero as meaning the working or providence of God when they refer to nature. (S VI i 241.12–244.27.)

[8] Z III 642.36–7; Works III 61. Cf. Z III 654.14–18; XIII 99.1–11.

[9] Z III 643.1–34. 'Fucus ergo est et falsa religio, quicquid a theologis ex philosophia "quid sit deus" allatum est.' (Z III 643.20–1.) Cf. Z III 202.35–204.15, with its references to sacrifices to God before Christ.

It is only from God that we can have true knowledge of man and of God, though the reason for the first has to do with man's lying and dissembling, and the reason for the second with the feebleness of man's understanding and the splendour and glory of God. (Z III 654.28–656.5.) D. E. Wolf misrepresents Zwingli in what he says about natural theology (Wolf, 'Luther, Zwingli, Calvin', Deutsches Pfarrerblatt, 40 (1936) 634). There is no sense in which human knowledge is a preparation for knowledge of God, as Zwingli's rejection of the saying 'Where the philosopher stops, the theologian starts' in another context shows. (Z I 377.27–378.9.)

[10] Z III 667.9–12, 30–2; Works III 89–90. Cf. Z III 907.24–9, 908.4–19.

[11] S VI i 241.17–27, 539.31–4.

The knowledge of God is not, however, intended to be a merely theoretical or intellectual knowledge of God. It is meant to lead to faith in him and love for him. True knowledge of God gives the basis for such faith and love.[12] In *James*, when expounding faith (Jas. 2: 19), Zwingli speaks of saving faith as involving knowledge of God and faith in, and love for, the God who is known. Knowledge by its nature precedes love, but it does not automatically lead to it. Such knowledge can come to us through the outward preaching of the gospel, whereas loving the God who is known comes from the Spirit alone.[13] In this sense it can be said that the more we know God, the more we love him. Indeed we are created for the knowledge of God, so that we may love him above all things.[14]

In the epilogue to *A Commentary* Zwingli places the distinction between man and animals in the knowledge of God. 'There is no difference between the life of man and that of beasts if you take away the knowledge of God.' Knowledge of God means knowing what God is and not just that he is— and that involves the law: knowing what God wills, what he forbids, and what he requires of us.[15] Knowledge of God is moreover related to knowledge of ourselves, leading to a knowledge of ourselves and therefore our penitence, but it is also in a sense dependent on our knowledge of ourselves.[16]

Knowledge of God is said by Zwingli, in an enigmatic sentence, to precede knowledge of Christ. This is part of his response to the challenge that in discussing piety he has made no reference to salvation through Christ and to grace, though he has already discussed God, Man, and Religion. It would be most natural to take this sentence in the historical sense, that God made himself known to men before he made himself known to them in Christ. Therefore they already knew him, however inadequately, before they knew him in Christ. Such a view fits entirely with Zwingli's presentation in *A Commentary* and also with the strongly historical and biblical discussion of God in *A Friendly Request*.[17] It might, however, if one argued from the immediate context, be taken in a trinitarian sense. Then the meaning would be that in order to understand who Christ is one must first know the doctrine of God as Father, Son, and Holy Spirit.[18]

[12] Z III 654.14–25. Cf. the failure of the Gentiles to worship him as they ought, despite their knowledge of him. (Z III 641.25–38; S VI i 539.14–23.)

[13] S VI ii 272.42–273.20. Cf. the reference to true and saving knowledge as coming from the Spirit in S VI i 539.31–34. Zwingli distinguishes *agnoscere* from *cognoscere*. 'Cognoscere intelligentis est; agnoscere grati est et memoris. Cognoverunt ergo Gentes deum, sed non agnoverunt eum, id est, non coluerunt eum fideli et grata mente.' (S VI i 80.11–14.)   [14] S VI i 629.16–26.

[15] Z III 907.16–17, 908.4–10; S VI i 539.3–23. Cf. Z VI iii 140.9–11.

[16] Z III 908.19–33; S VI i 321.24–29, 360.34–43, 766.13–16.   [17] Z I 215.9–216.25.

[18] Locher, *Die Theologie Zwinglis*, p. 55, n. 14.

In its discussion of the nature of God *A Commentary* begins with the being of God and then considers his goodness. The language of some of the discussion is philosophical or scholastic, and that is how some scholars have interpreted it, but the basis of the discussion is manifestly biblical. Zwingli considers the being of God first and then his goodness. In 'I am that I am' (Exod. 3: 14) 'God disclosed himself wholly; for it is just as if he had said, "I am he who am of myself, who am by my own power, who am being itself . . ."' God's aseity is the first thing that man should know about the nature of God. By the words which follow in Exodus 3: 14 God 'indicated that he alone is the being of all things'. He bestows being in such a way that nothing could possibly exist for a moment unless he existed.[19]

Zwingli then asserts that being is good, arguing that 'this is likewise clear from his word'. In particular he appeals to Genesis 1: 31 and Luke 18: 19. From the first he affirms that God's goodness is not derived from anything else and that he is the source of all good. (He expresses this by saying that all things which are are God. It is one of those expressions that have the superficial ring of pantheism.)[20] In developing his statement about God Zwingli draws on philosophical expressions such as entelechy, but in effect defends himself by offering biblical testimony for the idea and then by pointing to Paul's drawing on a non-biblical writer in Acts 17: 28.[21] From this basic understanding of God he elaborates his understanding of the providence of God.

*The Providence of God* is closer in many ways to *A Commentary* than to any other work of Zwingli, but it is much less obviously and straightforwardly biblical. It does not argue the case for the providence of God directly and explicitly in the light of Christ or the biblical revelation, but proceeds by logical argument, drawing on non-biblical sources, with biblical testimony brought in only from time to time and often at the end of the argument rather than at the beginning.[22] Yet *The Providence of God* appears even more philosophical than it is. It begins its discussion of God

---

[19] Z III 643.35–644.10, 644.35–645.5. The stress on aseity is in the patristic and scholastic tradition.

[20] Z III 645.9–25.                              [21] Z III 645.26–36, 646.27–34.

[22] The first chapter, to take but one instance, proceeds by way of logical argument. See, e.g., Z VI iii 71.12–75.18. At the very end Zwingli admits that he has 'made larger use of argument than of the testimony of scripture'. (Z VI iii 229.20–230.4; *Works* II 233.) Philosophical terms are used to describe God, yet some of their force is removed by the way they are used. Thus the term *primus motor* is identified as *deus noster*. (Z VI iii 88.2.) However, although Zwingli is aware of his philosophical approach and the objections to it, he does not desert it, but draws on examples to support the view he has been presenting before drawing on scripture. (Z VI iii 94.5–11.) In any case Zwingli had long held the view that there was truth outside the biblical revelation, though its truth depended on the Spirit.

with the term 'highest good' (*summum bonum*). The term is drawn from Greek philosophy, although it is also a patristic and scholastic term. However it is not new in Zwingli, but it, or something equivalent, is used throughout his works, and in a biblical, rather than in a philosophical, way. The term should be understood primarily in the light of Zwingli's use of it, not in the light of its origin. As early as 1522 in *Choice and Liberty Respecting Food* he is asserting in the light of Jeremiah 2: 13, Matthew 19: 16–17, and James 1: 17 that God alone is good and is the source—indeed the only source—of all good. There is a contrast therefore between God and the creature.[23]

It is this idea that lies behind Zwingli's use of *summum bonum*, as is obvious from its context in *The Providence of God*.

The highest good is not so called because it is above all goods, as if there were some goods that were good in their own nature, but were surpassed by this good, just as gold surpasses the value of silver, though both are valuable. It is called the highest good because it is the only thing good by nature, and every good that can be imagined is itself really this highest good. This Christ set forth by the words: 'Why callest thou me good? There is none good but God' (Matt. 19: 17) . . . the things which are called good . . . are good not by nature, but by sharing his goodness, or rather, by derivation. That is, they are good in so far as they are from the highest good, in the highest good, and to the glory of the highest good.[24]

The sense of God as the source of all good, on whom all other things depend, and the rooting of the term in the words of Christ, colour the use of the term here and certainly lie behind Zwingli's understanding of it. He can indeed use it, as in his exposition of 'I am the Lord your God, who brought you out of the land of Egypt, out of the house of bondage' (Exodus 20: 2), in a profoundly historical and christological way. The goodness of God, who is the highest good, is shown, for example, in the giving of manna and in Christ who is the pledge of his goodness.[25]

---

[23] Z I 126.8–24. Cf. Z I 313.15–29; III 269.15–270.11. 'Denn dieser nam "got" bedütet das guot, das die gwüssest zuoflucht unnd hilff und brunn des guoten ist.' (Z II 219.7-8.) Moreover God as the highest good is related to God as Father. (Z II 224.1–15.) The christological context is notable in the use of the term in Z III 44.11–14. Zwingli draws on many non-biblical terms to describe God. This was not in itself remarkable in his day, surprising as it may seem in ours. Locher has shown in several cases how the non-Christian force of a term was qualified by Zwingli's use of it, e.g. *Deus Optimus Maximus* (*Die Theologie Zwinglis*, pp. 91–3).

In the German translation of *The Education of Youth* (Z II 538.12–13; V 431.36) *Christus optimus maximus* becomes *Gott*.          [24] Z VI iii 70.9–71.11; *Works* II 131 (adapted).

[25] 'Domini nomen magnificentiam, potentiam ac virtutem, dei vero bonitatem ac munificentiam nobis summi illius boni significat . . . Parum autem esset, si se sic nominasset, nisi et hoc praestitisset . . . Bonitatem Iudaeis praestitit, dum e petra aquam, e coelo manna cibum dedit, dum eos ut aquila pullos suos fovit. Quae bonitas nobis ineffabiliter in Christo praestita est, qui pignus est bonitatis divinae, gratiae et misericordiae.' (Z XIII 389.13–30.)

*The Providence of God* begins with God as the highest good and only later considers God as being.[26] Moreover it has argued the case that all things depend on God for their existence before turning to the biblical passages, such as Exodus 3, in which the idea is based. Again there is the insistence on God's aseity and the dependence of all things on him for their existence.[27] As Zwingli develops the relationship of God and creation he uses phrases which superficially imply pantheism (or perhaps rather panentheism), but pantheism is fundamentally out of keeping with Zwingli's sense of the sharp distinction between the creator and the creature and the utter dependence of the creation on the creator. Passages that may seem pantheist manifest on examination a strong sense of dependence on God for being, sometimes with particular reference to Romans 11: 36.[28] Other passages show the distinction between God and the world. Thus a statement such as

The latter [i.e. the *summum bonum*] must be so good that absolutely no good can be imagined which is not from it, in it and, in fact, itself ... To be of the universe is, therefore, to be of the deity. Hence the opinion of those philosophers is no absurdity who said that all things are one, if we only understand them rightly, namely, in the sense that to be of all things is to be of the deity, in that all things are endowed and maintained by him

is followed by the words 'we are not the deity'.[29] There are also passages in which nature seems to be identified with God, but the whole purpose of Zwingli in such passages is to attribute to God what others have attributed to nature.[30]

## The Providence of God

Zwingli's entire theology, like his religious experience, is shaped by his sense of the sovereignty of God and of man's utter dependence on him. For him our salvation, indeed our whole life, comes from God and depends on him. It is in this theological and religious context that Zwingli's doctrine of providence is to be understood. (This does not deny, but rather helps to account for, his interest in Pico della Mirandola and in

[26] The concern with providence makes it natural to begin with goodness, whereas *A Commentary* begins with being. The relationship for Zwingli between the words 'God' and 'good' gives to goodness a certain priority. See, e.g., *Z* VI i 452.1–454.20.

[27] *Z* VI iii 100.6–101.16.

[28] *Z* III 645.19–25 and VI iii 92.19–93.5 have a reference to Rom. 11: 36. In the second passage *ex ipso* is replaced with *ipsum*. Zeller (pp. 36–42) derives Zwingli's pantheist sounding expressions from Stoicism, whether directly from Seneca, Pliny, and others, or indirectly through Augustine and other fathers, even perhaps fifteenth-century Neoplatonists.

[29] *Z* VI iii 219.24–220.12; *Works* II 226.

[30] *Z* VI iii 111.7–114.6. Cf. *Z* XIII 10.5–18 and *S* VI i 619.38–40.

non-Christian writers such as Seneca.) His understanding of providence is misunderstood where discussion concentrates on his most philosophical writings, *A Commentary* and *The Providence of God,* to the neglect of earlier writings and the numerous passing references to providence, not least in the biblical commentaries.[31]

Zwingli had a deep personal trust in God and a sense of being an instrument in his hands. This finds expression in the poem written when he was attacked by pestilence in 1519.

> To thee I cry:
> If it is thy will
> Take out the dart,
> Which wounds me
> Nor lets me have an hour's
> Rest or repose!
> Will'st thou however
> That death take me
> In the midst of my days,
> So let it be!
> Do what thou wilt;
> Me nothing lacks.
> Thy vessel am I;
> To make or break altogether.

This expression of utter trust in God and surrender to him is placed significantly in the part of the poem entitled 'At the Beginning of the Illness'.[32] Whatever the force of that position, there can be little doubt that such an experience of deliverance from death would have had a powerful effect on Zwingli, and would have intensified his sense of God's overruling providence and of being an instrument in his hands.

This kind of faith is evident in his letters. Thus he wrote to Myconius on 24 July 1520: 'I beseech Christ for this one thing only, that he will enable me to endure all things courageously, and that he break me as a potter's vessel or make me strong, as it pleases him.'[33] His sense of the

---

[31] Hans Büscher deals in turn with Aquinas, Calvin, and Zwingli. The main weakness of his treatment of Zwingli is that he deals only with *The Providence of God* and does not see it in the context of Zwingli's expositions of providence. His critique of Zwingli is in part in terms of Luther. ('Von der göttlichen Vorsehung', (Diss. Münster, 1958).)

[32] Z I 67.11-24; *Works* I 56. Zeller (p. 32) regards Stoicism and Augustinian Platonism as helping to Zwingli's personal faith in election and as serving the theological working out of that faith. While in Glarus Zwingli read and annotated Pico della Mirandola's *Liber de providentia dei contra philosophastros*. See, e.g., Usteri, *Initia*, pp. 638-46. Pico's influence is uncertain, although Zwingli read him before he had formulated his understanding of providence and predestination.

[33] Z VII 344.15-17; Jackson 148. Rich connects the poem and the letter, and would date the

88     THE THEOLOGY OF HULDRYCH ZWINGLI

providence of God is not, however, limited to issues of life and death. Thus in a letter to Vadian on 28 March 1524, he speaks of the immense pressure under which he works, so that in attending to people's needs he forgets what he had intended to write. But he adds at once, 'In all these things I recognize the providence of God . . .'. He also seeks to help others to see their suffering in the context of God's overruling love.[34]

His own sense of the providence of God and the way he develops his understanding of providence in his early writings suggest a more fundamentally biblical and personal basis to his affirmation of the sovereignty and providence of God than many critics have allowed. In *A Solemn Exhortation*, after appealing to Schwyz not to worry about the loss of riches or the lack of foreign assistance, involved in withdrawing from their part in mercenary service, Zwingli simply asks, 'If God is for us, who is against us?'[35] His confidence in God is expressed in the repeated use of this and the following Pauline question: 'He who did not spare his own Son but gave him up for us all, will he not also give us all things with him?' (Rom 8: 31–2.) These words show the biblical and christological basis for that confidence in God out of which his doctrine of providence is elaborated.

A sense of the providence of God permeates Zwingli's writings and is expressed in a variety of circumstances. *An Exposition of the Articles* relates to divine providence matters as diverse as the use of the word 'all' in 'Drink of it, all of you' and the present freeing of Christians from the pope as their former subjection to him.[36] However, the most important

poem from the same period (*Die Anfänge*, pp. 104-19). Cf. the letter to Myconius on 23 Aug. 1522: 'Totum itaque me illius benignitati permittam: regat, vehat, festinet, maneat, acceleret, moretur, mergat! Eius enim vasculum sumus; nobis uti potest et ad honorem et ad ignominiam.' (Z VII 565.10-14.) See also the letter to Haller on 29 Dec. 1521. After quoting various biblical passages, including Matt. 5: 11-12, which are an encouragement to those experiencing persecution, and speaking of his own willingness to die for Christ, Zwingli writes: 'Aliquando vero nostra haec infelicia tempora intuens, quibus temeritas et ingratitudo, ne dicam iniusticia, omnia tenent, omnia pervadunt, omnia vastant, in tam diversam trahor sententiam, ut ne mihi quidem plane constem, quid sentiam, nisi quod, dum ad me redeo, divino nutu omnia haec fieri cognosco, ut hoc pacto, qui ad deum accedere fide nolebant, deploratis rebus omnibus ad hunc unum confugere cogantur: dum scilicet omni humana ope fuerimus destituti, huc tanquam ad Iovis χρησφύγετον concurramus.' (Z VII 486.6-14.)

[34] Z VIII 166.14-167.4. See the letters to Michael Cellarius and Johannes Wanner. (Z VIII 715-716, 768-9.) The sense that God uses everything for the good of the elect or those who trust him is expressed in a wide variety of contexts throughout Zwingli's life, usually in relation to biblical precedents. (Z I 170.13-21; II 73.11-12; VI i 175.15-17; VI iii 210.9-10, 217.8-12; XIII 286.28-31; S VI i 272.40-5.)

[35] Z I 187.3-5. Cf., in a different setting, Z II 193.15-33.

[36] Z II 132.31-133.3, 312.4-7. God is always the same, and his providence can be seen in the present as in the past. He redeemed Israel in Egypt, and has now once again seen the oppression of his people and sent redemption. (Z III 9.20-10.3.)

references to providence are in the exposition of articles 16 and 20. They show that the bible is not brought in as a kind of afterthought to buttress an argument which Zwingli has already established on non-biblical grounds, as is sometimes alleged of his treatment in *The Providence of God*. In expounding article 16 he affirms that everything good comes from above from the Father of light (Jas. 1: 17) and then refers to God in his providence administering everything and turning everything evil to good.[37]

Later there is a more detailed consideration of providence—in the exposition of an article related to Christ as mediator, in which he declares that God wishes to give us all things in his name, so that outside this life we need no mediator except him. In a discussion of works and merit Zwingli refers to Matthew 10: 28-31, one of the texts he frequently cites in discussions of providence. In these words we hear that everything happens out of God's ordaining and providence; not a sparrow falls to the ground without God's ordaining it. Hence nothing, however small, happens unless it is ordained by God. Likewise God knows the number of hairs on our head. Indeed there is nothing so small in us or in any creature, that is not ordained and sent by the all-knowing and all-powerful providence of God. How much more then are our works ordained by God, and therefore they cannot be ascribed to us.[38]

After the fundamental statement about God's providence, Zwingli deals with the objection: If I cannot be good of my own power, but God must make me good, why does God not make me good or leave me uncondemned? His response is that he has not been in God's council, but he learns from Romans 9 that God is not unjust simply because he uses his creature according to his will, just as a potter cannot be called unjust by his vessels because he makes out of clay one vessel for worthy, another for unworthy, use. 'Therefore he disposes of his vessels, that is to say us men, as he wills. He chooses (*erwellet*) one to be fit for his purposes and use; the other he does not will. He can make his creatures whole or break them, as he wills.' After pointing out that Pharaoh could not have resisted the signs he saw, unless God had hardened his heart, Zwingli argues that the understanding of free will which we have taken from the heathen makes us ascribe to ourselves what God has done in us, not acknowledging his almighty providence.[39] The affirmation of God's providence arises from faith, not from philosophical argument.

[37] *Z* II 96.27-34. To say that all good comes from God is to deny that man is capable of God apart from God.                                                  [38] *Z* II 178.32-179.20.

[39] *Z* II 179.20-180.29. Cf. *Z* II 272.4-6. Romans 9 was to be important in Zwingli's discussion of election. However, the issue of election is not present at this stage, although the reference does imply both election and reprobation.

An unbeliever may object that he may as well therefore leave it to God to do what he intends. Zwingli replies that if God has made someone a good tree he will bring forth good fruit, because the Spirit of God will be active in him. The believer knows himself to be an instrument and vessel through whom God works, and he ascribes everything to God. By contrast you can recognize an unbeliever, as either he does no good work or if he does he ascribes it to himself and not to God. God wills to make of such a person a vessel of wrath, that is of damnation, by which he shows his righteousness. 'God makes people good or bad as he wills.'[40]

Against his catholic opponents Zwingli affirms that God is the cause of all effects, adding 'We have the strong word of God on our side'. He has argued his case from scripture, but then proceeds to draw on other biblical testimonies (John 6: 44-5; 15: 4-5, 16; Luke 17: 7-10; 1 Cor. 3: 5-6; 12: 3-6; 2 Cor. 3: 4-6; Phil. 2: 13). Zwingli states that the excursus on providence was to show that it is God (not we) who effects what is good in us and that we are simply instruments through whom he works.[41]

It is evident that in his early writings the doctrine of providence is not fundamentally a philosophical doctrine, but a biblical one. It is not at this stage concerned primarily with the world or with God as creator, but with the Christian life and with God as saviour. It is not something the unbeliever can grasp, but something the believer knows from experience. All this is confirmed by the treatment of the subject in other writings that precede *The Providence of God*.[42]

In *A Commentary* there is a discussion of providence in the sections on God and on merit. (In it Zwingli's position is sharply distinguished from the semi-pelagianism of Erasmus and much medieval theology.) In the first section, when referring to our knowledge of God, he asserts that every-thing is of God, a view of God's sovereignty which runs through Zwingli. Providence is seen as related to the understanding of God as the being of all things and as good, an understanding rooted in passages such as Genesis 1: 31 and Exodus 3: 13, Luke 18: 19, Acts 17: 28, and Romans 11: 36. God is the being and life of all things, sustaining and governing them.

---

[40] Z II 180.30-181.23.

[41] Z II 184.1-186.20. After this Zwingli refers to Augustine, possibly Zwingli's reference to John, Augustine, and Paul in Z V 713.2-714.2 is to this sense of everything as coming from God, which he supports here from these three.

In *The Education of Youth* providence is immediately rooted in the words of Christ in Matt. 10: 29-30 and Luke 12: 24, 27. Belief in providence means that we take refuge in God, seek everything from him, and do not give way to anxiety or greed. (Z II 538.30-539.26.)

[42] The short discussion in *The Education of Youth* is related to the creation, but in terms of Christ's teaching. (Z II 539.1-26.)

Nothing can intervene that is able either to impede his power or defeat his purpose.[43] God would indeed not be God, if anything lay outside his providence.

It is evident, therefore, that God not only is a sort of stuff, as it were, from which all things have being and motion and life, but is at the same time such wisdom, knowledge, and foresight, that nothing is hidden from him, nothing unknown to him, nothing beyond his reach, nothing disobedient to him. Hence not even the mosquito has its sharp sting and musical hum without God's wisdom, knowledge, and foresight. His wisdom, then, knows all things even before they exist, his knowledge comprehends all things, his foresight regulates all things. For that which is God would not be the supreme good unless it were at the same time supreme wisdom and foresight.[44]

It is a sign of temerity rather than faith to demand of God a reason for his acts and designs. The only proper response is to contemplate with reverence what God has wished to disclose to us, and not to wish impudently to touch what he has hidden.[45]

At this stage in his argument Zwingli states that 'it is time to bring forward the witness of the word itself to everything that has been said so far about the wisdom and providence of God'. It is not as if he has not developed the argument from scripture, but the method has been as much logical as theological, as it is later to be in *The Providence of God*. Nevertheless the biblical testimonies are not adduced as an afterthought and Zwingli can say 'the whole scripture of the old testament views everything as done by the providence of God'.[46] He has followed the example of Paul in Romans 1 in looking first at the world in which God has manifested himself, deliberately accommodating himself in this way, as Paul did, to those for whom he was writing. When he turns to the bible he is content with a few references from the old testament (Prov. 8: 22–36, Jer. 51: 15, and Ps. 104) before giving a number from the new testament (drawing on the teaching of Christ in Matt. 5: 36; 6: 25–34; 10: 29; Luke 12: 7; and John 9: 3; 11: 3–4).[47]

Even in this section on God the close relation of providence to the issue of free will and merit is evident. 'For the whole business of predestination, free will, and merit rests upon this matter of providence.'[48] The importance of this relationship is even more evident in the section on merit. He does not develop further the arguments from *An Exposition of the Articles*,

---

[43] Z III 641.14–18, 643.35–645.35.

[44] Z III 647.7–16; *Works* III 66. Cf. Z IX 30.15–28.

[45] Z III 647.27–31, 648.3–6.      [46] Z III 648.21–2, 649.1–3; *Works* III 68–9.

[47] Z III 640.28–650.15, esp. 641.23–5, 648.21–650.15.      [48] Z III 650.18–19; *Works* III 70.

though he faces the problem that God may be seen as the author of evil. He deals with it by stating both that we are often unaware of the cause and purpose of things and therefore do not wish to recognize divine providence in them, although it uses us and all things in its freedom, and that what is base to us is not base to providence, for this comes from the law to which we are subject, but not God—rather he is himself what he demands of us through the law.[49] Zwingli uses the analogy of reason as determining man's external actions to throw light on God's providence in the world. 'Yet, far stronger and surer is divine providence in controlling the whole universe; for—if one may compare little things with great—God is in the universe what reason is in man . . . how is that we do not confess that in the same way all things are so done and disposed by the providence of God that nothing takes place without his will or command?'[50]

In the writings following *A Commentary* there is no significant development in Zwingli's view of providence, although reference is frequently made to it. In the old testament commentaries all kinds of events are naturally ascribed to the providence of God and thus are to be ascribed to God and not to man or to chance. Thus Jacob's receiving the blessing was due, not to his father's blindness nor to his mother's deceit, but to the providence of God, which nevertheless used Isaac's blindness and Rebekah's cunning.[51] However, it is only the believer who sees God at work in all things in his power and providence. The unbeliever ascribes these things to man or nature, as if nature were something other than the power and providence of God.[52] The prefiguring of Christ in the old testament is also ascribed to the providence of God.[53] Yet there is a mystery in the purposes of God's providence, and people are not to seek to scrutinize it, unless, like Moses and Aaron, they are given a clear sign that they should ascend the mountain. This is an evident indication that Zwingli's doctrine of providence is in no sense the expression of a rationalistic approach to theology, as has been alleged.[54]

The frequent allusions to providence in the old and new testament commentaries testify both to the ordinariness and the importance of the doctrine in Zwingli. It is discussed in a letter to Fridolin Brunner on 25 January 1527, touched on in *The Berne Sermons* a year later, referred to

---

[49] Z III 842.30–843.15.

[50] Z III 842.15–30; *Works* III 271–2. Cf. Z VI iii 109.11–13, 114.1–6.

[51] Z XIII 168.17–26, 179.31–3. Sometimes the concern is with human counsel, as in Z XIII 198.18–20, sometimes with chance (242.8–10). The context is frequently an attack on free will, as in Z IX 31.1–2; XIV 708.18–19; S VI ii 172.33–4.

[52] Z XIII 10.5–18.

[53] Z XIII 299.29–37.

[54] Z XIII 385.4–11.

in some detail in the commentary on Matthew, and then expounded at length in *The Providence of God*.[55]

This work stands out as the least biblical and most philosophical of all Zwingli's writings. It is not as if there is any fundamental change in his understanding of providence, but the nature of the argument and the non-biblical presentation of the doctrine mark it off from all his earlier discussions of the issue. It is reasonable to assume that the literary and historical context accounts for this, at least in part.[56] Most writers adapt themselves to those they are seeking to persuade. At the same time their writings reflect themselves as well as their readers. Zwingli is aware of a less biblical approach and admits 'that I have made larger use of argument than of the testimony of scripture', though he affirms that it is 'the foundation for the whole argumentation'.[57] He consciously uses a philosophical approach, but defends it on the basis that all truth is of the Holy Spirit. He offers scriptural evidence or examples, but they come at the end of the argument rather than at the beginning. Nevertheless the argument proceeds in terms of 'the understanding of faith' (*fideli intellectu*).[58]

Zwingli seeks to make a logically coherent case for the doctrine of providence, beginning, as in *A Commentary*, from the nature of God—here from the nature of God as the highest good. His first thesis is 'Providence necessarily exists, because the highest good necessarily cares for and orders

[55] Z IX 29.1–31.25; VI i 451.17–461.7; XIV 757.18–20; S VI i 271.30–273.24, 416.5–17. In the Berne sermon Zwingli is expounding the Apostles' Creed and deals with providence under the first article, in a manner reminiscent of *A Commentary*, though with less biblical reference. Lack of time is the reason he gives for the lack of biblical testimony, but clearly other anxieties also underly his somewhat philosophical approach. (Z VI i 456.2–19.) In *St Matthew* he is commenting on 10: 29–30.

Büsser emphasizes the similarity between Zwingli and Lactantius in *The Providence of God*, especially in the doctrines of providence, creation, and man. ('Zwingli und Laktanz', *ZWA* 13 (1971) 375–99.)

[56] Many explanations have been given, some stressing more Zwingli's humanism, others the issues he was facing, e.g., the renaissance emphasis on chance. See S. Rother, *Die religiösen und geistigen Grundlagen der Politik Huldrych Zwinglis* (Erlangen, 1956), pp. 139–47, esp. pp. 139–41. (The references to chance in *The Ox* in 1510 are revealing: Z I 10.8–9, 11.15.) As a parallel note the relation that some see between the somewhat humanist discussion of philosophy in the preface of Bucer's commentary on Romans and the preparation for the founding of a college in Strasburg. See H. Strohl, *Bucer, humaniste chrétien* (Paris, 1939), pp. 17–35.

[57] Z VI iii 229.20–230.4; *Works* II 233. He refers to Moses, Paul, Plato, and Seneca as witnesses, though at least Moses and Paul come first. Z VI iii 83.15–16. Seneca and the Stoics appealed strongly to Zwingli as they did later to Calvin. In a discussion of Calvin's commentary on Seneca's *De Clementia*, F. Wendel comments that 'Zwingli's *Sermon on Providence* sometimes reads almost like a commentary on chosen passages from Seneca'. See *Calvin* (London, 1963), p. 29.

[58] Z VI iii 94.5–11, 75.12–13. In the middle of the chapter on election, the most obviously biblical chapter, the way he uses scripture emerges in the words, 'Nunc ad scripturae testimonia imus, quibus, non iam, quae ad electionis definitionem pertinent, firmantur, sed totum quoque providentiae negocium sub oculos ponitur.' (Z VI iii 160.20–2.)

all things.' He argues that the highest good must be true and therefore know and understand all things, and must be the highest power and therefore able to do all things. Thus since the highest good wills 'by its goodness to do what it clearly sees and can do, it follows that he who can do all things, must provide for all things'. If this were not the case he would not be God.[59] After this Zwingli defines providence as 'the perpetual and immutable rule over and administering of all things'. He describes this in terms of God's generosity and liberality. He uses the term 'unchangeable' to attack any notion of free will or the idea that God might need to change his mind, and he refers to all things because nothing is independent of God.[60]

Next Zwingli argues that all things have their being from God, a point he eventually presents with the use of biblical testimony, drawing as he has before—notably in *A Commentary*—on Exodus 3: 14, Romans 11: 36, Acts 17: 28, and Matthew 10: 29–30. (The chapter draws heavily on non-biblical sources: Aristotle, Plato, Pliny, Plutarch, Pythagoras, and above all Seneca.) He seeks to establish that God is the first and only cause of all things and that so-called secondary causes are only means or instruments in God's hands. This is as true of the apostles remitting sins as of the ground bringing forth or the fire giving warmth. (We see here the vital role of the doctrine of providence for Zwingli in affirming that everything is of God and in denying the role of anything creaturely in our salvation, in particular word and sacrament.) 'It is the kindly power of the deity that gives everything.' From this one can draw the conclusion that nothing happens by chance, for the hairs of our head are numbered. In effect to affirm the contrary is to deny providence and to deny God.[61]

In his detailed exposition Zwingli deals with some of the objections brought to the doctrine of providence, in particular that God is in the end reponsible for sin. This leads him to a defence of God's wisdom and his goodness. God's goodness 'did not cease when it did not guard against the fall of man, but manifested itself in a twofold manner, in creating man and restoring him when created'. In order to know righteousness men (and

---

[59] Z VI iii 70.7–8, 75.17–76.1 (*Works* II 133), 76.1–77.4. 'Si numen est . . . providentiam quoque esse oportet.' (Z VI iii 218.5–7.)

[60] Z VI iii 81.5–6, 81.13–82.2, 82.10–83.2.

[61] Z VI iii 92.19–93.3, 94.5–11, 100.5–103.4, 105.18–106.4, 111.7–10, 112.18–24, 113.23–114.9. Of the non-biblical material Zwingli says simply that God alone is true, and therefore he that speaks the truth speaks from God. (Z VI iii 110.12–14.) Zwingli spoke of all he had written in the book as being from one source, the nature and character of God, adding 'Quem fontem Plato quoque degustavit et Seneca ex eo hausit.' (Z VI iii 106.18–107.1.) The comment on Gen. 1: 11 offers a fine exposition of the view that it is God who is at work in the whole of creation. (Z XIII 10.5–18.)

angels) had to know unrighteousness. This happened through transgression of the law, but as God is not under the law he did not act unright-
eously. 'Thus by creating man so that he could fall, God manifested his
goodness. For by the fall the splendour of the divine righteousness was
made apparent.' God's wisdom is also shown, for it knew man would fall
and yet not after the fall, but likewise from all eternity, it determined on
his redemption. The proper response therefore of man to God is to
wonder at this wisdom, not to question it.[62]

The goodness of God is seen also in predestination or election. Zwingli
insists on a distinction between his approach and that of others in
originating predestination in God's goodness and not only in his
righteousness. The mercy and righteousness of God are held together in
the goodness of God.[63]

In a final chapter Zwingli gives examples of events that happened not
by chance, but by the providence of God. There is indeed a persistent
attack on the idea of chance, for a single example of chance would destroy
providence and thus God would not be God. In citing the rain in the
stories of Noah and Elijah he points out that it does not matter whether it
happened 'by a combination of natural forces adapted to do this at the
time or by a new miracle' as long as we know that the timing was foreseen
by providence before the foundation of the world. However, God does
miracles to make those who 'wage war against the sovereignty of the deity'
recognize a greater force than visible things possess. Yet Zwingli is not one
to stress miracles, and recognizes that many things were once thought
miracles which are not now. He finds greater wonder in what happens in
the natural course of events, for all things occur through the power of
God. All things happen by providence, even the illness that befalls those
who spend themselves in God's service and the health that befalls the
wicked. Indeed nothing is created of which the end and the attendant

---

[62] Z VI iii 141.10–12 (*Works* II 175), 141.20–144.14, 145.15–146.1 (*Works* II 177), 148.5–149.7,
18–20. Zwingli's view here, even more clearly than in *An Account of the Faith*, has become supra-
lapsarian. (Z VI ii 795.5–8.) He frequently returns to the problem posed by God as the author of
all things, using a variety of illustrations: 'Unum igitur atque idem facinus, puta adulterium aut
homicidium, quantum dei est autoris, motoris ac impulsoris, opus est, crimen non est; quantum
autem hominis est, crimen ac scelus est.' Thus the same deed (murder or adultery) is with God an
act, and not a crime, for God is not under the law and is not driven by affections which need to
be placed under the law. (Z VI iii 152.13–153.11.) (A denial that God is the author of evil things is
to be found in *S* VI ii 253.44–254.7. The issue was raised in *A Commentary*. Z III 842.30–843.15.)
Moreover God's providence is not limited to the deed of the murderer, but leads the murdered
person to eternal life and then acts through the judge. (Z VI iii 155.9–21.) Zwingli refuses to take
refuge in dualism, but runs the risk of seeming to make God the author of sin. See Locher,
*Zwingli's Thought*, pp. 205–7.
[63] The chapter on predestination is discussed in the next section.

circumstances have not been foreseen and settled long before they take place.[64]

The strong sense of providence and of God as the cause of all things expresses itself in passages which appear extremely deterministic. God is seen as the author of every human action.[65] He orders not only the beginning and end of our life, but also the whole course of our life in between.[66] One can say 'everything that is done, whether we call it accidental or premeditated and determined upon, is done by the immediate providence of God, whether it has to do with inanimate things or with things endowed with life, mind, and understanding . . .'.[67] Yet for Zwingli only the unbeliever interprets this in a deterministic way, and so regards all human action as vain. By contrast believers, with their knowledge of God, 'know that life must be ordered according to God's will' and therefore 'that they must refrain from whatever the law forbids'. Moreover failure, which to the unbeliever is 'a reason for despair', is 'an incentive to regeneration' for believers.[68]

Providence for Zwingli is never simply a matter for the mind, seeking to understand the mystery of the world or the mystery of God's being. It evokes in the godly a response of wonder, gratitude, and surrender to God. The sense of wonder is expressed at the end of chapter 5 in which Zwingli has engaged in a defence of God's goodness and wisdom in relation to man. 'When we see him created and redeemed, we contemplate the fact with reverence and cannot praise enough the wisdom, goodness, power, and providence of the creator in all things.' At the end of the epilogue he affirms the practical value of recognizing God's providence. If we recognize good things as from providence, we shall be thankful and watchful. If we recognize evil things as from providence, we shall gain comfort and endurance and shall in the end be victorious.[69]

---

[64] Z VI iii 196.5-13, 194.18-24, and 195.4-8 (*Works* II 209), 197.1-11, 216.7-10, 189.17-190.2. It was not by chance that the ass was standing with the colt at the cross roads (Matt. 21: 2), that the cords were lying in the temple (John 2: 15), that the boy had the five barley loaves and two fish (John 6: 9), that the fig tree was planted there years before Christ cursed it (Matt. 21: 19), or that a piece of fish was left over (Luke 24: 42). (Z VI iii 203.18-204.19.)

[65] Z VI iii 152.13-153.9. For the influence of Duns Scotus in this context, see Z VI iii 145, n. 4.

[66] Z VI iii 189.10-190.4.

[67] Z VI iii 211.8-11; *Works* II 220.

[68] Z VI iii 222.13-223.14; *Works* II 228-9 Zwingli's view of providence leads to activity rather than passivity. He rebukes those who neglect their health and say that they will live if it is God's will. He recommends a proper, though not anxious, care for one's health as something done for God and at his ordaining. (Z IV 875.2-19.)

[69] Z VI iii 149.14-17 (*Works* II 179-180), 223.24-225.14.

If . . . poverty, ugliness, illness, childlessness, lack of appreciation and defeats fall to our lot, and we attribute them to providence, what comforts it brings us amid such hard lines! We say to ourselves, 'These things are given me by divine providence. . . . You are God's tool. He wills to wear you out by use, not by idleness. Oh, happy man, whom he calls to his work.'[70]

As Zwingli makes clear elsewhere, belief in providence does not lead to indolence and to leaving everything to God, at least not in the elect. In them the Spirit of God is present and unceasingly active in doing good, for God uses them as instruments to effect his will.[71] Moreover they know that God requires their work.[72] Nor does the doctrine lead to a disregard of others on whom God's judgement seems to be falling. Rather we should pray that God will have mercy on such a person and illuminate his mind, so that he may not perish.[73]

## Predestination

The close relation between providence and predestination is made explicit by Zwingli. In *A Reply to Emser* he speaks of predestination as the innermost part of providence and in *A Commentary* he asserts, 'For the whole business of predestination . . . rests upon this matter of providence', 'providence is the mother of predestination, as it were', 'predestination . . . is born of providence, nay is providence'.[74] Predestination is to be understood within the providence of God and needs to be set in the context of Zwingli's repeated insistence on God's grace and sovereignty.

Predestination is not mentioned much in Zwingli's early writings, though it does occur from time to time. In a letter on 11 July 1521 Myconius raised the issue of free will, the view of some that it did not matter how they lived if they were elect (or alternatively not elect), and the charge of injustice made against God. We do not have Zwingli's reply, but the letter demonstrates that this was a matter with which he had to deal.[75] In his

---

[70] Z VI iii 224.7–14; *Works* II 229 (adapted).

[71] S VI i 215.31–216.2.

[72] 'Hoc interim observandum quod tametsi divina providentia omnia in omnibus operatur, nihilo tamen minus opera nostra et laborem, ut exerceamur, requirit, nec plus tamen efficiemus quam velit ipse.' (S VI i 273.14–16.)

[73] S VI ii 240.5–18.

[74] Z III 278.34–6, 650.18–19, 842.9–11, 15–17; *Works* III 70, 271–2. Locher deals with points of comparison and contrast between Zwingli and Aquinas and Calvin in his chapter on Zwingli's doctrine of predestination (*Zwingli's Thought*, pp. 121–41).

[75] Z VII 463.1–19. Myconius's reference to Paul, Augustine, Jerome, and Ambrose (to whom he ascribes *De vocatione gentium*) shows some of the main sources of the discussion which was a major point of theological debate. Usteri points to Zwingli's marking of the discussion in Origen, and to references to free will and the distinction between *praescientia* and *praedestinatio* in the fathers (*Initia*, pp. 114–115, 125–6). Probably in 1516 he read Eck's semi-Pelagian

attack on free will and works Zwingli speaks of the providence of God, and of the fact that all comes from God, rather than of predestination. Similarly, in his exposition of article 20, he attacks the idea of merit in terms of the grace of God, the fact that everything good comes from God, the providence of God, and also the death of Christ. He does not, however, consider predestination, and even where he quotes 'You did not choose me, but I chose you . . .' (John 15: 16) he does not deal with predestination.[76] Yet some of the issues that come up in his treatment of predestination emerge at this stage in relation to providence: the problem of human freedom and that of God's justice in condemning me for something I can do nothing about, the fact that God is the cause of all things and that man is an instrument through whom God works, and the ascription of salvation to faith.[77]

In *A Reply to Emser* (1524) predestination still does not have an independent role in Zwingli's theology. It is in the shadow of his teaching on providence and grace.[78] *A Commentary* is in part Zwingli's reply to Erasmus's *Freedom of the Will*, a reply that antedates Luther's. His attack, however, is in terms of the wider concept of providence rather than the narrower one of predestination, although the two can be spoken of as one.[79] However, in *Original Sin* in 1526 election has a clear role. After discussing original sin in the first part, Zwingli turns in the second part to the

---

*Chrysopassus seu VI Centuriae de praedestinatione*, with its distinction of *praescientia* and *praedestinatio* (ibid., pp. 647–52). He also drew, if sometimes inaccurately, on the schoolmen, in particular Aquinas. (See further the comment on *praescientia* in Meyer, 'Die Entstehung', pp. 309–10, n. 101.)

In the early Zwingli, references to the elect are frequently no more than a repetition of the biblical text, e.g. Z I 288.3–20 and II 166.25–167.6.

[76] Z II 174.1–7, 177.29–31, 179.14–20, 184.31–3.

[77] The unbeliever poses the problem of freedom by saying in effect: 'I will do nothing good and will see what God does through me. If he has made me good, I am good; if I am evil, it does not help if I do good, as I shall be damned.' (Z II 180.30–41.) Zwingli answers the challenge to God's justice by referring to Rom. 9, affirming that God is not unjust in dealing with his creature according to his will. Who are we to quarrel or reason with God? Indeed God shows his righteousness in making of someone a vessel of his wrath. (Z II 179.20–180.29, 181.17–19.) For God as cause and man as instrument, see Z II 181.7–10, 183.21–184.20; for salvation and faith, Z II 182.1–13.

In a letter to Zwingli about anabaptists in April 1526, Michael Wüst refers to those who appeal to Rom. 8 and say that they will not pray, for that is the work of the Spirit who dwells in them. They argue that God will act in accordance with what he has predestined, not in accordance with what we pray. (Z VIII 563.15–564.6.)

[78] Z III 278.34–279.6. Part of the problem is that predestination or election can be understood as involving man's merit and therefore their link with providence or grace needs to be affirmed. Cf. Z III 650.18–19. Bucer makes use of the doctrine of election as early as 1524 in *Against Treger*; see W. P. Stephens, *The Holy Spirit in the Theology of Martin Bucer* (Cambridge, 1970), ch. 1.

[79] Z III 844.25–30.

question whether it condemns all people to death, and immediately answers, 'The bliss of everlasting life and the pain of everlasting death are altogether matters of free election or rejection by the divine will.' He then attacks those who attach salvation to baptism and circumcision, since it comes 'to those elected of God, not to those who do this or that', and they were elected before they were born. We should not make judgements about others 'since God's election is hidden from us'. Zwingli criticizes those who regard Gentiles or the unbaptized children of Christians as damned. Christ did not say, 'He who is not baptized will not be saved'. Of Gentiles Zwingli asks, 'For what do we know of the faith each one has written in his heart by the hand of God?' He is aware that such a view might seem to detach salvation from Christ and insists that such Gentiles come to God through Christ alone. Zwingli's fundamental concern is to show that salvation comes from election and not from participating in the sacraments. This applies to children as much as to adults. Indeed he argues the case for the children of Christian parents.[80]

Urbanus Rhegius wrote to Zwingli on 28 September 1526 in response to Original Sin, which had been dedicated to him. He raised the questions of universalism and of the necessity of faith for salvation. He disputed Zwingli's interpretation of Mark 16: 15–16 as applying only to adults who hear the gospel, and cited additionally 'Without faith it is impossible to please God.' (Heb. 11: 6.) 'We know that no one can be saved, unless he is in Christ. We judge that no one can be grafted in Christ without faith. To anyone who does not receive Christ, power is not given, by which he becomes a son of God and heir.'[81]

In his reply on 16 October Zwingli argues that Mark 16: 16 must be understood from its context, in particular the reference to 'Preach the gospel'. Hebrews 11: 6 must also be understood from its context as applying to those who hear the word and fall away or those who hear it and receive it. These passages do not apply to children. Election, however, remains firm, even though the elect are drawn through Christ alone; it is necessary also for those who come to Christ to be elect. Zwingli will make no judgement about the children of Gentiles, but holds that the children of Christians

---

[80] Z V 377.28–380.26, 385.23–30; Works II 10–12. Zwingli had discussed Mark 16: 15–16 in 1524 and 1525. (Z VIII 274.4–12 and IV 316.11–32.) The anabaptists, just as much as the papists, think salvation is tied to symbols and do not see the free election of God. (Z V 387.11–13; XIII 106.32–4.)

[81] Z VIII 726–7. Earlier Zwingli related salvation to faith rather than to election. Thus in the context of a discussion of purgatory in An Exposition of the Articles he referred to Heb. 11: 6 and Mark 16: 15–16, saying that those who died without faith were condemned. (Z II 426.19–25.)

are children of God by virtue of the covenant. They are his children through the redemption of God's Son. Faith (or in another place the love and fear of God) is a sign of election in adults, but its absence in children is not a sign that they will be damned.[82]

Election has a key role in Zwingli's debate with anabaptists, in particular in *A Refutation* in 1527. It coheres with Zwingli's emphasis on God's sovereign grace and it enables him to make a stronger case for infant baptism. In the third part of the work Zwingli develops his treatment of the covenant and of election. In the section on covenant he states that God elected a people from whom his Son would take his body, and then elected Abraham so that from his posterity might be born one who would save the whole human race. However, God's election of Israel did not mean that no one would be saved who was not of that people, for God's election is always free. (Zwingli does not limit God's freedom and election to his dealings with Israel, and says that they are evident also in his speaking through the sibyls.) Indeed for Paul it is God's election now of the Gentiles, as formerly of the Jews, that means that there is simply one people and one church.[83] Then comes the section on election in which some of the main elements in Zwingli's view emerge. (He almost certainly did not take the initiative in introducing election into the debate with the anabaptists, but probably discussed it because they used it as an argument against him.)[84] His discussion is based on Romans. He points out that election arises from God's purpose and is in no sense dependent on man or his merit. When faced with the challenge that salvation is ascribed to faith, Zwingli points behind faith to election and refers to Romans 8: 29–30, in particular to the words: 'And those whom he predestined he also called; and those whom he called, he also justified; and those whom he justified he also glorified.' 'We see then that the first thing is God's deliberation or purpose or election, second predestination or marking out, third calling, fourth justification.' By use of synecdoche he explains that attributing salvation to faith is the same as attributing it to election, predestination, or calling, which all precede faith, faith being present wherever there is justification. Paul attributes salvation in particular to faith, as it is the element best known to us.[85]

---

[82] Z VIII 737.7–738.27.

[83] Z VI i 156.11–13, 156.42–157.3, 160.8–12, 162.8–11, 166.13–16. Elsewhere election also points forward to redemption in Christ. (Z XIII 46.3–6.)

[84] See Z VI i 172.6–184.6, esp. 175.20–176.1. On the issue of predestination and free will Zwingli was divided from the anabaptists, as he was from Erasmus.

[85] Z VI i 173.15–174.28. Synecdoche is a figure of speech in which a part is put for the whole, or the whole for a part. Zwingli's examination of the idea of faith as saving us occurs also in his

On the basis of this exposition Zwingli turns to the case of his anabaptist opponents. They referred to Paul's words in Romans 9: 11–13 that
when they were not yet born and had done nothing good or bad God said,
'Jacob I loved, but Esau I hated.' They argued that Hebrew children were
not of God's people, as his people was made up of the elect, and Esau was
described as hated. Zwingli's initial reply is that not only believers are sons
of God, but also those who are elect before they are believers and who may
die before they believe. It is not true that because someone is elect he
believes, since Jacob was elect before he believed. Nor is it true that
because someone does not believe he is not elect, for the elect are always
elect before they believe. The statement 'He who does not believe will be
condemned' must therefore be understood in this context. It means that
those not elect will be condemned. References to believing or not believing do not concern either those who have not yet reached the age when
they can hear or those to whom the gospel has not been preached. Unless
one takes this view, election would depend on faith rather than faith on
election.[86]

Zwingli asserts that the apostles were sure of the election of those who
believed and of the rejection of those who did not, for faith is the fruit of
election. He affirms this in general of those who have reached the
maturity that ought to show the fruit of election. However, as this does
not apply to children, we ought not to judge them. The children of
Christian parents are in the covenant of Abraham and that makes us sure
of their election until the Lord declares something else. (We can of course
make mistakes in our judgement, as the apostles did with Simon Magus.)
Zwingli holds that the children of Christians who die as children are elect,
because of God's promise in Matthew 8: 11 and because they have shown
no disbelief. If, like Esau, they do not die as children, then we shall later
have evidence of their faith or lack of faith. It is foolish, however, to say of
someone like Esau, 'Would that he had died as a child', for that is to ignore
the providence of God. 'He could not die, whom divine providence
created to live and to live impiously.'[87]

The conclusion of the argument for Zwingli is that 'election is above
baptism, circumcision, faith, and preaching'. It is not, however, in any

---

controversy with Luther. He thinks in terms of faith's depending on calling and election, even if
election is not mentioned in the text. (Z V 781.21–6.)

[86] Z VI i 175.20–178.8

[87] Z VI i 178.8–181.17. Zwingli is not primarily concerned with the assurance of salvation,
but with showing that we cannot judge whether infants are saved by the presence or absence in
them of faith. If someone believes, he is elect; but a person may be elect who does not yet believe.

sense above, or independent of, Christ, since the elect are destined to be saved through Christ.[88]

Predestination or election is frequently referred to in Zwingli's later works and particularly the commentaries. The most sustained treatment, however, is in *The Providence of God*. The thesis he discusses indicates two distinctive emphases: his preference for the word 'election' (over the word 'predestination') and his originating of predestination in the goodness of God, although reference is also made to God's wisdom. The goodness of God includes his righteousness and his kindness or mercy, though Zwingli recognizes that righteousness can be used to include mercy and kindness; in that case the terms 'goodness' and 'righteousness' are the same.[89]

Zwingli's definition of election, 'the free disposition of the divine will in regard to those that are blessed', has three parts. The third part shows that election concerns those who are to be made blessed, not those who are to be damned, 'though the divine will makes a disposition with regard to them also'. The first two parts affirm that election is altogether from God, uninfluenced by man in any way. In speaking of 'free disposition' he dissents from the view he ascribes to Aquinas in which God predestines a man when by his wisdom he sees what he is going to be like. In attributing election to the will of God he is not denying the place of wisdom and providence, but making it clear that election is independent of our acts. Zwingli adduces Exodus 7: 3-4; 9: 16; 33: 19 and Romans 9: 18 to show that election comes from God's will and Romans 9: 9-12 and 11: 6 to show that it has nothing to do with man's work or merit.[90]

There is in Zwingli, as in scholastic thought, an emphasis on the simplicity of God. In his exposition of predestination he is concerned to place

---

[88] Z VI i 184.3-6, 181.19-22. For Martin Cellarius's reaction to Zwingli's fundamental position on election in *A Refutation*, see Z IX 207.8-13.

[89] Z VI iii 150.3-152.12. Cf. Z XIII 129.13-19. In *An Account of the Faith* Zwingli states: 'It is of his goodness that he has elected whom he will' and then, when some have expected a contrast with election, he makes a contrast with goodness (or mercy), 'but it is of his justice to adopt and unite the elect to himself through his Son, who has been made a victim for satisfying divine justice for us.' (Z VI ii 796.28-30; Jackson 458 (*Works* II 40).) As the article is concerned with Christ's sacrificial death, it is not surprising that there is no reference to the reprobate. That would otherwise have formed the natural contrast between God's goodness in election and his righteousness in reprobation. However, the holding together of goodness (in the sense of mercy) and righteousness in election is important and corresponds with Zwingli's unified understanding of God. But Zwingli is inconsistent, using goodness sometimes to include righteousness (or justice) and sometimes as mercy to contrast with it (its varied use in the bible being a factor here). This confuses his holding mercy and righteousness (justice) together within the goodness of God.

[90] Z VI iii 155.22-165.4. The concern throughout Zwingli's discussion of election is to deny man's free will, works, or merit. See, e.g., Z XIV 708.18-19; S VI i 755.40-4; VI ii 229.23-4; see also Additional Note, pp. 106-7.

its source in the will of God rather than in his wisdom, since that could be taken to imply that God's election depended on his seeing in advance how we were going to act. But Zwingli's view of the simplicity of God means that wisdom is as much involved as the will, although at the same time the will remains the principal cause. 'For among God's endowments there is no discord. The deity is simple. Hence nothing can be done by him to which all his attributes do not equally contribute. For they are yet one simple and indivisible thing, however much distinctions are made between them in our understanding.' The same concern for simplicity is seen in relation to providence, where a single example of chance would deny the providence of God. 'And if his power were over all, and not also his providence, all the attributes of the deity would not be equal, and accordingly the deity would not be the supremely simple.'[91]

In an excursus on faith Zwingli draws out the relationship between election and faith in the light of Romans 8: 30. 'Therefore faith is given to those who are elect and ordained to eternal life, but so that election precedes and faith as a symbol follows election.' 'Faith is a sign of election . . .' Paul's statement in Romans is a key one, showing that our receiving everlasting glory depends entirely on God's decision and will. Since faith, which in any case is God's gift, follows God's election, ascribing salvation to faith means ascribing it to God's election, for without election there would be no faith.[92] As, however, election leads to faith and faith leads to love, faith is a sign to us that we are elect, and faith and love, or the lack of them, may be a sign to us whether or not others are elect.

Faith gives the elect a certainty that they have been elected by God. (This again Zwingli derives from the end of Romans 8.) They know that 'God has been reconciled to them through his Son'. Zwingli says quite simply 'their election is known not only to God but also to those who are elect'. Equally—in the light of Mark 16: 15—unbelief in those to whom the gospel has been preached is a sign of damnation. However, some do not respond to the gospel as soon as it is preached, as it is only after a time that the Spirit draws them. For that reason we should pass judgement only on those 'who persist in unbelief until death'. We should not in any case pass judgement on those who do not hear the gospel preached. (Here Zwingli refers to Socrates and Seneca who, though they did not know the one God, served him in purity of mind.) Indeed Zwingli can regard the good works of the elect, as long as they are done from love of God and neighbour, as

[91] Z VI iii 159.5-15, 196.10-12; *Works* II 185-6, 210. Cf. the way Zwingli unites the mercy and justice of God in his goodness. (Z VI iii 151.20-152.1.)
[92] Z VI iii 178.2-22, 183.11-184.2.

evidence to them and to others that they have faith—and by implication therefore are elect.[93]

Election does not mean that the elect are preserved from sin. Zwingli uses biblical precedent to affirm the contrary. He allows that the elect may fall into sins as monstrous as the sins of those who are rejected by God. For the elect, however, they are the cause of their rising again, but for the rejected they are the cause of despair, as David, Paul, Mary Magdalene, and the thief, among others, testify. All the deeds of the elect, both good and bad, God turns to good. If someone were to say, 'I will therefore indulge my inclinations, for if I am elect, I shall attain felicity however I live', that would indicate that he was not elect or did not yet have faith or knowledge of God. For those who have knowledge of God know that life must be lived according to his will. The elect therefore, knowing this, see that they must abstain from whatever the law forbids.[94]

However, it is important to realize that Zwingli is not fundamentally concerned to show that we can know ourselves or others to be elect, because of our or their faith and works. He is attacking the idea that salvation is attributable to our faith or works, or comes to us as a reward. Faith is dependent on election and it produces good works as a fire does heat. The cause of all things is in God, and therefore free will and merit cannot be maintained.[95]

Finally Zwingli deals with the election of children. He affirms that when 'the children of believers die it is a sign of divine election', for they are taken away so that they may not be stained by evil. 'For dying is just as much a sign of election in them, as faith is in adults.' In the children of believing parents there can be no stain, for original sin has been expiated through Christ and no stain of evil deeds can defile them, for they are not yet under the law. Children who survive show themselves to be rebellious

---

[93] Z VI iii 179.4–184.15, 181.7–12, 15–17, 182.3–5, 182.18–183.1, 184.9–15. The closest parallel to the relation between election and faith in the early Zwingli comes in the believer's knowing that if he believes in Christ, then he is drawn of God (John 6: 44). (Z I 374.3–9.) Zwingli is more reticent about reprobation than election. In the second disputation before he had formulated his doctrine of election he was concerned to leave to God the question as to who was damned and who was not. (Z II 757.3–18.) 'Darumb zimpt uns hie nit frevenlich zuo urteilen, wer verdampt syg oder nit, sunder söllend wir das got in sin urteyl setzen.' (Z II 757.15–17.)

[94] Z VI iii 217.8–10, 222.13–223.14. In Zwingli's earliest reformation writings God protects those who trust in him, so that if they fall they are not harmed by the fall. But at that stage this is not related to election. He gives the examples of David and Peter who were led to repent and reform. (Z I 169.26–170.21.)

[95] Not only in Z VI iii 184.1–187.18, but also in the whole discussion of election. In this context Zwingli is highly critical of Erasmus. (Z VI iii 185.16–20.)

Zeller (pp. 14–31) attributes to Zwingli a greater concern for people to know that they are saved, relating this to works, faith, and election, than is evident in Zwingli's writings.

like Esau, who was rejected, or godly like Jacob, who was elect. Zwingli holds children in the church as elect, just as he does adults, until their life demonstrates the contrary. He regards the children of Christian parents as among the sons of God because of the word of promise.[96]

Election is dealt with in Zwingli's commentaries and later works, but without any important differences from *The Providence of God*. One element which comes frequently is that we can know of ourselves that we are elect by our faith or by our faith and love—and even that we can know this of others. Sometimes the second of these is denied, although the first is affirmed, as in *An Account of the Faith*, which discusses election in the context of the church.

This [church] is known to God alone, for . . . he alone knows the hearts of the children of men. But, nevertheless, those who are members of this church, since they have faith, know that they themselves are elect and are members of this first church, but are ignorant of the members other than themselves . . . For the Spirit cannot deceive. If he tells us that God is our Father, and we with certainty and confidence call him Father, secure of eternal inheritance, it is certain that God's Spirit has been shed abroad in our hearts. It is therefore certain that he is elect who is so secure and safe, for they who believe are ordained to eternal life.[97]

The commentaries frequently state that the elect know they are elect because of their faith and the work of the Spirit, but there is also reference to works and love as evidence as well. We may judge others by their faith and also by their works, as good works are the fruit of faith. Usually, however, a note of caution is sounded here, since, unlike God, we can judge only by appearances. The absence of faith and works of love is an indication that someone is rejected.[98] Again the context of such comments should be heeded. It is often a denial that salvation can be attributed to faith or works, and an affirmation that they depend on election and flow from it. The fundamental function of the doctrine of election is to deny

---

[96] Z VI iii 187.19–192.5, esp. 190.14–192.1. Zwingli's doctrine of providence safeguards for him the fact that a reprobate person like Esau could not have died in infancy. He mentions various passages in reference to the word of promise, e.g. 1 Cor. 7: 12–14.

[97] Z VI ii 800.19–35; Jackson 463 (*Works* II 43–4). A similar view is expressed in *An Exposition of the Faith*: 'Therefore, seeing that the election and faith of others is always concealed from us, although the Spirit of the Lord gives us the certainty of our own faith and election . . .'. (S IV 61.3–6; LCC XXIV 269 (*Works* II 264).)

[98] S VI i 348.20–37, 364.1–10, 385.6–12, 764.13–15; VI ii 106.41–3, 155.44–156.19, 259.3–8. 'Verba ergo prophete sic intelligenda sunt: Si quis bonos mores in pessimos mutaverit et resipuerit, aequitatem et iusticiam fecerit, proximum dilexerit, certum est eum esse a deo ad vitam aeternam electum.' (Z XIV 708.14–17.) 'Bona enim opera . . . non causa sunt aut merita salutis aeternae, sed potius indices fidei et electionis.' (S VI i 349.41–3.) 'Quemadmodum vero fides te tibi notum facit, filius dei sis nec ne; ita et mandatorum dei observatio, te notum facit proximo.' (S VI ii 155.45–7.)

human merit or free will.[99] It is therefore primarily an affirmation of the sovereignty of God and of our total dependence on him that are for Zwingli at the heart of Christian faith.

The emphasis on election causes problems in Zwingli's theology, especially in relation to word and sacraments, but also in relation to Christ's role in salvation.[100] He affirms that election is through Christ, relating this in particular to his sacrificial death, and that no one can be saved apart from Christ. 'It is of his goodness that he has elected whom he will; but it is of his justice to adopt and unite the elect to himself through his Son, who has been made a victim for satisfying divine justice for us.'[101] Yet Zwingli does not make clear what kind of faith in Christ the elect Gentiles had. For him God is able to give them faith and to save them through Christ, even if the gospel of Christ is not preached to them.[102] Moreover sonship is on occasion related to election apart from faith.[103]

## ADDITIONAL NOTE

Zwingli's emphasis on the will of God is to be understood in the context of God's sovereignty. The locating of election in the will of God, rather than in the wisdom of God, makes it clear that God's decision is entirely free and it removes any possibility that the decision could be influenced by man. (Z VI iii 156.2–160.12.) God's actions are determined by nothing and no one outside himself. He acts according to his will and pleasure. In explaining too precisely the basis of our redemption in terms of the righteousness and mercy of God 'we may presume to say too much of his purposes', so that one should simply say that it pleased him. (Z III 676.28–33.) There is in the end no going behind the will of God, as though God has to satisfy something outside himself. 'It so pleased him to whom

[99] e.g. S IV 63.25–7; VI i 347.38–349.23, 35–44; VI ii 155.22–156.19.

[100] The relation of election and the death of Christ was an issue in medieval debate, e.g. in Biel's comment on Scotus. See H. A. Oberman, *The Harvest of Medieval Theology* (Michigan, 1967), pp. 215–17. The one work in which election has particular prominence is *Questions Concerning the Sacrament of Baptism*. Before dealing with the forty-six questions on baptism Zwingli offers some fundamental propositions, primarily about election, which he holds will deal with the issue of baptism and all other issues. He insists 'with Paul that the elect were elected in Christ from the foundation of the world'. (S III 571.15–576.6, 579.31–3.)

[101] Z VI ii 796.28–30; Jackson 458 (*Works* II 40). Cf. S VI i 242.11–12. Even in the later Zwingli election receives a variety of emphasis. It is not prominent in *An Exposition of the Faith*, but in *An Account of the Faith* it features in the exposition of the second article on God, in the third and fifth articles on Christ and our redemption, and in the sixth article on the church.

[102] S VI ii 69.21–36. Zwingli does not say that Christ died only for the elect, though his death is life giving only for those drawn by God. (Z VI i 473.19–22.) He is a saviour only for believers, although it is also said that all men are created and redeemed through him. (Z IV 66.20–8.)

[103] 'For not only believers . . . are the sons of God, but those who are elect are sons even before they believe, just as you yourselves prove by the example of Jacob.' (Z VI i 176.6–9; *Selected Works* 241.)

whatever pleases him is lawful and whom nothing pleases which is not good and holy and just.' (*Z* VI iii 125.21–22; *Works* II 164.) Yet the will of God has nothing to do with wilfulness. There is a consistency in God, as there is in his omnipotence: 'The omnipotence of God accomplishes all things according to the word of God: it never does that which is contrary to that word ... And that is not impotence, but true omnipotence.' (*Z* IV 831.23–6; LCC XXIV 215.) Cf. *Z* VI i 373.18–27; *S* VI i 546.35–48.

# 4. Christ

ZWINGLI testified clearly to the influence of Erasmus on his faith as a reformer. With hindsight we can see how much of the Erasmian mould was broken, but Zwingli seemed more aware of the continuity with Erasmus in his understanding of Christ than of the discontinuity. In *An Exposition of the Articles* he spoke of his indebtedness to Erasmus, while criticizing him for inconsistency in the place he gave elsewhere to the saints.

I do not want to keep from you, most beloved brethren in Christ Jesus, how I have come to the opinion and firm faith, that we need no mediator except Christ, and that between God and us no one can mediate except Christ alone. Some eight or nine years ago I read a comforting poem of the most learned Erasmus of Rotterdam, addressed to the Lord Jesus, in which Jesus laments in many beautiful words that we do not seek all that is good from him although he is the source of all good, a saviour, comfort, and treasure of the soul. Then I thought: It is always so. Why do we seek help in the creature?[1]

Although the sense of Christ as example and teacher is part of Zwingli's debt to Erasmus, it is not that to which he refers here. It is rather the stress on Christ as God—as the mediator between God and man, as saviour, as the source of all good. The form this was to take in Zwingli's theology may not be Erasmian, but the discovery was and it is set in the context of Zwingli's strong contrast between God and all that is created, in this case the saints.

We should also learn ... that everything in which we place our trust is a god to him who offers it trust and worship. For the name 'God' means that good which is the surest refuge and help and source of the good. ... If you have your confidence in a saint, then you have him for a god; for 'God' is the good in which we have confidence that it will accomplish for us the good we need.[2]

The intercession of the saints is linked with the idea of merit. It means that the creature is trusted rather than the creator, which is idolatry. By contrast, however, with placing confidence in the saints Christ says, 'Come unto me, all that labour and are heavy laden, and I will give you rest.' He calls us to himself. He does not point us to someone else.[3]

[1] Z II 217.5–14.
[2] Z II 219.5–17.
[3] Z II 171.19–23, 221.23–222.6. The text 'Come unto me ...' is very frequently used by Zwingli. It occurs throughout his writings and is a feature of their title-page. However, it is not

The example and teaching of Christ are important elements in Zwingli before his Zurich ministry. They are a part of the humanist rediscovery of the new testament. His clear presentation of Christ's teaching was applauded by Beatus Rhenanus in a letter of 6 December 1518. 'But you in preaching to your congregation show the whole doctrine of Christ briefly displayed as in a picture; how Christ was sent down to the earth by God to teach us the will of the Father . . .' Such preaching, drawn from scripture and properly expounded by the fathers, without being corrupted by the schoolmen, is contrasted with the preaching of heathen or Jewish doctrines, which leads to a people burdened with irrelevant ceremonies.[4] This humanist stress on the teaching of Christ colours Zwingli's understanding of Christ throughout his ministry and gives it one of its particular emphases. It is most strikingly present in the second article at the first disputation. 'The sum and substance of the gospel is that our Lord Jesus Christ, the true Son of God, has made known to us the will of his heavenly Father, and has with his innocence released us from death and reconciled God.'[5] The stress on Christ as teacher is not, however, a stress on his humanity, but rather on his divinity. It is because he is Son of God that he can teach us the will of the Father, in contrast with all other teachers. Moreover he not only teaches righteousness but also bestows it. A similar emphasis is evident when Zwingli points to the Spirit's teaching inwardly in the heart of believers that what Christ has taught is true.[6]

The moral concern, characteristic of Erasmian humanism, is a constant feature of Zwingli's theology and is expressed in a continuing emphasis on Christ as our example. His example moreover is a particularly effective way of teaching.

to be understood of Christ apart from his sacrificial death. In *St Matthew* it is set clearly in the context of Christ's death expiating the sins of the whole world. (*S* VI i 282.34–46.)

The contrast between Christ and the saints is present also in the later writings and commentaries, for salvation is the grace offered to us in and through Christ. (*S* VI i 553.8–16; *Z* VI ii 796.14–23.) Mary was held in high regard by Zwingli. He spoke of her as the highest creature after Christ, but also affirmed that the greatest honour we can give to her is to honour her son. (*Z* I 427.5–21; V 188.10–20.)

[4] *Z* VII 115.5–116.7. Such preaching was typical of Erasmian humanism, but Payne (pp. 64–70) rightly points out that there were other elements in Erasmus's view of Christ than teacher and example, even if these were dominant. For instance, his understanding of Christ as redeemer is combined with them in the term 'captain' or 'commander', from which comes Zwingli's *Hauptmann*, although for Erasmus the stress in the term is not on Christ as redeemer.

[5] *Z* II 27.17–20; *Selected Works* III. (A similar combination in *Z* IX 63.12–64.1 and *S* VI ii 138.27–39.) The seeming priority given in the article to Christ the teacher is qualified in the exposition that follows. (*Z* II 28.32–7.) The teaching to which he particularly refers is the Sermon on the Mount (Matt. 5–7), the Farewell Discourses (John 14–17), and John 5–6.

[6] *Z* II 28.32–7; V 625.21–8; IX 64.1–5.

Is it not a great and effective means of teaching humility, that the Son of God, otherwise like his Father, condescended to accept the weakness of men (Phil. 2: 6) that we might all give up pride and come to God? That he was born poor in a manger, then brought up in the midst of hard labour, does not that teach contempt of riches, the gaining of one's bread not by violence or usury but by the work of the hands? (Eph. 4: 28).[7]

The appeal to Christ's example can be an affirmation of Christ as divine. In his sermon on the Virgin Mary Zwingli complained of those who turn elsewhere for their teaching and example and ignore Christ 'the eternal divine truth and infallible pattern'.[8] There are, however, certain respects in which the example of Christ is not to be followed, as for instance in his not marrying, for this, Zwingli argued, was unsuited to his being God. Yet Christ commended marriage by being born of a betrothed mother. A distinction was made between what we may imitate, such as obedience and humility, and those things that belong to the perfection of his divinity.[9]

There are places where the presentation of Christ's example seems more distinctively human in emphasis, as in *The Education of Youth*, but even there it is the believer who is emulating the example of Christ, and therefore ultimately following his example is not a human, but a divine, work.[10] At points the example of Christ is also used in controversy. Thus Christ was baptized as an example to us. In this case, as in others, he did something not because he needed to, but for our sake.[11]

Nevertheless it is not on Christ as example or teacher that the main emphasis of Zwingli's christology lies. He frequently offered summaries of the gospel which include two vital elements, however differently expressed: that Christ was Son of God and that he died for us (in particular that by his death he satisfied the righteousness of God).[12] These lie at the heart of his christology and make it clear that christology is close to the centre of his theology.

[7] Z I 216.29–217.4; *Works* I 169. In the next sixty-four lines Zwingli gives four further examples of Christ's deeds as teaching us and nine examples of his doctrine as teaching us. In the pastor as well 'the living example teaches more than a hundred thousand words'. (Z III 21.17–19.)

[8] Z I 418.19–23. Cf. Z III 13.6–12.

[9] S VI i 204.26–36.

[10] Z II 543.22–32; V 438.9–22. Cf. S VI i 557.38–9, where imitating Christ is for those who have the Spirit of Christ.

[11] Z IV 265.31–266.4; S VI i 557.29–39.

[12] See, e.g. Z II 27.17–20; III 140.22–4; VI i 310.18–21; and S VI ii 63.39–44. Up to his last work, *An Exposition of the Faith*, Zwingli stresses the example of Christ alongside his person and work. 'The Son of God has, therefore, been given to us as a confirmation of his mercy, as a pledge of pardon, as the price of righteousness, and as a rule of life, to make us sure of the grace of God, and to teach us the law of living.' (S IV 48.9–12, *Works* II 243.)

## The Person of Christ

As the stress in Zwingli's theology as a whole is on God rather than on man, so the stress in his christology is on Christ as God rather than on Christ as man. The fundamental fact about Christ is his divinity, for it is by virtue of his being God that he saves. Many men have died for others, but no one should rely on them, for they were creatures. 'In Christ what is so wonderful is that, while he is God, through whom all things are created and governed, he died even for us, who was the life of all.'[13]

Christ's person is discussed primarily in terms of his being our saviour. It is because he is God that he can fulfil the will of God, and it is because he is man that he can be a sacrifice. Yet it is in Christ as God, and not as man, that we trust. His humanity, however, is a sure pledge of grace, for it was offered up in death, that the divine righteousness might be satisfied and reconciled with us, so that with confidence we might take refuge in God's grace and mercy.[14] The indispensability of both natures is related to Christ's sacrificial death in Zwingli's Berne sermon on the creed. The godhead cannot suffer, so the humanity was necessary, for it could suffer. At the same time no man could satisfy God's righteousness, but only God. Therefore God combined both divine and human natures in Christ. This sharp distinction between the divinity and the humanity led Luther to accuse Zwingli of holding that a mere man, rather than the Son of God, had died for us.[15]

The stress in Zwingli's christology on Christ's sacrificial death led to an emphasis on the virgin birth. The virgin birth was necessary as his divine nature could not suffer any stain of sin to attach to it. On the other side, his human nature had to be pure if it was to be the means of satisfying God's righteousness, for in the old testament the sacrificial victim was without stain.

And this could not have been unless he had been born of a virgin, and without male intervention. For if the virgin had conceived from the seed of a man, would

---

[13] Z VIII 792.27–793.8, 28–30. Cf. S VI i 532.4–6.

[14] Z II 162.9–15 and V 782.9–18. Cf. Z II 30.19–21. 'The deity of Christ raises us from the dead and is our life. The humanity of Christ was the means through which expiation was made on the cross.' (S VI i 738.39–40.)

[15] Z VI i 464.5–19 and VI ii 120.12–22. Cf. Z III 779.18–22, 33–6. For Luther, see WA 26.342.14–17.

R. J. Goeser holds that the dualism which affects Zwingli's understanding of the sacraments affects his christology. 'The human nature of Christ is not a part of the atonement or salvation because it is bodily or physical and the Spirit cannot be confused with what is physical. Thus the separation of the two natures in Christ, with respect to the divine nature, is determined by Zwingli's peculiar separation of Creator-Spirit from the creaturely-physical.' ('Word and Sacrament: A Study of Luther's Views as Developed in the Controversy with Zwingli and Karlstadt' (Diss. Yale, 1960), p. 72).

not the birth have been thereby polluted? And if a woman who had before known a man had conceived him, even from the Holy Spirit, who would ever have believed that the child that was born was of the Holy Spirit?[16]

Zwingli frequently alluded to the reference in Hebrews to Christ's being like us in everything, except that he was without sin. Indeed he experienced the punishment, suffering, and distress that belong to human life, to the day of his death.[17]

The contrast, not to say opposition, between the divine and the human made expressions such as 'The Word became flesh' problematic for Zwingli. His stress on the divinity in Christ led him by the use of alloiosis to speak of the Son of God's assuming humanity.[18] (In this way Zwingli could deal with a number of passages about incarnation in the new testament which did not fit easily into the structure of his theology. At the same time Christ's incarnation—especially in connection with the ascension—and not simply his death was drawn into Zwingli's understanding of our salvation.) He drew the analogy between God's uniting to himself our flesh and a king's marrying a slave, an act that far surpasses simply freeing or adopting her. Moreover if anything outward had been able to make us sons of God, Christ would have assumed our flesh in vain.[19] Elsewhere he emphasized that Christ descended and assumed human nature into himself, so that we might ascend, being renewed by grace and assumed somehow into the divine nature. He became man, so that through his grace he might transform us somehow into gods. In his discussion of the ascension, an important element in his christology, Zwingli referred to the eyes of our mind being fixed on Christ in heaven. He united our nature to the godhead and exalted it so that we should have a certain hope of victory with him, who is flesh of our flesh, our brother, and our head.[20]

It was primarily in the eucharistic controversy with Luther that Zwingli engaged in debate about the person of Christ. He stressed the distinction of the two natures, although insisting on the unity of the person of Christ. He used the idea of the sharing of properties or alloiosis to bring out the distinction of the natures within the unity of the person rather than the interpenetration of the two natures, with the human nature

---

[16] Z III 686.7-28; *Works* III 112. Cf. S VI i 205.24-5. Zwingli went on to argue for her perpetual virginity.

[17] Z V 682.6-13 and VI ii 129.19-27.

[18] See Additional Note 1, p. 127.

[19] S VI i 379.27-380.4. Cf. 'Sic deus carnem nostram adprehendit, sanctificavit et induit, sibique ita coniunxit, ut nunquam dimittat, imo ad dextram dei eam exaltaret.' (S VI i 379.37-8.)

[20] S VI ii 56.7-14, 74.35-41.

sharing in the divine and the divine in the human. The sharp distinction made by Zwingli between the two natures led to the accusation of Nestorianism. It is, however, the influence of scholasticism that can be traced in his formulations.[21]

Before the eucharistic controversy with Luther, Zwingli's view of the distinction of the two natures and the unity of the person of Christ is evident. It is clearly in the tradition of the Tome of Leo and Chalcedon.[22] Even during the controversy it is evident in non-controversial contexts and is a fundamental element in his understanding of Christ and his interpretation of the gospels, where he insisted, 'The distinction and property of the natures is always to be observed.' It is not 'as if we wish to separate the natures in Christ, for the one Christ is God and man, but we desire rightly to distinguish between the works and properties of each nature and not to confound them'. Thus as God Christ knew all things, but as true man he did not know the day in Mark 13: 32. Zwingli compared this with a councillor's knowing something as a councillor in the council, but not knowing it when asked outside as a private person.[23]

The detailed discussion of the sharing of properties took place in debate with Luther, especially in A Friendly Exegesis, Zwingli's Christian Reply, and Two Replies to Luther's Book. Zwingli uses the term 'sharing' or 'interchange' of properties (communicatio idiomatum) but his more characteristic word is the rhetorical term 'alloiosis' (or in the German writings Gegenwechsel). That—out of concern for the grammarians—he used a grammatical or rhetorical term, and not the traditional theological one, does not affect the fact that the substance of what he said is in the tradition of Chalcedonian and scholastic theology.[24]

A short description of alloiosis is 'Where we name the one nature and understand the other, or name what they both are and yet understand only the one.' An example is calling man nothing but earth, when it is the body that is earth, not the soul, and man is body and soul. Thus in the new testament there are references to Christ (who is God and man) that may refer to him either according to his divine or according to his human nature, so that, for instance, the words 'Christ lives in me' refer to him as God and not as man. On some occasions each nature stands for itself, but on other

---

[21] e.g. Z V 679, n. 3, and 682, n. 3. See Additional Note 2, pp. 127-8.

[22] Z III 140.12-143.19. Cf. III 688.13-689.20.

[23] S VI i 311.8-9, 557.15-28, 728.39-41. The analogy of the councillor shows how much the two natures exist alongside each other, though clearly united in a certain way in one person.

[24] Z V 679.6-701.19, 922.1-959.12; VI ii 126.1-159.15. An Account of the Faith summarized this view of Christ, though without using the terms 'alloiosis' or 'sharing of properties'. (Z VI ii 792.11-794.30.) On his use of alloiosis, see Z V 679.7-681.1, 942.11-21.

occasions the divine is taken for the human and the human for the divine. An example of this is found in 'The Word became man' (or 'God became man'). As God cannot become anything more, the sentence must be understood figuratively, and—through exchange—of the humanity. Thus man became God or—in the words of the Athanasian Creed—'Christ is one, not that the godhead is changed into the manhood but that the manhood is taken up into God'.[25]

Zwingli claimed that his position was rooted in the bible rather than in philosophy (although holding that philosophy was on his side) and that Luther's opposed view (that the body is everywhere) was not only untrue but also un-Christian, because it conflicted with the word and teaching of Christ. Zwingli rejected Luther's charge against him that alloiosis came from human reason, arguing that all orthodox theologians were driven to it by God's word. In the reference to God's word Zwingli had in mind especially, but not only, St John's gospel. The usage of the fathers he regarded as supporting his view, although in itself that was of course not a compelling argument.[26] The rule of faith was a persuasive reason for using alloiosis.[27]

The passages that Zwingli drew on to illustrate alloiosis show the sharp distinction he made between the two natures of Christ. Passages such as John 3: 13; 5: 17, 30; 6: 55, 62; 10: 30; 12: 26, 30, 44; and 14: 6, 25, 28 made sense for him only as they applied either to the humanity or the divinity of Christ.[28] Moreover passages in different gospels that contradicted each other, such as Matthew 20: 23 and Luke 22: 29–30, could be reconciled when one was seen as applying to Christ's humanity and the other to his divinity, and similarly passages in the same gospel such as John 10: 30 and 14: 28.[29] The distinction between the natures had to be preserved to safeguard each of them, but perhaps especially in Zwingli's theology to safeguard the divine nature. He was concerned that Luther was limiting God by confining him to Christ and enclosing him within the humanity of Christ, whereas he is infinite. God is also outside the humanity of Christ,

---

[25] Z V 923.1–928.17. Cf. Z V 680.1–681.3; XIV 858.21–3.

[26] Z VI ii 170.9–13, 128.31–129.18, 131.14–34, 165.28–166.1. Cf. Z V 681.9–12 and 925.14–17.

[27] Z V 693.5–9.

[28] These and other passages are discussed in Z V 679.6–701.19, 922.1–959.12; VI ii 126.1–159.15. Zwingli supports the use of alloiosis against Luther with the example of 'Before Abraham was, I am' (John 8: 58). He asks whether it applies to the humanity as well as to the divinity. If Luther says no, then alloiosis is established. If he says yes, then Christ was not born of Mary, as she was not born before Abraham, or else Christ had two human natures, one before Abraham and one from Mary. (Z VI ii 138.18–139.7.)

[29] Z VI ii 131.27–132.8.

in all creatures, and was so before Christ became man.[30] Zwingli argued that Christ himself was concerned to safeguard the divine by refusing to accept the word 'good' when it was used of him, for the person using it saw him only as man and not as God. His reply therefore, was 'Why do you call me good? Only God is good.'[31] The same kind of concern was seen in the words 'He who believes in me believes not in me, but in him who sent me.' Here Christ was saying that trust belonged to him as God, but not as man. Zwingli accused Luther by contrast of attributing to Christ's humanity the infinity which Christ refused, and in effect of teaching that trust should be put in the creature rather than the creator.[32]

Zwingli affirmed the unity of the person as consistently as the distinction of the natures, although the eucharistic debate made him emphasize the latter. He drew on two particular analogies from the fathers. His preference was for that of soul and body (two opposed substances) in man to show that the one Christ is both God and man. In conjunction with this comparison he frequently used that of a red-hot sword, which cuts and burns. The cutting and burning correspond to the power, nature, and working of the two natures. Thus Christ's divinity performs miracles, enters the mind, and dwells there, while the humanity hungers, suffers, and dies. He objected to Luther's misuse of the analogy to support his view of consubstantiation.[33]

Zwingli resisted equally Luther's view that if you could show that God was somewhere where the man was not, then you would divide the person of Christ. He pointed out that God is in hell, but not the man Jesus Christ, and yet the person of Christ is not divided, any more than in the soul's leaving the body. Zwingli drew on the analogy of the sun where the body is in one place and yet the light shines everywhere, and also used Luther's analogies of the voice's being heard in many places or the eye's seeing everywhere, although the man and the eye are in one place. With these analogies he was able to hold to the unity of the person and the distinction

---

[30] Z V 934.11–936.10. Cf. C. Sigwart, *Ulrich Zwingli* (Stuttgart, 1855), pp. 127–8.

[31] Z V 700.1–17. Zwingli added that Christ would not allow goodness to be ascribed to his human nature, and that we ought therefore not to attribute to the body when eaten what belongs to the one who alone is good—something that neither Christ nor the apostles did.

[32] Z V 687.21–34. There is a clear sense of what belongs or does not belong to God, so that Zwingli could say that even if there were clear passages of scripture attributing forgiveness of sins to the body when eaten, yet it would be by alloiosis, since forgiveness of sins belongs to God. (Z V 688.4–8.) Cf. 701.6–10. There is also concern to safeguard Christ's true humanity. (Z VI ii 807.7–9.)

[33] Z V 682.6–683.10, 923.23–925.13; VI i 464.17–465.5; VI ii 130.16–31; S IV 48.39–42. The Athanasian Creed used the analogy of body and soul, as did Augustine and Cyril of Alexandria, while John of Damascus, like Origen before him, that of a red-hot sword. Luther used the latter analogy in *The Babylonian Captivity of the Church* (*WA* 6.510.5–6) and elsewhere.

of the natures.[34] Sharp as was his insistence on the distinction of natures, Zwingli never failed to affirm the unity of the person of Christ. Christ is never simply God or man, he is always true God and true man. We can say that the one who suffered is God, but not that the godhead suffered. In his comments on the third Marburg article, with its reference to the un-divided person of Jesus Christ being crucified for us, Zwingli used the example from the story of the Good Samaritan which says the man 'fell among thieves', although only his body was wounded. The person of Christ therefore is undivided, even when only one nature does or suffers something. It is moreover the whole Christ to whom sanctification should be attributed, even though it is attributed to the humanity of Christ in Hebrews 2: 11.[35]

The unity of the person was stressed by Zwingli in *An Account of the Faith*.

I believe and understand that the Son assumed flesh, because he truly assumed of the immaculate and perpetual Virgin Mary the human nature, yea, the entire man, who consists of body and soul. But this in such manner that the entire man was so assumed into the unity of the hypostasis, or the person of the Son of God, that the man did not constitute a peculiar person, but was assumed into the inseparable, indivisible, and indissoluble person of the Son of God. . . . So God and man is one Christ, the Son of God from eternity, and the Son of Man from the dispensation of time to eternity . . .[36]

The unity of the person in the Son of God is particularly stressed in the way the dependence of the body on the soul is developed in *Two Replies to Luther's Book*, in a passage which shows the influence of Thomism in Zwingli.[37]

The different understanding of Christ that Zwingli and Luther had was perhaps the major reason for their disagreement about the eucharist. While Luther held together the two natures of Christ, in the one person, Zwingli sharply distinguished them. What Zwingli ascribed to the divinity, Luther—because of his different understanding of the sharing of proper-ties—ascribed to the humanity. This led, for instance, to a view of the omni-presence of the body, which was unthinkable for Zwingli. For him

[34] Z VI ii 156.10–157.31, 167.22–168.25, 807.10–19.

[35] Z VI i 282.21–283.5; VI ii 164.35–165.17, 521.15–19, 549.8–17; S VI i 296.3–10. Cf. S VI i 322.46–323.7 and 705.1–5.

[36] Z VI ii 792.17–93.14; Jackson 454 (*Works* II 36). Cf. S IV 48.18–46. The importance of his understanding of the person of Christ is evident in the fact that it is included in the first of the twelve articles in *An Account of the Faith* and forms the second article in *An Exposition of the Faith*. This relates in part to the centrality of the eucharistic controversy.

[37] Z VI ii 149.25–151.19.

Christ is like us in everything except sin, so that his body must be limited to one place, as ours is. But equally Zwingli ascribed to the humanity of Christ what Luther ascribed to the divinity. Luther held that if only the human nature suffered for him then Christ is a bad saviour, indeed needs a saviour himself. By contrast Zwingli maintained that if Christ could suffer according to his divinity, then he would not be God. We may say that the one who suffered is also God, not that the godhead suffered.[38]

The humanity of Christ does not have the vital place in Zwingli's theology that it has in Luther's, even though it is indispensable for our salvation. Moreover the dominant place afforded to the divinity and the sharp distinction made by Zwingli between the divine and the human seem at points to call in question the genuine humanity of Christ. (There is little sense that the divine is expressed within the constraints imposed by the incarnation.) For example, Christ prays, not because he needs to, but as an example to us, and he asks questions not to learn, but again in order to give us an example.[39] There is also a certain unreality about the temptations, as if they were for our sake, rather than part of what it meant for Christ to be human. The rather stark comment in Mark that Christ 'could not' do any mighty work becomes he 'would not', although Zwingli's explanation of the words makes the interpretation less extreme. Moreover when Christ took food for his glorified body, he did it, not because he needed to, but that he might show the reality of his human nature. Here again, however, Zwingli removed some of the sting of his statement by referring to the way we do things to build up our neighbours rather than from necessity.[40]

Zwingli rejected the idea that the humanity of Christ was nothing or worthless, insisting that his aim was to affirm the one Christ in his two distinct natures; but this meant no trusting in, or adoring of, his humanity.[41] Nevertheless the distinction between the natures and the necessity of the divinity for our salvation made the humanity in some ways primarily an

---

[38] e.g. Z VI ii 146.23–148.23, 159.16–162.28, 165.2–5. Zwingli criticized Luther's assertion that the person must be divided if what is done is divided, based on the view that doing and suffering belong to the person not the nature. Zwingli argued in terms of man's being soul and body. (Z VI ii 152.13–154.18.)

[39] Z III 726.33–7; S VI i 309.13–19, 480.22–33, 500.43–5, 612.25–6, 632.21–4.

[40] S VI i 570.10–13, 497.41–498.8; S VI ii 60.47–61.5. The description of God as emptying himself in Phil. 2 is re-expressed in terms of God's graciously coming to the help of man who is poor and needy, for he does not need us. (This is related to the use of human forms of speech when talking about God in the bible: Z V 939.1–23.) In S VI ii 213.26–30 it was paraphrased as the assumption of humanity into God.

[41] Z V 952.28–953.23. In the second disputation Jud refers to the fact that even the schoolmen rejected the adoration of Christ's humanity. (Z II 696.7–8.) Zwingli made the same point in Z IV 119.5–8 and VIII 792.18–21.

instrument of salvation, although it always kept the important independent role of example.[42] On occasion, however, the earthly life of
Christ is vividly recalled in Zwingli's writings.[43]

### The Work of Christ

Zwingli attacked a host of views on the simple ground that to hold them
nullified the death of Christ. This is a striking indirect testimony to the
centrality of Christ's death in his theology. In this context he referred to
placing one's trust in the sacraments (whether in baptism, the sacrifice of
the mass, or the bodily eating of Christ), in anything outward, or in any
creature (whether the intercession of the saints, indulgences, one's own
works or merits or those of others). The doctrines attached to these views,
together with the doctrine of purgatory, are a denial of Christ's death (or
in some cases of his coming), so that he need not have died, or may be said
to have died in vain.[44]

Christ's death was understood by Zwingli primarily in terms of the
Anselmian idea of satisfaction, although, following scripture and the
fathers, he offered other interpretations. The detailed comparison of
Christ with Adam shows Zwingli's use of Irenaeus; yet at points even in
that comparison the Anselmian emphasis was manifest.[45] (In this context
Zwingli also referred, following Athanasius, to Christ's becoming man
that we might become gods.) Christ's death was seen as a victory over, or
liberation from, sin, death, and the devil—and therefore a liberation from
the law and from ignorance.[46] There is also on occasion an almost
Abelardian sense of the compelling power of God's love displayed in
Christ.[47]

The Anselmian understanding of the atonement is rooted for Zwingli
in God's righteousness and his mercy. We have failed to keep the law,
indeed cannot keep it, because—following Adam's fall—we are sinners.

[42] Z VIII 794.10–22; VI i 170.8–11.

[43] As a means of teaching in Z I 216.25–217.18 or of showing Christ's righteousness (in comparison with Adam) by which he brought healing in Z III 681.4–691.11.

[44] Among many references one may note: the sacraments: Z VIII 235.26–8; baptism: Z IV
628.14–20; the sacrifice of the mass: Z II 660.1–12; XIII 178.38–179.2; bodily eating: Z V 897.1–3;
VI i 310.25–8; the prayers of the saints: Z III 272.31–6; indulgences: Z V 277.12–17; our works: Z
II 273.26–30; III 691.13–15; our merits: Z III 652.17–23; V 278.13–15; purgatory: Z II 427.22–7; V
193.11–12, 279.22–9. The challenge to all these is christological. In most cases it is Christ's death
that is being denied or nullified, though on occasion the reference is to his coming, as in S VI i
380.2–4, 608.1–2.                                                            [45] Z III 683.31–685.7.

[46] Z I 67.7–10, 130.27–131.9, 217.7–10; VIII 86.5–10; S VI i 381.9–14; VI ii 262.3–21, 294.31–5.
There is also a sense of Christ's death as dealing with the claims of the devil. (Z III 690.14–17.)

[47] e.g. Z II 39.1–7. For Zwingli, unlike Erasmus, the main emphasis is Anselmian rather than
Abelardian.

We deserve God's punishment. God is righteous and therefore cannot simply pass over sin; but in his mercy he sent his Son, who accomplished God's will and satisfied God's righteousness with his innocence.[48] Zwingli dismissed the view that good works, by which people were accustomed to cancel their sins, would be undermined if one said that Christ had paid for everything, by affirming that this is God's way and that we should not presume to teach him a better one. 'Christ is your salvation. You are nothing. You can do nothing. Christ is the beginning and the end. He is everything. He can do everything. . . . He is our righteousness and that of all those who have ever been righteous before God.'[49] Zwingli never tired of referring to Christ as our pledge, and constantly appealed to the Pauline word, 'He who did not spare his own Son, but gave him up for us all, will he not also give us all things with him?' (Rom 8: 32.)[50]

Christ is our salvation, because he is both God and man. As he is God he can fulfil the will of God; as he is man he can be a sacrifice that satisfies the righteousness of God.[51] We are in fact redeemed (or recreated) as well as created through him. Indeed we can be made alive only through the one through whom we were created.[52] This sense of unity between creator and redeemer is paralleled by the unity within the godhead of mercy and righteousness—sometimes held together in the goodness of God, though goodness, like mercy, can also be contrasted with righteousness. Zwingli did not allow an opposition or choice between God's righteousness and his mercy; they are both 'sacrosanct and inviolable'. We should fear the righteousness of God no less than rely on his mercy, for God gave his Son to satisfy his righteousness. Writing this in a letter to Haner, Zwingli referred to his treatment of the matter in *A Commentary*.

Since his justice, being inviolably sacred, had to remain as intact and unshaken as his mercy, and since man was indeed in need of mercy, but wholly amenable to

[48] Z II 36.25–39.19. Zwingli could give this as a summary of the gospel without quoting scripture because, he argued, every believer knows it and unbelievers deny it in spite of scripture. (Z II 39.10–13.)

[49] Z II 40.22–41.11. Christ was sent because it was impossible for men to satisfy God's wrath or righteousness. Christ alone satisfies them. (S VI i 320.34–7.) Cf. S VI i 214.3–6. The term 'pledge' occurs with striking frequency in *A Commentary*.

[50] Z II 139.1–5, 496.19–22; III 785.3–8; VIII 794.15–18. References to Rom. 8: 32 occur frequently in Zwingli's writing, e.g. Z II 39.6–7; III 695.2–4; V 629.5–7. Zwingli often refers to salvation as being for all, as in Z III 697.18–24, but he understands 'all' as meaning Gentiles as well as Jews (S VI i 743.33–7) or, as Bucer and Calvin did, all kinds of people, and so in effect the elect.

[51] Z II 162.5–13. Cf. Z VI i 464.5–17. The Anselmian note is clear in words such as 'For he is an eternal God and Spirit. And that means he is of sufficient value to redeem the offences of all men, more so indeed than the offences themselves can possibly require.' (Z II 541.29–31; LCC XXIV 107.)

[52] Z II 638.14–15; III 124.12–19, 681.30–682.1, 686.7–11. Cf. Z VIII 793.2–4.

God's justice, divine goodness found a way to satisfy justice and yet to be allowed to open wide the arms of mercy without detriment to justice. Not that he thus took precautions against the adversary or that the potter may not out of moistened clay make or remake any vessel he chooses [cf. Rom. 9: 21], but that by this example of justice he might remove drowsiness and sloth from us and show us what sort of being he was—just, good, merciful; or, not to presume to say too much of his purposes, because it so pleased him . . . While, therefore, God is alike just and merciful, though with a leaning towards mercy (for his tender mercies are over all the rest of his works), yet his justice has to be satisfied that his wrath may be appeased.[53]

Gäbler suggests that the doctrine of satisfaction is closely bound up with the doctrine of providence and deduced from God's qualities, not vice versa. There is some force in this reflection, but Zwingli related his doctrine of satisfaction both to scripture and to Christ. His assertion that Christ would have died in vain if sacrifice or works could have expiated sins shows how often the argument began with historical fact, in which the character of God is discerned.[54] There is even then an element of arbitrariness in the death of Christ. The stress (perhaps Scotist) on God's acting according to his will and pleasure implies that there could have been another way, though this was in fact the way God chose. This removes something of the inexorability of the Anselmian doctrine of satisfaction.[55]

[53] Z VIII 793.10–14; III 676.23–677.5. (*Works* III 100). Cf. III 694.37–695.20. In Z III 676.23–8 God's goodness is seen to unite his righteousness and mercy. (Moreover God's righteousness is satisfied by Christ's righteousness in Z III 684.36–9.) In Z VI ii 796.25–30 goodness is used in the sense of mercy, but not in opposition to righteousness. 'All his works therefore savour of mercy and justice. Therefore, justly his election also savours of both. It is of his goodness that he has elected whom he will; but it is of his justice to adopt and unite the elect to himself through his Son, who has been made a victim for satisfying divine justice for us.' *An Exposition of the Faith* speaks of his goodness as being righteousness and mercy, with his righteousness requiring atonement, his mercy forgiveness, and his forgiveness a new life. (*S* III 47.30–2.) In a comment on Mark 12: 29–33 Zwingli referred to God's righteousness and mercy as being united in the heart of believers, with his righteousness leading to penitence for our sins and his goodness and mercy lifting us up and consoling us when we despair. (*S* VI i 531.7–14.) Elsewhere he spoke of God's showing us both mercy and righteousness in Christ. (Z XIII 304.17–24.) The appeasing of God's righteousness is also described as a work of mercy. (Z V 629.1–5.)

[54] Z XIV 612.10–20; III 676.23–33, 695.33–696.3. The issue is raised in Gäbler, *Zwingli*, pp. 65–7. Zwingli admits that he has not used scriptural evidence in presenting what the gospel is, but he explains why. (Z II 39.10–13.) In *Original Sin* he refers to passages where Christ speaks of the necessity of his death and regards them as the basis of the argument, 'Constituit igitur divina providentia filio suo mundum sibi reconciliare. Nefas ergo esto vel inquirere, an alia ratione aliove autore negotium perfici potuerit.' (Z V 391.20–2.)

[55] e.g. Z III 686.7–11. Cf. 'Divine providence, therefore, determined to reconcile the world to himself through his own Son. Let it be, therefore, a sacrilege to inquire whether the thing could have been accomplished by other means or another author.' (Z V 391.20–2; *Works* II 27.) An interesting comparison could be made with Z XIII 347.22–6. Zwingli constantly insists on the atonement as effected in the historical sacrifice of Christ. 'Eucharistiae tribuitur ipsa expiatio,

## The Place of Christ

In his discussion of true and false religion in *A Commentary* Zwingli gave almost forty pages to a consideration of the nature of religion, God, and man, before turning to Christ and the gospel. Both the order and the treatment could lead to the charge that Christ played a secondary role in his theology. Zwingli defended himself against those 'who are sure to say . . . that in discussing piety so far I have made no reference to salvation through Christ and to grace':

First, because I cannot say everything at once and in the same place; secondly, because all that I have said of the marriage of the soul to God applies to Christ just as much as to God (for Christ is God and man) and finally, because knowledge of God in the nature of the case precedes knowledge of Christ.[56]

There is some justification in his reply and in his earlier affirmation of Christ. In the discussion of God he indicated that despite the presence of truth in non-Christian writers we, to whom God has spoken through his Son and through the Holy Spirit, are to look to the sacred scriptures.[57] Yet in spite of the indispensable, and in many ways central, place Christ had in Zwingli's theology, Christ is not the beginning, middle, and end of his theology. Moreover the Christ on whom Zwingli concentrated is Christ as God rather than Christ as man.

The central place of Christ in Zwingli's faith is evident in the opening articles of the first disputation. (Some would see in this the influence of Luther at that period.) The central concern is the gospel which is summarized in Christ. He is described as the only way to salvation of all who were, are, or shall be, so that any one seeking or pointing to another, murders the soul. He is the guide and captain promised and given to the entire human race, so that he may be the eternal salvation and head of all believers who are his body.[58] It is as saviour that he holds this central and indispensable

cum illa tunc solum facta sit, cum Christus deus et homo pro humana natura mactaretur . . .'. (Z VI iii 165.9–10.)

[56] Z III 675.27–34; *Works* III 99.

[57] Z III 643.20–7.

[58] For articles 1 to 7 see Z II 21–53. The opening articles are specifically related to Christ. The exposition of article 18 begins by stating that the article is grounded in the office of Christ as high priest. (Z II 112.1–4.) Zwingli sets God's wanting to give us everything in Christ in a comparison of our fall in Adam and our redemption in Christ. (Z II 168.24–31.) One thing is necessary to salvation—Christ. Indeed our entire salvation and righteousness are in him. (Z I 372.22–6, 373.22–3.)

For Zwingli the later conflict with Luther has to do with his insistence on the centrality of Christ for salvation. 'Haec, inquam, est absolutio nostra, expiatio, satisfactio ac peccatorum omnium remissio, cum Iesu Christo, dei filio, fidimus; iam enim scimus omnia nobis cum illo et per illum donari.' (Z V 715.14–716.1.)

position. Persistently Zwingli asserted that it is through Christ alone that we come to God, relating this in particular to John (especially 14: 6), Acts 4: 12, 1 Timothy 2: 5–6, and Hebrews.[59] His death and resurrection are determinative for our salvation and no one entered heaven before his resurrection and ascension.[60] The centrality of Christ could be seen almost symbolically in the fact that he is exactly at the mid-point between creation and the end of the world.[61]

The relation to Christ of those living before him or without knowledge of him raises questions about the centrality and indispensability of the death and resurrection of Christ. The questions are intensified by the affirmation that they (or some of them) are saved. Zwingli made this assertion both of believers in the old testament and of elect Gentiles. But for him, as for Augustine, those in the old testament who believed, believed in Christ. The difference between them and Christians is that they believed in the Christ who is to come, while Christians believe in the Christ who has come. This was stressed in the baptismal and eucharistic controversies.[62] It is moreover not just a general belief in Christ, but belief in his sacrifice. The belief of the people of old in the sacrifice of Christ is shown in their making sacrifices which foreshadow his sacrifice.[63]

Zwingli stressed the difference between the old and new testaments, as well as the similarity. Opposition to catholic opponents in the early days of

[59] Z I 218.22–34; II 157.15–158.35, 579.24–580.15; III 213.22–32, 695.33–700.18; V 379.22–9; XIII 67.23–68.3; XIV 745.10–11; S VI i 522.21–3. Cf. 'Christum ergo solum esse, per quem ad patrem acceditur, vel hoc argumento pateat, quod si ulla via potuisset ad deum iri, nihil fuisset opus, ut Christus moreretur.' (Z III 695.35–696.3.) That his unique position relates to his humanity as well as to his divinity is clear from passages such as S VI i 479.32–6.

In the early writings Zwingli opposes Christ or his merit to us or our merit as the cause of our salvation. This holds through all his writings and excludes any sense of salvation as being other than through Christ. '. . . ut Christi meritum una sit solaque nostrę salutis causa . . . Quicquid igitur nobis a deo contingit, per Christum contingit; solus enim meruit, ut iustitię suę deus erga nos parcat . . . Tale est meritum Christi, ut citra ipsum inpossibile sit venire ad deum.' (Z II 580.4–8.)

[60] Z III 769.16–25; VIII 270.27–32. Cf. Z VIII 762.20–7. The doctrine of election does not make the death and resurrection of Christ of secondary importance or even dispensable. They remain crucial. 'Causa vero, cur promiserit, alia non fuit, quam quod beatitudo nobis contingere nequibat, quantumvis conantibus et sudantibus, cum lapsus primi parentis expiatus non esset. Cum autem Christus iam pro nobis mactatus divinam iustitiam placavit ita, ut per ipsum solum accedatur ad deum, iam novum foedus iniit deus cum humano genere, non sic novum, ut hanc medelam vix tandem invenerit, sed quod olim paratam, quum tempestivum esset, adhibuerit.' (Z IV 500.27–31.) Zwingli makes the point in the eucharistic controversy that the crucifixion would not have been necessary if 'the disciples were children of everlasting life the moment they partook of his flesh and blood in the last supper'. (Z IV 817.24–7; LCC XXIV 205.) Cf. Z V 348.9–20.

[61] In an exposition of Dan. 7: 25 in Z XIV 751.1–7.

[62] Z VIII 232.35–233.5; IV 826.5–8; S VI i 300.10–15, 728.31–5.

[63] Z XIII 80.16–19.

the reformation made him stress the difference, as opposition to anabaptists led him to stress the similarity, but both elements are present in his
theology both before and after the baptismal controversy.[64] What marks
Zwingli's later works is the attempt to hold the two together. In *A Friendly
Request* he expounded Paul's reference to the gospel in Romans 1: 16 in
terms of God's gracious manifestation of himself in the old testament. (The
main difference that there is with the coming of Christ is the drawing of the
Gentiles as well as the Jews.) This exposition in July 1522 is not fundamentally different from his comments on Genesis 12 in 1527, although the later
treatment (as one would expect after a period of controversy) is more carefully elaborated.[65] Especially, but not only, in debate with the anabaptists
Zwingli emphasized that it was the same God, the same Christ, the same
Spirit, and the same people of God in both testaments.[66]

There are differences between the old and new testaments, but they are
not essential differences. In *A Refutation* Zwingli responded to the question 'What difference is there between the old and the new testaments?'

Very much and very little . . . Very little if you regard those chief points which
concern God and us; very much if you regard what concerns us alone. The sum is
here: God is our God; we are his people. In these there is the least, in fact, no
difference. The chief thing is the same today as it ever was. For just as Abraham
embraced Jesus his blessed seed, and through him was saved, so also today we are
saved through him. But so far as human infirmity is concerned, many things
came to them in a figure to instruct them and be a testimony to us. These are
therefore the things which seem to distinguish the old testament from the new,
while in the thing itself or in what pertains to the chief thing they differ not at all.
First, Christ is now given, whom formerly they awaited with great desire. . . .
Second, they who died then in faith did not ascend into heaven, but [went] to the
bosom of Abraham; now he who trusts in Christ comes not into judgement, but
hath passed from death into life. Third, types were offered as is shown in Hebrews.
Fourth, the light shines more clearly . . . Fifth, the testament is now preached and
expounded to all nations, while formerly one nation alone enjoyed it. Sixth,
before there was never set forth for men a model for living as has now been done

---

[64] In *Choice and Liberty Respecting Food* the relationship of the new testament to the old is in
terms of 'how much more' or of the new as superseding the old; yet the old testament is used as
part of the argument for Zwingli's case. (Z I 134.3–20.)

[65] Z I 215.9–216.29; XIII 67.10–68.3. He insisted in one of his earliest writings 'that not more
at one time than at another God is revealed as merciful or as wroth, but at all times alike'. (Z I
100.25–8; Jackson 415–16 (*Works* I 81).) This has implications for the relation of the old and new
testaments, although it is not used in that context.

[66] Z IV 826.5–8; VI i 169.6–15, 186.28–31; XIII 304.7–17; XIV 172.3–6; S VI i 735.15–17.
'Neque Christus novus aliquis deus est, sed ille aeternus, cuius diem ut videret magna exulta-
tione et summo desyderio cupivit Abraham.' (Z XIII 304.11–13.) See further Additional Note 3,
p. 128.

by Christ. For the blood of Christ, mingled with the blood and slaughter of the Innocents, would have been able to atone for our faith but then we should have lacked the model.[67]

Zwingli did not appear to see any great difference on earth between believers before Christ and those after Christ, although he did allow that believers before Christ did not have the Spirit as abundantly as those after his death.[68]

The Gentiles' relation to Christ raises the question of Zwingli's christology even more acutely. Zwingli argued from Malachi 1: 11 that Gentiles before Christ sacrificed to the one true God and he used various passages of scripture to show that Gentiles responded to God. Their sacrifices are then related, however, to the one sacrifice of Christ.[69] Zwingli insisted that the Gentiles' salvation was through Christ, just as much as that of Jews and Christians. Thus in *Original Sin*, after an admiring reference to Seneca, he commented, 'Who, pray, wrote this faith upon the heart of man? Let no one think that these things point to the taking away of Christ's office, as some men charge me with doing; they magnify his glory. For through Christ must come all who come to God.'[70] Zwingli was

[67] Z VI i 169.19–170.11; *Selected Works* 234–5. Cf. S VI ii 91.9–14. See also Z XIII 67.10–68.3, which speaks of the light of the gospel as not shining so brightly in the old as in the new testament, adding the suggestion that this has to do with human blindness; and Z XIII 398.18–20, which mentions a clearer and more certain knowledge of God. (In this context he quotes Augustine's relating of old and new testament: 'Dicit Augustinus: novum testamentum in veteri latere, vetus in novo patere.' He refers to the law as a tutor to Christ, but adds that there were many in the old law, like Abraham, who knew and served God without the tutor.) The contrast made in Z I 357.29–358.2 between promise and performance is taken up in Z IV 637.15–19. In Z III 13.6–12 the word of God is less clearly expressed in the old testament than in Christ.

[68] S VI i 722.29–36.

[69] Z III 202.35–204.15. Cf. Z II 187.10–15. In the first of these passages Zwingli mentions Josephus' reference to Alexander the Great and Pompey, as sacrificing to the true God, and quotes the old testament example of the Queen of Sheba and Melchizedek. He also cites in his support the testimony of Origen. These views about the Gentiles arise almost incidentally in the context of a discussion of the mass. They are not related, as they are later, to the doctrine of election, which is not a developed part of Zwingli's theology at this stage. They are related to it in *The Providence of God*. 'Nihil enim vetat, quo minus inter gentes quoque deus sibi deligat, qui sese revereantur, qui observent et post fata illi iungantur; libera est enim electio eius.' Zwingli then states that he would prefer to be Socrates or Seneca than the pope. For though they did not know the one God, they busied themselves with serving God in purity of heart, whereas the pope 'would offer himself as God if only there were a bidder at hand'. (Z VI iii 182.18–183.3; *Works* II 201.)

[70] Z V 379.22–9, *Works* II 12–13. 'Brevitur, inconcussa est electio, et lex in hominum mentibus scripta, sic tamen, ut, qui electi sunt et qui legis opus faciunt ex lege in cor scripta, per solum Christum ad deum veniant.' (Z V 580.15–18.) In the phrase 'through Christ' Zwingli's emphasis would lie on Christ as divine, with the risk that the incarnate Christ would be undervalued. However, in many contexts where it is used the historical reference is clear, e.g. Z XIII 67.10–68.3.

concerned with children and adults. He defended the salvation of Gentile children, by arguing that otherwise the salvation brought by Christ would be less extensive than the disease brought by Adam. He said of Gentiles who show by their works that the law is written in their hearts that they have faith, for works are done as a consequence of faith—and that comes not from us, but from God. All this is set in the context of his argument that original sin is removed not by baptism or anything outward, but only by the blood of Christ.[71]

Zwingli affirmed the necessity of Christ and of his death for the salvation of all, though without relating this to the proclamation of Christ in word and sacrament. The sovereignty of God in election is not limited to, or by, word and sacrament, any more than it was limited historically to Israel. In his letter to Ambrosius Blarer of 4 May 1528 he related this wider redemptive action of God in electing the Gentiles to the fact that the Spirit created not only Palestine, but also the whole world.[72] However, he asserted elsewhere that the Gentiles' worship of God was not so sincere, nor their knowledge of him so clear as that of the Israelites, with the implication that they came to know God better through God's chosen people.[73] He did not assume that all the apparently good works of the Gentiles were in fact good works springing out of faith. Where they did not arise from faith they were not pleasing to God. He made it clear, however, in *The Resurrection and Ascension of Christ* that no one is saved without faith and that God can give faith to Gentiles. For him there is no contradiction between God's sovereignty in election and Christ's role as mediator in the salvation of the Gentiles. All people are saved through Christ, by which he means

---

Zwingli also used, as he had done before, the biblical examples of Jethro, Moses' father-in-law, and Cornelius. He drew on Augustine in arguing that Gentiles who do the law do so by grace, by faith, by the Spirit of God, and are to be counted among those justified by the grace of Christ. (*S* VI i 242.6-243.1.) In *An Exposition of the Articles*, in a discussion of the law of nature, Zwingli speaks of the Spirit as at work in the Gentiles. They knew the law of nature not from their own understanding, but from the illumination of the Spirit. However, only a few of them knew it; others simply pretended to know it or spoke about it. (*Z* II 327.3-13.)

[71] *Z* V 387.32-391.22. Faith, in this discussion, is opposed to works, but is not explicitly related to Christ.

[72] 'Non continebatur tum religio intra Palęstinę terminos, quia spiritus iste coelestis non solam Palęstinam vel creaverat vel fovebat, sed mundum universum. Pietatem ergo etiam apud istos aluit, quos elegit ubiubi essent.' (*Z* IX 458.25-459.4.) Three lines later he says: 'et ethnicus, si piam mentem domi foveat, Christianus sit, etiamsi Christum ignoret'. In *A Refutation* he writes: 'It was then the special people whose were the promises, even though he spoke also through sibyl prophetesses among the Gentiles, that we might recognize the liberty of his will and the authority of his election.' (*Z* VI i 162.8-11; *Selected Works* 226-7.) Cf. *Z* XIII 301.11-15.

[73] *Z* XIII 377.36-378.18.

the mercy of God shown in Christ. They can be saved, however, whether or not the gospel is preached to them.[74]

It is the famous (or infamous) vision of heaven in *An Exposition of the Faith* that presents the issue most dramatically. It comes as the climax of the section on Eternal Life, which opens with the confident assertion that 'there is for saints and believers an everlasting life of joy and felicity' and attacks the anabaptist belief that the soul sleeps until the resurrection. It is intended as an encouragement to the King of France, promising that if he acts like David, Hezekiah, or Josiah, he will see God.

After that you may expect to see the communion and fellowship of all the saints and sages and believers and the steadfast and the brave and the good who have ever lived since the world began. You will see the two Adams, the redeemed and the Redeemer, Abel, Enoch, Noah, Abraham, Isaac, Jacob, Judah, Moses, Joshua, Gideon, Samuel, Phinehas, Elijah, Elisha, Isaiah and the Virgin Mother of God of whom he prophesied, David, Hezekiah, Josiah, the Baptist, Peter, Paul; Hercules too and Theseus, Socrates, Aristides, Antigonus, Numa, Camillus, the Catos and Scipios; Louis the Pious and your predecessors the Louis, Philips, Pepins and all your ancestors who have departed this life in faith. In short there has not lived a single good man, there has not been a single pious heart or believing soul from the beginning of the world to the end, which you will not see there in the presence of God. Can we conceive of any spectacle more joyful or agreeable or indeed sublime?[75]

This vision causes no surprise in the context of Zwingli's theology, except for his confident naming of particular people. Strictly speaking, his own theological conviction would mean that he could not know whether

[74] 'Philosophi et gentes multa in speciem honestissime fecerunt, sed quia fide carebant, non erant eorum opera grata deo.' (*S* VI i 601.13–15.) 'Salus et vita aeterna electione constat, neque enim manus eius clausa est aut abbreviata, ut inter gentes neminem servet. Potest enim deus infundere fidem in cor gentium, quam deinde operibus comprobant et ostendunt, qualiter non temere de Socrate, Seneca, aliisque multis sentio. Dicat quis: Sed non crediderunt. Respondeo: Si non credunt, non servantur . . . Nam etsi illis evangelium externum de Christo non praedicatur, per Christum tamen potest eos servare deus. Quicunque enim servantur, per Christum servantur, hoc est, per misericordiam dei quam mundo in Christo obtulit. Nemo enim tam iustus tamque innocens esse potest, qui coram iustitia dei consistere possit. Omnibus ergo ad misericordiam dei per Christum confugiendum.' (*S* VI ii 69.21–36.) Several of the discussions concerning the salvation of Gentiles are in the context of baptismal controversy, sometimes with particular reference to Mark 16: 16.
[75] *S* IV 65.26–41. Zwingli's universalism is not fundamentally of a humanist kind with its emphasis on man's free will, but is related to God's free election and Christ's redemption. There is considerable agreement between Zwingli and Augustine here, although Zwingli names particular Gentiles and does not limit himself to Gentiles living before Christ. See R. Pfister, *Die Seligkeit*, pp. 97–103. Bucer also drew on Augustine in his understanding of the relation of the Gentiles to Christ. He tackles the issue more systematically than Zwingli. See Stephens, *Martin Bucer*, pp. 121–8.

somebody else was saved. But the naming of Gentiles such as Socrates and the Scipios is not astonishing, although the omission of Seneca may be, for the whole statement is qualified by the reference to piety and faith, and that for Zwingli implies salvation not through works, but through Christ.

## ADDITIONAL NOTES

1. On the incarnation Zwingli writes, 'He who is Son of God from all eternity, when he assumed manhood became also son of man, not in the sense that he who was Son of God lost the destiny or status of divinity, or changed it into the condition of a man, nor that he converted the human nature into the divine, but in the sense that God and man became one Christ, who in that he is Son of God was the life of all—for all things were made through him—and in that he is man was the offering by which the eternal righteousness, which is also his righteousness, was propitiated.' (Z V 681.13–682.6.) Zwingli appeals to the Athanasian Creed, 'non conversione, inquiens, divinitatis in carnem, sed adsumptione humanitatis in deum'. (Z V 684.4–5.)

In *St John* there is simply the comment that the Son of God, by nature God, became man, although reference is made later to the human nature's being assumed into the unity of the person in the one Christ. (*S* VI i 685.3–4, 705.2–5.) Zwingli commented thus on divinity and humanity in *Two Replies to Luther's Book*: 'Dann die gottheyt ist ein ewigs, unangefangens, unlydenhaffts guot; so ist die menscheyt ein geschaffenn, lychtvelligs, lydenhaffts ding.' (Z VI ii 133.14–16.)

In *The Eucharist*, where he insists on the distinction between the divine and the human in Christ, he states 'nam quod ad subsistentiam adtinet, non obsto theologorum omnium sententiae, qua sentiunt humanitatem Christi non in se, sed in unitate hypostaseos constitisse'. (Z IV 496.24–31.)

2. Krodel (pp. 107–8, n. 12) asserts Erasmus's influence rather than that of Duns Scotus on Zwingli's christology. Payne (pp. 62–4) stresses Erasmus's emphasis on the distinction of the two natures, though he emphasized the human rather than the divine. Blanke (Z V 679, n. 3) contrasts the Chalcedonian approach with its distinction of the two natures in Christ with earlier formulations of the sharing of properties in Gregory of Nazianzus, Gregory of Nyssa, and Cyril of Alexandria. Zwingli followed the former approach, Luther the latter. The sharp distinction of the natures is characteristic of Nestorianism, but the Zwinglian emphasis on the unity of the person is anti-Nestorian. The suggestion of Nestorianism made in Zwingli's lifetime by Lutheran and catholic opponents such as Burgauer (at the Berne disputation) and Eck (in his attack on the first article of *An Account of the Faith*) is misplaced. (Z VI i 366.7–9, 27–8; VI ii 41.11–14; and *S* IV 22.33–23.21.)

Locher sees the root of the differences between Zwingli and Luther in all areas of doctrine in the different emphasis they have in their christology, with Zwingli's emphasis on the divinity and Luther's on the humanity leading Zwingli to stress the revelation of *God* and Luther the *revelation* of God. (*Zwingli's Thought*, p. 173; 'Grundzüge', pp. 502–3.) Reinhold Seeberg comments, 'Aber für das Grosse in Luthers Christologie—dass eben Christi menschliche Worte und Werke die Offenbarung Gottes sind—hat er kein Verständnis.' (*Lehrbuch der Dogmengeschichte IV* 1: *Die Entstehung des protestantischen Lehrbegriffs* (Leipzig, 1933), p. 461.)

3. Zwingli challenged the idea of two covenants, as implying two peoples and two Gods. 'For the same testament and covenant, i.e. the same mercy of God promised to the world through his Son, saved Adam, Noah, Abraham, Moses, David, which saved also Peter, Paul, Ananias, Gamaliel, and Stephen.'. '. . . it is one and the same testament which God had with the human race from the foundation of the world to its dissolution. . . . God therefore made no other covenant with the miserable race of man than that he had already conceived before man was formed. . . . So there could be no other testament than that which furnished salvation through Jesus Christ.' (*Z* VI i 164.2–165.1, 168.33–35, 169.4–6, 8–11; *Selected Works* 229, 233–4.) His conviction that there is only one covenant or testament shaped his interpretation of Paul's reference to more than one. (*Z* VI i 163.8–165.2.) Cf. his exposition of Rom. 9: 4 in *S* VI ii 108.4–7.

# 5. The Holy Spirit

THE importance of the Spirit in Zwingli's thought can be seen in descriptions of his theology as spiritualist or pneumatological.[1] These words raise the questions whether or not the Spirit in Zwingli is the Holy Spirit and how the Spirit is related to the word—incarnate, written, and preached.

The emphasis on the Spirit corresponds in part to the emphasis on the centrality and sovereign freedom of God in his theology and the contrast between God and man.[2] Thus the need to be taught of God can be expressed in terms of being taught by the Spirit of God or the Holy Spirit, even where there is no mention of the Spirit in the biblical texts referred to. Yet this does not mean that the Spirit and God are used simply as synonyms.[3]

## The Spirit and Christ

The Spirit is the Spirit who created and sustains the world, but he is also closely related to Christ. He was active in his birth and life and through his death and resurrection was given to the disciples. He came at Pentecost in the place of Christ. He both leads to faith in him and is given to those who have faith in him, and he forms in them the life of Christ. The strongly christological character of the Spirit in Zwingli is the proper context in which to see Zwingli's varied utterances on the Spirit.

In his exposition of 'The Spirit was not yet' Zwingli stated that the passage does not refer to the being of the Spirit, who always was from the beginning, but to the gift and operation of the Spirit at Pentecost. He was promised by Christ and through the death of Christ he is given to those who believe. In affirming this, Zwingli does not deny that the Spirit was with the godly in the old testament, but not so abundantly.[4] Indeed Christ

---

[1] On the use of 'spiritualist', see Additional Note 1, p. 137.

[2] e.g. faith comes from the Holy Spirit and not from the creature. (Z VI ii 206.25–7; S VI i 759.10–11.) The sovereign freedom is expressed in surprising places, such as the exposition of Genesis 47: 12, 'And Joseph provided his father, his brothers, and all his father's household with food . . .' 'Sic animarum cibator deus dat spiritum suum cuicunque, ut vult.' (Z XIII 267.32–7.)

[3] The terms are used in succession in such passages as Z III 337.32–338.3; IV 67.4–15; S VI i 487.41–8; VI ii 172.1–5. They are distinguished in S VI i 314.23–4. Zwingli speaks in successive lines of God, the Spirit, and Christ when referring to the new life of the Christian, an indication both of his trinitarian way of thinking of God and of the fact that in each person of the godhead it is God who is at work. (Z II 650.2–7; VI ii 118.7–8.)

[4] S VI i 722.29–36. Cf. Z II 26.29–32.

and the apostles observed Jewish rites, until through the Holy Spirit the light of faith dispersed the shadows of the old testament—and that happened through Christ's death.[5] Zwingli contrasted the state of the disciples before and after they received the Spirit. During Christ's life they talked with him and received his teaching, but they were weak and fearful. They fell, they fled, they distrusted and denied him, until they were made strong and whole by the coming of the Spirit. Then they preached Christ boldly.[6]

The Spirit came in the place of Christ's bodily presence—a point Zwingli used constantly to argue against Christ's bodily presence in the eucharistic bread. Indeed if the eating of the bread and wine strengthened faith, then there would have been no point in the sending of the Spirit to the disciples.[7] The Spirit is sent by Christ, and it is by the Spirit that Christ is now present and active.[8] Through the Spirit Christ works to make us sure of salvation.[9] It is the Spirit who leads us to faith in Christ and who comes with faith in Christ. He it is who effects Christ's saving work in us and conforms us to his character.[10] This close link of the Spirit with Christ occurs both where there are explicit new testament passages influencing Zwingli's thought and where there are not. In his exposition of John 14: 26 he goes beyond the text in declaring that the Spirit will teach nothing new, as he brings to remembrance what Christ taught the disciples. In that way the Spirit is bound closely to Christ.[11] Moreover Zwingli frequently uses the criterion in 1 John 4: 2–3 for testing the spirits: for example in *A Reply to Emser*, where he has already applied the Pauline test of unity and peace.

[5] *S* VI i 533.44–8.

[6] *S* VI i 377.43–378.1. Cf. *S* VI i 487.43–8.

[7] *Z* V 946.5–11; XIII 179.2–4. In the first of these passages reference is made to John 16: 7, a text to which Hoen's letter drew attention, but which was also stressed in Erasmus's *The Enchiridion*. (*Z* IV 516.27–31, 519.15–20.) Elsewhere the stress is on other Johannine texts, such as John 14: 16. Zwingli also pointed out that the Spirit does not have a human nature. (*Z* VI ii 117.26–118.12.)

[8] *Z* II 80.15–16; *S* VI i 751.26–30. The text 'I will not leave you orphans' is paraphrased in part with the words 'Then after the ascension I will be present with you in my Spirit.' (*S* VI i 751.41.)

[9] *Z* XIII 56.4–8.

[10] *Z* II 61.25–7, 80.12–19, 650.2–7; III 760.25–8; V 900.14–17; IX 64.1–5; *S* VI i 760.5–15. In the second of these passages the Spirit is referred to as God's and as Christ's in successive sentences. Zwingli argues from Matt. 12: 31–2, Luke 12: 9–10, and John 3: 36, that the sin against the Holy Spirit, the sin which is not forgiven, is to deny God or not to believe, whereas the person who believes in Christ is not condemned. It is called the sin against the Holy Spirit, because faith comes from the drawing of the Holy Spirit. The person who is not drawn by the Spirit does not believe. (*Z* II 408.25–409.27.) Blasphemy against the Holy Spirit is described as attributing God's work to a creature or to the devil and not to God; and such blasphemy is unbelief. (*Z* II 410.22–411.6.)

[11] *S* VI i 752.41–4.

Zwingli interprets Christ's coming in the flesh in terms of his coming for us and contrasts with this the seeking of salvation other than in God.[12]

Yet the Spirit is not limited to those who have explicit faith in Christ. The Spirit was present with Adam before the fall and is present both with the saints of the old testament and with some who stand outside the biblical covenant.[13] This is related to Zwingli's understanding of the Spirit as the Creator Spirit and to his doctrine of election. As the Spirit was not limited to Palestine in the creation, for he created the whole world, so he is not limited to Palestine in his continuing work.[14] The Spirit's work is also manifest in the writing of the law in the hearts of the Gentiles in Romans 2: 14–15. This cannot come from man's reason, because reason is concerned with itself rather than with others. What makes the inward man godly must come from God and not from man.[15] Yet the renewing in the Gentiles of the image of God by the Holy Spirit is related to Christ, precisely because they are those who were elected in Christ before the foundation of the world. However, Zwingli does appear to see a contrast between the work of God's Spirit in them and the later work of Christ's Spirit.[16] In any case the work of the Spirit is not independent of Christ, quite apart from the fact that his work must always be seen in the context of the trinity.

[12] Z III 264.5–17. Cf. Z II 71.17–32 and S VI i 761.9–13 with its reference to the glory of God and of Christ. The test of the prophet in S VI i 380.10–25 is whether he has the Spirit of Christ. In a discussion of councils, in expounding the first article, Zwingli appeals to Christ as the touchstone of the Spirit. If what is said manifests Christ, then it is from the Spirit of God. (Z II 25.20–26.19.)

[13] Z II 631.18–19; S VI i 722.29–36.

[14] 'Non continebatur tum religio intra Palęstinę terminos, quia spiritus iste coelestis non solam Palęstinam vel creaverat vel fovebat, sed mundum universum. Pietatem ergo etiam apud istos aluit, quos elegit ubiubi essent.' (Z IX 458.25–459.4.) (There are few references to the Spirit and creation in Zwingli.) After this passage, but not directly related to it, Zwingli refers to Gentiles who can be Christian, although they do not know Christ, using the analogy of the person who is a Jew, not because of outward circumcision but because of circumcision of the heart (Rom. 2: 28–9). In this context the Spirit is not directly related to the historical Christ, nor his work to the preaching of Christ. (Z IX 459.5–10.)

[15] Z II 634.19–34. Zwingli follows Augustine in relating the law of nature to the Spirit. 'Also kumpt ouch das gsatzt der natur allein von got, und ist nüt anderst dann der luter geist gottes, der innwendig zücht und erlücht. Darumb ouch die Heiden das gsatzt der natur nit uss irem eignen verstand, sunder uss dem erlüchtenden geist gottes, inen unbekant, erkent habend.' (Z II 327.3–7. Cf. Z II 262.35–6, 325.16–17.)

[16] S VI i 242.6–12, 32–9, 244.26–7. In other places Zwingli does not make a sharp distinction between the Spirit of God and the Spirit of Christ. (Z II 80.12–19.) Of course the works of God towards his creatures are the works of all three persons, since they are one in their being. (Z VI ii 118.7–8.)

## The Spirit and Scripture

The written word of scripture is also closely linked with the Spirit, for the Spirit is the author and interpreter of scripture.[17] As the Spirit is always consistent with himself, the utterances of councils and popes as well as of others will be seen to be from the Spirit, only as they are consistent with scripture. The appeal to scripture was made by Zwingli at different times in debate, with all his major opponents: catholics, anabaptists, and Lutherans. Against the catholic assertion that where a council is properly assembled there is the Spirit of God, Zwingli appealed to the scriptures, saying that the Spirit of God would be with them if first of all the scriptures were their master.[18]

With the anabaptists the problem was different. Zwingli alleged that wherever it suited them they denied scripture and asserted their own spirit.

For as often as by the use of clear passages of scripture they are driven to the point of having to say, I yield, straightway they talk about 'the Spirit' and deny scripture. As if indeed the heavenly Spirit were ignorant of the sense of scripture which is written under his guidance or were anywhere inconsistent with himself.

Against their speaking without the authority of scripture he cited Christ's own appeal to it, despite the fact that his signs and teaching were a sufficient proof that he spoke from God. Zwingli referred to the Johannine injunction to test the spirits with its use of Christ's having come in the flesh as the criterion, and alleged that the anabaptists failed the test by denying that he is by nature Son of God and that he is the propitiation for the sins of the world. Indeed the spirit activating them is not the Spirit

---

[17] Introducing the biblical passages in support of his view on fasting, Zwingli wrote, 'Therefore read and understand, open the eyes and ears of the heart and hear and see, what the Spirit of God says to us.' (Z I 91.20–2.) The Spirit and scripture are consistent with each other. 'Et spiritus per omnia consentit scripturę, et scriptura spiritui ... Consentanea enim est scriptura θεόπνευστος (2 Tim. 3, 16) ei spiritui, a quo suggesta et suppeditata est.' (Z XIV 181.11–18.) To Eck he wrote in 1526, 'dann hie allein das götlich wort und der geist gottes rychter sin söllen'. (Z IV 757.19–20.) Note the order 'word and Spirit'.

[18] 'Für das erst: Ob der geist gottes by üch syg, erfindt sich zum ersten, so ir sin wort üweren wegfürer hand und nüt handlend, dann das clarlich im gotswort ussgetruckt würt, also, das die gschrifft üwer meister ist, und ir nit meister über die gschrifft sind; so ist der geist gottes by üch.' (Z II 62.24–8.) A further, related, criterion is found in whether their decisions do away with human opinion and exalt the word and glory of God.

At the end of The Clarity and Certainty of the Word of God Zwingli offers twelve tests of being taught by God, with the presupposition that we must be versed in scripture. They concern trusting in God and not in ourselves, in other words God's glory and not our own, living for others and not ourselves, becoming sure of God's grace, being renewed and finding that the fear of God brings joy rather than sorrow. (Z I 383.1–384.19.)

who brooded over the waters at the foundation of the world, but the one that hurled itself into the swine.[19]

In *Two Replies to Luther's Book* Zwingli declared that no one should boast of the freedom of the Spirit who teaches or acts against God's word. It is not enough to claim that if Luther has God's Spirit he should not be judged. Two years earlier in writing to Christians in Esslingen he rebutted Luther's charge of being an enthusiast (*Schwärmer*) and accused Luther of being one, precisely because Luther was raging away without the support of God's word.[20]

The appeal to scripture was made by Zwingli as a general principle of interpretation, quite apart from particular controversies. Christ's own willingness to confine himself within scripture, when he told the scribes to search the scriptures, as they testify of him, is part of the basis of the argument. Scripture is to be the touchstone of our spirit, and our spirit, inspired as it may be by the Holy Spirit, needs to be restrained by the reins and ropes of scripture.[21]

Although Zwingli insisted from beginning to end that the bible is the criterion by which you can tell whether something is of the Holy Spirit, he was aware that the bible could be misunderstood and misused. The reader needs to be imbued with the same Spirit who wrote it, if he is to understand it aright. This emerged in its simplest form in his early catholic controversies, with an appeal to 1 Corinthians 2: 14-16 which is typical of the reformers.[22] It is the Spirit who judges what is of the Spirit and that means in practice the community or individual who is imbued by the Spirit. (Indeed Zwingli saw certain references to the Spirit as applying to the mind of the believer as taught by the Spirit, rather than directly to the Spirit.[23]) This conviction underlay the disputations, where it was assumed that those who were taught by the Holy Spirit would be able to judge in accordance with God's Spirit and decide whether scripture was misused or who had scripture on his side.[24]

---

[19] Z VI i 24.2-6; 194.22-195.22. See Additional Note 2, pp. 137-8.

[20] Z VI ii 234.6-20; V 421.17-422.15.

[21] Z V 733.29-734.25. Cf. S VI i 205.35-45, 680.9-11. Although this argument is developed in the context of the eucharistic controversy with Luther, it is presented as a general principle.

[22] Z I 380.6-26. 'Demnach berueff mit andacht die gnad gottes über dich, das er dir sinen geist und sinn gebe, das du nit din sunder sin meinung in dich fassest.' (Z I 377.10-12.) Zwingli expresses the need for both the Spirit and scripture: 'We are therefore to be taught by scripture and the Spirit.' (Z III 350.22-3.)

[23] S VI ii 105.41-4, 106.6-10. The argument from the Holy Spirit as indwelling the church is used against anabaptists as well as catholics. (Z IV 395.25-397.9.)

[24] Z I 499.7-12.

In the analogy, which he used elsewhere, of a horse drawing a load with ropes or a carpenter using an axe or chisel, Zwingli stressed the necessity of both elements—in effect scripture and the Spirit. Our spirit, imbued by the Spirit of God, is represented by the horse or carpenter and it can do nothing worth while without the implements, which represent scripture; indeed scripture has a restraining role. However, it is our spirit, imbued by the Spirit of God, that is the chief thing. Nevertheless the intention here is precisely and explicitly not to give free rein to the interpreter, for the point of the passage is to affirm that 'scripture is the touchstone of our spirit'. In a parallel passage in *St Luke* there is a similar analogy and the same kind of emphasis.[25] On occasion Zwingli speaks of the determining role of the Spirit of faith (as in deciding what is to be believed in dreams) without explicitly referring to scripture, but this does not mean that the Spirit acts without scripture or contrary to it.[26]

One of Zwingli's best-known illustrations has sometimes been used both to show the priority of the Spirit and the Spirit's independence of scripture; but this is not its purpose. In *An Answer to Valentin Compar* Zwingli described an old countryman who had helped to make the laws before they were written down. If the old law book had been lost, it would have been no use having someone adjudicate between various new law books, as he would not have known what was right. By contrast the old countryman would have been able to tell. Zwingli saw the godly old man as representing the believer in whose heart God has written the law. From the inward faith and knowledge given to him by God he would be able to confirm whether the outward letter conformed to God's teaching. With this example Zwingli made what was for him the fundamental point: that believers could judge whether or not the teachings of the papists conformed to the faith thay have in God and the knowledge of God, which they have learnt from him. There is no statement here that the believer judges scripture independently of scripture. What he is judging is the word that men teach or preach. All this is set in a wider context in which Zwingli was arguing that faith is the gift of God and does not come from words spoken by the church.[27]

[25] Z V 733.29–734.25; S VI i 679.42–680.14. 'Si litera scripturae non esset, quisque iuxta libidinem suam loqueretur. Scriptura ergo regula et funis est, iuxta quam omnia dirigenda sunt. Spiritus veritatis, hoc est, fidelis mens spiritu dei illustrata arripit literam et eam moderatur. Litera non cogit spiritum aut sensum, sed spiritus enarrat literam et illustrat.' (S VI i 680.9–14.)

[26] Z XIII 240.14–22.

[27] Z IV 71.8–72.8. Zwingli is dealing with Compar's attack on the sixty-seven articles. In his reply to the first of Compar's main points Zwingli refers to the rejection of the apocryphal gospels by ordinary Christians (not by the pope or the bishops) because they did not conform to God's holy word, which could be a reference to scripture. (Z IV 74.10–19.) The reference in Z I

## The Spirit and the Word

The relation of the Spirit to the outward word of preaching must be seen in the context of a theology that stresses the freedom and sovereignty of God and saving faith as the gift of God. Such a theology can give no independent power to anyone or anything apart from God. Inevitably therefore the emphasis lies on the Spirit rather than on the word, except where the word is quite simply God's word. This can be seen in *The Clarity and Certainty of the Word of God*. 'The word of God is so sure and strong that if God wills all things are done the moment that he speaks his word. For it is so living and powerful that ... things both rational and irrational are fashioned and despatched and constrained in conformity with its purpose.' That this view of the word has a different accent from Luther's emerges when Zwingli moves from the power of the word to its clarity. Then the role of the Spirit becomes evident. The word is understood not because of human understanding, but because of 'the light and Spirit of God, illuminating and inspiring the words'.[28]

The combination of Spirit and word in Zwingli expresses the fact that it is God who makes the word effective. The terms can be conjoined or contrasted, thereby giving Zwingli's theology a more positive or a more negative aspect. In expounding Isaiah 59: 21 with its reference to the Spirit and the word, Zwingli stressed that the Spirit is placed first, for without the Spirit the flesh misunderstands the word. The church therefore has both the word preached by the prophets and the Spirit who illuminates where he wills.[29] Here there is a sense of unity between the two, with no hint of opposition.

The Spirit may be spoken of as working in the preacher or the hearer. This applied to the apostles in their day, as it does to us in ours. 'Moreover, they that were to spread Christ through all the world receive also the Spirit of Christ. For as he had been sent, so also are they sent [John 20: 21];

---

382.23 is not in any significant sense an appeal from scripture to the Spirit, but rather an indication of the origin of scripture in the Spirit.

[28] Z I 353.8-13, 365.14-21; LCC XXIV 68, 78. The same fundamental position is expressed later in terms of faith in Z XIII 144.26-145.29.

[29] 'Spiritum anteposuit. Absque spiritu enim verbum dei rapit caro in contrarium sensum. Constat autem coelestis doctrina verbo et spiritu. Haec promittuntur ecclesiae. Habet ergo prophetas, qui docent praedicando, habet et spiritum, qui illuminat, ac mentes deo conciliat instinguendo et ingruendo, ubi ipse vult.' (Z XIV 391.1-7.)

The order can vary. In *A Commentary* it is word and Spirit, for 'we are to be taught outwardly by the word of God and inwardly by the Spirit'. (Z III 900.6-7.) In *An Exposition of the Articles* it is the Spirit and the word, for it is not the preacher who causes someone to believe, but 'the Spirit and the word of God do that'. (Z II 111.9-11.) For this reason prayer is linked with the preaching of the word, as in Z II 630.2-20.

therefore they had to have the same Spirit, being engaged in the same work.'[30] The necessity for the Spirit with the word was also expressed in prayer for those who hear the truth to be given the Spirit, so that they may receive the truth and fashion their life in accordance with it.[31]

Although Spirit and word are combined in Zwingli at all periods, yet his characteristic emphasis is on the Spirit, even where there is no strong contrast between the two. Where a contrast is made, it is usually to secure the freedom or sovereignty of God in enabling people to believe. In the exposition of the seventeenth article, Zwingli moves from saying that the Spirit and the word of God make people believe to saying that the Spirit effects everything in everyone, and that man is nothing other than a steward of the word of God.[32] Where there is a contrast, the purpose seems rather to affirm the Spirit than to deny the place of the word. Without the Spirit teaching inwardly the outward word is in vain, for everyone must be taught by God. 'Yet it does not follow for that reason that the outward word is not necessary, for Christ commanded the apostles to preach the gospel through all the world.'[33]

The agreement at Marburg between Zwingli and Luther is in keeping with Zwingli's theology, even if it is not the way he characteristically expressed himself. It is the Spirit who is the subject of the sentence, not the word. It is the Spirit who creates faith, and who does so in his own freedom.[34] In the end it is the word that needs the Spirit, rather than the Spirit who needs the word. In this regard what Zwingli said about the sacraments would apply equally to the word.

Moreover, a channel or vehicle is not necessary to the Spirit, for he himself is the virtue and energy whereby all things are borne, and has no need of being borne; neither do we read in the holy scriptures that perceptible things, as are the sacraments, bear certainly with them the Spirit, but if perceptible things have ever been borne with the Spirit, it has been the Spirit, and not perceptible things, that has borne them . . . Briefly, the Spirit blows wherever he wishes . . .[35]

---

[30] Z III 737.34-7; *Works* III 172. Cf. *S* VI ii 68.10-14.

[31] *S* VI i 262.44-8. Cf. *S* VI i 380.10-14.

[32] Z II 111.7-19. A similar vein emerges in the exposition of the thirty-ninth article which urges the authorities to introduce true knowledge of God among their people. This will happen only with the pure word which makes people new, but immediately the qualification is added, 'not the spoken word, but the Spirit of God who works with his word'. (Z II 330.21-5.)

[33] *S* VI i 752.44-8. Cf. *S* VI i 217.36-41, 362.15-20; VI ii 273.12-20. The Pauline reference to faith as coming from hearing can be seen in this light. (Z II 538.16-24; V 432.2-13.)

[34] Z VI ii 522.12-17, 550.5-10; see Additional Note 3, p. 138.

[35] Z VI ii 803.10-22; *Works* III 466-7. If the Spirit were conveyed by outward means, his sovereign freedom would be lost. The quotation continues: 'Therefore, the grace of the Spirit is not conveyed by this immersion, or that drinking, or that anointing, for if that happened one would know how, where, by what, and to what the Spirit is borne.' (Z VI ii 803.26-9.) There is a certain

The relation of the Spirit and the word is not precisely formulated, although both are in the end given by God and are combined in his purpose. Zwingli's concern was to stress that God (or the Spirit) is the true teacher. This led him almost inevitably to set this over against human teaching and hence to lay less stress on the word. Yet it was through the preaching of the word that Zwingli expected reformation to take place.

## ADDITIONAL NOTES

1. The term 'spiritualist' is normally used negatively to indicate that Zwingli stressed the Spirit rather than the word—often to emphasize that he divorced the Spirit from the word. This is fundamentally Luther's view of Zwingli, whom he considered a spiritualist like Carlstadt. See, e.g. E. Seeberg, *Zwingli, Schwenckfeld und Luther*, pp. 43–80. Cf. 'In der Tat tritt neben die Christus-Offenbarung die des h. Geistes.' (W. Köhler, *Die Geisteswelt Ulrich Zwinglis. Christentum und Antike* (Gotha, 1920), p. 65). The term 'pneumatological' is normally used positively to indicate that Zwingli stressed the Spirit, but as the Holy Spirit, without divorcing him from the word. See. F. Schmidt-Clausing, *Zwingli* (Berlin, 1965), pp. 82–112, and 'Das Prophezeigebet', esp. pp. 12–22.

Gestrich (pp. 10, 73, 119, n. 138) argues that the primary issue is not whether the Spirit is the Holy Spirit, which he does not dispute, but how the Spirit is related to the mediation of grace through word and sacrament and above all to scripture. In this he describes Zwingli as a spiritualist. He sees four roots to his spiritualism, the main two being Augustine's theory of illumination and Erasmus's dualism of flesh and spirit. Burckhardt, in his study of Zwingli, seems less concerned with his theology of the Spirit than with the four elements he sees in Zwingli's theology: the reformation or biblical, the spiritualist, the mystical, and the rational (*Das Geistproblem bei Huldrych Zwingli*).

2. The allegation that the anabaptists deny Christ as Son of God by nature and the propitiation of the sins of the world is probably made against Denck, Hätzer, and Kautz. See e.g., Z VI i 26.2–27.2 and footnotes on pp. 26, 27, and 57. Zwingli also referred to their claim to be in the Spirit, and not in the flesh, when they were guilty of immorality. (Z VI i 27.8–13.) In letters to Zwingli from Michael Wüst and Capito in the previous year, 1526, there are examples of anabaptist claims that it is the Spirit who prays or speaks in them. (Z VIII 563.15–19, 624.4–11.)

In *The Ministry* (1525) Zwingli challenges the anabaptist claim to the Spirit in what they say. (Z IV 413.2–4.) They assert that the Spirit enables them to understand scripture and that they do not need knowledge of the biblical languages. Zwingli insists on the necessity of languages precisely because of hypocritical claims to the Spirit and because scripture is the test of whether something is of

contrast with Zwingli's earlier words in *The Canon of the Mass*: 'Ut igitur spiritu tuo vivificemur, ne quęso verbum tuum a nobis unquam auferas. Eo enim veluti vehiculo spiritus tuus trahitur; nam ipsum ociosum ad te non revertitur.' (Z II 606.27–9.)

God. This is related to Paul's understanding of prophesying in 1 Cor. 14 and leads to the prophecy in Zurich. (Z IV 417.10–419.6.) Cf. Z IV 394.19–395.23, 398.3–10. Against the tendency of individual anabaptists to claim the inspiration of the Spirit Zwingli also argues for the role of the congregation in testing whether something is of the Spirit. (Z IV 395.25–31, 420.3–24.)

3. *The Marburg Articles* states, 'Von dem usserlichen wort. Zum achten, das der heylig geyst, ordenlich zuo reden, niemants soelichen gloubenn oder syne gabe on vorgend predigt oder müntlich wort oder evangelion Christi, sonder durch unnd mit soelichem müntlichem wort würckt er und schafft er den glouben, wo und in welchen er wil. Rom. X.' (Z VI ii 522.12–17.)

In a letter to the Elector of Saxony Melanchthon wrote: 'In articulo de Ministerio Ecclesiastico sive verbo, et usu Sacramentorum, graviter hallucinantur. Docent enim, Spiritum sanctum non per Verbum et Sacramenta, sed sine Verbo et Sacramentis donari. Idem etiam docebat Muncerus, et ea ratione privatis speculationibus sese dabat. Id quod sequi necesse est, si quis Spiritum sanctum sine verbo acquiri posse existimet.' (S IV 184.42–185.2.) By contrast Oecolampadius defends Zwingli and himself from attack in a letter to Haller. By use of the distinction *potentia absoluta* and *potentia ordinata*, which Zwingli does not use, he gives a positive exposition of the Marburg agreement: 'Scis enim duplicem esse potentiam Dei, unam absolutam, alteram ordinatam, ut vocant. Cum igitur dicimus, Spiritum fidei per verbum nobis communicari, de solito ordine Dei loquimur: nolentes interim angusto limite divinam potentiam concludi. Hunc autem esse ordinem et morem Dei, docet Paulus dicens: Quomodo credent ei, de quo non audierunt? Quare ergo illi inferunt, quasi ex libertate deordinationem faciamus: servat enim et sic suam libertatem Spiritus sanctus, ut solis electis se communicet. Quod si minus admisissemus, nonne ministerium verbi, ut Catabaptistae quidam, abstulissemus? Interim non derogamas potentiae divinae absolutae, quod etiam ante auditum verbum externum, hominem instruere possit. Proinde non dicimus, gratiam Spiritus sancti esse alligatam, ut illi calumniantur: sed fatemur Dominum per Spiritum sanctum cooperari praedicantibus, ut Marcus habet.' (S IV 192.15–28.)

# 6. Man

THE profound ambivalence in Zwingli's understanding of man is manifest in *A Commentary*.[1] The biblical and the Neoplatonist views of man are both evident, although the biblical predominates. Moreover, though man's being made in the image of God is mentioned, it is simply the prelude to a description of man's fall and the fundamental corruption of his nature. The biblical emphasis is characteristic of most of Zwingli, with the notable exception of the chapter on man in *The Providence of God*.

## The Image of God

The biblical idea of the image of God does not feature largely in Zwingli's thought, although its influence may be seen in many places. It is expounded in *The Clarity and Certainty of the Word of God* in the early twenties and again in *St Matthew* in the late twenties. In the first Zwingli states that it is in the mind or soul and not in the body that man is made in the image of God, for God did not assume bodily form until later, that is, in Christ. A sign of the image of God in man is that 'he looks to God and to the words of God'. The universal desire for eternal blessedness after this life is something that distinguishes man from plants or animals. Zwingli sees the difference as deriving from God's act in creation, for whereas the animals were brought forth by the earth, man was created by God's taking the earth and forming it into a man. Man's desire for life was inspired in him by the Spirit of God breathing into him, so that man became a living soul. God did not, however, give animals life with the breath of his lips, nor is it said of them that they became a living soul.[2]

After exploring the image of God largely in terms of Genesis 2, Zwingli moves to the Pauline contrast—especially in Romans 7—between the new, or inward, and the old, or outward, man. For him man is made in the image of God 'in order to have fellowship with him'. The new man is fundamentally man made in the image of God and renewed according to that image.

[1] E. Künzli gives a more practical picture of Zwingli's understanding of man in 'Der Mann bei Zwingli', *ZWA* II (1961) 351–71.

[2] Zwingli refers to Augustine's view that the intellect, will, and memory which constitute the soul are a likeness of God as trinity, but asserts that there are many ways in which we experience the likeness of God more specifically than with the intellect, will, and memory. He then offers the comparison with animals. (Z I 344.6–7, 345.4–349.11.)

Paul says clearly that our inward man—which is created in the divine image—has a desire to live according to the law and will of God, but that it is opposed by the outward man—in the members of which—that is, in which—sins dwells, that is, a proneness to sin (*der süntlich prästen*): for by the word sin Paul here means the weakness (*die prästhaffte*) which gives rise to sin.

Although Zwingli does not develop the contrast explicitly, the inward man is in effect the soul. God is the bridegroom and husband of the soul, and nothing gives greater joy to the soul than the word of its creator. The fact that the inward man is renewed (2 Cor. 4: 16) shows that it is not destroyed, rather the old man obscures and darkens the new which is unsullied by the weaknesses or sins (*prästen*) of the body. However, man cannot of himself do anything to change the situation, for the image is not his but God's. It is only through Christ that the inward man is freed from the imprisonment of sin. The outward man is always subject to the weakness (*prästen*) of sin; therefore we have to see that the inward man is not dominated by the outward, so that we serve the flesh and its desires.[3]

The second way in which Zwingli speaks of the image of God is in terms of the law written on the heart by the Holy Spirit. The reference is to the law written on the hearts of the Gentiles in Romans 2: 14-15. In expounding 'In our image and likeness' in *Genesis* (1527) he prefers this meaning of the image to that of the mind or to man's dominion over creatures, and he sees the image as restored through Christ.[4] This interpretation is equally present in his early writings where the natural law is seen as the Spirit of God or the leading of the Spirit. That law is expressed in the words 'Whatever you wish to be done to you, do to others' (Matt. 7: 12) and 'Love your neighbour as yourself' (Matt. 22: 39).[5]

The other main treatment of the image of God is in *St Matthew*, in the exposition of natural law in Matthew 7: 12. After referring to Romans 1 and 2, Zwingli quotes Cicero to show that the heathen also recognized the law of nature, although they speak of nature while the Christian speaks of

---

[3] Z I 349.12-353.5; LCC XXIV 66. The translation of *präst* is problematic. Bromiley, uses 'weakness' as Finsler does in the footnotes to the critical edition. See also n. 41 below. Zwingli uses *präst* in German where Augustine used *morbus*.

[4] 'Hoc quidam ad dominium super creaturas referunt, quod homo cunctis veluti deus praesit; alii hoc ad animum trahunt. Ego vero ad imaginem hanc et similitudinem esse puto, quod nos naturae ius dicimus: "Quod tibi vis fieri, aliis facito!" Haec imago dei inscripta est et inpressa cordibus nostris ... Qui ergo iustitiam colunt, qui deum quaerunt, qui deum innocentia vitae Christumque omnibus perinde atque sibi benefaciendo [cf. Matth. 22: 34-40] exprimunt, hi demum antiquam imaginem dei referunt, quae per Christum repurgata et ac instaurata.' (Z XIII 13.34-14.10.)

[5] Z II 262.24-6, 324.18-327.13. Zwingli makes it clear that the nature referred to in the law of nature is not man's corrupt nature. (Z II 298.1-3.) In his doctrine of sin the law of nature, with its knowledge of good and evil, is important for man's responsibility and guilt.

the will of God or the image of God. The image has not been altogether extinguished, even in the most impious and evil men.[6] On this occasion Zwingli develops Matthew 7: 12 in the light of the commands to love God and to love one's neighbour in Matthew 22, both passages regarding their commands as expressing the law and the prophets.

Therefore the law of nature is nothing other than true religion, to wit the knowledge, worship, and fear of the supreme deity. No one but God alone is able to teach this knowledge and this worship. This law of nature, which is written by God in man's heart and confounded by evil, is renewed by the grace of Christ. For as at the beginning this light is shone upon man by the Spirit of God, so afterwards it is restored and confirmed by the Spirit of Christ.

In this discussion of the image of God there is clear reference to the corruption of the flesh in Adam and the renewal of the image in Christ, indeed a contrast between the work of the Spirit of God in making the image and that of the Spirit of Christ in remaking it.[7]

The exposition of 'Come to me' (Matt. 11: 28) has several similar features, including a reference to Cicero and the Gentile equivalent of the image of God, and a strong christological reference. Man has been created to know and enjoy God. God has revealed himself to man, for he has imprinted his image on him. Hence in all men, even the impious, there is a fear of God. Men fear the righteous judgement of God, but he comes to their aid in the life and death of Christ. It is through Christ that we find peace.[8] In contrast with what is generally held about the later Zwingli, the later presentation of the image of God is in many ways as biblical and as christological as the earlier presentation in *The Clarity and Certainty of the Word of God*.

[6] *S* VI i 241.12–244.27. Cf. 'Ex his et aliis quae apud Ethnicos leguntur passim, facile inducor, naturam rationemque illis fuisse quod nos dei voluntatem aut ordinationem dicimus, aliquando etiam imaginem dei, quae aut insculpta sit primum hominibus, aut deinde spiritus sancti operatione per fidem et charitatem illustrata et renovata. . . . Haec imago dei homini impressa nonnihil vitiis deturpata et inquinata. Haec lucernula densissimis tenebris obfuscata et obliterata est, non tamen omnino extincta. Nam et in impiissimis et sceleratissimis hominibus se prodit, et peccatis reclamat, ac quantam quidem potest renititur ac repugnat.' (*S* VI i 242.6–17.) Zwingli supports his view with a long quotation from Augustine.

[7] *S* VI i 243.44–244.27. The exposition of the next verse has a somewhat unexpected reference to the image of God in man, who is described as spirit and flesh, as a kind of amphibian, comparable to passages in *A Commentary* and *The Providence of God*. In the same passage, however, the reason is described as flesh, as is everything on which man determines apart from the word of God. (*S* VI i 245.16–42.)

[8] *S* VI i 281.42–282.46, 421.25–422.11. There are other passing references to the image of God in the commentaries, e.g. 'Animo hominis imago dei indita est; veritatem ergo dum audit, aut obtemperat aut formidat.' (*S* VI i 326.1–2.)

*Flesh and Spirit*

Fundamental in Zwingli's understanding of man is his sense of man as fallen, as a sinner. This is expressed in the biblical contrast of flesh and Spirit, though also in the Greek contrast of flesh and spirit or body and soul. It is not as if one gives way to the other; both can be found throughout his writings, though the biblical view is dominant and is on the whole the one necessary for his understanding of salvation in Christ.[9] In it flesh is the whole man, not a part of man, and describes man as fallen. *An Exposition of the Articles* has both elements. It can contrast flesh and Spirit in this way: 'To live according to the Spirit is to withdraw oneself from the reason and the power of the flesh, that is human nature, and trust in the Spirit of God alone.'[10] At the same time man, who consists of body and soul, is compared with a mixture of water and wine or of wax and clay. Water and wine, when mixed, lose their taste, until drunk and changed into blood. In the sun wax melts and the clay is baked hard, and in water wax becomes hard and clay is washed away. So in man two things strive with each other, the spirit against the flesh and the flesh against the spirit, for the body retains its nature, just as water mixed with wine struggles to retain its nature. Yet even here the conflict in man of soul and body is set within the Pauline conflict of Spirit and flesh and is in part reinterpreted by it.[11]

*A Commentary* shows the same ambiguity in its description of the conflict in man. The dominant note is the biblical one of flesh and Spirit, and the view of flesh as the whole man rather than as part of man. 'And think not that I mean here the flesh that we have in common with the cattle (for who does not know that there is no good thing in that?). . . . I am speaking of the whole man who is nothing but flesh if left to himself (as God himself said in Genesis 6: 3) . . .'. (Flesh can of course still be used of man's

[9] The Greek contrast of flesh and spirit is particularly important for man's receiving salvation and hence especially for Zwingli's understanding of word and sacraments. Gestrich (p. 67) states: 'Die starken Gegensätze, die für Zwinglis Theologie konstitutiv gewesen sind, bilden nicht Antike und Christentum, Wissen und Glauben, Rationales und Irrationales, sondern einzig und allein: Fleisch und Geist!' It is, however, striking that Zwingli attributes the strong contrast of flesh and Spirit to Luther, suggesting that he sees the Pauline contrast rather than the Greek contrast as fundamental. 'Quis enim luculentius aut purius quam tu inimicicias carnis et spiritus ex apostolorum fontibus propinavit?' (Z V 723.3–724.1.)

[10] Z II 81.3–5. Cf. Z II 95.5–6. Pfister stresses that Zwingli's Greek dualist view of man, with its implicit denial of man's guilt for sin, is incompatible with Zwingli's understanding of Christ and salvation. It also has no influence on his doctrine of original sin.' (*Das Problem der Erbsünde*, pp. 15–16.)

[11] Z II 46.5–47.14. It is all set in the larger context that we can do nothing apart from the grace of God.

bodily life.) The conflict is between man as flesh and the Spirit. Man, as he responds to the Spirit, is called the inward man, man as he responds to the flesh is the old man. The life of the Christian is a continual battle between the two. When someone trusts in Christ, he becomes a new man. It is the mind that is renewed. However, the mind is not seen as having of itself a special relationship with God, for before this it was ignorant of God, and where there is ignorance of God there one has nothing but the flesh, sin, and self-esteem. Later, when he moves from Romans 7 to Romans 8, Zwingli interprets the reference to the Spirit as being to the spiritual man who has been raised by the Spirit of God and who looks to God alone—and he states that the spiritual man means the pious mind. The conflict of flesh and Spirit is then expressed in terms of the pious mind and the carnal man or the flesh, that is man subject to the flesh or self-love.[12] In the epilogue, however, the conflict is one of flesh and spirit, expressed in terms of body and mind, in which the body resists because by its nature it despises what the mind values. It desires earthly things because it has no hope of seeing God. Indeed God has willed that man be an amphibian among creatures, living sometimes on earth, sometimes in heaven, and while on earth sometimes winning, some-times yielding. He wins if he remains loyal to Christ, his head.[13]

Regarding man as consisting of body and soul is part of the Christian tradition. The unity of the divine and human natures in Christ is described in terms of the union of body and soul in man.[14] The contrast of body and soul is not necessarily in conflict with that between flesh and Spirit, as is evident from the exposition of Genesis 6: 5, where the whole man, who consists of soul and body, is called flesh.[15] It is the Holy Spirit who makes men spiritual, who would otherwise be carnal.[16] Of course the ambiguous use of the word 'flesh' in the bible leads to some of the ambiguity in Zwingli. It can mean quite simply man, or—in a neutral sense—man's bodily nature, or man as sinner.[17] The difference of body and soul can moreover be expressed without a sense of their opposition, as in the gift of the sabbath which serves the needs of body and soul.[18]

---

[12] Z III 712.38–720.29, esp. 713.17–23 (*Works* III 145), 713.35–714.9, 28–9, 717.5–15, 719.35–720.20. 'Ecce, ut manifestum fieri incipit, quod homo, quatenus homo est, et quatenus iuxta ingenium suum vel cogitat vel agit, nihil nisi quod carnis est . . .'. 'Sed de toto homine, qui, utut ex anima corporeque rebus natura diversis compactus est, caco tamen adpellatur, quod pro ingenio suo nihil quam carnale mortiferumque cogitet.' (Z III 658.13–15, 660.10–13.)

[13] Z III 909.22–8, 910.22–8.                                    [14] e.g. Z V 924.16–20.

[15] Z XIII 45.8–10. Cf. *S* VI ii 93.2 and 203.17–21. This view of man is present in the later Zwingli as well as in the earlier. (Z III 660.10–13.)

[16] *S* VI i 694.20–9.

[17] Z I 206.16–22; V 969.11–32; *S* VI i 500.46–8, 714.26–8; VI ii 46.29–33, 87.4–8, 102.1–4, 40–3.

[18] Z XIII 394.22–35.

The chapter on man in *The Providence of God* presents by contrast a view of man that is largely non-biblical in inspiration. It begins with a quotation from a muslim Abdala, probably drawn from Pico della Mirandola, that man is the most wonderful of all things to be seen in the world. Man is unlike the spirits in having an earthly and visible body and unlike the animals in having understanding and reason. From this we can infer that God made man both to be an image of himself and to be the one, from all the creatures made from the earth, who should enjoy God—and also to foreshadow in a way the fellowship God would have with man through the incarnate Christ. However, body and mind are so made that there is warfare between them.

When the mind begins to contemplate God, to talk and commune with him about the things it has in common with him, suddenly the flesh, fashioned from clay, draws it back.

But however much the flesh refuses to listen to any counsel but what the belly dictates, whenever it succeeds in getting the ascendancy over the spirit, yet the nobler and kindlier mind never ceases to warn, advise or dissuade as occasion offers.

Although Zwingli refers incidentally to the fall, nevertheless the conflict of body and mind does not derive from the fall, for 'the flesh is just as much part of man as the spirit, and he received both from God the creator himself'. At this point Zwingli discusses the law, the most explicitly biblical section of the chapter, and then identifies this non-biblical opposition of flesh and spirit with the opposition made in Romans 7, insisting that for man to be man (and not angel or animal) each part of him must retain its characteristics. Indeed both mind and body are sustained in their life by God and reflect his will.[19] Although there are biblical references, the thought of the chapter has been more powerfully influenced by non-biblical insights than by biblical ones, and the role of Christ (like that of the fall) is peripheral to the discussion. Here, more than almost anywhere else, the humanist influence can be seen in Zwingli's theology. But it has always to be asked whether there is an immediate reason for this, as in *A Commentary*, where at the end of the chapter on man Zwingli writes, 'I have brought in these things from the heathen in order that, if possible, even those who are devoted to philosophy may receive eyes with which to

---

[19] Z VI iii 115.13–140.19, esp. Z VI iii 115.16–17, 116.4–117.7, 121.10–12 and 122.14–17 (*Works* III 162 amended), 124.10–13 (*Works* III 163), 136.9–137.12, 139.2–7. Reference is also made in the epilogue. (Z VI iii 220.19–222.4.) Büsser points to the particular influence of Seneca in the chapter on man. (Z VI iii 16–17.)

see what man is.'[20] However, with the single exception of *The Providence of God*, it cannot be said that it is particularly after 1525 that this view is developed, or that the stress on the corruption of human nature ceases with *A Commentary* in 1525.[21]

Zwingli uses the terms *anima*, *animus*, *cor*, *mens*, and *spiritus* almost interchangeably.[22] They express something that distinguishes man from the animals and it is this core of a man's being that is addressed by God. It is in other words the soul rather than the understanding.[23] At points the way of expressing it is more directly biblical, at points more philosophical. In part in his references to the heart or soul, the mind or spirit, or indeed the inward man, Zwingli is contrasting what God does with what man does. God alone knows the heart and can change it; man can see only what is outward and can affect only what is outward. There is also the conviction—related to passages such as Hebrews 9—that outward things as a means of salvation have been done away by Christ, for they could not cleanse the conscience. (With Christ it is the Spirit who gives life.) To think otherwise is to restore Judaism.[24] Moreover if outward things could purify the soul, then salvation would be at our disposal for we can do outward things, such as baptism. But that is contrary to God 'who alone can purify the soul or inward man'.[25] In his later writings Zwingli speaks of God's using outward things, because man is made with senses. This is related to the view of man that places him between animals and angels.[26]

---

[20] Z III 664.23–5; *Works* III 86. Several passages in *St Luke* have a similar dualist view of man: S VI i 584.13–36, 635.45–636.32, 652.2–9.

[21] Pollet, *DTC* 3790.

[22] See, e.g., Z III 759.18–760.1, 777.3–21, 782.6–17; V 621.31–2, 673.6–8; XIV 611.39–612.9; S VI i 219.25, 652.2–9; VI ii 203.16–17.

Schmid (*Zwinglis Lehre*, p. 112) argues for a distinction, albeit occasional, between *mens* and *spiritus* in the light of 'Sed spiritus est superior portio mentis, dei capax.' (S VI i 547.25–6.) *Spiritus* is used similarly in S VI i 333.24–6, but in contrast to the body, not the mind.

[23] He stands here in the Augustinian tradition. Zwingli also refers to God's stimulating and drawing the will as well as the mind or soul. (S VI i 673.45–674.1.) The reference to the intellect in the epilogue to *The Providence of God* is not especially typical. Zwingli moves almost at once from the use of *intellectus* to the use of *mens*. (Z VI iii 220.19–221.27.) Cf. Z VI iii 116.4–8.

[24] Z IV 216.26–217.13; VI ii 805.23–6.

[25] Z IV 267.1–9.

[26] S VI i 582.18–29. However, faith does not come from something outward unless the Holy Spirit draws inwardly. (S VI i 261.27–8.) The body, of course, can lead away from God. (S VI i 636.9–13.) God's use of outward things is also present earlier, e.g. in the letter to Fridolin Lindauer on 20 Oct. 1524, where the contrast is made between the inward and the outward man. (Z VIII 236.3–19.) The contrast is made in a variety of contexts. Thus the commands to do with divine or inward righteousness, such as not coveting, refer to the inward man, those to do with human or outward righteousness, such as not stealing, refer to the outward man. (Z II 484.15–28.) The outward man is known to others, the inward man is known to God and oneself. A distinction can be made between commands that concern the inward man, which therefore apply to everyone and

Nevertheless the work of the Holy Spirit is inward, in the heart. It cannot be seen, any more than the wind can be.[27]

For Zwingli there is a clear distinction between body and spirit. 'For body and spirit are such different things that if you take one it cannot be the other . . . Hence, to eat bodily flesh spiritually is simply to assert that the body is spirit.'[28] He regards as axiomatic the statement: 'That which is born of the flesh is flesh, and that which is born of the Spirit is spirit' (John 3: 6). This has clear implications for his understanding of how God deals with man. In the eucharistic controversy it is also a major factor in Zwingli's difference from Luther. 'If, therefore, the natural body of Christ is eaten by our mouth, what but flesh will be produced from flesh naturally masticated?' 'As the body cannot be fed upon a spiritual substance, so the soul cannot be fed upon a bodily substance.'[29]

There is not, however, something in man that of itself can respond to God. The mind or spirit of man is not in that sense a point of contact with God. In those passages where Zwingli has been thought to hold this view, it is clear that man's response is a matter of his faith, not of something inherent in his mental or spiritual nature.[30] The response of faith will lead to a union of the spirit or soul with God, but that is not anything inherent in it apart from God. The union is through faith, and it may be compared with the union of the human and the divine in Christ.[31]

## Sin

Zwingli's understanding of sin and original sin is formulated in the course of controversy with catholics, anabaptists, and Luther. If his writings are studied chronologically, they reveal his fundamentally biblical view of sin,

those that concern the outward man, which may vary from person to person. (*S* VI i 218.42–3, 219.17–22.) The distinction between the inward and outward man does not mean any division in us, any more than there is division in Christ in his being God and man. (*S* VI i 388.7–8.) The phrase 'inward man' can refer to man as he responds to God in faith, as he gives ear to the Spirit. (*Z* II 649.10–16; III 713.35–714.3; V 502.12–15.)

[27]  *S* VI i 694.30–40.
[28]  *Z* III 787.7–13.
[29]  *Z* V 506.19–507.4, 957.7–958.3; VI ii 809.18–19, 810.9 (Jackson 474–5; *Works* II 52–3).
[30]  This is true of the passage in *St Matthew* mentioned by Pollet (*DTC* 3790). Zwingli refers to the power of the Spirit, and goes on: 'in mente aliquid esse, quod superne illapsum trahat et invitet. . . . Oportet ergo quod aliquid prius sit in homine quam audiat verbum externum, quod verbum praedicatum et auditum vel recipiat, vel respuat, fides videlicet vel infidelitas.' (*S* VI i 333.20–8.) Cf. *S* VI i 445.9–23. It is also true in the earlier writing, *The Clarity and Certainty of the Word of God*, where, after the discussion of the image of God, the different responses to the sower in Matthew have to do in effect with faith. (*Z* I 359.10–361.27.) It is the word of God that shines on human understanding and enlightens it. (*Z* I 361.31–2.)
[31]  *Z* VI i 311.13–25. Cf. *S* VI i 717.45–718.1.

and a work such as *The Providence of God*, with its non-biblical approach, is
seen to be an occasional work, unrepresentative of his writings as a whole.
The initial controversy is concerned to establish that salvation is
through Christ alone and the discussion of sin is set in that context, with
Zwingli asserting that man is totally corrupted by sin and unable to do
anything for his salvation. Thus in *An Exposition of the Articles* it is after
articles 2–4, which affirm Christ as saviour, that article 5 considers the
nature of sin. Indeed it is so that our healing or salvation may be understood better that he describes the underlying sickness, beginning with an
account of Adam.[32]

Adam was created good, with freedom according to his will to keep, or
not to keep, to God and his commands. Adam, however, turned from God
to himself and wanted to become like God. He disobeyed God's command
and consequently suffered the penalty of death. As a result all his
descendants are dead. Dead people, however, cannot make themselves
live; only God's Spirit can do that. They, like Adam, cannot fulfil God's
will, for in sinning Adam withdrew from the Spirit of God, and where the
Spirit of God is absent there is death and powerlessness to do good.
Zwingli summarizes his discussion of sin in four points. Apart from a brief
reference to the sin against the Holy Spirit, which he interprets as unbelief,
and sin as the sacrifice for sin, he speaks in effect of original and actual sin.
There is sin as the weakness, defect, or sickness of a corrupt nature; it is
also called the flesh. As a result of this we are unable to do good and are
children of wrath. Then there are those sins that grow like branches out of
this sickness or defect, and come out of the corrupt flesh, as from a
spring.[33] Later Zwingli underlines the nature of man's sinfulness by insisting that Genesis 8: 21, if properly translated, states that the thoughts of the
heart are evil, not, as in the Vulgate, that they tend to evil, a translation
which leads some to speak of man's free will. The truth is that man is in his
very nature evil.[34]

[32] Z II 33.7–9.
[33] Z II 33.9–38.18 (esp. 33.11, 18–20, 38.6–13, 34.27–31, 35.32–36.2, 28–32) and 43.19–45.34.
See also Z II 162.34–163.6, 32–5. In *An Exposition of the Articles* Zwingli thinks it more probable
that the unbaptized children of Christian parents are not damned than that they are. (Z II
455.18–456.3.) This could indicate that he already distinguishes original sin and original guilt,
although at this stage that might seem inconsistent with the limitation to Christian parents.
Payne (p. 42) stresses Erasmus's preference for using the word 'sin' for personal or actual sins.
Zwingli differs clearly from Erasmus in his stress on man's total depravity. The voluntarist stress
links Zwingli with Scotus. Pfister notes that, with the schoolmen, Zwingli teaches the unity of
Adam with the human race, but that like Scotus and unlike Augustine and Aquinas he does not
explore the inheriting of sin through procreation (*Das Problem des Erbsünde*, pp. 7 and 71).
[34] Z II 98.31–100.3.

The discussion of sin in *A Short Christian Introduction* is also set in the context of salvation. It is concerned with the origin of sin, precisely so that we may see ourselves to be sinners and yield ourselves to God's mercy.[35] We are all sinners and are all dead, as we are all born of Adam; and a sinner and dead man cannot give birth to one who is not a sinner or who is alive. The death moreover is not only bodily, but is also the loss of the grace and friendship of God, of the indwelling and leading of the Spirit of God, so that Adam and his descendants with their corrupt nature can do nothing good. We are therefore by nature children of wrath. Sin is an inborn sickness and a powerlessness, which bears evil fruit. It comes from Adam's inordinate desire, his wanting to be like God.[36] After the section on sin, and before the section on the gospel, comes an exposition of law. Without the law we do not know about sin (and as children we live without the law), but the law shows us what sin is. Through it we learn our sickness and powerlessness, and as only the blameless can come to God, we despair of coming to him of ourselves. Then it is that God's grace in Christ is made known to us.[37]

The understanding of sin in the early Zwingli is completed in *A Commentary*. It is striking that in the chapter on man, the whole concern is with man as sinner. Sin is dealt with as much there as in the later chapter on sin. Man indeed is so profoundly sinful that only God can enable him to know himself.[38] As before, Zwingli draws largely on Genesis and Romans. Sin is rooted in the fall in which Adam sought to be equal with God and which led at once to the death of the soul. Now, however, there is a stress on the fact both that this sprang out of self-love—not that that was the nature given to him by God—and that the resulting disease of man is most fittingly described as self-love. There is the same twofold understanding of sin. It is 'that disease which we contract from the author of our race, in consequence of which we are given over to love of ourselves', and 'transgression of the law'; 'sin that is transgression is born of the sin that is disease'. Zwingli again stresses the totality of sin which has infected the whole man. From this position he attacks the notion of free will, pointing out of Adam that 'on no reasonable inference does it seem likely that one who was so bent upon running away and hiding that he could scarcely be dragged out would have returned if the Lord had not followed him up in

---

[35] Z II 630.30–3.
[36] Z II 631.3–8, 13–25, 632.27–633.9.
[37] Z II 635.29–636.6, 25–30.
[38] Z III 655.12–13, 27–8. Cf. 'Tam ergo necessaria est fides homini ad sui cognitionem quam ad dei.' 'Solius divini spiritus est, ut homo sese cognoscat.' (Z III 661.18–19, 692.21–2.)

MAN                                   149

his flight'. The sin against the Holy Spirit, which is never forgiven is lack of
faith 'for it never lays hold of or worships God'.[39]

Zwingli's writings up to this point show him as affirming strongly the
Augustinian and Lutheran view of the total corruption of sin, although
some of his accents are different from theirs. The fall arose from the desire
to be equal with God, but also from self-love. From being in communion
with God, and under the guidance of the Spirit, Adam lost the favour of
God and the power of the Spirit. His life after the fall was one of death,
powerlessness, and self-love. Self-love corresponds with concupiscence in
Luther, though in the earliest writings the stress in Zwingli is on death and
powerlessness, rather than self-love. (There is frequent reference to
original sin as self-love in Zwingli's later writings.)[40] Because of the fall the
descendants of Adam are dead and sinful. The sin born in them is
described as disease or weakness. It affects the whole of man, so that he is
not able of himself to do anything good. It is out of sin as disease that sin as
transgression flows. The whole discussion of sin is related to salvation in
Christ and is in strong opposition to the scholastic and Erasmian understanding of what man can do.[41]

Zwingli's controversy with the anabaptists led to an important re-
expression of his doctrine of sin. In *Baptism, Rebaptism, and Infant Baptism* in
May 1525 he stresses sin as voluntary transgression of the law and
distinguishes original sin from original guilt. (Against the anabaptists he
argues for the baptism of infants. The traditional view of baptism is that it
deals with original sin, a view that is inconsistent with Zwingli's symbolic
understanding of baptism. As a result he has to consider whether children
have original sin and, if so, whether and how they can be saved.) The excursus begins with the statement that original sin is a *präst*, or defect, which a
person has from birth without his own guilt, whereas sin is an act done of
one's own choice. Original sin which is inborn in us 'is a defect which of
itself is not sinful in the one who has it. It also cannot damn him, whatever
the theologians say, until out of this defect he does something against the
law of God. But he does not do anything against the law, until he knows the
law.' Zwingli supports this position with a series of references to Romans,
especially 'Knowledge of sin comes through the law' (3: 20) and

---

[39] Z III 654.27–667.29 and 706.34–723.20, esp. 657.3–4, 18–27, 664.33–5, 708.10–13 (*Works* III
138), 19–21, 709.36–7, 661.20–5, 658.9–16, 667.5–12 (*Works* III 89), 721.25–8.
[40] For Aquinas, as for Augustine, self-love is the cause of sin. Zwingli uses the term *con-
cupiscentia* in the sense of self-love. (Z III 712.7–9.)
[41] Zwingli uses the word *präst* (Latin *morbus*), for which various translations are possible:
sickness, disease, lack, defect. See Pfister, *Das Problem der Erbsünde*, pp. 23–5. Locher prefers the
translation 'incurable breach' (*Zwingli's Thought*, pp. 202–3).

'Where there is no law, there is also no transgression' (4: 15). Therefore 'the children of believers cannot be damned on account of original sin, as long as they do not know the law'. Zwingli also quotes the words from Ezekiel, 'The son shall not bear the guilt of the father' (18: 20) and 'The soul that sins shall die' (18: 4). In other words 'the child is not damned for the father's sin', though he has the defect out of which, when we know the law, sin springs.[42]

Zwingli is then forced to reformulate his doctrine of original sin in response to Luther's attack on his position as Pelagian and in reply to a letter from Urbanus Rhegius in Augsburg.[43] *Original Sin* (August 1526) examines the terms for sin and original sin, considers the appropriate name for original sin, indicating how and whom it damns, and shows that it cannot be cured by any other medicine than the blood of Christ. Zwingli uses the word 'disease' (*morbus*) for original sin, but not in the sense of something temporary, in contrast to a defect (*vitium*) which is lasting. 'I use it as combined with a defect and that a lasting one, as when stammering, blindness, or gout is hereditary in a family . . . On account of such a thing no one is thought the worse or the more vicious. For such things, which come from nature, cannot be put down as crimes or guilt.' He draws an analogy between our condition following Adam's sin and that of someone born a slave whose ancestors had been taken prisoners of war and who were not killed, but graciously saved as long as they and their descendants were slaves. He supports this with the words of Paul, 'Death reigned from Adam to Moses, even over those who had not sinned in the way that Adam did' (Rom. 5: 14). From this he argues that Adam did what caused the penalty of death to be inflicted on his descendants. The word 'sin' may be used for the resulting disease or defect, as Paul used it, for example in Romans 7: 17, as long as one then understands by sin 'a condition and penalty, the disaster and misery of corrupted human nature, not a crime or guilt on the part of those who are born in the condition of sin and death'. Zwingli states that he is not, however, 'contending for a name'.[44]

---

[42] Z IV 307.11–312.4 and 315.10–25, esp. 307.16–21, 308.26–30, 309.30–310.2, 311.30–1, 315.15–21. 'So vil kurtzlich von der erbsünd, dass sy ein präst ist und nit ein schuld, ein straff der ersten misstat, nit ein eigne missthat eins yeden.' (Z IV 312.3–4.) Scotus's voluntarist understanding of sin probably lies behind Zwingli's emphasis on sin as voluntary transgression of the law.

[43] Luther commented, 'Zwingli hat niemals Christus erkannt, denn er irrt im Hauptartikel, nämlich dass die Erbsünde keine Sünde sei. Wäre dem so, wie leicht könnte der freie Wille bejaht werden!' (Z V 359–60.)

[44] Z V 370.23–7, 371.11–372.3 (*Works* II 4–5), 372.4–373.29 (*Works* II 6). Zwingli makes the scholastic distinction between original and actual sin. See, e.g., Z V 376.25–7 and XIII 38.32–5. 'The flesh, then, is one thing, its works another, and the flesh is not sin, but that which the flesh

When he turns to the question whether original sin damns, he makes a varied response. He defends his earlier statement that it does, by referring to its nature and force. 'From a sinner we are all descended as sinners. If sinners, therefore enemies of God; if enemies, therefore also damned.' However, the statement has to be qualified in various ways. He does not accept the view that it damns those who have not been baptized, affirming that salvation depends on election not on baptism. But, with particular reference to the children of Christian parents, he argues that their condition is similar to that of those descended from Abraham. Jacob, for example, was beloved by God before he was born and therefore original sin could not have damned him. Zwingli supports this with reference to the covenant in Genesis 17: 7 with Abraham's seed, which includes the children of Christian parents, 'If, therefore, he promises that he will be a God to Abraham's seed, that seed cannot have been damned because of original guilt . . .'. A further argument relates more directly to the work of Christ as making good the evil done by Adam, a point made in relation to Romans 5: 19–21. This could have led Zwingli to affirm that the whole race, and not just the church of believers, was restored, but he is held back from that by some points against it and by not knowing whether anyone else has held it. Certainly it applies to the children of Christians, as they are within the covenant. Then he returns to the quite separate argument that as long as children are too young to know the law they cannot transgress the law and consequently are not damned.[45]

With varieties of emphasis this remains Zwingli's position. It is the nature of original sin taken by itself to damn, for it leads to actual sin. However, Christ has made good what Adam did. He has obtained salvation from original and actual sin, so that it does not damn those who trust in him, or their children. This approach seems to imply original guilt, as the argument from Christ's work is used for the children of Christian parents who have not committed actual sin. However, this approach helps to satisfy the concern to relate salvation at every point to Christ. The other approach stresses the relationship between transgression and damnation, and between knowledge of the law and transgression. This emphasis, with its distinction between original sin and original guilt, recedes in the later Zwingli, while the doctrine of election, which gains importance in this

doeth is sin. The flesh, therefore, the disposition of man, the original defect or sin, this propensity, is that which desires things contrary to the Spirit.' (Z V 377.16–20 (*Works* II 10).)

[45] Z V 380.31–2, 377.31–3, 384.30–4, 385.23–386.2 (*Works* II 20), 387.16–20, 387.32–389.26, 390.5–12. Zwingli's main emphasis is on the Anselmian view of the atonement. In this context, however, the Irenaean view is stressed. The combination of the two in *An Account of the Faith* is instructive. (Z VI ii 794.31–800.15.)

period, is used to reject the view that would damn those who have not been baptized. It is bound up with the idea of covenant, but Zwingli explicitly relates the immunity of infants from original sin not 'to the holiness of their parents, but to that of God who elects'. After making this point he goes on to say that Christ makes good what Adam did. These points are also related because both election and Christ's restoration come from the goodness of God.[46]

The fourth of the Marburg articles which Zwingli signed does not involve a contradiction of his position, though it does not express it unequivocally. Zwingli does hold that original sin damns, if you consider its nature and if you do not relate it to the work of Christ. However, Zwingli's position is more subtle than that bald statement. The article does not include the distinction he makes, at least sometimes, between original sin and original guilt, nor his insistence that there is no damnation until there is transgression. However, since salvation depends on election and election is in Christ, the article does cohere with his basic theological position. In the conversation with Melanchthon beforehand, Zwingli included in his agreed summary a reference to the fact that there is no law for children, but the punishment of the law with damns.[47]

Although *An Account of the Faith* is an anti-Lutheran work, it does not show a fundamentally different understanding of original sin from the Marburg articles. The statement is longer, which enables Zwingli to rehearse his views of the fall as springing from self-love and the desire to be equal with God. God made man a slave, although he could have punished him with death; and since then all his descendants have been born in slavery. Original sin is not properly speaking a sin, as there has been no transgression of the law, but a disease. However, following Paul, it can be called a sin—indeed 'such a sin that those born therein are God's enemies and adversaries'. We die because of Adam's sin and guilt. 'I know that we are by nature the children of wrath, but I doubt not that we are received among the sons of God by grace, which through the second Adam, Christ, has restored what was lost in the fall.' This restoring of the whole human race in Christ means that one must not regard the children of the heathen as damned, quite apart from the fact that salvation depends on God's

[46] Z V 387.27-31, 384.13-15.

[47] The article reads: 'das die erbsünd sye uns von Adam angeboren und ufgeerbet und sye ein soeliche sünd, das sy alle menschen verdamnet, unnd wo Jesus Christus uns nit zuo hilff kommen were mit sinem tod und laeben, so hettend wir ewig daran sterben und zuo gottes rych und saeligkeyt nit kommen muessen.' (Z VI ii 521.20-4.) His own form of words, after reference to original sin as disease, includes the statement: 'In parvulis non est lex, sed pęna legis, quę tale malum sive peccatum est, ut damnet.' (Z VI ii 507.11-12)

election. However, we can be sure of the election of the children of Christian parents, the implication being that they will not be damned by original sin.[48]

Like the other reformers, Zwingli understands man from the experience of salvation in Christ. It is this that enables him to see how fundamentally untrue is man's own understanding of himself. Moreover he gives his account of man precisely in order to help men to see their need of salvation. This helps to explain why man's sinfulness plays a more important part in Zwingli's thought than man as made in the image of God, although the latter is presupposed, especially when it is interpreted in terms of the law of nature. Like Augustine and Luther, he affirms man's total corruption and his incapacity to contribute to his own salvation. This insistence on man's total corruption is to be understood in opposition to the medieval stress on works and the emphasis in Erasmus and others on man's free will. Zwingli distances himself from scholasticism here, although he is indebted to the schoolmen at other points, not least in his distinction between original and actual sin and the voluntarist stress in his understanding of sin.[49]

Zwingli's view of man is at heart a biblical, not to say Pauline, one, but throughout his writings there is also a Greek dualist view of man, which emphasizes the contrast of body and soul. This affects some ways he has of speaking of the image of God in man and the origin of man's sinfulness, but it does not fundamentally alter his view of man, which is determined by his understanding of salvation in Christ. The Greek view does, however, influence for him the way word and sacraments mediate that salvation, although a more important factor even then is Zwingli's emphasis on the sovereignty of God.

[48] Z VI ii 796.31–800.15, especially 796.31–798.6 (Jackson 459; *Works* II 40), 798.28–9, 798.38–799.24 (Jackson 461; *Works* II 42).

[49] See Pfister, *Das Problem der Erbsünde*, pp. 63–73, for an account of the points of comparison and contrast between Augustine, Aquinas, Duns Scotus, and Zwingli. Köhler affirms the influence of Origen on Zwingli's view (Köhler, 'Die neuere Zwingli–Forschung', p. 364).

# 7. Salvation

FUNDAMENTAL to Zwingli's understanding of salvation is that it is from God and in God. He saw the teaching and practice of the medieval church as radically opposed to this. His concern, which was that of pastor and theologian, was to re-express the centrality of God in the salvation of mankind.[1]

The debate about election was an aspect, but by no means the whole, of his argument that salvation is from God. Salvation lies deep in the purpose and election of God, and a proper grasp of this makes it clear that salvation has to do ultimately with God and not with our response of faith.[2] Salvation, however, does not merely have to do with God's will, through which we were elected before the foundation of the world, but it has to do with Christ. It is he who is our salvation. Christ moreover is not simply the one in whom we were elected, in a sense that lies above or before history, but he is the one whose incarnation, death, and resurrection have made salvation possible. Salvation is related to the incarnation or to the death or resurrection of Christ, though most characteristically to his death.[3] The salvation accomplished through Christ is brought home to us by the Spirit; and so the work of salvation is seen as altogether from God—Father, Son, and Spirit.[4]

It is primarily, though not only, against his catholic opponents that Zwingli affirmed that salvation is of God.[5] It is from God's word, not man's.[6] Those who seek it other than in God are seeking it in the creature,

[1] In the exposition of article 16 Zwingli points out that we can do nothing without the Spirit. If we wish to receive the Spirit we must pray to God, and as soon as we call on him God will be present and enable us to believe and do what pleases him. It is all of God, who causes us to call on him in the first place. (Z II 89.19–90.7.)

[2] Z VI i 172.6–174.24.

[3] Z I 396.11–18; II 40.20–8, 246.23–5; III 700.16–18; S VI ii 47.6–9, 63.39–44. His merits are described as the sole cause of our salvation. (Z II 579.39–580.8.) He is the author of man's salvation. (S VI i 687.38–41.) He is in fact salvation. (Z II 79.18–20, 82.9–11.) The sum of salvation is to believe in Christ, the Son of God, and to know the benefit that we receive from his death. (S VI i 749.29–30.) In A Reply to Emser, after asking, 'What is the whole new testament but the firm and sure confirmation of the grace of God?' Zwingli at once refers to Christ as our salvation and our only way to the Father. (Z III 271.26–272.8.)

[4] Z II 89.32–90.3; S VI i 553.13–16, 569.11–15. Cf. Z I 366.30–3 where the reference to God drawing us is related to the Spirit.

[5] Salvation does not come from outward things, but from the Spirit, and therefore not from the sacraments. In this context Zwingli opposed Lutherans and anabaptists as well as catholics. (Z XIII 106.32–4; S VI i 383.39–384.7, 386.18–20.)          [6] Z I 382.20–31.

whether on earth or in heaven.[7] The term 'creature' embraces anyone or anything that is not God: images, saints,[8] the pope,[9] or ourselves, whether our vows, our works, or our merit.[10] All this is quite simply idolatry, for it is turning not to God, but to the creature for help and refuge. It is the mark of those who do not believe in God.[11]

## The Gospel and the New Life

Whereas the sixty-seven articles placed the gospel at the beginning of the disputation, for that was the centre of the conflict, A Commentary made it the climax of a discussion about God, man, and religion.[12] After sections on God and man Zwingli describes the relation between the two in the story of Adam: man's turning from God, the source of all good, his hiding from God and not daring to appear in his presence, and God's pursuing man, who would never have come back to him of his own accord. The initiative was entirely God's, and through it man saw both the wretchedness of his own condition and the grace of God.[13] This in effect

---

[7] Z VI i 271.21–8; S VI i 553.8–16. The distinction can be made—as it has been at least since the first half of the nineteenth century—between Zwingli's attack on idolatry, ascribing to the creature what belongs to the creator, and Luther's attack on works. The first is a paganizing, the second a judaizing of the church. On the positive side Zwingli's emphasis is on giving God alone the glory and Luther's on justification by faith. See Guggisberg, pp. 212–13. The attack on idolatry, which is characteristic of Zwingli, includes an attack on works. See, e.g. Z III 50.11–51.1.

[8] Z II 656.15–27. In the period before the reformation there seems to have been an immense increase in images, processions, and pilgrimages in Zurich. According to Farner (III 19–20), the increase in images was a hundredfold. Zwingli's attack on idolatry needs to be set in this context.

[9] At the end of A Commentary , after quoting Jer. 2: 13, Zwingli writes, 'Vicarium Christo subrogavimus, quem et nostra stulticia audiendum dei loco decrevimus.' (Z III 910.34–5.) Cf. Z III 61.25–62.10; VIII 207.23–208.13.

[10] Z II 271.20–272.20; S VI i 258.34–9; VI ii 133.6–8.

[11] Z IV 89.10–33. Opposition to idolatry is a fundamental element in Zwingli's theology. His attack on it is announced in the sixty-seven articles, where he affirms that God forgives sins through Christ alone and that it is idolatry to ascribe this other than to God. (Z I 463.28–464.2.) Trusting in money is also idolatry. (Z II 219.12–14.) By contrast the believer hangs on God and his word alone, just as a faithful wife listens only to her husband. (Z III 669.16–670.8.) A person who seeks grace other than in God is not a Christian. (Z II 646.6–10.)

[12] This exposition of the gospel is drawn from the sections on religion, the Christian religion, the gospel, and repentance. (Z III 665–706.) The many definitions of the gospel in Zwingli all centre in Christ and his dealing with our sins. 'The gospel is the pledge and certainty of the mercy of God: Christ Jesus.' 'As he has given him for us, there is no sinner so great, that he can despair of God, when he sees that he has given his Son for us.' 'That briefly is the sum of the gospel, namely: that God has given us a saviour and redeemer for our sin, his only begotten Son.' 'Thus Christ is the message, the messenger himself, the pledge of grace, the reconciler, and reconciles himself. Therefore this word "believe in the gospel" is nothing other than: believe in Christ, trust in Christ, rely on the grace of Christ.' (Z IV 64.18–19, 66.2–4, 25–7, 68.31–4.) Cf. S VI ii 245.29–31.

[13] In his exposition of Gen. 3: 9 Zwingli refers to God's showing man to himself, so that he knows his disobedience and misery, and at the same time showing his own generosity, so that man, from despairing, trusts in God's grace. (Z XIII 26.14–23.)

foreshadowed God's initiative in Christ. Man could not satisfy God's righteousness, although some people are sufficiently ignorant of God's righteousness and their own unrighteousness to imagine that they can satisfy God with so-called good works. Therefore God in his goodness found a way to be merciful and to satisfy his righteousness—in Christ. Christ is thus man's restorer as well as creator. In that context Zwingli opened the discussion of the gospel by saying what it is (sins are forgiven in Christ's name) and what it does (it saves the believer). Repentance goes with this forgiveness; and the knowledge of oneself, which leads to repentance, comes from the Spirit.

The gospel, however, is not simply a way of dealing with man's past, an ending of the estrangement between man and God, it has to do with creating a new man. (In his earliest reformation writing Zwingli spoke of the preaching of the gospel as firing people with the love of God and neighbour.[14]) Zwingli even said that it would have been better not to send a redeemer at all than to send one and then for us not to change.[15] The call to repentance that goes with the gospel is a call to a complete change of life. (The section on repentance in A Commentary immediately follows that on the gospel.) Repentance moreover is a constant feature of the Christian life, not simply something which marks its beginning. (This is elaborated in the discussion of law and sin which concludes the first and fundamental part of A Commentary.)

The stress on repentance, however, must be seen with Zwingli's strong and persistent emphasis on the new life. In his exposition of 'Put on the Lord Jesus Christ' (Rom. 13: 14), he stated that through one's whole life one should live and act as Christ did, adding that it is Christ who does this in us, so that we are conformed to his living image. He concluded with the words 'the life of a Christian is nothing other than acknowleding oneself a sinner, trusting in God's mercy through Christ, and building a life in holiness and innocence according to Christ's example'.[16]

---

[14] Z I 88.10–89.2. Cf. Z I 259.25–8. The stress on love is important, even if not as pronounced as in Bucer.

[15] Cf. the comment on John 6: 57: 'Mundum veni modo redimere, sed etiam mutare. Qui ergo me fidunt, ad meum exemplum vitam suam transformabunt.' (S VI i 716.43–5.) The passage almost exactly reproduces the words in A Commentary. (Z III 781.20–7.)

[16] S VI ii 126.12–29. Cf. S VI i 568.27–31. References to living an innocent or blameless life are frequent. (S VI i 246.14–18, 645.44–47; VI ii 129.1–3.) The Christian does not simply put on the new man once for all, but must change his life every day or else he mocks the name of Christ. (Z III 19.1–29.) 'Vide obiter, an Christiana vita sit perpetua poenitentia necne?' (Z III 717.25.) The Christian life is also an unceasing battle, but we win if we do not forsake Christ the head. (Z III 910.21–4.)

Zwingli deals with the objection that faith in the grace of Christ makes people indifferent to sin. For him such faith is not real. He compares the Christian with someone who has broken his leg. He does not feel he can go on breaking it, simply because he has found a doctor who can cure it. Rather he remembers the pain he experienced when it was broken. 'So those, who when they hear that Christ has made atonement for the sins of all, exultantly exclaim, "We will sin, for all things are freely pardoned through Christ," have never felt the pain of sin.'[17]

The stress on the new life is characteristic of Zwingli. It emerges in all his writings, whether in extended expositions or in passing comments, and is expressed in a wide variety of ways. It is seen in opposition to anabaptists, whom Zwingli accused of talking, rather than living, the life of Christ, and catholics, whom he accused of cutting the Christian life off from its source in Christ.[18]

The example of Christ, so important in humanist circles, remained part of Zwingli's theology as a reformer, but living in accordance with Christ's example was the gift of God and not the goal of human striving.

All the writings of the apostles are filled with this idea, that the Christian religion is nothing else than a firm hope in God through Jesus Christ and a blameless life wrought after the pattern of Christ as far as he gives us.

To be a Christian is not to blather about Christ, but to walk as he walked.[19]

The purpose indeed of Christ's coming is that we may be like him.[20] However, it is not simply a likeness to Christ that is intended. Zwingli spoke of our being deified or being changed into God. This is the work of the Spirit, so that Christ lives in us, or, as he also says, the Spirit of Christ or God lives in us.[21]

It is the fact that Christ, or the Spirit, or God is in the believer that leads to the transformation of his life.

---

[17] Z III 700.19–701.28, *Works* III 130–1. Cf. the link between faith and the new life in his comment on Rom. 6: 4, 'Christiana ergo vita fiducia est firma in deum per Christum, et innovatio vitae in Christo, carnis mortificatio etc.' (S VI ii 95.24–6.)

[18] S VI ii 271.8–21. Köhler points to the connection Zwingli makes between justification and the living of the Christian life as early as his use of Origen in the marginal notes on Romans ('Die Randglossen', p. 95).

[19] Z III 705.7–10 (*Works* III 135); III 407.18–19.

[20] S VI ii 330.6–12.

[21] See the exposition of the thirteenth article. (Z II 72.14–73.18.) This idea comes both early and late in Zwingli. A later example is in *The Resurrection and Ascension of Christ*: 'Aeternus dei filius descendit, et naturam nostram adsumit in se, ut per gratiam eius innovati, in divinam quodammodo naturam assumpti, ascendamus . . . Factus est homo, ut nos per gratiam suam in deos quodammodo transformaret.' (S VI ii 56.7–14.)

The believer does the commands out of love; the godless hates them. The believer does not do them in his own strength, but God effects in him love, counsel, work, as much as he does.

Our works are good in so far as they are of Christ . . .

Our works therefore are good in so far as they are gifts of God and are done from the Spirit of God.[22]

They may equally be said to be of God because the faith out of which they spring is the gift of God.[23]

Zwingli's attack on works, like Luther's, is an attack on works that are held to be good, but are not (either because they do not arise from faith or because they are not commanded by God),[24] but also an attack on regarding our works as the basis of our salvation or standing with God. In *A Commentary* Zwingli criticizes the scholastic idea of doing what is in us by showing how far from truly good such works are.[25] These are rejected, however, in order that people may do truly good works, which come from living faith. Only works that come from faith in God are good works, for it is through faith that a man becomes good and it is from a good man that good works come. It is in effect the same to say that they are from God as to say that they are from faith.[26] A living faith necessarily leads to good works, just as a good tree cannot but produce good fruit.[27] Faith is active in love, and where there is no love then it is certain there is no faith.[28] Indeed true faith can no more exist without love or good works than fire without heat.[29] Zwingli went so far as to speak of love or works as a sign of election

---

[22] Z II 237.14–17, 238.27–239.3; S VI i 349.29–30. Within seven lines Zwingli speaks—in this context—of Christ, God, and the Spirit of God. (Z II 47.25–31.) The sense of the new life as coming from Christ's living in the believer is present in Zwingli's earliest reformation writings. (Z I 118. 22–5.) The new life is also the work of the Spirit in us, so that without him we become worse every day. It is necessary for us to be renewed every day, because we sin every day. (S VI i 333. 40–4.)

[23] S VI i 697.42–4.

[24] S VI i 520.19–21, 519.26–9. These two may be distinguished although they are ultimately one. See the discussion in *An Exposition of the Faith* (S IV 61.9–62.8). Zwingli refers to the importance of the right intention in what others do for us, and argues that it is similar in what is done for God. It must spring out of faith—and those with faith look to God's will or law as their standard in everything. He attacks the good works invented by the papists. Cf. S VI ii 263.38–45.

[25] Z III 678.35–680.11. Zwingli gives half a dozen reasons to show why those doing even a godly work like almsgiving do not do it in such a way as to deserve reward from an impartial judge. Moreover the idea of doing what is in us makes Christ superfluous.

[26] Z III 849.36–7; S VI ii 220.21–6.

[27] Z I 118.21–25; III 383.18–23; S IV 63.39–42; VI ii 272.3–7. Cf. S VI i 217.8–10, 525.22–3. See Additional Note 1, pp. 167–8.

[28] Z III 44.10–14; S VI i 655.9–10; VI ii 175.33–7, 220.26, 271.30–8. The Christian life is described as nothing but love. 'Vita vero Christiana, quid in universum est, quam charitas?' (Z III 742.13–14.) In Z II 43.15–17 Zwingli insists that there is no faith without both hope and love.

[29] S IV 63.14–15; VI i 348.48–349.3; VI ii 272.3–7. The link between faith and the new life is

and faith, and their absence—at least humanly speaking—as making it certain that election and faith are not present. However, Zwingli also recognized that hypocrites do many outwardly good works without faith, and therefore he denied that faith is present because works are present.[30]

Zwingli recognized early in controversy with catholics that just as there were more passages of scripture that ascribed salvation to works than those that ascribed it to faith, so there were passages that spoke of God's rewarding our works. He pointed out that the believer is a son, not a slave, and therefore he does not work for a reward but simply to the glory of God, leaving the matter with God.[31] Moreover, where God gives and promises something to our works, he is doing it to his own work, for he gives the will and the deed.[32]

*Righteousness and Faith*

Righteousness in Zwingli is set within an Anselmian view of the atonement. After a ten-point comparison between Christ and Adam in *A Commentary*, Zwingli refers to Paul's comparisons in Romans 5 saying that they show

how the divine righteousness has been appeased for us by the righteousness of Christ alone. For his innocence, given to us, has become as much ours as the life which we also derived from him ... As life, I say, was given to us from him, so also was righteousness, which has been made ours from him and through him; for from him we are all that we are. He put on flesh that he might become ours. He had no need of it, but we had the greatest need of him. To become one of us, therefore, he, great God that he is, righteous, holy, merciful, creator, became man, that we through his fellowship might be raised to gods.[33]

It is through Christ's righteousness (and not a righteousness from our own works) that we come to God, and his righteousness becomes ours because 'he is our head and we are his members'.[34]

In *Philippians*, where Zwingli expounds 'not having my own righteousness' he speaks of two kinds of righteousness, the one of the law and the

expressed in other ways. Thus, if we truly believe that it is the Son of God who is nailed on the cross for us and who has freed us from the death of sin, then we shall certainly be transformed into other men. (*Z* III 257.9-18.)

[30] *S* VI ii 259.5-8, 274.7-12. See also *S* VI i 349.41-3, 364.4-9, 706.20-2; VI ii 115.13-14. In *S* VI i 391.25-31 works are a sign to others of a person's faith (and hence his election). However, he sees them as a sign to oneself and others in *The Providence of God*. (*Z* VI iii 184.9-15.) The believer knows himself saved, because his faith in the gospel gives him such certainty with God, whereas he cannot be certain of others, as they may be hypocrites. (*Z* IV 301.3-10.) But see *Z* XIV 708.5-17.

[31] *Z* III 44.15-25.

[32] *Z* V 278.19-24; XIII 170.12-24; *S* VI ii 81.17-22. See Additional Note 2, p. 168.

[33] *Z* III 684.36-685.7; *Works* III 110-11.          [34] *Z* II 235.35-236.12.

other of God. The righteousness of God or of Christ has to do with Christ's righteous dying and making satisfaction for us. This righteousness becomes ours through faith, which is from the Spirit of God alone and not from anything created; and it is by this righteousness that we are, and are reputed, righteous before God. The righteousness therefore of Christians is to trust in Christ and to be adopted into him. In this Paul attributed nothing to himself.[35]

In the later commentary on Matthew a fundamentally similar view is expressed, although with greater emphasis on the renewal of the believer's life. Zwingli refers to the righteousness with which we are able to stand before God as the righteousness of faith. He also speaks of two kinds of righteousness. The first is an outward righteousness (with men), expressed in works and ceremonies. The other is the righteousness of God by which a man is inwardly pure and holy and does good from the heart. It involves the renewing of a person's spirit and mind. God gives this righteousness through his Son and the Spirit, and it is a righteousness that expresses itself outwardly. However, the person who is righteous in this way is displeased even with his good works and sees how impure the things are that he does. When he has done all he has been commanded, he knows himself to be an unprofitable servant and a sinner. So far is he from trusting his own righteousness that he always prays: 'Father, forgive us our trespasses'.[36]

For Zwingli, however, righteousness is never simply imputed. It is also imparted. Christ does not only teach true righteousness, but also bestows it, and the righteousness he bestows and teaches is described in *A Friendly Exegesis* as inward righteousness, which is the same as the Spirit. Christ also gives outward righteousness, which flows from inward righteousness.[37] In this way the righteousness of Christ is never simply an atonement for our sins, it is the initial and continuing source of a life like Christ's. In this it is like faith which does not simply rely on the righteousness of Christ rather than human righteousness, but also, because of its source in God, overflows in love and good works.

From the beginning Zwingli affirmed that faith comes from God and not from human understanding.[38] Moreover it does not come from

---

[35] *S* VI ii 215.46–216.9.     [36] *S* VI i 203.15–34, 260.6–35.

[37] *Z* V 625.21–8. Zwingli used the words *Rechtmachung* and *Rechtwerdung*. (*Z* II 29.29–30.1, 172.22–7, 642.6–12.) In *Romans* the reference is to 'quomodo homo reddatur iustus apud deum' (*S* VI ii 78.12–14), whereas in *St John* it is 'tamen quia credunt, iusti censentur' (*S* VI i 753.42–6). In *The Providence of God* he wrote, 'sic enim "iustificandi" verbo pro "absolvendi" utuntur Hebraei. Nunc ergo quae alia est iustificatio nisi fidei?' (*Z* VI iii 178.20–2.) His translation, which seems to lay a greater stress on being righteous, does not allow that justification is other than of faith.

[38] Zwingli said this about Mary's faith in God's promise in his sermon on the Virgin Mary in

anything outward (whether word, sacrament, or miracle), but only from God. It is true that we may need to have preachers, but they do not make the heart believe. That is the work of God, and in particular the work of the Holy Spirit.[39] As Zwingli developed his doctrine of election, the fact that faith comes from God was expressed with new force, since only those believe who have been chosen and drawn by God.[40] In no sense is faith at man's disposal; it is always the gift of God.

Faith in Zwingli is always fundamentally faith in God—not of course faith in God as opposed to faith in Christ, but faith in God as opposed to faith in anyone or anything that is not God. His concern here was theological and pastoral, for putting faith in something other than God (like seeking salvation other than in God) imperils men's souls.[41] Even faith in Christ is faith in him as God and not as man, for faith in Christ as man would be faith in the creature rather than in God.[42] In his frequent quotation of Hebrews 11 Zwingli stressed the contrast between things invisible, meaning God, and things visible, meaning anything created. In that context he said that where we are pointed to Christ it is because he is God and man. No one should be pointed to his humanity, for he himself said, 'Whoever trusts in me, trusts not in me', that is, he should not trust in Christ as far as he is a man.[43]

---

1522. Five years later he returned to the same example in the eucharistic controversy with Luther, when he distinguished between words that promise and words that do not. He contrasted our trusting in words that promise and our simply believing those that teach or command. (Z I 410.25–411.18; V 783.11–785.28.) On Zwingli's understanding of faith Köhler says 'Das Herzstück von Zwingli's Theologie ist der Glaube' ('Zwingli als Theologe', p. 62).

[39] Z II 111.9–11; III 42.11–20; IV 227.28–228.2; VI ii 206.23–207.4; XIV 340.28–9; S VI i 248.28–9; VI ii 233.5–6. Faith is not a matter of our choice, as if the gospel were guaranteed by the church, for then we should choose it either because so many others do or because the pope and bishops affirm it to be right and good. (Z IV 67.21–68.2.) Faith and the increase of faith come from God. It is all of God, who knows, as we do not, why he gives faith at once to some, but more slowly to others. (Z II 182.8–13, 183.12–16.)

[40] Z V 781.21–7. Zwingli refers here to John 6, where there is a reference to being drawn, but not to being elected. (Z VI i 172.14–173.6.)

[41] See, e.g., the opening articles of the first disputation. After expounding the substance of the gospel in Christ, Zwingli declared, 'Hence Christ is the only way to salvation for all who ever were, are and shall be' and 'Who seeks or points out another door errs, yea, he is a murderer of souls and a thief.' (Z I 458.13–19; Selected Works, 111.)

Faith as trust in the promises and mercy of God is an element in Erasmus, although he also understands it as assent, and justification for him was not by faith alone. See Payne, p. 86–7. Already in Einsiedeln, in the light of Erasmus, Zwingli interprets faith in Heb. 11: 1 as trust: 'fides hic pro fiducia, qua inconcusse speramus'. (Z XII 102.21.)

[42] Zwingli argued this distinction on the basis of John 12: 44, especially in the eucharistic controversy. (Z V 687.21–9, 782.4–12; VI ii 209.22–210.1.)

[43] Z VI ii 207.26–210.4. Zwingli was of course arguing against Luther's eucharistic views, in particular faith in the bodily eating of the body of Christ.

It has been argued that faith in Zwingli is faith in God rather than in Christ, and that it is characteristically a general faith—in God's providence rather than centred in what God has done in Christ. This is not the case, although Zwingli's accents are not Luther's. There is a strong faith in the providence of God, associated with passages such as Matthew 6: 25–32. But throughout Zwingli's writings, as in the new testament, faith is related both to God and to Christ, and where faith is related to God it is often specifically associated with Christ and his merits.[44]

In an attack on the Lutheran view of the sacraments he states:

Faith is a matter of fact (*rem*), not of knowledge or opinion or imagination. A man, therefore, feels faith within, in his heart; for it is born only when a man begins to despair of himself, and to see that he must trust in God alone. And it is perfected when a man wholly casts himself off and prostrates himself before the mercy of God alone, but in such fashion as to have entire trust in it because of Christ who was given for us. What man of faith can be unaware of this? For then only are you free from sin when the mind trusts itself unwaveringly to the death of Christ and finds rest there.

It is in part because of the certainty of faith that Zwingli rejects the idea that sacraments strengthen faith. Faith does not need the sacraments. 'For if your faith is not so perfect as not to need a ceremonial sign to confirm it, it is not faith. For faith is that by which we rely on the mercy of God unwaveringly, firmly, and singleheartedly, as Paul shows us in many passages.'[45]

Zwingli distinguished justifying and saving faith from what—perhaps following Melanchthon—he sometimes called historical faith, a holding something to be true. Even demons could have historical faith, believing that Christ was born, suffered, and was raised, and that he was Son of God. But they did not believe that this was all for them, for their salvation.[46]

---

[44] Pollet (DTC 3799) suggests that faith is in God rather than in Christ. However, faith in Christ or his merits features in Zwingli's later works as in his earlier ones. (Z II 182.4–8; S VI i 760.13–15; VI ii 112.7–9.) Faith in God is often related to Christ. (Z II 61.23–5; III 760.10–18; S VI i 246.11–13; 282.38–46, 541.44–5; VI ii 129.1–3.) Even a general discussion such as that in *The Providence of God* is specifically related to Christ and his death. (Z VI iii 177.14–16.) Salvation is specifically linked with faith in Christ, e.g., in Z III 694.40–695–4. Faith as trust in the merit of Christ is not opposed, but rather related, to faith in God's providence as ordering all things. (Z II 182.14–19.)

[45] Z III 760.10–18, 761.25–29; *Works* III 182, 184.

[46] S VI i 692.12–32. Zwingli uses the singular ('I' and 'me') and not just the plural ('we' and 'us') in this context, even if he does not use *pro me* here, *pace* Gestrich (p. 108, n. 87). The singular *pro te* is used in Z III 100.28–30. 'Non est igitur satis aut scire aut credere deum talem esse, nisi scias et credas eum tibi talem esse, id est: ut deus tuus sit. Hoc tum fiet, si eum vere colis, amas, si ab eo totus pendes.' (Z XIII 100.28–30.) In an attack on images he asserted, 'It does not save us to know how he was crucified or that he was crucified, but that he was crucified for us, and that he who was crucified is our Lord and God.' (Z IV 121.29–32.)

Saving faith comes only from the Spirit of God, whereas historical faith can come from outward things, such as word and sacrament.[47] Knowledge, as Zwingli used the term, can also correspond with these two kinds of faith, one of which may be preliminary to saving faith, the other being so closely bound up with it that salvation can be summed up in terms of knowledge of God and of oneself. Simple knowledge of God can come from preaching, whereas it is the work of the Spirit that we trust and love the God of whom we have learnt.[48]

There is confidence and certainty in the Zwinglian view of faith, perhaps related in some measure to the place given to Hebrews 10 and 11. (It is notable that the section on faith in *The Providence of God* begins with the quotation of Hebrews 11: 1.) Faith is

the essential thing to the soul, not a cursory notion that pops lightly into a mind that wavers and believes or thinks now this, now something else.
. . . since, I say, faith is this light and food of the soul, nothing else can happen than that faith should be to the just man, that is, the man who thus has faith and security in regard to the goodness of God and his inheritance therein,—that faith should be his life and strength, through devotion to which he is defended against all adversity. But this power is not from man . . . but is from God alone.[49]

In *St Matthew* Zwingli refers to faith as the pledge and seal with which God seals our hearts, speaking of it both as the pledge of the Spirit and as a trust in God's mercy from which no created thing can pluck us. He could speak of faith in this way because it does not come from man, but springs from the action of the Spirit in us and is his gift. Later in the commentary the association of faith and the Spirit is made more explicit. The believer's certainty is related to his receiving the pledge of the Spirit who cries Abba,

[47] '. . . no external things, but only the Holy Spirit can give that faith which is trust in God. The sacraments do not give faith, but only historical faith . . . For it is only those who have been taught inwardly by the Spirit to know the mystery of the divine goodness who can know and believe that Christ suffered for us . . .'. (*S* IV 55.9-20; LCC XXIV 260-1 (*Works* II 254-5).)

[48] 'Cognitio dei et sui ipsius summa est salutis, ut homo cognoscat quam malus, quam impurus sit, ut cognoscat quam bonus sit deus, huncque amplectatur, iuxtaque eius voluntatem ambulet, quae voluntas cognosci debet. Hoc praecipuum est in Christianismo, ut deum agnoscamus, et ei iuxta voluntatem eius serviamus.' (*S* VI ii 220.13-20.) See also *S* VI i 203.27-9; VI ii 224.48-225.3; 324.22-4. Zwingli sometimes makes a distinction between *cognoscere* and *agnoscere* to indicate two kinds of knowing. (*S* VI ii 79.33-6, 80.10-14.) Cf. *S* VI i 649.22-3; VI ii 272.44-273.20. For trust in Christ as the sum of salvation, see, e.g., *Z* V 895.7-9.

[49] *Z* VI iii 169.17-21, 177.16-22; *Works* II 193, 197. It is faith, not the bread, that is food for the soul. In *Hebrews* Zwingli writes on Heb. 11: 1, 'Ea fides cum non nisi doctore spiritu dicitur, ductoreque illo apprehenditur, non constat ex humano ingenio . . . Est ergo fides hoc loci non opinio, arbitrium, vel humana quaedam et frigida suspicio, sed fiducia firma, certa, indubitata, cui innititur homo apud deum, divinitusque hominis menti indita.' (*S* VI ii 314.4-10.)

Father.[50] As faith is the work of the Spirit in the believer, it is not surprising that it can be described as guarding us from falling, looking in all things to God and dictating what is approved by him, teaching us to seek forgiveness when we fall and enabling us to live lives that are blameless and holy.[51] For Zwingli in the end whatever is ascribed to faith is quite simply to be ascribed to God.

## The Law and the New Life

Differences in stress and substance are evident between Zwingli and Luther in the understanding of gospel and law. Initially Zwingli spoke as Luther did of law and gospel, but the order gospel and law is more characteristic of his theology. In his letter to Franz Lambert and others in Strasburg on 16 December 1524 some of the varied elements in his view emerge. He held that law brings knowledge of sin and can be a stimulus to faith, but his emphasis lay on the fact that only those who believe really hear the law, so that faith is the foundation on which law is built. Faith indeed delights in the law. At the same time however the law terrifies those who trust in God, while by contrast those who do not believe despise it.

Therefore if a magistrate is not a believer, he will not hear the law of God. Therefore faith must be preached, so that it may be the foundation on which the law is built. But what am I saying here, that faith is the foundation of the law? This is an unusual statement. Let no one be offended! What I say is true. For unless faith is present, you will sing the song of the law in vain, as is clear because only they hear the voice of the shepherd who are of his sheep. Do you want the law to be accepted by anyone? Teach faith and pray God to draw him, otherwise you will plough the sea shore. However meanwhile I observe this, that I preach the law and faith at the same time on account of the variety of believers.[52]

Although Zwingli's understanding of the law differed at important points from Luther's, there are obvious similarities as they drew on the same new testament passages. His early writings stressed the impossibility of fulfilling the law, and Christ's giving it to us so that we recognize our shortcomings and take refuge in him.[53] But Zwingli was critical of

---

[50] S VI i 348.10–28, 383.43–384.7, 385.7–14. Prayer is indissolubly linked with faith, for no one can pray 'Our Father' who does not believe that God is his gracious Father. Prayer expresses our dependence on God. (Z II 223.27–224.20, 226.28–34.) 'Oratio igitur hoc colloquium est, quod ex fide cum deo habes, tanquam cum patre et tutissimo certissimoque opitulatore.' (Z III 853.17–18.)

[51] S VI ii 235.20–37.                                    [52] Z VIII 263.18–265.24.

[53]. Z I 103.32–104.7. In the commentaries equally there are frequent references to our despair if we seek to fulfil the law ourselves. Zwingli also speaks of the preaching of the gospel (as

Luther's negative way of describing the law. The law itself is holy and one ought not, like Luther, to speak of it as frightening us, bringing us to despair, or causing us to hate God. Despair and hatred of God are not an effect of the law, but come from the weakness of the flesh which cannot keep the law. Therefore the law, which shows us God's perfect will, condemns us—that is, through the law we see that we cannot come to God and hence we are rightly condemned. But as Zwingli put it, in expounding James 1: 25, the law does not condemn any more than light shining on people who are deformed makes them deformed.[54]

Fundamental to Zwingli's understanding of the law is his description of it as God's unchangeable will. It reflects profoundly the nature or character of God.[55] Moreover it can be called gospel because it should be seen from the standpoint of believers, not of unbelievers. In the exposition of the sixteenth article Zwingli stated,

I understand gospel here to be everything which God has made known to us through his own Son. It is also gospel when he says: You shall not be angry with one another ... I understand it thus: The true believer is gladdened and nourished with every word of God, even if it is against the desires of his flesh.

It is indeed the Spirit of God who teaches him inwardly this way of seeing the law. For the law is spiritual, since it comes from the Spirit and does not will anything but what the Spirit wills. What is said of God's commands and prohibitions applies also to his promises. The unbeliever despises God's grace, but not the believer—for what to the believer is salvation and teaching is to the unbeliever despair and folly. In this way the tension between gospel and law is eliminated.[56]

With his view of the law as God's unchangeable will Zwingli resisted the Roman view that the commands of God were simply counsels. For him they were real commands of God; and it is in his commands alone that God makes his eternal will known to us. In *A Commentary*, however, Zwingli made it clear that civil and ceremonial laws which concern the outward man are not eternal, for the former can vary according to time and place and the latter were abolished altogether by Christ. He argued— in the light of Romans 2: 14 and Matthew 7: 12—that it is the laws which concern the inward man that are eternal. They are summed up in Christ

distinct from the law) as leading to repentance. 'Sequitur ergo, quod beneficia dei quae per Christum humano generi exhibuit et nunciavit mundo pientissimus pater, prius praedicanda sint populo. Hinc enim nascitur displicentia et dolor peccati, et amor iusti et recti.' (*S* VI i 485.40–3.)

[54] *S* VI ii 260.24–261.25.
[55] *Z* II 231.33–233.15, 234.17–235.3, 236.18–22; *S* VI ii 260.40–6. Cf. *Z* VI iii 128.10–130.2.
[56] *Z* II 76.12–78.16, 79.11–18, 159.32–160.19, 232.2–233.2. See Additional Note 3, p. 168.

or in love, for Christ and love are said to be the end of the law (Rom. 10: 4 and 1 Tim. 1: 5).[57]

Towards the end of his exposition of the twenty-second article Zwingli summarized his view in four points.

(1) The will of God wills eternally what is right and good. (2) From this arises the eternal law, which may never be done away or changed. But we are not capable of keeping it. (3) Therefore the eternal will of God must remain and God's grace must come to our aid. (4) It has done so through Christ our mediator. He is our righteousness.[58]

Christ's fulfilling of the law has radically changed our relation to it.[59] He has freed us from the law, in the sense of freeing us from the curse or condemnation we were under through our failure to keep it. 'As he alone has fulfilled the will of God, he is our righteousness, through whom we come to God.' But he has freed us from the law 'not so that we are never to do what God commands and wills', but rather so that we should do what God wills out of the love stimulated by God's grace and friendship.[60] We are free from the law both because we do it from love and because, with the Spirit indwelling us, we do not need it, for the Spirit teaches us. The Spirit is said to be above the law. He is our guideline and gives us the desire to do God's will.[61]

---

[57] *Z* II 481.18–23; III 706.34–708.8. Cf. *S* VI i 680.27–681.2; VI ii 97.46–7. The sabbath is an example in *Z* IV 128.14–129.30 and *S* VI ii 224.21–36.

[58] *Z* II 238.3–11.

[59] Christ fulfilled the law in two senses: in showing what God wants from us, and in doing what we could not do, to satisfy divine righteousness. Therefore the law is renewed by Christ by being expressed more clearly, and it is done away in that transgression of the law cannot condemn us, if we believe that Christ has fulfilled the law and has purchased access to God as a pledge for us for ever. (*Z* II 496.6–22.) In *St Matthew* Zwingli writes of four ways in which Christ fulfilled the law: his undergoing of everything—e.g. circumcision; his accomplishing what was predicted of him; his doing everything that was prescribed in exact accordance with the mind of the lawgiver; his fulfilling of the law for us, that is, satisfying the divine righteousness, and bearing the punishment, which we deserved for violating the law. (*S* VI i 223.31–41.)

[60] *Z* II 235.4–236.33. Cf. *Z* II 647.4–648.5; III 710.3–5. On Christ's freeing us from the curse of the law, see *Z* II 79.28–80.12; III 710.22–32; *S* VI ii 98.7–9. See also Additional Note 4, pp. 168–9.

[61] These two sources of freedom from the law, equally characteristic of Bucer, run through Zwingli's writings. (There is also in Erasmus a stress on love as not needing the law as well as a sense that the law has a positive use for the Christian.) Examples of our doing what the law requires out of love can be seen in *Z* II 237.14–18; VIII 192.4–8; *S* VI ii 98.7–9, 269.30–4. 'This is the way we have been made free: He that loves does all things freely, even the hardest. God, therefore, has put into our hearts a fire by which to kindle love of him in place of love of ourselves . . . We do for love that which we know will please God.' (*Z* III 710.8–21; *Works* III 140–1.) The law is about love of God and love of neighbour, and in the example of the sabbath Zwingli showed how love both frees and guides a Christian. (*Z* IV 128.14–129.30.) Typical examples of the freedom given by the Spirit are: *Z* II 80.6–81.23, 83.30–84.24, 159.16–21; *S* VI ii 98.7–9, 262.12–28, 269.27–34. 'Wherever the Spirit of God is in a man, he rejoices and delights in the law.' (*S* VI i 232.14–15.)

Zwingli says that the law was not given to believers (following 1 Tim. 1: 9), because all his life the believer looks to Christ alone, who lives in him and is his consolation. If God dwells in someone he does not need the law, for God leads him—and where the Spirit of God is, there is freedom.[62] However, the faith of many is faint, and therefore we need to warn them to show their faith by deeds. 'Hence we preach the law as well as grace. For from the law the faithful and elect learn the will of God . . .'[63]

In the end the law can occupy the place it does in Zwingli's thought because of Christ.

The person who lays hold of Christ in the law has a true deliverer. For Christ is the perfection of the law, for justification to everyone who believes, giving himself up to death for us that he might redeem us from all iniquity. For he was born under the law that he might deliver us from the curse and yoke of the law, imparting the Spirit of love, through whom we fulfil the law and will of God not by compulsion but freely and willingly. . . . The law binds our conscience and presses heavily, until Christ dwelling in us through faith gives a docile heart which loves the law, a new heart and a new spirit, through whom Christ rules and sweetly leads us . . . and we live in conformity with the Son of God, nay rather we do not live, but Christ lives in us.[64]

## ADDITIONAL NOTES

1. In his exposition of Jas. 2: 14 Zwingli directs his attack in two directions: against Jews and papists who separated faith from works and sought righteousness from their own works without faith, and against those (possibly Lutherans) who gloried in the word 'faith', but who do not accompany it with works. (S VI ii 271.1–21.)

There is a difference of accent between Zwingli and Bucer. Zwingli speaks of man as created for work, as a bird is for flying. Bucer, after speaking of birds as created for flying, says that no more than a creature can surrender what it was created for, can a true believer live without good works. However, the work for which man is created is for Zwingli of course a fulfilling of God's will. 'Sic hominem condidit deus, ut perpetuo agat et conetur quae recta et divina sunt, perpetuoque sit sollicitus et sedulus, nec tamen plus efficiet, quam velit deus . . .

[62] Z II 648.7–650.9. Cf. Z II 82.8–31. The new life lived by the Christian is not his own work, but God's. Moreover the law is not needed because Christ who dwells in the believer is his law. (Z II 82.9–12.) But Zwingli also spoke of the law as leading those who believe in Christ, for they are zealous to conform themselves to the law of God. (S VI ii 90.36–40.) Cf. S VI i 636.5–21.

[63] S IV 63.31–45; LCC XXIV 273 (Works II 269). In his letter to Bucer of 16 June 1524, Zwingli writes of the danger of speaking of the law as if it were antiquated or of the believer's being free from the law, adding that he never omits the law. (Z VIII 192.22–193.11.)

[64] S VI ii 262.12–28.

Homo enim ad laborem conditus est, ut avis ad volatum.' (S VI i 208.40–209.12.) Elsewhere he says, 'Ad hanc cognitionem dei . . . creati sumus, ut scilicet hunc amemus, idque super omnia.' (S VI i 629.24–6.) For Bucer, see BW I 66.8–12.

2. Zwingli follows Augustine in asserting that it is his own work that God rewards; indeed everything depends in the end on God's election of us before the foundation of the world. (S IV 62.21–44.)

Gestrich (pp. 182–3) speaks somewhat surprisingly of Zwingli's not having broken entirely with the doctrine of merit. He quotes a remark about works done according to God's law 'ardua questio est an illa mereantur'. He largely ignores the discussion that follows, as Zwingli considers the two positions and the texts that favour them, and statements such as 'Therefore God did not elect us because of works, for he elected us before the foundation of the world. Therefore works are not meritorious' and 'For how can a person merit anything when it is by grace that he exists and by grace that he receives all that he has?' (S IV 62.9–11, 25–6, 43–4.) Already in An Exposition of the Articles Zwingli has spoken of God as rewarding his own work in the case of Cornelius and Tobias. (Z II 187.15–16.)

3. For Zwingli's views on gospel and law, see also his letter to Bucer of 16 June 1524, 'Breviter: iusto, id est fideli, omne verbum dei, sive legis sit sive promissionis, cibus est, lux et gratiarum actio.' (Z VIII 193.9–11.) He makes the comparison between God's disclosing his will and nature to us and a king's entrusting his views and plans and nature to a councillor and the way that such a person would leap and exult for joy. (Z VI iii 130.2–4.) Cf. Z II 232.11–13 and S VI ii 261.13–17. In an extended exposition of Jas. 1: 25 Zwingli refers to the law as a mirror in which is reflected God's will and his love for us, as well as our sin. From his making himself known to us to be loved, it is certain that he loves us; for if he did not love us, what reason would there be for making himself known to us? We learn that he loves not only man, but all his creatures; for if he had not loved them he would not have created or sustained them, he would not live or work in them. (S VI ii 261.3–5, 21–9.) Hubmaier contrasts the way that the flesh is terrified by the law with the way the believing soul thanks God for it. (LCC XXV 127.)

4. In his first reformation writing, Choice and Liberty Respecting Food, Zwingli tackles the objection that people will never fast if they are allowed to eat meat. Apart from insisting on Christian liberty in an area where God has given freedom, he argues that fasting should be a free act, and not compulsory. (Z I 99.15–16, 106.8–107.11.)

A Short Christian Introduction has a section on the abolition of the law. We are freed from the ceremonies of the old testament which are outward. They are a type of Christ and were abolished with the coming of Christ. We are furthermore freed from the punishment of the law, if we trust in Christ for salvation. Moreover, as we trust in God we are freed from the laws which concern the inward man. For as God needs no law, so neither does the person in whom God dwells, because God leads him. We are also freed from the laws which have been laid on us to make us good, including all the papal laws not based on God's word, such as vows, indulgences, and confession, as well as from human teachings not based on God's word, such as purgatory, images, and the intercession of the saints. (Z II 646.11–651.16.)

# 8. The Word

THE texts a theologian chooses, the way he uses them, and the way he combines them with others, reveal both his theology and his cast of mind. In his understanding of the word, Zwingli (unlike Luther) did not stress a text such as 'So faith comes from what is heard, and what is heard comes from the preaching of Christ' (Rom. 10: 17). He used this text, but he interpreted it in the light of what were for him much more fundamental texts: 'No one can come to me unless the Father who sent me draws him' (John 6: 44), 'It is written in the prophets, "And they shall all be taught by God"' (John 6: 45), 'I planted, Apollos watered, but God gave the growth. So neither he who plants nor he who waters is anything, but only God who gives the growth' (1 Cor. 3: 6–7). The stress is not on the one preaching nor on the word we preach, but on God who draws, teaches, and gives the growth.

These texts are present in Zwingli's earliest writings and are used equally in his later ones. In *Archeteles*, when he recalled in order the different new testament books from which he had preached over the previous three years and the reasons that lay behind the choice of them, he added, 'This is the seed I have sown. Matthew, Luke, Paul, and Peter have watered it, and God has given it splendid increase, but this I will not trumpet forth, lest I seem to be canvassing my own glory and not Christ's.'[1] But although Zwingli's characteristic emphasis is on God who gives the growth, yet he emphasizes the necessity of sowing (that is, the preaching of the word) without which God gives no fruit. In this, however, God does everything and the one who waters and plants is nothing, though scripture

---

[1] *Z* I 285.25–8; *Works* I 239. The text was widely used by others, e.g. Melchior Macrinus in a letter to Zwingli on 25 Jan. 1523 and Oecolampadius in a letter on 12 July 1526. (*Z* VIII 15.6–8, 659.1–2.) Oecolampadius spoke of God's commanding us to plant and water, reflecting Zwingli's conviction as well that the planting and watering are important and are willed by God. Bucer used the text frequently, emphasizing in the twenties rather more God's giving the growth and in the thirties that it is through planting and watering that God gives the growth. See Stephens, *Martin Bucer*, pp. 196–212.

Zwingli used the text later against Luther, along with John 6: 44, to stress the inward action of God. (*Z* VI i 64.16–22, 99.20–100.5.) In *The Providence of God* he interprets Rom. 10: 17 in the light of John 6: 44 and 1 Cor. 3: 6–7, distinguishing the work of the preacher and the work of the Spirit: 'For the apostle's work is also from the hand of God, but indirectly, the internal drawing is the work of the Spirit acting directly.' (*Z* VI iii 186.12–187.18; *Works* II 203.) God is the real cause of all things.

sometimes—as Zwingli frequently pointed out—ascribes to us what belongs to God because of the close relationship between the head and the members.[2]

The texts 'No one can come to me unless the Father who sent me draws him' and 'They shall all be taught by God', like 1 Corinthians 3: 6–7, were used initially in controversy with Rome. In *The Clarity and Certainty of the Word of God* they were used in conjunction against the view that we need human teachers, whether the fathers, the pope, or councils. 'Even if you hear the gospel of Jesus Christ from an apostle, you cannot act upon it unless the heavenly Father teach and draw you by the Spirit.' 'You do not know that it is God himself who teaches a man, nor do you know that when God has taught him that man has an inward certainty and assurance.'[3]

Although the texts can be used almost synonymously, they often serve different purposes. The reference to being drawn by the Father was useful in debate, whether with anabaptists about election or with Luther about the preaching of the word. In the exposition of election in *The Providence of God* the text is used to indicate the limitations of the outward word which, as scripture and daily experience show us, does not bear fruit of itself.[4] Although John 6: 44 speaks of the Father drawing, it is equally proper to speak of the Son drawing, as in John 12: 32, for then the reference is to Christ as God and not as man. There are also frequent references to the Spirit drawing.[5]

Zwingli's primary concern from beginning to end is to show that the power and initiative is God's. There is no contrast here between the early and the late Zwingli. References to the power of the word in the early Zwingli, which may be influenced by Luther's thought, are to the word as God's word. If God himself speaks the word, then it has power.

The word of God is so sure and strong that if God wills all things are done the moment that he speaks his word. For it is so living and powerful that even the things which are irrational immediately conform themselves to it, or to be more accurate, things both rational and irrational are fashioned and despatched and constrained in conformity with its purpose.[6]

[2] S VI i 593.14–17; VI ii 68.45–69.7. 'Deus operatur omnia in omnibus, nihil est qui rigat, nihil qui plantat, sed qui incrementum dat deus. Is deus omnia facit, movet os et plectrum praedicantis, trahit et illustrat cor audientis.' (S VI ii 69.5–7.)

[3] Z I 366.12–367.5, 371.5–7; LCC XXIV 79, 83. The need to be taught by God is frequently repeated in this writing. (Z I 368.31–2, 377.19–21.)

[4] Z VI i 109.18–110.4; VI ii 64.16–20; VI iii 186.12–187.2.

[5] S VI i 743.33–41; VI ii 171.44–172.5; VI i 333.20–1.

[6] Z I 353.8–13; LCC XXIV 68.

In the reformation preaching of the gospel Zwingli saw God at work and believed that the word would lead to the deliverance of the people and the overthrow of the papacy.[7] Like Luther and Bucer, he uses Isaiah 55: 11 to indicate the power and effectiveness of the word, but his comment on the text in *Isaiah* is brief and makes it clear that the reference is to God's word or command. It does not concern the word that men preach.[8]

In this context to ascribe power to the word is to ascribe it to God, for the word is seen as God's word over against the words of men.[9] This point, made originally in controversy with his catholic opponents, was taken up later against Lutherans and catholics when they ascribed to the word what belonged to God.[10] Even in the ministry of Christ a distinction must be made between the word which was spoken and the power of God which lay behind it. He preached often to the Pharisees and scribes, and yet they did not respond, but were rather hardened by the word. This is related to the fact that Christ was a man, just as the apostles were and we are.[11] We can do nothing by our own power, but only by being endowed with power from on high.[12]

Although the power is entirely of God, yet he does use instruments to do his will in the whole of his creation. This is expressed powerfully in *The Providence of God* with its stress on God as the true cause of all things.

Do we not see here that the apostle and the word which he uses for the setting forth of the truth are instruments, not causes, and that the one cause, by which even the apostle exists and preaches, is the deity? And to put it briefly, the ground does not bring forth, nor the water nourish, nor the air fructify, nor the fire warm, nor the sun itself, but rather that power which is the origin of all things, their life and strength, uses the earth as the instrument wherewith to produce and create.[13]

---

[7] Z VIII 199.19–27, 200.16–19; III 448.17–449.2. Cf. 'Tuond umb gots willen sinem wort gheinen drang an; dann warlich, warlich, es wirt als gwüss sinen gang haben als der Ryn; den mag man ein zyt wol schwellen, aber nit gstellen.' (Z III 488.6–8.)

[8] Z XIV 379.5–9. The text is used positively in Z III 636.9–12 to indicate that wherever the gospel is preached it cannot but be that it will be received by many.

[9] e.g. Z III 670.40–671.6. Something may be attributed to us, when in fact it is of God. (S VI ii 232.1–10.)

[10] 'Quomodo ergo adfirmant quidam verbum secum ferre omnia, et mox quum verbum profertur perficere quod significat? et quod solius dei est, illi verbo tribuunt externo. Quod si per verbum virtutem dei intelligunt, quid novi dicunt?' (S VI i 328.2–6.)

[11] S VI i 251.44–252.3, 256.29–34, 263.2–24. When something is attributed to the apostles, it is because of the close relationship of the head and the members or by analogy with the way a servant speaks of the house as his house. See also S VI i 266.36–43.

[12] S VI ii 68.12–14.

[13] Z VI iii 112.18–24; *Works* II 156.

It is not that God needs instruments, unlike man who can do nothing without them, but he uses them on our account. This is true of the world of nature as of the world of men.[14] But it can also be said that God has acted in this way because it has pleased him to.[15]

God uses man as an instrument, as he does herbs for healing, although he does not need instruments. Moreover the fact that it is God who changes men's hearts and minds does not make the work of preaching unimportant.[16] The outward word was ordained by God, even if faith does not come from it, but from the word that God speaks in the heart. The fact moreover that Christ commanded the apostles to preach the gospel throughout the world refutes the view that the outward word is not necessary.[17] In expounding 'And he chose twelve whom he called apostles' (Luke 6: 13) Zwingli responds to the question, what need Christ had of apostles when no one believes who is not called inwardly, by appealing to the fact that God has made man with senses and in need of admonition, unlike the angels who see him continually.[18]

There is in Zwingli a sense that God honours the ministry of those he has called and makes the word they preach effective.[19] (This is expressed most clearly in the commentaries.) Indeed in expounding 'And thou, child, shalt be called a prophet' (Luke 1: 76) Zwingli speaks of the sending of a prophet as sure evidence of God's mercy. Although God could enlighten people's hearts by his Spirit, yet his order was to send a prophet to prepare the way of the Lord by his preaching. His comment on the words 'He gave them power' (Luke 9: 1) shows how close an association there can be between God's action and man's preaching, for it means 'nothing else than

---

[14] S VI i 205.6-11; Z XIII 10.5-18, 51.29-38, 329.7-22. This aspect of Zwingli's thought features prominently, as one would expect, in the commentaries. 'Sic rursus potuit uno verbo aquas revocare, sed ventum ad hoc excitavit, ut videamus, quod et antea saepe dictum est, deum, tametsi virtute sua soloque nutu et verbo omnia possit, uti instrumentis tamen, quae ad hoc creavit.' (Z XIII 51.33-6.) 'De angelis nonnihil superius attigimus, quibus deus nos visitat, erudit ac consolatur; qui tametsi omnia virtutis suae verbo operatur, utitur tamen ministerio angelorum propter nos.' (Z XIII 184.6-8.)

[15] S VI ii 239.33-240.2.

[16] S VI ii 254.40-1; Z XI 476.21-8.

[17] Z III 263.9-25. The stress in this passage is nevertheless on the inward word. His reference to the parable of the sower should have led him, however, to a closer association of the inward and the outward word than emerges here. (S VI i 752.44-8.)

[18] S VI i 582.19-32.

[19] Z XIV 418.16-22. There is nothing automatically effective about the preaching of the word, but Zwingli's prayer is that God will use it. In this context it should be recognized that a man's theology is expressed just as much in liturgy as in doctrinal controversy. 'Lassend uns gott ernstlich bitten, das er sin heilig ewig wort uns armen menschen gnädigklich offnen welle und in erkantnuss sines willens ynfuoren, ouch alle, so an sinem wort irrend, wider an den rechten wäg wyse, damit wir nach sinem göttlichen willen läbind.' (Z IV 686.16-19.)

to make them sure, that everywhere where they will preach, he himself wills to work at the same time'. This, however, does not imply that the power is theirs. It is always God's power. Nevertheless Zwingli makes it clear in *Romans* that it is not the case that no one can believe or be saved unless he hear the outward word, although God's custom is always to send out prophets to preach his word.[20] This positive note is sounded strongly in *An Account of the Faith* in 1530.

For in speaking canonically or regularly we see that among all nations the out-ward preaching of evangelists or bishops has preceded faith, which nevertheless we say is received by the Spirit alone. ... Whithersoever, then, prophets or preachers, of the word are sent, it is a sign of God's grace that he wishes to mani-fest the knowledge of himself to his elect; and where they are denied, it is a sign of impending wrath.[21]

Such a positive view of the preaching of the word entirely fits Zwingli's practice and his concern to allow the free preaching of the word in every place. Regardless of the various alliances he sought to achieve, he remained utterly convinced of the power of the gospel when preached.[22] His view of the word is also manifest in his attack on images. In a letter to Bucer in 1524 his case against them was not simply that they are not commanded by God in scripture, but that we cannot learn Christ from them, for they affect only the senses. We need to be taught by the word. As Zwingli put it later, all one can learn from an image of Christ is, for example, that he was handsome. It does not save us to know how or that he was crucified, but that he was crucified for us and that he is our Lord and God.[23]

Yet God is not bound by the word. He can act with it or without it. This was an element in Zwingli's thought even when he stressed God's

[20] *S* VI i 550.8–22, 609.5–20; VI ii 114.1–8. *S* VI ii 58.30–40 refers to God as being present with his people, adding 'Deinde et foris loquitur per verbum, per sacramenta, per omnes denique creaturas, ut excitet nos, et ad sui laudem provocet.' 'Ex his ergo discimus praedicationem externi verbi et sacramentorum praecedere ...'. (*S* VI i 567.26–7.) There is a revealing reference in *Archeteles*: 'recordor aliquando vitio versum esse, quod dixeram deum per me loqui cum eius verbum promulgarem'. (*Z* I 287.31–2.)

[21] *Z* VI ii 813.8–16; Jackson 478–9 (*Works* II 56–7). In *An Exposition of the Articles* (1523) this was more negatively expressed: 'Ob man glychwol den predgenden haben muoss, so macht er doch das hertz nit gleubig; der geist und wort gottes thuond das.' (*Z* II 111.9–11.) In *The Education of Youth* the necessity of both word and Spirit is maintained. 'Ideo verbis purissimis instillanda est, oreque dei usitatissimis, fides. Iungendae simul preces ad eum, qui solus fideles facit, ut quem nos docemus verbo, ipse adflatu suo inluminet.' (*Z* II 538.21–4.) Cf. 'Spiritus arguet mundum, quod tamen per apostolos facit: tribuitur ergo apostolis quod dei solius est.' (*S* VI i 759.9–10.)

[22] 'Where the grace of God is not preached, man is a beast ...'. (*S* VI i 609.21–2.)

[23] *Z* VIII 194.9–35; IV 120.14–121.32. If images were, as was claimed, books for those who cannot read, then why not send them to unbelievers for them to learn faith from them? Christ, however, did not command us to teach with images, but to preach the word.

ordaining and using of the word. In *Two Replies to Luther's Book* Zwingli drew an analogy between the rain and snow from heaven making the earth fruitful without anyone to distribute them and God's letting fall the dew of his grace and Spirit.[24] In a discussion of the sacraments Zwingli states that God can act with or without an instrument, something which is true of the preaching of the word as it is of God's work in the natural order.[25]

Zwingli presents a far from uniform picture of the relationship between the outward word and faith or the Spirit. This can be seen by considering both the word and the Spirit and the outward and the inward word. There are occasions when he clearly linked the word and the Spirit, so that the two seem almost indissolubly joined. It is not simply that the word is not effective without the Spirit, though that is a constant element in his theology, but there is the sense that the Spirit and the word go together. There are examples that Zwingli drew from his own preaching, where he spoke of preaching by the Spirit or by the inspiration of the Holy Spirit.[26] Already in *An Exposition of the Articles* he mentioned the Spirit of God as working with his word. The same thought, but with a slightly different emphasis, is present in *The Providence of God*, where he has referred to Paul's statement that faith comes from hearing.

Paul's meaning, then, is only that it is necessary, as far as is shown by scripture examples, that the word be preached, in order that then God, who giveth the increase, may start the seed of faith by means of this tool, as it were, but with his own hand as the immediate cause. For the apostle's work also is from the hand of God, but indirectly, the internal drawing is the work of the Spirit acting directly.[27]

Elsewhere he wrote of the Spirit as working in preacher or hearer or both so that the word preached was received.[28] But he also insisted that it was

[24] Z VI ii 99.15–30.
[25] Z VI iii 271.10–12. 'Si spiritus mysteria eruere quis velit, lucis spiritualis instrumentum externum verbum est, per quod deus nonnunquam operatur, nonnunquam vero sine verbo, sola mentis inlustratione.' (Z XIII 11.17–20.) Cf. Z XIII 51.29–38; 360.21–4. In the context of the Gentiles Zwingli could speak of God's saving people through Christ, even though the gospel of Christ is not preached. (S VI ii 69.31–3.)
[26] Z I 487.18–488.3. Cf. Z III 465.1–2. There are, of course, numerous examples that speak of the necessity of the Spirit with the word, or of the word's not being effective without the Spirit. (Z V 591.3–8; S VI ii 273.18–20.)
[27] Z II 330.23–5 (cf. Z XIV 391.1–7) and VI iii 187.2–7 (*Works* II 203). Zwingli used a number of strong expressions to describe the relationship of the Spirit and the word. 'Ut igitur spiritu tuo vivificemur, ne quęso verbum tuum a nobis unquam auferas. Eo enim veluti vehiculo spiritus tuus trahitur; nam ipsum ociosum ad te non revertitur.' (Z II 606.27–9.) Cf. Z VIII 635.9–15.
[28] For the Spirit in the hearers or preacher, see S VI i 262.39–48; VI ii 68.12–13.

176 THE THEOLOGY OF HULDRYCH ZWINGLI

necessary for the Spirit (or faith) to be present before the word was preached, although it is perhaps more characteristic of him to place the preaching of the word before the gift of the Spirit. An example of this order is drawn from the annunciation, where first comes the outward word and then the Spirit. Zwingli did not use this analogy in the way Luther did and there is for him no strict connection between the word and the Spirit. Sometimes the point is, as it was for Paul, that the word is preached and only some time afterwards does the Spirit make it effective.[29]

The distinction of inward and outward is made early in a discussion of the sacraments, but not used till later of the inward and outward word.[30] Indeed the contrast of inward and outward word, so characteristic of Denck, is not especially characteristic of Zwingli. He spoke of the outward word, but much more often made the contrast, not with the inward word, but with what God does inwardly, in the heart or mind. The contrast is between the word that man speaks to the ear and the word that God speaks to the heart.[31]

This distinction was used in two main contexts: against catholic opponents to affirm that believers judge the outward word which is presented to them in the light of what God has taught them inwardly, and against primarily Lutheran opponents to argue that the outward word does not itself bring faith or the Spirit, nor does it perform what it says.

In *A Reply to Emser* Zwingli presented the view that the church which relies on God's word judges whether the word that is preached is God's and does so in the light of the word God speaks in the heart. This word is not contrasted with scripture to which Zwingli appealed at several points in the discussion.

Now you know what church it is that cannot err: namely that one alone which rests upon the word of God only—not upon that word which Emser supposes I merely look at, which consists of letters or sentences, but upon that which shines in the heart and recognizes every word, by whomsoever spoken, whether it is the Father's and Shepherd's or not.

---

[29] *S* VI i 602.48–603.3; 348.11–14; *Z* VI iii 182.3–5. *S* VI i 333.19–28 and VI ii 59.12–15 are examples that seem to imply that the Spirit (or faith) must be present before the word, otherwise it is not received or understood.

[30] e.g. in Wyttenbach's letter (15 June 1523) with references to being inwardly taught by the Spirit and to the believer's knowing himself to be purified inwardly by faith as outwardly by water. (*Z* VIII 85.21–86.5.)

[31] Inward word could refer to the sense or meaning of the outward word or to the Spirit in *Z* VIII 317.25–34. The opposition of inward and outward word is characteristic of anabaptists and spirituals, such as Denck and Franck: e.g. the seven articles that Kautz announced for public debate on Whit Sunday 1527, the first was: 'Das äussere Wort ist nicht das rechte, lebenhafte oder ewig bleibende Wort Gottes, sondern nur eine Zeugniss oder Anzeigung des innern, damit dem

Whoever hears the scripture of the celestial word explained in church judges that which he hears; yet what is heard is not the very word which causes us to believe, for if we were rendered faithful by that word which is read and heard, evidently all of us should be faithful. . . . It is clear, then, that we are rendered faithful only by that word which the Heavenly Father proclaims in our hearts, by which also he illumines us so that we understand, and draws us so that we follow. . . . nevertheless, the word of faith, which resides in the minds of the faithful, is judged by no man, but itself judges the external word. . . . However, the faithful judges not by his own judgement, but by that of the Divine Spirit.[32]

The inward word is not given a precise content, although for Zwingli its content would be in keeping with scripture rightly understood. It is its origin that is important, and its origin is God, and not man. In other words it is God who judges, and not man. It is also revealing that the context of the discussion is the church and the proper understanding of the church as a communion of saints or believers, and not as a gathering of bishops.[33]

In *An Answer to Valentin Compar* the following year Zwingli considered inward and outward word in the course of attacking the idea that the church guarantees the gospel.[34] He used the example of a countryman who had helped to make the laws before they were written. If the old law book were lost and there were a dispute about other books, the old man would know what the old law was. He represents the believer in whose heart God had written his law. From his faith and knowledge he would know what conformed to God's teaching. It is therefore the inward man who must judge the outward word or, as Zwingli put it later, 'The outward word must be judged by the inward word, which God has written in the heart . . .'. Again there was the insistence that bishops were to be judged by the believing church, rather than that the bishops were to guarantee the word.[35]

äussern auch genug geschehe.' (*S* VIII 77, n. 1.) The second article, with its declaration that nothing outward has power to console or confirm the inward man, is more typically Zwinglian.

[32] Z III 259.32–260.3, 263.9–26; *Works* III 373, 376–7. The section Z III 263.7–26 is repeated with only a few verbal changes in *I Corinthians* some two and a half years later (following the dating of Meyer, 'Die Entstehung'). It is significant that the commentary begins by asking how mortal man can judge concerning the eternal word of God, and replies in the words, 'The spiritual man judges all things' (1 Cor. 2: 15). It adds the clear statement 'Verbi ergo praedicati iudex est non homo, sed spiritus divinus in corde pii hominis habitans . . .'. (*S* VI ii 180.30–46.)

[33] Z III 262.2–4. There is no opposition between the inward word and scripture in this section. Rather Zwingli bases his argument on scripture and appeals to scripture, referring both to 'the infallible judgement of the Word of God' and to 'arguing the matter by the scriptures'. (Z III 268.15, 31.)

[34] He was responding to Compar's statement 'das die nit gott lestrend, die die euangelia klein achtetind on bewärnus der kilchen'. (Z IV 64.11–12.)

[35] Z IV 71.8–72.8, 75.10–31, 77.8–14.

The controversy with mainly Lutheran opponents concerned the view that the word, when preached, brought faith or that the words of institution, when spoken, made the body of Christ present.[36] Zwingli insisted on the sovereignty of God who gives faith to whom he will and when he will. For him it was evident from scripture and daily experience that the outward word did not lead to faith—otherwise everyone who heard the word would believe. The point was made in *A Christian Answer* that we must be taught by the word and not by images—not the word that men speak, but God's word in our hearts.[37] This word spoken in the heart by God is in effect the inward word, although the phrase is not used often by Zwingli, and it is used on occasion not in his way, but in the way used by his opponents. That is almost certainly the case in *A Friendly Exegesis*, where he wrote, 'Therefore it is by the Father who draws us that we trust in Christ, and not even through the inward word.'[38] Although controversy caused Zwingli to set outward and inward over against each other, they were not necessarily opposed, but properly belonged together.[39] However, he had not reached the point where, like Bucer, he could develop his understanding of election to see that God usually made the outward word effective—where the hearers were elect.[40]

In the end Luther and Zwingli were talking and arguing at cross purposes. They understood word and sacrament differently because their understanding of God and Christ was different. For Luther the power of the word was vital to his understanding of God's dealing with men in Christ. For Zwingli the power of the Spirit who can and does use the word, but who need not use it, was vital to his understanding of God's dealing with men in Christ. Zwingli stressed the distinction of the divinity and

---

[36] Z V 591.3–10. Cf. Z IV 249.5–6. Outward words may be a means or an instrument, but they are not 'volbringende instrument'. (Z VI i 343.8–11.)

[37] 'Das wort muoss uns leeren: nit des menschen, wiewol er's redt zuo sinem bruoder, sunder das wort, das gott mitt sinem geyst in unseren hertzen ufftuot und ze verstan gibt, das wir es bekennend und imm anhangind.' (Z III 170.16–19.)

[38] Z V 583.12–19. Gäbler, like others, regards this as Zwingli's view (*Zwingli*, p. 68). Zwingli used the phrase 'inward word' in the Berne disputation. (Z VI i 343.21–2.) But it is striking that in the previous speech of thirty-two lines he used the term 'outward word' a dozen times, but 'inward word' not once. Cf. Z V 520.7–20, 531.24–532.13, 534.13–22 where the use is clearly dependent on his opponent's use. The contrast of outward and inward word corresponds with the two uses of the word 'call' in 'Many are called' (Matt. 20: 16) which refers to outward preaching and 'Those whom he called he also justified' (Rom. 8: 30). (Z XIV 270.28–32.) Cf. Z VI i 341.25–342.3, 9–13.

[39] Z IX 460.6–10.

[40] He could have developed passages such as Z VI i 341.25–342.3 and S VI i 353.24–9. (The latter passage also refers to the outward word 'by which God reveals himself to us'.) Some passages point to the necessity of the outward word while contrasting it with the inward word. (S VI i 752.38–48.) By itself of course the outward word can lead only to historical faith.

humanity in Christ, Luther their interpenetration. Zwingli stressed the divinity of Christ, Luther the divinity in the humanity. Zwingli stressed God's sovereignty over word and sacrament, Luther God's sovereignty in them. For Zwingli the creature was set over against God as leading us from him to idolatry, for Luther the creature was a mask for God through which he comes to us. Their theological approach and their religious concern were different, which meant that there could be no underlying agreement.[41]

There was of course an agreement at Marburg, in which their different emphases are combined in a common statement. Like most agreements, it did not state one position or the other unequivocally. The eighth article is not expressed as Zwingli would have expressed it apart from Marburg, but its basic elements can be found elsewhere in his writings. He did speak of the necessity of preaching the word or the gospel. He did allow that through the word the Spirit acts to give faith. He did of course insist—and this is the strongly Zwinglian note—that this happens where the Spirit wills and in whom he wills. Naturally he interpreted the article in the light of his position.[42]

[41] Zwingli did not really grasp the theological and religious point of Luther's understanding of the word and drew on subtle and in many ways skilful biblical arguments against the idea that the outward word brings with it what it refers to. Hence, for example, his careful distinction between words of promise and words that relate facts or that command or prohibit, to show that the words of institution were not words of promise. (Z V 522.22–529.6, 783.11–785.28.)

[42] 'Zum achten, das der heylig geyst, ordenlich zuo reden niemants soelichen gloubenn oder syne gabe on vorgend predigt oder müntlich wort oder evangelion Christi, sonder durch unnd mit soelichem müntlichem wort würckt er und schafft er den glouben, wo und in welchen er wil. Rom.X.' (Z VI ii 522.13–17.) Cf. his comments in Z VI ii 550.5–10 and 551.11–12, 17–21. The phrase 'ordenlich zuo reden' would seem to be a Zwinglian qualifying of Luther's position. There is moreover the clearly Zwinglian view that it is the Spirit, and not the outward word, who gives faith. Cf. S VI ii 114.4–8.

# 9. The Sacraments

THE sacraments in Zwingli can be properly understood only in the context of his life and theology. It is not this doctrine or that one that impinges on the sacraments, but all of them in one way or another. The sovereignty of God, the person and work of Christ, the presence of the Spirit, all affect Zwingli's understanding of the sacraments, as does his doctrine of scripture, salvation, man, and the church. Some have a more decisive role than others, but they all interpenetrate in the way he formulates his view. The sacraments were moreover at the heart of medieval religion and were therefore naturally at the heart of the conflict provoked by the reformation. Zwingli's view of them is expressed largely in controversial writings, which gives a greater emphasis to the opinions he rejects than to those he holds. Constant controversy may also have been one of the factors preventing him from expressing a more positive view.[1]

The word 'sacrament' itself is rejected by Zwingli, both because it is wrongly understood by people and because it groups together rites that are better understood individually. In *An Exposition of the Articles* (1523) he points out that 'sacrament' is derived from *sacramentum*, meaning an oath. It could therefore be used of those things that 'God has instituted, commanded, and ordained with his word, which is as firm and sure as if he had sworn an oath thereto'. That, however, would exclude things we call sacraments of which God has not spoken, such as confirmation; and it would include what we do not, such as alms and excommunication. Nevertheless Zwingli accepts the use of the term 'sacrament' for the body and blood of Christ, if it means 'a sure sign or seal'. The sacrament can also be to believers who are weak an assurance of the forgiveness of their sins by Christ. The sacraments are called pledges. But we should not use the same term

---

[1] Bucer's view of word and sacrament is more positively expressed in the thirties than in the twenties, in a way that is consistent with his theology as a whole and not by a change in his theology. The doctrine of election plays an important part in this. In 1536, when his views are regarded by many as Lutheran, he could speak positively of Zwingli. 'Christ alone effects the whole of salvation in us, and he does it not by some other power, but by his Spirit alone. However, for this he uses with us the word, both the visible word in the sacraments and the audible word in the gospel. By them he brings and offers remission of sins . . . Zwingli recognized that; hence, when he denied that the sacraments dispense grace, he meant that the sacraments, that is the outward action, are not of themselves effective, but that everything belonging to our salvation depends on the the inward action of Christ, of whom the sacraments are, in their way, instruments.' (*In sacra qvatvor evangelia, Enarrationes perpetvae* (Basle, 1536) p. 485 B.)

to cover both things instituted by God and things instituted by men. In any case the term 'sacrament' is a Latin word which Germans do not understand or need, as each of those rites called a sacrament has its own name. Moreover the word is one that Christ did not use.[2]

Between *An Exposition of the Articles* and the discussion of the sacraments in *A Commentary* in 1525 some important changes take place in Zwingli's presentation of the sacraments. The term 'oath' is seen as referring to our oath or pledge rather than to God's oath, and the idea of the sacraments as an assurance of forgiveness disappears. The changes take place in discussions primarily of the Lord's supper, the first one particularly in reflection on 1 Corinthians 10. In his discussion of verses 16–17 in *A Proposal Concerning Images and the Mass* (May 1524) Zwingli refers to the sacrament as 'an inward and outward union of Christian people'. We eat and drink 'so that we may testify to all men that we are one body and one brotherhood'. We are moreover obliged to give ourselves for one another just as Christ gave himself for us. Alongside this new view the old view is present that the sacrament is 'a sign and assurance of the testament', the testament being the forgiveness of sins. We take the sign and assurance of the testament both for the hunger of the soul and for the renewal of the brotherhood. However, by sharing in the sacrament no one can strengthen or testify to the faith of someone else.[3]

*A Christian Answer* (August 1524) gives further expression to this new position. We publicly bind ourselves to our brethren in the pledge or covenant (*Pflicht*) which Christ has instituted. Before his death he gave us a will or sacrament with which we pledge ourselves eternally to each other, just as he has bound us to God.[4] *A Reply to Emser*, written at the same time, speaks of the eucharist as being given so that 'by this sacred pledge (*initiatio*) as it were' we may be united into the one army and people of God.[5] Zwingli also begins to relate the oath of allegiance that Christians

---

[2] Z II 120.23–121.2, 122.5–7, 127.22–8, 125.6–7, 124.13–15, 125.19–25, 126.33–127.5. Zwingli also refers to Peter Lombard's definition of a sacrament as a sign of a holy thing. (Z II 121.3–4.) (For the continued concern about the misunderstanding of the word 'sacrament', see, e.g., Z III 487.3–7, 762.32–5.) Through the years Zwingli returns to this scholastic summary of Augustine's view, though in various forms, e.g. 'Credo igitur, o Caesar, sacramentum esse sacrae rei, hoc est: factae gratiae signum.' (Z VI ii 805.6–7.) In Zwingli there is a clear distinction between the sign and what it signifies. Here he stands, like Erasmus (see Payne, p. 98), in the Franciscan tradition. In *The Lord's Supper* he argues that in canon law also the word 'sacrament' is used to mean simply a sign. (Z IV 801.5–15.)

[3] Z III 124.32–127.27, esp. 124.32–125.4, 10–14, 126.9–11, 25–31, 127.23–5. The great stress on unity as a function of the sacraments expressed here and elsewhere in Zwingli (e.g. in Z III 226.16–228.28) is also found in Augustine and Erasmus.

[4] Z III 227.11–228.28, esp. 227.26–228.11.

[5] Z III 282.29–32. The term is used of baptism, e.g. in Z VIII 269.19–21.

make to the meaning of the word 'sacrament', as an oath.[6] This illustrates in part the way in which the accent has shifted from God to Christians as the subject of the sacraments. The covenant or oath Christians make to each other is illustrated by analogies from Swiss national life, although its origin is not to be found there, but rather in the interpretation of 1 Corinthians 10.[7]

A change also takes place in what is said about the sacraments as strengthening faith. In this the dualism in Zwingli's understanding of man plays a part. The letter to Thomas Wyttenbach in June 1523 speaks of those who are weak in faith as strengthened by the sacraments. They strengthen faith, but do not give it where it does not exist. The spirit, which is inwardly taught by the Holy Spirit, is made more sure and joyful by a visible sign. In this context Zwingli refers to the body as weighing down the soul, and blinding the spirit with its mists. However, the later strong contrast and separation in which the bodily has no effect on the spirit is not explicit here. Although the strong in faith do not need the sacrament for the strengthening of faith, yet they come to it for spiritual enjoyment and to delight (*amoenare*) their faith.[8]

Zwingli's letter to Fridolin Lindauer in October 1524 has a contrast between the outward and the inward man rather than the weak and the strong in faith. The sacraments are said to be given for the instruction of the outward man which grasps matters through the senses, whereas the inward man cannot learn or become a believer through outward things. So that God may satisfy the whole man, that is the inward as well as the outward, he commands that the person who already believes should be baptized. He does not do this because he wants the spirit to be purified in this way, for a substance that is incorporeal cannot be purified by a corporeal element, but so that the outward man may be initiated by the visible sign and become certain of the thing that happens with the inward man by the light of faith or the manifest word of the grace of God.[9]

The sacraments are now no longer called assurances of salvation, though they are in some sense an assurance for the outward man. Whereas before this the man who was strong in faith, probably by virtue of the clear word of God's grace, did not need the sacraments to strengthen his faith,

---

[6] Z III 348.6–22. Erasmus also speaks of the meaning of 'sacrament' as an oath.

[7] Z III 533.4–534.13, 534.28–535.30. 'Also in disem sacrament verbindt sich der mensch mit allen glöubigen offenlich . . . Nun ist diss sacrament ein offner eyd und pflicht, das sich der mensch für einen Christen hierinn usgibt und offnet.' (Z III 535.18–19, 27–9.)

[8] Z VIII 85.13–26, 85.34–86.21.

[9] Z VIII 236.3–13. He relates this to Augustine 'qum dixit, etiam, qum verbum accedat ad elementum, fide tamen omnia confici'. (Z VIII 236.13–14.)

although the man weak in faith did, now it is man as a person with senses for whom the sacraments are useful, for it is the senses to which the sacraments appeal, not the spirit. As Zwingli is to put it in *Those Who Give Cause for Tumult* (December 1524), 'our eyes want also to see, otherwise Christ would not have instituted baptism and the eucharistic bread'.[10]

In his second main discussion of the sacraments in *A Commentary* the change of position from *An Exposition of the Articles* is evident. Again Zwingli criticizes the use of the term 'sacrament' as obscuring and confusing the meaning of the things to which it is applied. However, because it has come into use he is prepared to accept it, but only for baptism and the Lord's supper, since they are initiatory ceremonies or pledges.[11] He arrives at this fundamental element in his understanding of the sacraments by pointing out that the word 'sacrament' meant for Varro 'a pledge which litigants deposited at some altar, and the winner got back his pledge or money'. It is also an oath, a use still current in France and Italy; and finally it is a 'military sacrament by which soldiers are bound to obey their general according to the rights or laws of war'. The word was not used 'among the ancients to mean a sacred and secret thing', nor does it properly represent the Greek word 'mystery' in Ephesians 5: 32. In the light of all this Zwingli states that 'a sacrament is nothing else than an initiatory ceremony or a pledging. For just as those who were about to enter upon litigation deposited a certain amount of money, which could not be taken away except by the winner, so those who are initiated by sacraments bind and pledge themselves, and, as it were, seal a contract not to draw back.'[12]

From this standpoint he attacks three other positions: catholic, Lutheran, and anabaptist. The first is expressed in the way ordinary people understand the word 'sacrament'; hence Zwingli's desire not to use the term. 'For when they hear the word "sacrament" they think of something great and holy which by its own power can free the conscience from sin.' However, a sacrament 'cannot have any power to free the conscience, if it is simply an initiation or public inauguration'. Underlying Zwingli's attack on this position is his understanding of God and salvation. God alone is able to free the conscience, 'for it is known to him alone, for he alone can penetrate to it'. He supports this by reference to Solomon's words, 'For you alone know the hearts of the children of men' (2 Chron. 6: 30), and those of the Pharisees, 'Who can forgive sins, but God alone?'

10 Z III 411.16–18.
11 Z III 762.23–763.5.
12 Z III 758.15–759.18; *Works* III 180–1.

(Luke 5: 21). An implication of all this is that no created thing can know a man inwardly or cleanse his mind or conscience.[13]

Zwingli accepts the Lutheran view when it speaks of a sacrament as 'the sign of a holy thing', but not when it insists 'that when you perform the sacrament outwardly a purification is certainly performed inwardly'. His opposition to this view springs from his understanding of faith and of the freedom of the Spirit, and from the testimony of what happened with baptism in the new testament. Faith 'is born only when a man begins to despair of himself, and to see that he must trust in God alone'. The change that happens in the believer as he becomes a new man through the work of the Spirit is something of which he is aware. Water does not contribute to this, for you could cover people with the River Jordan and say the baptismal words a thousand times, but people would not feel a change of mind. However, because of superstitious views of the sacraments, people may of course think 'they have found, nay, actually felt, salvation, when they have not felt anything at all within, as is shown by their subsequent lives'. Acts 19 gives an example of this, while in Acts 10 Cornelius received the Spirit and was sure of the grace of God before baptism. Then Zwingli presents a more fundamental objection to the view that, at the same time as we administer the sacraments outwardly, what they signify happens inwardly. With such a view 'the freedom of the divine Spirit would be bound, who distributes to each, as he wills, that is: to whom, when, and where he wills'. However, the examples given from the new testament show that the Spirit is not bound by signs.[14]

The anabaptists rightly reject the catholic and Lutheran positions. However, they hold that 'a sacrament is a sign which is given only when atonement has been made in the mind, but is given for the purpose of rendering the recipient sure that what is signified by the sacrament has now been accomplished'. But, Zwingli asks, what is the need of baptism to make someone sure, when, if he believes, he is already sure of God's forgiveness?[15]

Zwingli's view differs from all these. Sacraments are signs 'by which a man proves to the church that he either aims to be, or is, a soldier of Christ, and which inform the whole church rather than yourself of your faith'. By baptism and the Lord's supper we are initiated; by the first we give our name, that is, enter the church, and by the second, remembering

[13] Z III 757.10–13, 759.18–760.4; *Works* III 179, 181.
[14] Z III 757.13–17, 760.4–761.8; *Works* III 179, 182.
[15] Z III 757.17–20 (*Works* III 179), 761.8–22. Note the reference to the increase of faith in Z IV 14.8–15.

Christ's victory, we show ourselves members of his church. 'In baptism we receive a token (*symbolum*) that we are to fashion our lives according to the rule of Christ; by the Lord's supper we give proof that we trust in the death of Christ . . .' This faith in Christ involves the living of a new life in accordance with Christ's commands.[16]

*Baptism, Rebaptism, and Infant Baptism*, published two months after *A Commentary*, offers a positive, as well as a negative, view of the sacraments. Christ is seen as one who has done away with outward things so that we are not to look for justification in them. (In Christ it is the Spirit who gives life—not outward things.) However, Christ has given us two outward signs 'as a concession to our frailty'. Zwingli uses the word 'sacrament' of these, but only after stating that no outward thing can take away sin. Sacrament is rather equivalent to a pledge of allegiance (*Pflichtszeichen*).

If a man sews on a white cross, he proclaims that he wishes to be a confederate. And if he makes the pilgrimage to Nähenfels and gives God praise and thanksgiving for the victory vouchsafed to our forefathers, he testifies that he is a confederate indeed. Similarly the man who receives the mark of baptism is the one who is resolved to hear what God says to him, to learn the divine precepts and to live his life in accordance with them. And the man who in the remembrance or supper gives thanks to God in the congregation testifies to the fact that from the very heart he rejoices in the death of Christ and thanks him for it.[17]

Zwingli makes a sharp distinction between the sign and what it signifies: signs cannot be what they signify, or they are no longer signs. He also compares the two main signs of the old testament and of the new, a comparison that was to be influential in his sacramental teaching. These covenant signs he distinguishes from other signs. He allows that 'some signs are given the better to confirm faith, or in some sort to reassure the flesh, which does not allow faith any rest', but they are miraculous signs, not covenant signs. The fundamental reason given for this is that outward things cannot confirm faith, as faith does not come from them, but from God. This raises the question whether miraculous signs can confirm faith. He admits that they were given to this end, 'but even this does not mean that they add anything to faith or augment it, but that they satisfy the curiosity of the flesh which is constantly itching to see and to know'. However, if a person has no faith, miraculous signs do not give him faith, as examples

---

[16] Z III 761.22–38 (*Works* III 184), 775.26–30, 807.20–4. 1 Cor. 10: 16–17 is used as evidence that in breaking bread we show each other that we trust in Christ. (Z III 801.29–802.13.)

[17] Z IV 217.6–218.13; LCC XXIV 131. From 1525 Zwingli uses *Pflichtzeichen* as the equivalent in German of *sacramentum*. (Z IV 218.3–4.)

from the bible show. Zwingli confesses that earlier he erroneously held the view that sacraments do confirm faith.[18]

There is an important change in Zwingli's understanding of covenant signs in 1525, deriving from his understanding of the covenant. He has naturally used the term 'covenant' of God's covenant with man, but in 1525 this view is developed and related to the sacraments as signs of the covenant of grace made by God with man, that he will be their God and they will be his people.[19] Until this the sacraments have been seen as the covenant or pledge made between the Christian and his fellow Christians. This development takes place in terms of the eucharist, but is of particular importance in Zwingli's controversy with the anabaptists, as it gives greater coherence to his arguments for infant baptism.[20] This change gives a stronger theological and historical dimension to Zwingli's understanding of the sacraments.

Although there is a clear change of emphasis and expression in Zwingli's later writings, there is not that fundamental change of position that some have asserted. The most obvious change is in *An Exposition of the Faith*, which merits separate attention. The other writings can be grouped together, especially *Two Replies to Luther's Book*, *An Account of the Faith*, *The Providence of God*, and to some extent *The Letter to the Princes of Germany*.[21]

The fundamental role of the sovereignty of God in Zwingli's understanding of the sacraments is clear in *An Account of the Faith*. It dominates the first half of the article on the sacraments. The reason why they cannot confer grace is that grace is given by the Spirit. 'Moreover, a channel or vehicle is not necessary to the Spirit, for he himself is the virtue and energy whereby all things are borne, and has no need of being borne.' In his sovereign freedom the Spirit does not need outward means and is certainly not bound by them, either in the sense that he must work where they are present, 'for if it were thus it would be known how, where, whence, and whither the Spirit is given', or in the sense that he cannot work apart from

---

[18] Z IV 218.13–17, 219.1–25, 226.29–229.7 (LCC XXIV 138–9), 292.4–6. See also Z VI ii 206.31–207.4. The comparison between old and new testament signs is made even more strongly in *A Refutation*, where Zwingli points out that in 1 Cor. 5 and 10 and Col. 2 Paul 'attributes to them baptism and the eucharist or spiritual feeding on Christ, but to us the passover and circumcision, so that all things are equal on both sides'. (Z VI i 172.1–4.) See also Z XIII 349.37–351.27.

[19] Z IV 499.1–502.5.

[20] In his study of the place of the covenant in Zwingli's theology, J. W. Cottrell argues strongly for the development of the covenant in the context of the eucharist. ('Covenant and Baptism in the Theology of Huldreich Zwingli' (Diss. Princeton, 1971).)

[21] Certain points in *The Letter to the Princes of Germany* are dealt with under *An Exposition of the Faith*.

them, for the Spirit blows where he wills. Elsewhere the freedom of the Spirit in relation to outward means is put more positively, where Zwingli says, 'And one and the same Spirit works all these things, sometimes without, sometimes with the external instrument, and in inspiring draws where, as much, and whom he wills.'[22] Although certain things are attributed to the sacraments in scripture, that is simply parallel to the way in which forgiveness of sins is ascribed to the apostles. If the sacraments were of themselves effective, then Judas would have repented. However, repentance is the work of the Spirit, as is faith, which the Spirit effects before the sacraments take place. Zwingli regards as sacramentarians those who 'attribute to the symbols what belongs only to the divine power and the Holy Spirit working immediately in our souls', and who thus lead people away from simple trust in God to trust in the power of symbols.[23] His concern is that glory shall be given to God and not to the sacraments.[24]

Zwingli's profound suspicion of outward things in religion is derived in part from Augustine's Neoplatonism with its stress on the inward over against the outward, the Spirit over against the visible. He is constantly quoted, notably in *The Letter to the Princes of Germany*.[25] However, the suspicion of outward things has also to be set in the context of medieval religion, with its superstitious attachment to people, places, and things, not least to the sacraments, and the financial exploitation of this by the church. This attachment is for Zwingli a restoration of Judaism, and puts man and his works in the place of God.

For if we think otherwise of the sacraments, as that when externally used they cleanse internally, Judaism is restored, which believed that crimes were expiated,

[22] Z VI ii 803.7-15, 22, 28-9; VI iii 271.10-12 (*Works* II 117). Contrast Zwingli's earlier expression about the word in 'Eo enim veluti vehiculo spiritus tuus trahitur; nam ipsum ociosum ad te non revertitur.' (Z II 606.28-9.) Now he holds: '. . . ut spiritum sanctum recipere non sit baptismi opus, sed baptismus sit opus recepti spiritus sancti.' (Z VI iii 267.10-11.) He alludes to Pentecost when the wind brought the tongues, not the tongues the wind, and to the old testament, when the wind brought the quails and carried away the locusts, not the quails and the locusts the wind. (Z VI ii 803.16-20.)
    Emphasis on outward things challenges the freedom of the Spirit; see the comment on Luke 4: 1: 'Quod putas mentes esse quas divinus spiritus (virtus dei omnibus praesens et omnia penetrans) illustret ac penetret, quae corporalem spiritus speciem nullam vident? patris vocem externam non audiunt? Spiritus ubi vult spirat et operatur in corde credentium, non res externae.' (S VI i 569.6-10.)
[23] Z VI iii 165.1-166.7. 172.9-174.2. Cf. the exposition of Isa. 6: 7 in Z XIV 174.4-19. Cf. Z VI iii 265.11-19.
[24] Z VI iii 270.18-21.
[25] Z VI iii 265.19-270.17, 277.6-12.

and grace, as it were, purchased and obtained by various anointings, ointments, offerings, victims, and banquets. Nevertheless, the prophets, especially Isaiah and Jeremiah, always most steadfastly urged in their teaching that the promises and benefits of God are given by God's liberality, and not with respect to merits or external ceremonies.[26]

The sharp distinction between the sign and what it signifies fits this basic theological position. In this context Zwingli happily accepts in *Two Replies to Luther's Book* the traditional definitions of a sacrament as 'a sign of a holy thing' or 'a visible form or figure of an invisible grace'. The sign is not the holy thing itself, although it takes the name of what it signifies. This is true of secular signs, as it is of biblical signs. Moreover it does not follow that what is signified is present with the sign, otherwise since baptism is the sacrament of the death of Christ, Christ would have to die wherever there was a baptism. It is rather a sacrament of something that has happened. Furthermore a sacrament does not make present what it signifies, but it shows and attests that what it signifies is there. Thus baptism does not make people God's children, but those who are already God's children receive the sign and testimony of God's children.[27] Zwingli can therefore speak of a sacrament as the sign of a grace that has been given.[28] The signs make their appeal to the senses, but what they signify must already be present to the mind or soul.[29]

The bible is full of examples of God making use of the outward to accomplish his purposes, and the commentaries naturally refer to this. It is allowed that God could act without means, but nevertheless he uses them. Thus in the story of the flood he used wind and rain, which he had created for this purpose, although he could have filled the earth with water by his word alone.[30] Unlike us, God does not need to use outward means; he uses them for our sake, not for his own.[31] This does not alter the fact that the power is entirely of God and that it does not reside in the means that are used. It is God who, for example, heals the sick, which he does through the

[26] Z VI ii 805.23–9; Jackson 469–70 (*Works* II 48). For salvation as bound to a place, see S VI i 386.18–20.

[27] Z VI ii 200.6–201.18, 202.26–203.9. Cf. Z VI iii 166.3–168.12 and Z VI iii 253.8–258.20: '. . . externals can do nothing more than proclaim and represent . . . Nevertheless Christ himself does not disdain to call the bread his body, which to quote Augustine's words, is only the sign of his body.' (Z VI iii 166.3–9; *Works* II 190.)

[28] Z VI ii 805.6–7.

[29] Z VI iii 168.4–12.

[30] Z XIII 51.29–36.

[31] S VI i 205.6–10, 499.3–14. Cf. 'Adhibet aliquando deus externa quaedam, ut caro nostra tranquilletur, quemadmodum in coena externum sacramentum sensibus exhibet divina sapientia.' S VI i 356.1–3.

outward means that he has chosen.[32] This position is at one with Zwingli's view that God is the cause of all things. 'And to put it briefly, the ground does not bring forth, nor the water nourish, nor the air fructify, nor the fire warm, nor the sun itself, but rather that power which is the origin of all things, their life and strength, uses the earth as the instrument wherewith to produce and create.'[33]

This sense that it is God who is at work in all outward things could have led to a more positive view of the sacraments as means that God uses, although it would still have been qualified by Zwingli's sharp distinction between the outward and the inward. In such a view God's sovereignty could have been safeguarded, and the doctrine of election could have been used, as Bucer used it, to indicate that the sacraments are effective only with the elect. The distinction of outward and inward could have been expressed by the use of the preposition 'with' (rather than Luther's prepositions 'in' and 'under') to express the relationship between what is signified and the sign. But the opposition of outward and inward is so strong in Zwingli's thinking that this development does not seem possible for him. Nevertheless in *An Exposition of the Faith*, and at some points in other writings, he does speak more positively of the outward signs, and seems to allow that things happen together on two levels.

The whole presentation of the sacraments in *An Exposition of the Faith* is essentially positive. Earlier, in the opening section on God and the worship of God, Zwingli makes it clear that we are not to trust in the sacraments, for that would be to make them God, whereas they are creatures not creator. They are signs of holy things, but they are no more what they signify than the word 'ape' when written down is an ape. Zwingli asserts that they do not have the power that belongs to God alone, but he heads his section on sacraments 'The Power (or Virtue) of the Sacraments.'[34]

The first two virtues are historical. First, the sacraments were instituted by Christ and, what is more, he received the one and was the first to celebrate the other. Second, they testify to actual historical events. The next three, perhaps four, virtues involve the relationship between the sign and what it signifies, of which one, the third virtue, is already familiar: they take the place and name of what they signify.[35]

---

[32] *S* VI i 609.5-11, 729.24-8.
[33] *Z* VI iii 112.20-4; *Works* II 156. In *The Providence of God* Zwingli stresses the importance in understanding providence of recognizing that secondary causes are not properly speaking causes. It is God who is the cause of all things. In keeping with this, the emphasis in his references to the sacraments is on God rather than the sacraments. (*Z* VI iii 83.24-5, 165.5-11.)
[34] *S* IV 45.26-30, 46.7-11, 32-4. Cf. Additional Note, p. 193.
[35] *S* IV 56.18-31. Cf. *S* IV 46.11-16.

The fourth virtue is that they signify high things. Here Zwingli uses the analogy of the ring used earlier in *The Lord's Supper*.[36] The value of the queen's ring comes less from the value of the gold than from the value of the person it represents, the king. 'In the same way the bread and wine are the symbols of the friendship by which God is reconciled to the human race in and through his Son.' The bread can therefore be spoken of as consecrated and not common, and it is called the body of Christ as well as bread.[37]

The analogy is expounded at much greater length in *The Letter to the Princes of Germany* as a statement of his view of the eucharist. There is here a stronger sense of something happening at two levels. A husband, before going on a long journey, gives his wife a ring with his image cut upon it, saying, 'Here am I, your husband, for you to keep and delight in in my absence.' He is a type of Christ, who, when going away, left his spouse, the church, his own image in the sacrament of the supper. 'As he is the strong foundation of our hope, so does the bread strengthen mankind, and as wine refreshes the heart of man, so does he raise up despairing consciences.' It is as if Christ said,

I am wholly yours in all that I am. In witness of this I entrust to you a symbol of this my surrender and testament, to awaken in you the remembrance of me and of my goodness to you, that when you see this bread and this cup, held forth in this memorial supper, you may remember me as delivered up for you, just as if you saw me before you as you see me now, eating with you . . .

Thus I say we have the Lord's supper distinguished by the presence of Christ. But in all this is not the presence of the body of Christ sacramentally and to the eye of faith, as I have always said, the gist of the whole matter?

. . . the repast of the supper, though not Christ's material body, rises to high value because it was given and instituted as an everlasting sign of the love of Christ, and because as often as it is celebrated it so represents him who so loves us that we gaze upon him with the eye of the mind and adore and worship him.

. . . in the supper the body of Christ is the more present to the contemplation of the believing mind, the greater one's faith and love is towards Christ.[38]

All this is still only representing Christ rather than presenting him,

---

[36] Z IV 856.16–19. Jud also used it. The analogy of the ring was probably drawn from the beginning of Hoen's letter, which Zwingli published in 1525. (Z IV 512.10–15.)

[37] S IV 56.32–46; LCC XXIV 263 (*Works* II 257). This use of the word 'symbol' can be compared with the use of 'pledge' (*pignus*) in S IV 57.27–9. Zwingli speaks of the necessity of the sacraments, but in terms of what they signify. Those who trust in God do not despise the sacraments, but rather rejoice in them. (S III 581.24–30.)

[38] Z VI iii 278.19–282.7; *Works* II 122–24: 'Sic in coena Christi corpus tanto praesentius est fidei contemplatione menti . . .'. (Z VI iii 281.24–5.) Zwingli refers to Ps. 104: 15, as he did in the letter to Thomas Wyttenbach. (Z VIII 85.16–18.)

but there is a clear relationship for the believer between what is happening outwardly and what is happening inwardly.

The fifth virtue is the twofold analogy between the signs and what they signify. There is an analogy to Christ, for the bread sustains human life as Christ sustains the soul, and to us, for the bread is made up of many grains as the body of the church is made up of many members.[39]

The next virtue is dealt with at greatest length. With the fourth it is the closest Zwingli comes to a traditional affirmation of what the sacraments do, when he says that they 'augment faith and are an aid to it'. They are a help in terms of the senses, for it is through them that we are so often led astray. The sacraments appeal powerfully to the senses. They are indeed 'like bridles which serve to check the senses when they are on the point of dashing off in pursuit of their own desires, and to recall them to the obedience of the heart and of faith.' 'Therefore the sacraments assist the contemplation of faith . . .'.[40]

In *The Letter to the Princes of Germany* Zwingli makes it clear that the sacraments were instituted to make use of the senses. He grants that 'all created things invite us to the contemplation of the deity, yet this invitation is an altogether dumb one. In the sacraments we have a living and speaking invitation. For the Lord himself speaks, the elements speak, and they speak and suggest (*suadent*) to the senses the same thing that the word and the Spirit do to the mind.' Therefore the believer does not neglect or despise the sacraments. Indeed Zwingli's encouragement of their use is eager rather than defensive.

For who can disdain the things of love? And is not the love of God and of one's neighbour eager to call to mind the goodness of God and to praise and magnify him with thanksgiving? Is it not eager to be united to its neighbour by the bond of the Spirit and to bear witness thereto openly? Does it not desire to have its faith propped up and restored, when it sees it wavering? And where in the world can he hope to find that better than in the celebration of the sacraments, as far as visible things are concerned?

However, the appeal to the senses in the sacrament, powerful as it is, is ineffective unless the person has faith, unless the Spirit is present and active in him.

But when these things are contemplated the sacraments not only set them before our eyes, but even enable them to penetrate to the mind. But what leads the way? The Spirit.

---

[39] *S* IV 56.48–57.11.
[40] *S* IV 57.12–58.5; LCC XXIV 263–4 (*Works* II 258–9).

Since, therefore, this presence amounts to nothing without the contemplation of faith, it belongs to faith that the things are or become present, and not to the sacraments. For, however much they lay hold on the senses and lead to reverence for the things that are done, these handmaidens can effect nothing unless their mistress, faith, first rules and commands on the throne of the heart.[41]

At points throughout his writings Zwingli refers to the fact that the weak in faith need the sacraments or that they serve the senses, though particularly in his later works. However, he does it in these two works more fully and positively than elsewhere. In the earlier writings it seems much more a matter of concession to the weak.[42]

The seventh virtue of the sacraments is that they act as an oath. Those who eat his body sacramentally are joined in one body, so that anyone who enters it without faith betrays the body of Christ, both the head and the members of the body.[43]

Zwingli's understanding of the sacraments moves from the earlier writings, where they are signs of the covenant with which God assures us, through a period where the emphasis is on them as signs with which we assure others that we are one with them in the church, to the later writings, where something of both these emphases is present. The positive view of the sacraments in the later writings is developed largely in terms of an appeal to man outwardly through the senses. The appeal is always only to believers, so that a sacrament may help in confirming faith, but does not give it.

A number of factors combine to make Zwingli deny that the sacraments give faith or the Spirit. Fundamental among them is the understanding of the sovereignty of God and the freedom of the Spirit, together with his view of faith, but there is also the Neoplatonist element in his view of man which denies that outward things can reach and affect the soul. This plays an important part from 1524, whether or not influenced by Hoen's letter, although it is somewhat modified in the last writings.

[41] Z VI iii 261.6-11, 269.34-270.15 (*Works* II 116-117), 262.2-7 (*Works* II 111), 265.5-9 (*Works* II 113). The German translation renders *suadent* as *gliebend* (Z VI iii 270, n. 4). Cf. S IV 55.9-23: the sacraments give historical faith, but only to believers do they testify that Christ did not only die, but died for us.
[42] Z II 143.16-22; III 411.16-18; IV 217.14-19; VIII 85.37-86.21; XIII 177.13-20; S VI i 356.1-4, 373.27-32, 555.3-14, 567.4-7; VI ii 58.35-37. Cf. Z IV 228.2-5. 'Minime, sed animo offertur istud contemplandum, sensui vero sensibile eius rei sacramentum. Liberius enim ac expeditius agit mens, cum a sensibus quam minimum alio vocatur. Cum ergo et sensibus obiicitur, quod simillimum est ei, quod mens agit, iam non levis est sensuum opitulatio.' (Z VI iii 260.8-261.3.)
[43] S IV 58.6-15.

Zwingli's thinking about the sacraments is closely linked to the church and they are conceived corporately in terms of the church rather than individually in terms of salvation. This is true of both ways in which they are understood as covenant signs: as our pledges to our fellow believers that we are one with them in God's people and as God's pledge to us that he is our God and that we are his people. Both these elements are developed in the course of controversy, though neither is ultimately dependent on the controversy. Yet undoubtedly controversy heightens the negative elements in Zwingli's theology, the denial of what he holds to be false views of the sacraments. The more positive notes in his later writings do not seem to depend on the absence of controversy, but they are in some ways confessional writings, which may have stimulated a more constructive formulation of sacramental doctrine.

## ADDITIONAL NOTE

On the power of the sacraments see Zwingli's statement on baptism in *Questions Concerning the Sacrament of Baptism*: 'Sacramentum dat, non rem ecclesia; sed rem significat. Solus enim Christus baptizat spiritu sancto et igni, quem Ioannes post se venturum dicebat, eum tamen ipse iam baptizaret. Est ergo baptismus externa ceremonia, quae tamen rem, non praestat. Et nemo dicit baptismum tantum esse ceremoniam, quae nihil significet: sic enim non esset cerimonia. Sed magnum est discrimen inter *significare* et *praestare*.' (*S* III 576.43–577.2.) The sacraments may be said to represent (*darstellen*), but not to present (*darreichen*), a distinction made for baptism by J. M. Usteri and for the eucharist by F. Blanke (Usteri, 'Darstellung der Tauflehre Zwinglis', *Theologische Studien und Kritiken*, 55 (1882) 269, and Blanke, 'Antwort', *Theologische Blätter*, 11 (1932) 18). W. Niesel expresses this in a negative and extreme way when he says, 'Die Sakramente sind nicht Werkzeuge Gottes, sondern Werkzeuge des Glaubens' ('Zwinglis "spätere" Sakramentsanschauung', *Theologische Blätter*, 11 (1928) 15).

# 10. Baptism

ZWINGLI's writings on baptism arise out of his conflict with the anabaptists. It was in the attempt to answer their challenge to infant baptism that he reformulated his view of baptism as well as developed his case for the baptism of infants. The baptismal controversy revealed other fundamental differences between them and Zwingli, especially in their understanding and use of scripture.

## Early Statements on Baptism

Zwingli's statements on baptism were few until the controversy broke after the second disputation in October 1523. It is clear that his emphasis lay on faith rather than on baptism,[1] but his attitude to infant baptism is ambiguous. In *An Exposition of the Articles* he appears to accept infant baptism and his concern is that those baptized as infants shall be properly instructed in the faith, as happens at Zurich. This means that they must not be confirmed until they are able to confess the faith. At the same time he recognizes that in the early church many were catechumens who received instruction before being baptized.[2] However, Zwingli was accused by Hubmaier and others of opposing infant baptism and he wrote in 1525, 'I thought it much better not to baptize children until they had come to years of discretion.'[3] (He relates this to the erroneous view he held of baptism as strengthening faith, pointing out that this was inconsistent with infant baptism, as children are unable to believe.) The fact that Zwingli did not

---

[1] e.g. baptism is explained in terms of faith in Z I 130.27–131.4. In a clear reference to Mark 16: 16 in Z II 426.20–5 Zwingli speaks only of faith in relation to being saved, and ignores the reference to baptism. In *The Canon of the Mass* he again ignores it, using the text along with others to reject the doctrine of purgatory. (Z II 594.9–595.1.)

[2] This discussion is in the context of confirmation, itself examined in the context of the sacraments. (Z II 122.20–124.2.) In expounding the sixty-seventh article he states that it is more probable that the unbaptized infants of Christian parents will be saved and not damned. (Z II 455.18–25.) This seems to imply doubts about the traditional doctrine of original sin and the relation of baptism to it, for the salvation of infants is not made to depend on baptism. He later admitted that he did once hold the traditional doctrine. (Z IV 247.31–2.)

Erasmus twice refers to Gerson's opinion that the unbaptized infants of Christian parents may be saved by God's immense mercy through the pleas of their parents. See Payne, p. 177. Knowles points out that Occam's views on justification were used to support the view that good pagans might be saved and that unbaptized infants might attain to heaven (D. Knowles and D. Obolensky, *The Christian Centuries*, II *The Middle Ages* (London, 1969), p. 448).

[3] Z IV 228.20–229.7.

stop the baptism of infants suggests either that he did not regard the matter as fundamentally important or that he did not regard the time as opportune for such a change. In view of what happened later the former seems more likely.[4]

In his letter to Thomas Wyttenbach in June 1523 baptism is shown as strengthening faith. Zwingli makes it clear that baptism does not give faith, for if someone does not have faith, then washing him in water a thousand times achieves nothing. It is faith that is required. A person who is strong in faith does not need baptism in order to be more sure or secure. But where faith is more primitive there is need, for in being baptized one knows oneself to be washed inwardly by faith, just as outwardly by water.[5] The contrast of inward and outward may be expressed in the passing reference in a letter to Bucer in June 1524 where the Spirit flowing from heaven is said to be the water with which Christ said one must be baptized, and faith comes from the Spirit.[6]

In his letter to Fridolin Lindauer in October there is a similar contrast between faith and baptism in water: baptism in 1 Peter 3: 21 is said to refer to faith and not to baptism in water, the sign standing for the thing signified, for it is by faith alone that we are saved. (In any case an incorporeal substance cannot be washed by a corporeal element.) The sacrament instructs the outward man which grasps things through the senses and is initiated by the visible sign. In this way the outward man becomes certain of what comes to the inward man 'by the light of faith and the manifest word of the grace of God'. Thus in commanding the person who already believes to be baptized, God satisfies the whole man, inward and outward.[7] There are in effect two grounds for baptism: God's command and the need of the outward man.

This development of the idea of the sacraments as strengthening faith is for Zwingli no more appropriate for infant baptism than the original idea. Nor is the idea of sacraments as pledges which Zwingli develops in the light of 1 Corinthians 10 in relation to the eucharist. In the end Zwingli has to find other ways of understanding baptism that can apply to adults and infants.

---

[4] Cottrell (p. 48) suggests that he continued the practice while working out a rationale for baptism to include infants as well as adults. He might justify his action by the principle, 'Anything which God has not forbidden is not sin.'

[5] Z VIII 85.34-86.5. In this discussion, with its distinction between those who are strong and those who are weak in faith, Baur (II 54, n. 1), following Usteri, sees the influence of Origen.

[6] Z VIII 194.14-15.

[7] Z VIII 236.3-20. Zwingli rejects the claim that sins are taken away by the sacraments as a denial of the incarnation and atonement. (Z VIII 235.23-236.3.)

*The First Defence of Infant Baptism*

In December 1524, when writing to Strasburg, Zwingli set out his first
detailed defence of infant baptism, although he had, he says, already discussed it twice successfully. His position is based on the view that in the
bible 'baptism is the initiation both of those who have already believed
and those who are going to believe'. He argues first from John the Baptist.
According to John 1: 26–7 and Acts 19: 4 he baptized people into Christ,
who was still to come and whom those baptized did not know. He was
enrolling them as by an oath of allegiance (*sacramento*) in the service of his
coming leader. Baptism therefore preceded knowledge of Christ. Zwingli
makes 'no distinction at all between the baptism of John and the baptism
of Christ', for the symbol and the oath of allegiance (*sacramentum*) were
the same, and even those with knowledge of Christ who were baptized by
the apostles would not have gone to the Father before the resurrection of
Christ. With this he sees himself as proving that 'baptism was given also to
those who were going to believe at some time, and they were baptized for
this purpose, that they might learn Christ afterwards . . .'. Second, he
argues more precisely for infant baptism on the grounds that baptism
according to Colossians 2: 11 replaced circumcision, and that circumcision, though a sign of preceding faith (Rom. 4: 11), was given to infants
whose faith came later. 'Therefore baptism like circumcision should be
bestowed on those who are going to believe later . . .'. Third, he draws on
the words of Christ in Matthew 19: 13–14 where Christ commanded the
apostles to let the children come to him, for of such is the kingdom of
heaven. He asserts that if anyone forbids children to be baptized, he forbids them to come to Christ. Zwingli then invokes Peter's words in Acts
10: 47 to ask who can forbid that they be baptized, since they are God's. He
also uses 1 Corinthians 7: 14 in support of this.[8]

After this Zwingli tackles four objections. First, it is said that there are
no statements or examples in support of infant baptism, therefore infants
should not be baptized. Against this he quotes the statement that baptism
is our outward circumcision and the example of John the Baptist and the
baptism of households described in 1 Corinthians 1 and Acts 16, in which
it is more likely than not that there were children. Second, it is argued that
the apostles examined beforehand the faith of those whom they baptized.
Zwingli says that this happened only sometimes, following the example of
Christ who sometimes asked those he was going to heal about their faith
and sometimes did not. Third, it is held that the words of Mark 16: 16

---

[8]  Z VIII 269.13–273.11.

imply that faith should precede baptism. To this Zwingli replies that the words, as the previous verse shows, apply to adults to whom the gospel is preached, and not to infants. Fourth, comes the objection that it will be more vivid and effective if everyone confesses his faith openly before being baptized. Zwingli answers that there will be a better opportunity of learning the faith if a boy is baptized, because of the obligation baptism places on a child to learn and on a parent to teach. Baptism, like circumcision, is 'a sacrament by which while still children we are bound to the learning of the law of the Lord and to the fashioning of our lives, by which also our parents are bound to form us in this way . . .'. Personal confession of faith follows in the eucharist. After these four points Zwingli concludes that the only matter in infant baptism over which one should dispute is not attributing to baptism what belongs to the grace of God alone, in other words thinking that the soul is cleansed by the water of baptism.[9]

The comments on baptism in *Those Who Give Cause for Tumult* do not add essentially to the case made out in the letter to Strasburg, except for two matters. Zwingli allows that there is no command to baptize infants in the new testament, just as there is also no prohibition. Moreover the fact that the new testament does not record that the apostles baptized infants does not mean that we should not baptize them, any more than the fact that they did not baptize in Calcutta means that we should not baptize there. Therefore in the absence of clear direction in the new testament one should turn to the old testament, where we find circumcision which has now been replaced by baptism. It was given to children without faith, although it was a sign of preceding faith. In this discussion Zwingli seems to imply that he does not lay great store by the matter, and could change his mind. Nevertheless he stands his ground, pointing out that Christ instituted baptism because our eyes want to see. It is to be feared, therefore, that if infants are not baptized, Christians will demand circumcision. People want their children marked with a sign.[10] Most of the main arguments Zwingli is to use in the baptismal controversy are deployed in the early writings, but they are developed and refined in the course of the controversy.

[9] Z VIII 273.12–275.22. More fundamental than the fact that nothing outward can affect the soul is the fact that salvation is entirely of God's grace.
   The argument from the obligation baptism places on parents to bring up their children according to the teaching of the church is repeated in Zwingli's last work on baptism. (S III 587.26–34.)
[10] Z III 409.14–410.13, 411.6–18, 412.5. 'Ouch nit, das mir an der kindertouff so vil gelegen sye . . . Und wo ich hieruss empfunde schmaach gottes erwachsen oder nachteil christlichem läben, läge mir nüts daran, das ich min meinung endren sölte.' (Z III 411.6–14.) See Additional Note 1, p. 216.

*The Development of the Controversy*

The anabaptists confronted Zwingli with the question of rebaptism as well as that of infant baptism, when in January 1525 they began baptizing those already baptized as infants. This changed situation required a different response. This is apparent in *A Commentary* in the space given to identifying the baptism of John with that of Christ.

Zwingli's view of baptism is differentiated from the respective positions of catholics, Lutherans, and anabaptists: that baptism can free or cleanse the conscience, that it makes a person sure that the Spirit does inwardly what the sacrament signifies outwardly, that it is a sign which makes a person sure of what has been done within him. Rather the sacraments are signs 'by which a man proves to the church that he either aims to be, or is, a soldier of Christ, and which inform the whole church rather than yourself of your faith'. Baptism is an initiatory ceremony or pledging.[11]

At the beginning of the exposition Zwingli refers to the distinction whereby baptism is used sometimes for baptism and teaching and sometimes only for the sign of baptism. Failure to see this distinction, which he develops in *Baptism, Rebaptism, and Infant Baptism*, causes the anabaptists to fight blindfold. Zwingli's concern, however, is to show the identity of John's and Christ's baptism, so that he can demonstrate that there was no need for a second baptism in Acts 19, an example used by the anabaptists in support of rebaptism.

Zwingli argues for the identity in this way. Christ and his disciples were baptized by John, and as Christ made no change in the baptism in either case, then clearly baptism began with John and there can be no difference between the two baptisms in essence, effect, or purpose. Moreover Christ's baptism was obviously not for his own sake, but for ours, to commend baptism to us. However, as he made no change in John's baptism, he must be commending baptism to us by means of John's baptism, and therefore the two must be the same. If that is the case 'there was no need to be baptized with the baptism of Christ'.[12] From that he goes on to show that such rebaptism did not happen. He does this by arguing both that baptism in the new testament sometimes means teaching and that the teaching (and

---

[11] Z III 757.10–20, 759.5–761.29; *Works* III 184. Zwingli stresses that the biblical formula is 'into the name' and not 'in the name'. To baptize into the name of the Father, of the Son, and of the Holy Spirit is 'nothing else than to dedicate, devote, consecrate, those who were previously of the world and the flesh to the Father, Son, and Holy Spirit'. (Z III 771.31–773.3; *Works* III 196.) Zwingli introduces this formula into the baptismal service.

[12] Z III 763.6–773.24, esp. 763.9–15, 768.28–769.2.

hence the baptism of teaching) in John and Christ was the same. What happened therefore in Acts 19 has to do with baptism in the sense of teaching. Those who had been taught had not in fact been completely taught. They had therefore been baptized in the sense of taught.[13]

## A Major Defence

After these relatively brief statements on baptism Zwingli published three major works, the first two in 1525, when the baptismal controversy was intense, and the third in 1527. Then in 1530 came a reply to Schwenckfeld. His concern is not, of course, with the doctrine of baptism alone, but with the threat posed to the reformation itself by the anabaptists' radical approach on baptism and social issues. He particularly attacks them for disturbing the peace of the Christian church on account of something outward, when they have affirmed that salvation is not bound up with outward things, and for their divisiveness in separating from the church to set up their own sinless churches. The problems are not limited to Zurich, but menace other places as well, including St Gallen, to which he dedicates *Baptism, Rebaptism, and Infant Baptism* .[14]

Before outlining his case Zwingli indicates his basic disagreement with the anabaptist and catholic positions. He accuses the anabaptists of doing what they accuse others of: adding to the word of God. When they say 'God does not command the baptism of infants, therefore we should not baptize them', they in effect add to God's word the prohibition of infant baptism. If, however, there is no law forbidding infant baptism, then there is no transgression and hence no sin in baptizing infants.[15] He challenges the catholics by asserting that Christian teachers have been in error since the time of the apostles 'in ascribing to water what it does not have'. No outward thing can make us pure and righteous, but only Christ. Indeed Christ did away with outward things, so that we should not seek salvation in them. As a concession to our weakness he has given us two outward things, baptism and the eucharist, but they are pledges, signs of holy things, and not the things themselves.[16]

---

[13] Z III 769.2–772.1. Payne (p. 290, n. 1) gives examples from Erasmus where flesh and blood mean teaching, but they are later than Zwingli's use of baptism to mean teaching.

[14] Z IV 206.6–207.10, 208.28–209.3, 210.24–211.7, 216.7–12.

[15] Z IV 211.8–212.4. Zwingli's first major work on baptism is presented in some detail, in part as an example of his controversial writings.

[16] Z IV 216.14–218.24. In the brief summary statement on baptism at the end, the catholic position is attacked. Zwingli states that no outward thing in this world can purify the soul, but only the grace of God. Therefore baptism cannot wash away sin. But if it cannot wash away sin and yet is instituted by God, it must be a covenant sign of God's people and nothing else. (Z IV 333.16–22.)

The work is divided into four sections: baptism, its institution, rebaptism, and infant baptism. There are no major changes or developments in Zwingli's view of baptism at this stage, if we accept that he does not really develop his idea of baptism as a sign of the covenant at this point, although he expounds the arguments at greater length, even if frequently with less clarity.[17]

First, Zwingli considers the use of the term 'baptism' in the bible. The distinctions he makes provide the basis for his case against catholics and anabaptists. He notes that the term is used in four ways: immersion in water, the baptism of the Spirit, outward teaching and outward immersion, and lastly outward baptism and inward faith. The first is seen in cases where there is a clear reference to water, as in John 3: 23; the second where there is a distinction between being baptized in water and being baptized in the Spirit, as in Acts 1: 5; the third where baptism cannot refer to water baptism, as in John 3: 22 and Matthew 21: 25; the fourth where it must refer to faith, because salvation is ascribed to it, as in 1 Peter 3: 21. The first three of these are different forms of baptism and they are given separately. Thus people can be baptized with water and not receive the Spirit, like Simon Magus; or they can be taught and not be baptized with water, like the Jews in Acts 18; or they can receive the Spirit without being baptized with water, like the thief on the cross. The inward baptism of the Spirit can be given by God alone and without it no one can be saved, though, like the thief, one can be saved without the outward baptism of teaching and immersion. The outward baptism of the Spirit, that is the gift of tongues, is not necessary for salvation and is given only to a few.[18]

Baptism is a sign, but it must be distinguished from miraculous signs. Fundamental in Zwingli's understanding of baptism is that it is a covenant sign or pledge. As such it does not strengthen faith, although he admits that for a period he thought it did and therefore thought one should not baptize infants, who are unable to believe. However, the idea of a pledge does not lead Zwingli to an anabaptist position. Indeed he disputes their claim that it is a pledge to live without sin, for that makes God a liar (1 John 1: 8, 10) and will bring back the hypocrisy of legal righteousness, as we seek to appear sinless to men. Baptism is rather a pledge to amend one's life and to follow Christ. In short it is the beginning of a new life, an

[17] Already in *A Commentary* he has spoken of baptism as teaching and shown the beginnings of the emphasis on covenant as God's covenant with man. Cottrell (pp. 159–66) makes a case for the clear development of baptism as a sign of God's covenant with us in *A Reply to Hubmaier*.

[18] *Z* IV 219.1–226.28. There is an implicit reference to the baptism of the Spirit in *Z* VIII 194.14–15 and to baptism as faith in *Z* VIII 236.16–20. The distinction between the inward and outward baptism of the Spirit occurs in *A Commentary* in *Z* III 764.25–765.5.

initiatory sign, like the cowl one has on entering an order, which one wears before learning the rules of the order. As scriptural support Zwingli quotes Matthew 28: 19-20, a favourite anabaptist text, where baptizing precedes the teaching of what the baptized are to observe, and Matthew 3: 11 and Mark 1: 4, to show that baptism is an initiatory sign or pledge. He then uses Luke 3: 7-8 to overthrow the view that only those who can live without sin should be baptized and John 1: 25-7 and Luke 3: 16 against the view that only those with the Spirit should be baptized. (In this context Zwingli rejects the view that infants cannot have the Spirit, for God works how and when he wills.) Romans 6: 3-5, with its use of 'into' rather than 'in', its reference to death, resurrection, and walking in newness of life, and its use of baptism as an example to show that we can no longer remain in the old life, is the strongest support for the view that 'baptism in water is an initiatory sign, with which we pledge ourselves to a new life . . .'.[19]

In considering what baptism effects Zwingli recognizes that the anabaptist controversy has had some beneficial results: showing both that human additions to baptism such as exorcism, spittle, and salt are worthless, and that the pouring of water does not wash away sin. He cites, as usual in this context, Hebrews 9, as evidence that bodily things do not purify the conscience. On this basis he tackles a text that seems to tell against him, John 3: 5. He asserts that the reference to water in John 3: 5 is not to baptism but, as is clear from other passages such as John 7: 37-8, to the water that quickens our soul, that is Christ, a view supported by passages such as Isaiah 55: 1 and Zechariah 14: 8. Moreover if water is taken literally in John 3: 5, then so should fire in Matthew 3: 11. However, for Zwingli it is not only catholics who ascribe too much to baptism, as in John 3: 5, but also anabaptists. They are rebaptized in order that their brethren may restrain them from sin. This makes Zwingli attack their rebaptism as monkery, sectarianism, and legalism, for a Christian should act from faith, not from compulsion.[20]

---

[19] Z IV 226.29-247.4: 'Das aber die wunderzeichen zuo vestung des gloubens ggeben werdend, kumt nit dahar, dass sy dem glouben etwas zuotragind oder merind, sunder das sy dem gwünndrigen fleisch gnuog tuond, welchs all weg ouch wüssen unnd sehen wil.' (Z IV 228.1-5.) In reference to Luke 3, Zwingli describes baptism as an initiatory sign and pledge with which we bind ourselves to God and testify this to our neighbour with an outward sign. (Z IV 241.27-30.)

[20] Z IV 247.5-254.9. Against the catholic and anabaptist overemphasis on outward baptism, Zwingli asserts his fundamental conviction 'that it is certain that no outward element or action can purify the soul'. (Z IV 252.21-6.) (He later accuses the anabaptists of not considering election, but, with the catholics, of thinking that salvation is bound to symbols. (Z V 387.11-13).)) The use in this section of frequent cross-reference to establish the meaning of a controversial passage is typical of Zwingli.

After the first section of the book dealing with what baptism is, the second section deals with its origin and institution. It does not so much present Zwingli's view as deal with his opponents' case. He argues against associating the origin and institution with Matthew 28: 19–20. For the anabaptists such an association was important to show that teaching should precede baptism. For Zwingli, however, the unity or identity of John's baptism and Christian baptism is a fundamental part of his case. He argues that baptism was instituted by God through John who was therefore known as the Baptist. As John came to prepare the way of the Lord (Mal. 3: 1) and in his coming baptized, it follows that he initiated the Lord's baptism. Zwingli dismisses the view that John's baptism was only a type of Christ's baptism, for that would place John in the old testament, whereas if you look at the teaching of John you see that he preached the kingdom of God, that is the gospel. There is an identity of teaching and baptism between John and the disciples and therefore between John's baptism and Christ's baptism. A further point favouring their identity is that Christ gave us an example by being baptized, but the baptism with which he was baptized was John's. If we wish to follow his example we must be baptized with the same baptism. Central to the anabaptist case is the contrast of the two baptisms and the instance of rebaptism in Acts 19: 1–5. Zwingli deals with the anabaptist objection that Paul baptized those already baptized by John, by arguing that the anabaptists have misunderstood the passage. Paul states that John's baptism concerned repentance and faith in Christ, which is the same as Christ's baptism. Drawing on his argument that baptism often means 'teaching' and the fact that 'into' is used rather than 'in', Zwingli seeks to establish that the people had been baptized in the sense of 'taught', though inadequately taught, by Apollos. Two other points in favour of baptism meaning 'teaching' here are that there is no record that Apollos baptized, and that when the people were baptized it was in the name of Jesus. That is exactly what would have happened if John had baptized them.[21]

The section on rebaptism also does not contribute much to Zwingli's theology of baptism, in part because he is concerned to correct his opponents by pointing out, for example, that baptism is not a papal invention and that one can know one has been baptized by asking one's godparents.

Zwingli's attack on catholic and anabaptist alike is based on his interpretation of certain key texts. His distinction between baptism in water and baptism of the Spirit is a weapon against the catholic identification of the two. His distinction between baptism as teaching and baptism as immersion is a weapon against the anabaptist argument for rebaptism based on Acts 19.

[21] Z IV 258.3.–277.13.

His fundamental assertion however is that rebaptism has no support in scripture. Moreover—and this is one point where anabaptists are as much in error as the papists—those who rebaptize seek something in it that they did not have before, and that goes with seeking salvation in outward things. If baptism renewed and strengthened the soul, one would be baptized as often as the need arose. However, baptism is a likeness or figure of the death of Christ, who died only once, and those who are rebaptized crucify Christ afresh.[22]

The final section deals with infant baptism, presenting the two major arguments for infant baptism to which he returns in his later writings. First, the children of Christians are no less children of God than their parents are, just as much as in the old testament. However, if they are God's, who will refuse them baptism? Second, as a sign, circumcision was to the ancients what baptism is to us. As circumcision was given to children, so should baptism be.[23] It must be said, however, that the arguments as he presents them lack the clarity and precision of his summary.

Zwingli has to deal with a fundamental anabaptist objection that Christ did not baptize infants, and therefore that we should not. Zwingli cannot and does not deny the fact, but he does challenge the conclusion drawn from it. He answers by saying that the anabaptists' statement would imply that women should not come to communion because there were no women at the last supper with Christ. There may not be a clear word to baptize children, but there is a command to baptize, and why should one distinguish in this between old and young any more than between men and women? Zwingli's counter-assertion is that there is no clear prohibition of infant baptism. Like Augustine, he has no doubt that infant baptism comes from the time of Christ and the apostles. The absence of explicit reference to it should not surprise us as—to cite a parallel—it is only because of misuse in Corinth that we have a detailed account of the eucharist. However, there is for Zwingli evidence in the new testament in favour of infant baptism. He draws on the gospel account of the children being brought to Jesus, and asks how else children are to come to him now apart from the covenant sign of God's people; and if they belong to the kingdom of God, then—by analogy with Peter and Cornelius in Acts 10: 47—why should one withhold from them the sign of God's people?

---

[22] Z IV 277.14–292.2, 334.1–5. Quoting John 13: 15, Zwingli uses Christ's example as an argument for baptism and against rebaptism. We are to follow the clear word and example of Christ. Therefore as Christ and the apostles were baptized in John's baptism and were not rebaptized, neither should we be. Those mentioned in Acts 19 were also, by implication, not rebaptized. (Z IV 283.17–30.)

[23] Z IV 333.23–9.

(We can be certain from this passage that children belong to God, whereas we cannot tell of adults whether they are believers.) Moreover, given the zeal of the parents in bringing their children to Jesus, we can be sure that they would have had them baptized. Zwingli reiterates that in outward matters, such as baptism, we must beware of saying that something did not happen because it was not recorded; after all there is no record that Mary and most of the apostles were baptized.[24]

The natural argument for the anabaptists was to point to baptismal passages where there was no reference to children or where faith was mentioned, which implied that children were not involved. Zwingli denied this implication for passages such as Acts 2. He also drew on 1 Corinthians 10: 1–5 as an argument for the baptism of adults and children, for the passage says that they were all baptized into Moses. With his view that baptism can mean 'teaching' Zwingli interprets this in terms of the teaching of the law and their being taught and pledged to the law of God. However, that teaching followed baptism in the cloud and in the sea. Thus for us baptism applies to all and comes before the law.[25]

In an excursus on original sin Zwingli denies original guilt. This probably fits the development of his case in terms of the need to affirm that children are God's, which would be contradicted if they suffered from original guilt, and therefore were liable to damnation. After the excursus he returns to reasons why it is more likely than not that children were baptized in the time of the apostles, citing the example of households that were baptized, and then he turns again to what he regards as the fundamental matter: that the children are God's. (He limits himself to the children of Christians, though he does not think other children are damned as long as they do not know what sin and the law is. However the judgement, he affirms, is God's, not his.) 1 Corinthians 7: 12–14 refers to the children of one Christian parent as holy, that is, counted among God's people. From this we can clearly deduce that the children of Christian parents are counted among the sons of God. Indeed they are more certainly children of God than we are. To the anabaptist objection that whoever does not believe will be damned (Mark 16: 16), Zwingli replies that the context refers to those to whom the gospel is preached. Moreover, in a typical argument from the old to the new testament, he states that if the children of Christians who did not believe were damned, then they would be worse off than the children of Jews. The matter can be summed up in two points: it is more probable than not that infants were baptized in the time of Christ; the children of believers are God's and therefore one should

[24] Z IV 296.1–303.11.     [25] Z IV 303.12–307.10.

baptize children. For Christ has only one church and only one baptism. We cannot therefore have a part of the church baptized, and a part not. The unity of the church is something fundamental in Zwingli's theology.[26]

He has already outlined the argument from circumcision, given to Abraham and his descendants as a covenant sign or pledge. It was not a confirming of Abraham's faith, for faith is a matter for God alone, but it is a pledge to lead one's children to God. Abraham himself believed before he was circumcised, but not the children whom God commanded to be circumcised. Baptism therefore serves the purpose that circumcision did in the old testament, namely that those who trust in God should lead their children to know God and cleave to him. In this the covenant sign is given first, with the teaching coming after, just as in the old testament circumcision is given before faith.[27] In expounding God's covenant with Abraham Zwingli still speaks of the covenant sign in terms of our pledge. He uses it both as pledging oneself and pledging to bring up one's children. In this way it is adapted to the baptism of adults and children and is specifically related to the institution of circumcision with Abraham.

To buttress the argument from circumcision Zwingli has to affirm the role of the old testament against the anabaptist appeal to the new. He does this by reference to the example of Christ who appealed to the old testament in Matthew 22: 29 and John 5: 39, as Paul did in Romans 15: 4 and 1 Corinthians 10: 11. We need to go to the old testament, not only about baptism, but also about other outward matters, such as the degrees of marriage. We find that circumcision there is equivalent to baptism with us, and that then children and women as well as men were figuratively (*bedüt-lich*) baptized and actually circumcised, so that all of us and our children should be baptized no less than they. Baptism in the old testament is a figure of ours (1 Cor. 10: 1-2). How much more should our children, who live under grace, be counted among God's people and given the covenant sign than their children who lived under the law. Zwingli uses Colossians 2: 10-12 to show that baptism is in the place of circumcision; and since baptism is in place of circumcision it should be given to children. The outward matters in baptism, that is, time, place, and person, are not important. From infant baptism, however, certain consequences follow: we need instruction in Christian doctrine and so the ministers must gather children to teach them the faith; and children are obliged to live in a Christian

---

[26] Z IV 312.5-318.19. Zwingli quotes from Augustine in favour of the practice of infant baptism in apostolic times. (Z IV 318.20-324.28.)

[27] Z IV 292.4-295.33.

way and parents to bring them up in a Christian way, which would not follow if the children were not baptized.[28]

A work must be judged by its purpose and whether it achieved it. Although his arguments did not persuade the anabaptists, they did persuade many who might otherwise have been swayed by them. The writing, in many ways typical of Zwingli's controversial works, lacks clarity and precision. This arises in part from his mixing of his own position and his reply to those of his opponents. It involves him in detailed exegesis of the crucial texts, in which the argument is sometimes more skilful than compelling. But in controversy it is often as important to throw doubt on the force of one's opponent's case as to establish one's own. The book is involved, which Zwingli seems to recognize by giving a summary at the end, but its main points are clear. Baptism, like other outward things, cannot save, but is a covenant sign or pledge. It should be given to infants, as they are part of God's people, and they should receive it as children, because baptism replaces circumcision which was given to children. Although there is no explicit reference to the baptism of infants in the new testament, it is more likely than not that they were baptized. Baptism, however, must not be repeated, for that is not supported in scripture and would amount to crucifying Christ again.

### Baptism and the Covenant

*A Reply to Hubmaier* marks an important development both in the understanding of baptism and in the case for infant baptism. Baptism is seen as a sign of God's covenant with us rather than as a sign of our covenant, and infant baptism is supported on the basis of our being part of the one covenant made with Abraham and consummated in Christ. The changed understanding of the covenant sign and of covenant unity is already expressed in *The Eucharist* in August 1525. 'Our baptism therefore looks altogether to the same thing as circumcision did formerly. It is the sign of the covenant God struck with us through his Son.' The covenant in Christ is a working out of the covenant made with Abraham. 'For the covenant struck with Abraham is so firm and in no way abrogated, so that unless you always keep it you will not be faithful.'[29]

---

[28] Z IV 325.17–332.14. See Additional Note 2, pp. 216–17.

[29] Z IV 500.9–39. Cottrell (pp. 180–5) argues suggestively that this understanding of the covenant and of covenant unity may have arisen in the detailed examination of Genesis that Zwingli was engaged in at this period in the prophecy. The commentary, published in 1527, could well reflect this. This idea of covenant was of course present in *An Exposition of the Articles*, but it does not feature in Zwingli's baptismal theology. There is a sign of this new understanding

Zwingli's view on baptism and his arguments for infant baptism in *Baptism, Rebaptism, and Infant Baptism* are repeated in *A Reply to Hubmaier*, together with the theses advanced at the end of it. Much of the work is taken up with a detailed reply to Hubmaier's book, which was an attack on Zwingli's position. The reply is both defence and counter-attack. Zwingli defends his position, for example on the identity of John's and Christ's baptism, on baptism as teaching, and on the need for anabaptists to show a text prohibiting infant baptism. He attacks Hubmaier's position, for example, for seeming to speak of the necessity of baptism as if one could not be saved without it, and as if it contributed to the forgiveness of sins. If that were the case Christ would have died in vain and it would be false to say that God alone forgives sins. There are, however, those whom God elected who have not been baptized. Baptism is only an outward sign of the covenant which all those in the covenant should receive.[30] Zwingli is willing.to accept Hubmaier's reference to baptism as a testimony to faith, but undermines it as an argument for adult baptism. Faith must be understood as the content of the whole covenant which we have with God, and not as the trust which a person has in his heart. When infants are baptized it is not in terms of their parents' saving faith, for they may be unbelievers, but in terms of the faith they confess with their lips.[31] More generally Zwingli attacks the anabaptists' sectarianism and their attitude to civil government.

The interest lies, however, in the second part of the work, where Zwingli presents his own views more positively. They are fundamentally unchanged, except for the new understanding of the covenant, which dominates the presentation. This view is also present incidentally in the first part. The covenant is God's covenant of grace, rather than our covenant, his promise rather than ours, with a consequent change in the meaning of the covenant sign, as the sign of God's covenant and promise, rather than our pledge to live a godly life. This understanding of 'sign' fits adult and infant baptism alike, whereas its earlier understanding as 'pledge' had a somewhat different sense in each. Moreover the covenant is not a new or different covenant, but 'we are in the covenant that God made with Abraham'.[32]

in *A Commentary*. Cottrell draws attention to the fact that the idea of covenant unity developed independently of the baptismal controversy.

[30] e.g Z IV 613.4–618.18. See Additional Note 3, p. 217.

[31] Z IV 621.8–30, 626.7–627.10, 632.26–634.2. In this context Zwingli refers to Augustine's remark about the faith of the church.

[32] Z IV 596.1–2, 636.24–6, 636.33–637.1. The covenant is God's promise to be our God and the God of our seed and also to send a saviour of the seed of Abraham. (Z IV 630.24–632.25.) Baptism 'is an enrolling in the people of God', 'an outward covenant sign which all should

The sections on baptism and rebaptism are brief and simply elaborate the earlier theses. Infant baptism is treated at length. Again the earlier theses are repeated, with Zwingli declaring both that they are the ground for holding to infant baptism and that Hubmaier has not touched them in his book. Zwingli's approach is twofold: to show first that children were members of God's people and second that our children are no less members of God's people than theirs. Zwingli describes the covenant made with Abraham, and renewed later with others, and points to the fact the children were given the covenant sign because they were no less in the grace and covenant of God than their parents. God would not have commanded that they be given the sign unless they were members of his covenant and people. The fact that only boys, and not women (who were in the covenant as well), were given the sign Zwingli explains by means of synecdoche, in which the whole race is included under the chief part. Other examples can be found in Acts 2: 46–7 and 1 Corinthians 10: 2. Similarly, although Christ did not explicitly say, 'The children are mine: baptize them as well', they are regarded, no less than the children of Abraham, as belonging to the people and church of God. Christians who were Jews would know that one should give the covenant sign to children. The objection that we cannot know whether the parents are believers and in the covenant Zwingli dismisses on the ground that since only God can know the heart, we must be content with outward confession. In any case membership of the covenant is of God's grace. The example of circumcision also shows that the teaching (in Deuteronomy 31) followed the sign.[33]

Having established that children in the old testament were counted in God's people, Zwingli seeks to show that our children are no less God's children, arguing that the Christian covenant or new testament is the same as the old covenant with Abraham. The point of reference is the covenant of grace with Abraham and not the law and Moses. The argument is not therefore, as before, in terms of the contrast between the two testaments, so that if something applied to them under the law, how much more does it apply to us under grace. Now it is rather in terms of the unity of the two. What is said about them applies to us as we are the same people, in the same covenant, with the same faith in Christ. The old and new testaments both testify to the fact that the Gentiles will become God's

receive who are in the covenant . . .'. (Z IV 593.5–6, 618.13–16.) Zwingli can use the terms *Pflicht-zeichen* and *Bundeszeichen* interchangeably, as he apparently does in Z IV 631.6–7, although the former more naturally represents the earlier understanding of the covenant as our pledge, and the latter the later understanding of it as God's covenant.

[33]  Z IV 629.1–634.2.

people in place of the Jews. Perhaps the most vivid example is the parable of the wedding of the king's son in Matthew 22: 1-14, which shows that we are not called to another wedding feast, but to the one that was originally prepared. Paul states that through faith we, as much as the Israelites, are children of Abraham. It is true that children cannot have faith, but by synecdoche we know that they are also included in the covenant and promise; because 'Christian people are also in the gracious covenant with God, in which Abraham stood, it is clearly proved that our children are no less God's than Abraham's.' They are members of the church of God, which is a sure comfort for the children of Christians. The implication of all this is self-evident for Zwingli. 'If they are children of God, it follows as Peter says in Acts 10 that we neither should nor may deny them outward baptism. . . . Why do you dispute then about baptism? Should we not give the outward baptism of water to those who are children of God?' Thus infant baptism is 'a source of unity and a clear, comforting sign of assurance that by virtue of the testament our children are certaintly God's'.[34]

The second of Zwingli's basic arguments for infant baptism, the one from circumcision, is manifestly secondary in *A Reply to Hubmaier*. It is dealt with in a paragraph in which baptism is shown to be for us the covenant sign which circumcision was for them. As before Christ the covenant sign was given to children, as to those who were in the covenant, so under Christ the covenant sign is given to children. If we did not do this, we should be acting as if children were not in the covenant or the church. In that case Christ would be less salutary for us than Abraham or Moses.[35]

*A Refutation*, Zwingli's third major work on baptism, published in 1527, shows no significant change in his views.[36] He draws primarily on the arguments used earlier in the controversy, and repeats the same two fundamental propositions to establish infant baptism. 'The children of

---

[34] Z IV 634.30–638.20, 641.5–14, 24–6. Zwingli sets out a table to show the unity of the two covenants, with the covenant sign as the only difference. Earlier he mentions as differences between the old and new testament that the covenant is with a new people and that Christ who was promised has now come. (Z IV 637.15–26, 638.5–639.11.) The emphasis on the unity of the covenant leads to Zwingli's case that our children are God's being based considerably on the old testament, whereas before it was based on new testament testimony. As before, he defends his use of the old testament in terms of the way Christ and the apostles used it. (Z IV 639.12–31.)

[35] Z IV 638.21–639.11. There is still, as here, some arguing from the lesser to the greater, stressing the contrast between the two testaments rather than the unity.

[36] The work includes a sustained attack on the lives of the anabaptists and on some of their other views, especially in the second part and in the appendix. (Z VI i 103.11–155.21, 188.1–195.22.) As often, the form of much of the work is dictated by the arguments to which Zwingli is replying. He makes considerable use of synecdoche in replying to the anabaptist position and in defending his own.

Christians are no less sons of God than the parents, just as in the old testament. Hence, since they are sons of God, who will forbid this baptism? Circumcision among the ancients . . . was the same as baptism with us. As that was given to infants so ought baptism to be administered to infants.'[37] Infant baptism is based on these two propositions, not on the fact that the apostles baptized infants, although Zwingli continues to give reasons to support his view that they did. It would not affect his position if in fact they did not, any more than the fact that Christ did not baptize affects our baptizing, for the apostles baptized, although he did not.

Apart from the familiar argument from households which would most naturally include children, there are various indirect arguments. He deduces two from Acts 15. First, 'It cannot be then that if the apostles were unwilling to baptize the children there would not have arisen some disturbance. But nothing is said of this, so there was no disturbance.' Second, infants were with their parents in the church. If, as the anabaptists held, the infants 'were not baptized, yet were circumcised, it follows that by a decree of the church children of Christians were cast out of the church and were remanded to the circumcision'. Zwingli argues thirdly, also conjecturally, that since Jews were devoted to outward things, Jewish Christians would probably have had their children baptized. Fourth, he refers to 1 Corinthians 10: 1–2 and Colossians 2: 11, Paul's making us and the Hebrews equal, and the outward things we have (baptism and circumcision) equivalent. However, Paul could not have held that our circumcision is baptism, unless children were baptized, as once they had been circumcised. Besides these factors Zwingli asserts that the only scripture the apostles could use was the old testament, which would lead them to see that baptism should be given to infants as circumcision had been.[38]

As before, the covenant plays an important part in the presentation of the case for infant baptism. The covenant is indeed with Adam in the first instance, but is now seen as purposed by God before the creation of man. There is no other covenant but this one covenant, for two covenants would mean two Gods. God has entered into the same covenant with us as he made with them, so that we might be one church and people with them. (Biblical references to two peoples and two covenants are held not to conflict with Zwingli's assertion of one covenant and one people.) The words of Christ in Matthew 8: 11 and in the parable of the labourers in the

---

[37] Z VI i 48.10–15; *Selected Works* 139.

[38] Z VI i 51.19–53.12, 184.8–187.19. Cf. Z IX 109.6–111.14 in his letter to Haller and Kolb on 28 Apr. 1527. Zwingli also adduces again the testimony of Origen and Augustine to the apostolic practice of baptizing infants. (Z VI i 187.20–35.)

vineyard point to this unity, as do passages such as Romans 11, Ephesians 2: 11-20, Hebrews 12: 22-4, and 1 Peter 2: 9-10.[39] 'Since therefore there is one immutable God and one testament only, we who trust in Christ are under the same testament, consequently God is as much our God as he was Abraham's, and we are as much his people as was Israel.' From this it follows that as the children of Hebrews were one with their parents in the covenant and received the sign of the covenant, so the children of Christians being counted in the church of Christ should receive the sign of the covenant, that is baptism. Moreover the equality between us and the people of old comes out in the way Paul attributes baptism and the eucharist to them and the passover and circumcision to us.[40]

Election now plays a part in Zwingli's defence of infant baptism, but is in no sense the basis of his case. Rather he makes use of it because it has been used against him by the anabaptists, who argued from the rejection of Esau in Romans 9: 11-13 that infants were not of God's people. Zwingli's reply is that only those whom God has elected are members of his people, and they are members even if as yet, like infants, they do not believe. The children of Christians are moreover in the covenant as the children of the Hebrews were. This makes us sure of their election until God pronounces differently about them, as he did in the case of Esau. At the end of the discussion he adds: 'baptism is not at all to be denied infants on account of God's election or reprobation, for neither to Esau nor to any other who was rejected was circumcision denied'.[41] The way Zwingli has developed his argument shows that election is not fundamental to his case for infant baptism, although it strengthens it.

*The Later Writings*

The later years show no change in Zwingli's fundamental position, although *The Marburg Articles* are in part in Lutheran, rather than in Zwinglian, language. The reference in article 9 to baptism as not an empty

---

[39] Z VI i 156.39-41, 169.4-6, 164.2-4, 163.8-19, 164.7-11, 165.3-16, 166.3-5, 166.13-168.31. Zwingli relates the salvation of the Hebrews as of Christians to Christ, without whom there is no salvation. 'Therefore as they had one and the same saviour with us they were one people with us, and we are one people and one church with them, even though they came before us a long time into the vineyard.' (Z VI i 166.3-5; *Selected Works* 230.)

[40] Z VI i 170.12-16 (*Selected Works* 235), 171.15-19, 171.28-172.5. Baptism and circumcision are equivalent, for each is a sign (*signaculum*) of the covenant. (Z VI i 171.28-9.)

[41] Z VI i 175.20-179.19, 184.2-4 (*Selected Works* 247). Zwingli rejects the view that infant baptism can be tolerated simply out of love, by affirming that it rests on the command of Christ. (Z VI i 181.23-183.19.)

The emphasis on election can detract from the importance of the outward means which God uses, for Zwingli insists that election is 'above baptism and circumcision; nay above faith and preaching'. (Z VI i 172.9-11; *Selected Works* 237.)

sign, but a sign and work of God, could be directed against Zwingli's position, but he takes it as a reference to any despising of the sacrament. For his part he stresses in his notes and comments the more obviously Zwinglian tone of the following clause which speaks of the sign as requiring our faith. Through this faith we are born again to life. Such faith moreover is, according to the next article, the work of the Spirit. In this way Zwingli distances himself from Luther's view of the efficacy of the sacrament, as he also does from the notion of faith in the infants who are baptized.[42] Article 14 on infant baptism was also capable of different interpretations by Luther and Zwingli. For Luther the reference to God's grace reflected his view of the sacraments as a means of grace, with baptism washing away the sins of the one baptized. For Zwingli they are signs of grace already given, with the word 'sacrament' designating the outward sacramental action.[43]

An Account of the Faith shows in brief compass many of the emphases present in Zwingli's later works and can be taken as representative of them. He does not devote a separate article to baptism, but discusses it in the context of salvation and the church in articles 5 and 6 and in the general setting of the sacraments in article 7. As in all his debates with catholics and Lutherans, he attacks the idea that baptism conveys grace. It is rather a sign of grace which is already present, and is a public testimony to that. Faith is not given in baptism, for baptism is given to an adult who has been asked whether he has faith. In the case of children God's promise precedes the baptism.[44] Baptism is given a corporate, rather than an individual, significance, for by it we become members of the visible church, and it is clearly related to the living of a new life.[45]

---

[42] Z VI ii 522.18–24, 550.11–18. The second half of the article reads, 'so ists nit allein ein ledig zeichen oder losung under den christen, sonder ein zeichen und werck gottes, darinn unser gloube gefordert, durch welchen wir zum laeben widergeborenn werdend'. Cf. Zwingli's rejection of baptism as a mere ceremony. (S III 576.39–577.2.)

[43] Z VI ii 523.10–11, 550.29–31. The article states 'das der kindertouffe recht sye und sy dadurch zuo gottes gnaden und in die christenheyt genommen werdend'. Zwingli's marginal note reads, 'Zuo gottes gnaden gnomen. Hoc est, sacramentaliter accipiuntur in gratiam. Quod nihil est, quam eum, qui in gratiam iam receptus est, fidei sacramento signari.' Cf. Usteri, 'Tauflehre Zwinglis', p. 276, n. 1: 'Nach Luther freilich sollten die Kinder getauft werden, damit sie von der Erbsünde rein würden, und das konnte und sollte der Artikel aussagen. Nach Zwingli hingegen dürften die Kinder getauft werden, weil sie durch Christi Verdienst schon von der Erbsünde befreit waren und dem Gnadenbund angehörten.'

[44] Z VI ii 804.13–805.5. Cf. Z VI iii 173.19–174.21; Z VI iii 256.13–17, 270.21–271.1; S VI ii 273.18–20. Grace is used in the sense of forgiveness. (Z VI ii 803.7–10.)

[45] Z VI ii 805.10–22. Part of the discussion of baptism is in the context of the church. Cf. S VI i 373.27–35, 374.8–12, 470.40–471.8: 'Glich als so einer spricht zu einem Ratsherren: Lieber, weisst du nit, warum du den schwartzen Rock treist, darum das du sehist, das, wie du erbarlich bekleidet bist, das du nit uneerlich lebist . . . Also ist auch der Tauff ein Zeichen, das wir den Lastren abstan söllent, recht und fromklich leben.'

Against the anabaptists Zwingli continues to argue for the baptism of infants, primarily in terms of their being members of the church by virtue of God's promise that the Gentiles will be gathered into the people of God. However, as the children of Jews belonged to God's people, so do the children of Christians, otherwise Christ would be hostile to us in denying to us what he gave to them. This argument is set in the context of a discussion of the salvation achieved by Christ. It is because of this salvation that infants are declared free of the curse of Adam, but also because of election. They are too young to show faith, but faith, as Zwingli frequently asserts, follows election and does not precede it. Indeed the children of Christians may be judged by us to be elect.[46] Zwingli argues, for example in the letter to the brethren in Berne, that in baptism faith is necessary, but the faith is not a person's inward faith, which God knows, but we do not, but the Christian faith which the church holds. Children are baptized with their parents' confession of faith, for whereas an adult can ask for baptism and confess faith, a child does this through someone else. However, infants are in no sense inferior here to adults, for, unlike adults who may be hypocrites, as were Judas, Simon Magus, and Alexander the coppersmith, infants cannot sin or dissemble.[47]

Zwingli's last substantial treatment of baptism was *Questions Concerning the Sacrament of Baptism* (1530). A response to forty-six questions raised by Schwenckfeld about baptism, to which Zwingli replies one by one, it is in no sense a systematic presentation of his views. Of particular interest is Zwingli's introduction to the questions, where he offers a number of propositions which he sees as cutting all the knots in the whole of religion.[48] The propositions largely concern election, which does not elsewhere feature largely in Zwingli's doctrine of baptism. Even here, however, it seems to be a weapon against the anabaptist linking of baptism and faith in support of believers' baptism, rather than the basis of his own case for infant baptism. It is election that saves. We cannot know who is elect among those enrolled in Christ's service. The church itself consists of the reprobate as well as the elect. From the discussion of election and some discussion of synecdoche, Zwingli makes four points in the eighteenth proposition. First, we cannot know who are elect and who reprobate, therefore the anabaptists are wrong to drive from the church the children of Christians, to whom belongs God's promise. Second, those who do not have faith are not

---

[46] Z VI ii 799.4–800.15.
[47] Z X 347.6–349.13. Zwingli refers also to Christ's regarding the faith of those who brought the paralytic to him.
[48] S III 571.26–8.

thereby damned, for faith follows election, not election faith. Third, if only those who have faith and repent should be baptized, then nobody can be baptized, for we cannot know for certain of people's faith. Fourth, the church includes elect members, both children and adults, and false members, both children and adults, and unbelievers, both those who will one day believe and those who will not.[49]

The familiar arguments reappear: that Christ alone baptizes with the Holy Spirit, while baptism is an outward ceremony which signifies, but does not perform; that baptism took the place of circumcision, as the fathers held; that the sacraments of the old and new testaments effect the same, as Augustine also held, for we have one and the same faith; that John's baptism is the same as Christ's; that neither Christ nor the apostles made any distinction between the baptism of infants and that of adults; and that baptism edifies because it offers to children in the church both a uniform education and a companionship which is useful and honourable, while preserving the church from schism.[50] Zwingli is concerned to show baptism's relation to Christ against the accusation that the argument from circumcision means replacing Christ by Moses. He counters this by pointing out that circumcision has to do with Abraham, not Moses, and by appealing to election as taking place in Christ before the foundation of the world.[51]

Fundamental elements in Zwingli's theology make him deny that baptism is a means of grace or that it is necessary to salvation. A contrary position would for him deny the sovereignty of God, the centrality of Christ, and the freedom of the Spirit. It would equally conflict with the clear testimony of scripture where some were baptized who were not saved and some were saved who were not baptized. Zwingli's whole understanding of God and of salvation is bound up in his doctrine of baptism, as well as his understanding of man, which would not allow that the soul could be affected by what is bodily. He could not argue for the necessity of infant

---

[49] S III 572.3–576.6, esp. 572.12, 573.7–9, 35–7, 575.19–39.

[50] S III 576.43–7, 579.12–13, 580.4–8, 582.13–583.5, 585.1–6, 587.26–45. Zwingli says that Christ, John the Baptist, and the apostles did not distinguish infant and adult baptism, thus assuming his case that infants were baptized. However, in the same paragraph he argues that the Hebrews would have objected if the society of the church had been refused to their children. (585.1–11.)

[51] S III 566.9–30, 579.24–580.14. Zwingli points out that we are called children of Abraham, which we could not be if Abraham did not have the same faith as we have. He then draws on baptism's taking the place of circumcision with particular reference to Col. 2: 9–12. Later he emphasizes the fact that whereas Abraham believed before being circumcised, Isaac, the son of Abraham, was circumcised before believing. (586.30–7.)

baptism in this sense, any more than he could argue for the necessity of baptism for adults. Baptism therefore had to have both a different meaning and a different purpose from those traditionally given to it.

In contrast with the traditional view of baptism as a sacrament, Zwingli sees it as an initiatory sign, a sign of the covenant, an idea developed at first in terms of our pledge to live the Christian life. This is less suited to infant baptism, as the child is not able to make a pledge, so that it is interpreted as the parents' pledging of the child and the child's being pledged to the law. As Zwingli begins to develop the nature of the covenant as God's covenant of grace, he is able to relate the term 'covenant sign' more adequately to God and the church. Thus whereas the term 'pledge' has a primarily moral reference, the later understanding of 'covenant sign' has a stronger theological and ecclesiological reference. The term is also capable of being used in fundamentally the same sense for adults and for infants. In this it contrasts not only with the idea of baptism as a pledge, but also with the earlier view that baptism strengthens faith, which cannot apply to infant baptism, as infants cannot believe.

It is primarily because of the controversy with anabaptists that Zwingli has to develop his doctrine of baptism. Nevertheless his understanding of covenant signs emerges first in his writings on the eucharist, not in his writings on baptism. In his debate with the anabaptists Zwingli relies on two major propositions for the baptism of infants: that children belong to God and should therefore be baptized, and that baptism replaces circumcision. The argument from circumcision is foreshadowed in the second disputation before the outbreak of the controversy.[52] In the earlier Zwingli, where the contrast between the two testaments is more strongly expressed, he tends to argue from the lesser to the greater, in support of not denying to the children of Christians what the children of the Hebrews received. As he comes to see the unity of the covenant, the argument changes, and the old testament has a more important part in it. At both stages he supports his use of the old testament by reference to the new testament.

Zwingli uses a number of important supporting arguments or counterarguments either to defend his position or to show the untenability of his opponents' position. They are based on a detailed exegesis of new testament texts. The most important concern the identity of John's and Christ's baptism, the distinction between baptism as teaching and as immersion, the nature of the faith required in baptism, the doctrine of election, and the use of synecdoche. With these Zwingli challenges the anabaptists' understanding of faith, their connection between faith and baptism, and

[52] Z II 710.10–13.

their consequent conviction that infants cannot be baptized and that believers baptized as infants should be baptized (or rebaptized). He also uses a range of arguments to show that it was more likely than not that the apostles baptized infants.

The use made by others of Zwingli's arguments on baptism shows that they were judged more compelling than has sometimes been supposed. His defence of infant baptism was not, as has been alleged, a matter of church politics, but was clearly related to his theology and to his profound sense of the unity of the church. Baptism could not have for him the role it had for others, nor the role it had for Bucer and Calvin. But he speaks of baptism and the eucharist as being so necessary that whoever scorns them does not hold the chief point of religion, which is to trust in God. For those who trust in God, far from rejecting the sacraments, rejoice in them.[53]

# ADDITIONAL NOTES

1. An anabaptist writing from this period may be noted in *Z* III 368–72. (There is dispute about its author. For Grebel's authorship see *Z* III 367–72; for Manz's see Walter Schmid, 'Der Autor der sogenannten Protestation und Schutzschrift von 1524/1525', *ZWA* 9 (1950) 139–49.) The author asks for scriptural evidence. He states, for example, that Christ did not teach, nor did the apostles practise, infant baptism. Baptism is for those who seek to lead a new life. Christ commanded those who had been taught to be baptized, and the apostles baptized only those who had been taught and who desired baptism. Christ more-over is held before us as an example, having been baptized at thirty, and circum-cised when eight days old. He sees infant baptism as a popish invention, and challenges Zwingli to make the case for it from scripture. (*Z* III 369.3–12, 371.2–15, 372.4–10.)

2. After attributing to his opponents the length of what he has written in *Baptism, Rebaptism, and Infant Baptism*, Zwingli summarizes what he has said in a number of theses. (*Z* IV 333.9–334.11.) This is followed by the baptismal order used in Zurich, an order stripped of exorcism, spittle, and salt. It begins with a characteristic statement of Zwingli's basic theological position. 'Our help is in the power of the Lord, who made heaven and earth' (Ps. 124: 8). It expresses his understanding of baptism, although the reference to being incorporated into

[53] 'Si ad salutis efficaciam sive causam spectes, non reddet salvum neque circumcisio, neque baptismus: sola enim numinis gratia et liberalitas beat. Si vero ad mysterium quod sacramenta significant, iam dicimus adeo necessaria esse, ut qui ea contemserit, antea caput religionis non teneat, quod est fidere uno Deo. Qui enim fidunt Deo, eius sacramentis gaudent; tam abest ut abiiciant. Sunt enim signa sanctae unionis et commercii, cum Dei et hominum, tum hominum inter se.' (*S* III 581.24–30.)

Christ needs to be taken, like similar references elsewhere, to dedication to Christ and entry into the church. (*Z* IV 334.10–336.20.) In the later order the minister says, 'Darumb lassend unns gott bitten disem kind umb den glouben, unnd das der usserlich touff innwendig durch den heiligen geist mit dem gnadrychen wasser beschehe . . .'. (*Z* IV 680.23–5.) The reference to 'gnadrychen wasser' is almost certainly not to be understood in the literal way which has puzzled most commentators (see, e.g., *Z* IV 672), but as a reference to the inward baptism of the Spirit. Cf. *Z* VIII 194.11–17. For a somewhat different view, see F. Schmidt-Clausing, *Zwinglis liturgische Formulare* (Frankfurt am Main, 1970), p. 86, n. 82, and 'Die liturgietheologische Arbeit Zwinglis', pp. 613–15. Too many writers have failed to see that the language of prayer differs from the language of controversy. Zwingli may deny that baptism or preaching are automatically effective, but he may pray for God to act in them.

3. Besides his detailed attack on Zwingli's view of baptism, Hubmaier—in *The Christian Baptism of Believers*—expresses his own view, drawing on new testament texts to show that preaching precedes baptizing and that confession and faith precede being baptized. Infant baptism cannot be baptism; therefore it is wrong to refer to their baptism as rebaptism. For Hubmaier baptism is necessary in obedience to Christ's command. He recognizes that people can be saved without it, where it is not available. (*Z* IV 613–617, n. 4, 626, n. 10.) In a letter to Oecolampadius in January 1525 Hubmaier said that he would baptize children where the parents were weak and insisted on it. He did this without conceding the point at issue. (*S* II i 339.4–11.) (It cannot be said that Zwingli always does justice to Hubmaier's views on baptism.)

# 11. The Eucharist

THE eucharist was a centre of controversy in the reformation because it focused the fundamental differences between the reformers and the medieval church and those among the reformers themselves. The controversy was moreover practical as well as theological, for a change in theology inevitably involves a change in practice, both in the church's forms of worship and the believer's forms of piety. In his conflict first with catholics and then with Luther Zwingli saw man's salvation itself as at stake, as indeed did they. For Zwingli, however, it was a matter of attacking a doctrine and a practice that imperilled the understanding and reception of God's gift of salvation; for his opponents it was a matter of defending a doctrine and practice that embodied that gift. It is this that explains the intensity of their battle.

We do not know what Zwingli's eucharistic theology was before he became a reformer, and there is considerable dispute about whether he had a mystical or symbolic view in his first years as a reformer.[1] The influence of Erasmus in a symbolic direction is probable, whether or not Zwingli held the mystical view of Christ's presence attributed to Erasmus.

## The Early Writings

It is not until 1523 that Zwingli's writings offer any discussion of the eucharist, although there are passing and revealing references in *Choice and Liberty Respecting Food* and *Archeteles* in 1522. In the former the references to enjoying or sharing in God (*got genossen*) and eating heavenly food seem to imply a non-symbolic view of the eucharist. However, other expressions cohere with the symbolic view which Zwingli certainly held from 1525, for example, references to trusting the gospel and not foods, and to God as not revealing himself more in one place than another or as not revealing himself as more merciful or wrathful at one time than another, since otherwise he would be subject to times chosen by us.[2]

In *Archeteles* Zwingli responds to the statement that no rite of the church should be changed by asking 'Why has the synaxis been changed

---

[1] For discussion of Zwingli's theology of the eucharist, see works in the Bibliography marked by a dagger.

[2] Z I 126.4–6, 129.5–7, 15–17, 97.20–98.2, 100.16–30.

which used to be given in both kinds according to the institution of Christ and the usage of the apostles?' Five lines earlier he affirms that 'faith is the sole cause of salvation' after asserting that whoever believes that Christ won the church by his blood belongs to the church. Later in an attack on the view that we should seek to appease God by our prayers, as if prayers were like money rather than an imploring of God's mercy, he appeals to Christ's sacrifice for us in Hebrews 9: 12 and Luke 22: 19–20.[3] Of these three passages only the first specifically refers to the eucharist, though the other two have a bearing on it. Although only communion in both kinds is explicitly affirmed, yet other elements important for the future are present: the use of the term 'synaxis', the stress on faith, the assertion of Christ's sacrifice on the cross.

The eighteenth article which Zwingli defends at the first disputation in January 1523 concerns the sacrifice of the mass. In it he denies that it is a sacrifice on the basis of Christ's once for all and eternally valid sacrifice, and states that it is 'a memorial of the sacrifice and an assurance of the redemption Christ has manifested to us'.[4] His exposition of the article is published six months later, and constitutes his first sustained discussion of the eucharist. There is the repeated denial that the mass is a sacrifice, based especially on the presentation of the priesthood and sacrifice of Christ in the letter to the Hebrews, and the insistence on communion in both kinds as corresponding not only with the institution of Christ and the custom of the apostles, but also with the former eucharistic practice in Switzerland.[5] Zwingli claims that for some years he has called it 'a memorial of the suffering of Christ and not a sacrifice'. He calls it a memorial precisely because the commemorating of a sacrifice that has happened denies the view of those who make the eucharist a sacrifice. The fact that Christ said 'Do this in remembrance of me' and not 'Offer this up to me' shows that he did not intend the eucharist to be a sacrifice, but 'a memorial and renewal of what happened once and is eternally powerful and precious enough to satisfy the righteousness of God'. 'Memorial' means renewing with remembrance of what Christ has done for us. This understanding is confirmed by Paul's interpretation of the term in 1 Corinthians 11: 26, where he speaks of proclaiming the death of the Lord till he come. Remembrance is 'an inward thanksgiving' for what Christ has done; his

---

[3] Z I 320.9–11, 1–8, 323.6–18.

[4] Z I 460.6–10.

[5] Z II 112.1–119.23, 120.11–14, 132.25–135.23. In discussing the definition of a sacrament as a sign of a sacred thing, Zwingli distinguishes a sign from what it signifies and asks how the eucharist can be a sacrifice if it only signifies. (Z II 121.2–7.) *The Canon of the Mass* draws on Heb. 7–10 in its attack on the sacrifice of the mass. (Z II 583.22–587.6.)

suffering has united us to God and this makes the believer so joyful that he cannot sufficiently praise the goodness of God.[6]

The ideas of presence and sacrifice are associated when Zwingli refers to the eucharist which is a memorial of Christ's sacrifice as 'an assurance to the weak that Christ has redeemed them', if they believe that Christ died for their sins on the cross.

When in this faith they eat his flesh and drink his blood and recognize that they are given to them as an assurance, then their sins are forgiven, as if Christ had only now died on the cross. Christ is so powerful and present at all times, for he is an eternal God. Therefore his suffering also is eternally fruitful, as Paul says in Hebrews 9, 'How much more shall the blood of Christ, who through the eternal Spirit offered and dedicated himself without blemish to God purify our conscience etc.'[7]

Here forgiveness is linked with a believing participation in the eucharist and there is a sense of Christ's presence in the sacrament, related to his being God.

Immediately after this comes the much debated sentence, 'But here the simple should learn that there is no dispute here about whether the body and blood of Christ are eaten and drunk (for no Christian doubts that), but whether it is a sacrifice or only a memorial.'[8] Zwingli's primary concern is with the sacrifice of Christ and not with the presence of Christ, but the statement implies that no one doubts that the body and blood of Christ are eaten in the eucharist. This would naturally mean that Zwingli himself had no doubt about it. It would not require any particular theory to be held, although it could rule out a symbolic view of the eucharist, unless taken in conjunction with what he says on the basis of John 6 and also with the distinction he makes between the sign and what it signifies.

The other evidence of *An Exposition of the Articles* is more ambiguous. It is true that Zwingli uses realist language about the sacrament, describing it as the body and blood of Christ, referring to 'heavenly food' and 'comforting food', and speaking of the food as Christ, as well as of enjoying Christ.[9] However, he not only rejects transubstantiation as something invented by

---

[6] Z II 137.32-3, 138.12-18, 136.15-137.31. See Additional Note 1, pp. 255-6.

[7] Z II 127.15-128.8.

[8] Z II 128.8-11. There is a somewhat similar statement in *A Short Christian Introduction*, where the context makes it clear that the body and blood of Christ are only food for the soul. (Z II 658.25-659.3.)

[9] Z II 133.19, 144.10, 140.23-4, 134.16. The subsequent statement that if we believe Christ to be our salvation we have found salvation in faith, even if we are denied communion in both kinds, could imply a strong doctrine of the presence of Christ, but it also makes the eucharist something dispensable, at best of secondary value. (134.16-18.)

theologians, but also speaks strongly of the necessity of faith and draws on John 6 in referring the terms 'body' and 'blood' to the death of Christ.[10] Indeed it is after stating that he will indicate how the content of the eucharist is to be understood that he discusses John 6. His exposition contains a variety of points: the word of Christ in which we find comfort and strength is that he gave his body and blood for our redemption; food for the soul is to be sure that Christ is our salvation; putting one's trust in the body and blood of Christ means putting it in his death; the words about flesh and blood have to do with faith; it is not a matter of bodily eating but of faith, which comes from the Spirit who makes alive. In short, 'the body and blood of Christ are nothing other than the word of faith, to wit, that his body slain for us and his blood shed for us have redeemed us and reconciled us to God. If we confidently believe that, then our soul receives food and drink with the body and blood of Christ.' For the sake of the simple, Christ has given a form of his body that can be eaten, so that they may be made sure in their faith with a visible action. However, unless a person believes that Christ is his salvation, the body of Christ is of no use to him; indeed he eats to his damnation. 'If he is alive in faith, the food strengthens him.' In this context Zwingli states that he is not concerned with what the theologians have invented concerning the bread and wine, as he knows through faith that Christ is his redemption and the food and comfort of his soul.[11]

A number of accents are found here which are important in Zwingli's eucharistic thinking both here and later. Apart from the clear repudiation of the sacrifice of the mass, transubstantiation, and communion in one kind, there is the stress on Christ's atoning death, on salvation as dependent on faith in Christ's body and blood as given for us and on the Spirit as enabling such faith, on faith as necessary for participation in the eucharist and as being strengthened by such participation. (The strengthening of faith is later called in question.) Christ's presence in the eucharist is related to faith (perhaps dependent on it) and perhaps also to his divinity. The nature of his presence is not made clear. Bodily eating is rejected. The preference for the word 'memorial' rather than 'testament' is characteristic of a subjective, rather than an objective, stress in the eucharist.

In *A Commentary* Zwingli explicitly states that he wrote 'many things with a view rather to the times than to the thing itself'. Concerned to reap

[10] Z II 121.4-11, 144.13-14, 134.16-18, 139.1-5, 140.16-19. Zwingli claimed that he had never believed in transubstantiation. (Z III 350.6-13.) In *The Babylonian Captivity of the Church* Luther rejected the reference of John 6 to the eucharist.

[11] Z II 141.14-144.16, esp. 141.14-15, 23-27, 141.33-142.1, 12-14, 23-6, 142.36-143.4, 12-30, 144.13-16.

as large a harvest as possible for the Lord, he made concessions in what he
wrote to people's tenderness so that he might build them up. Zwingli does
not indicate precisely which views he is retracting, but simply refers to
things not written earlier or not written so plainly or written differently.[12]
Köhler holds that in *An Exposition of the Articles* Zwingli has an Erasmian
view of Christ's presence and that what he refers to here concerns the
liturgy, rather than the theology, of the eucharist. A distinction between
liturgy and theology seems unlikely. It seems more likely that Zwingli
holds that he expressed his views of the presence of Christ in too
traditional or realist a way. Yet that makes his statement that no Christian
doubts that the body and blood of Christ are eaten and drunk seem
deliberately and unnecessarily misleading, since he himself doubted it in
the most straightforward sense of the words. However, all direct or
indirect statements about Christ's presence are qualified by the references
to faith and Zwingli effectively limits Christ's presence to those who have
faith. Where his views clearly change is that in *A Commentary* he does not
allow that the sacrament strengthens faith, whereas in *An Exposition of the
Articles* he does.[13]

Zwingli wrote a letter to Thomas Wyttenbach, his former teacher, on
15 June 1523, in response to his enquiries about the eucharist. It expresses
some points more openly and vigorously than the more public *An
Exposition of the Articles*, published in the following month. Zwingli's initial
statement on the eucharist is that it is eaten where there is faith, and that it
is given to strengthen faith. This is related to man's being a person with
senses and his need of visible signs.[14] The comparison is made with baptism
where you could use water a thousand times, but it would be in vain if
there were no faith. This is true of participation in the eucharist in which
bread and wine are eaten in vain if there is no faith. The faith is, however,
related, not to the eucharistic elements, but to 'the body of Christ slain for
us' for our salvation. This body is our only hope and is food for the soul.
The bread and wine can be called the body and blood of Christ only
catachretically, nevertheless 'it is not the bread that liberates or the wine
that makes the mind spiritually joyful, but the faith Christ commanded us
to have in his body and blood, because he redeemed us with his body and

---

[12] Z III 773.26–774.24; *Works* III 198.

[13] Köhler, I 83–7. Locher's reference to an anamnetic presence is acceptable in that it ties the
presence to faith. However, that still leaves Zwingli's statement about no Christian doubting
that the body and blood are eaten and drunk as unnecessarily misleading, to say no more. See *Die
Zwinglische Reformation*, p. 287.

[14] Z VIII 85.10–16, 24–6.

washed us with his blood'. Faith is fundamental, just as in baptism, where it is faith and not the baptizing that takes away sins.[15]

Earlier in the letter Zwingli rejects the doctrine of transubstantiation as inconsistent, drawing on the example of the changing of water into wine at Cana. Now he turns to the question of reservation which Wyttenbach has raised and affirms that a eucharist is such only in use and not apart from it. Christ is either in heaven at the right hand of God or on earth in the heart of the believer. The bread is given to be eaten in accordance with Christ's word in Matthew 26: 26, 'Take, eat'. Moreover the reference to the body follows, rather than precedes, this. Zwingli would wish the words of administration to be not 'The body of Christ lead you to eternal life', but rather Christ's words, 'Take, eat; this is my body . . .', said aloud so that they can be heard, for faith is to be in Christ who gave himself to redeem us. (The adoration of the bread is attacked by Zwingli as idolatry, as only God is to be adored and not Christ, in so far as he is a creature.) He draws on the analogy of a flint, which he has used in discussions, to illuminate his understanding of Christ's presence. There is fire in the flint only when it is struck. Similarly Christ is found under the form of the bread only when he is sought in faith.[16]

The concerns of the letter to Wyttenbach are clearly different from those expressed in article 18. The presence of Christ, rather than his sacrifice, is now to the fore. His presence is dependent on, or at least conditioned by, faith. (Little can be argued in terms of Christ's presence from Zwingli's undeveloped references to the participation of unbelievers, for in essence he is simply quoting 1 Corinthians 11: 27.) Transubstantiation is repudiated, without any detailed argument, as illogical and inconsistent. The whole emphasis is placed on the body and blood as given for us and thus on Christ and his saving death and our faith in this. The bread and wine in the sacrament are given to be eaten and the stress is on the first half of Christ's word 'Take, eat', rather than on the second half, 'This is my body'.

[15] Z VIII 85.34–87.1. Zwingli does refer to the presence of Christ in some sense in the sacramental bread at two or three points where he is thought to use realist language: 'quicquid hic agitur, divina virtute fieri, modum autem nobis penitus ignotum, quo deus illabitur animae . . .', 'ut eum ederent, qui in dextera dei sedet'. (Z VIII 86.30–2, 86.37–87.1.) The words following the comparison with flint 'sed mirabili modo' (Z VIII 88.9–10) are less clear, but they cannot alone bear the weight placed on them by Köhler (I 22 ff.). Zwingli speaks of Christ as 'qui tam abest'. (Z VIII 87.33.)

[16] Z VIII 85.26–34, 87.1–88.19. There is a sense of communion with Christ, although it is not dominant: 'sese in cibum nobis obtulit, quo se ipse nobis ac nos sibi sociat . . .'. (Z VIII 87.32–3.)

The emphasis on the action rather than on the elements becomes clearer later. 'Baptismus nunquam est aqua, sed actio; sic eucharistia nunquam est panis aut corpus Christi, sed gratiarum actio.' (Z V 711.18–19.)

Christ is present, in a way not defined, for those who believe, and their faith is strengthened where it is weak, or made joyful where it is strong. All this is set in the context of the eucharistic action, not apart from it. There is therefore a shift of accent from the elements to the action.

In *The Canon of the Mass* Zwingli defends the use of the term 'eucharist', although it was not used by Christ or the apostles, as it proclaims that the food and drink are 'the generous and good gift and grace of God'. The name therefore arises out of what is done, whereas the name 'mass' makes an offering out of what is given to us as a gift. Thus the eucharist is what God offers to us, not what we offer to God.[17] A number of passages point to Zwingli's understanding of the presence of Christ. In one passage he rejects transubstantiation, but allows that one may pray for the bread to become the body of Christ, stating that 'to those who eat with faith the bread and wine becomes the body and blood of Jesus Christ, however it happens (*quocumque tandem modo id fiat*)'. In the prayers with which Zwingli concludes the work he affirms that Christ was not content to be sacrificed for us, but 'gave himself as food and drink that we might lack nothing', that 'he gave himself as food for the soul under the form of bread and wine that the remembrance of his generous deed might not die', and that 'he is himself the host and feast'. He also uses the words of administration, 'The body (or blood) of our Lord Jesus Christ be effectual (*prosit*) for you to eternal life', of which he was critical earlier.[18] There is, however, nothing in the bread or wine apart from the Spirit and faith, 'for in vain we eat the flesh of your Son and drink the blood, unless through faith in your word we firmly believe before all things that this same Son of yours, our Lord Jesus Christ, nailed to the cross for us, atoned for the transgressions of the whole world. For he himself said the flesh is of no avail, it is the Spirit who gives life.' The cross remains the fundamental reality in Zwingli's thinking about the eucharist and his concern is that people should meditate on the cross rather than make the sign of the cross.[19] Other elements in his later writings are evident here, in particular the corporate emphasis and the relation between the eucharist and the living of the life of Christ.[20]

---

[17] Z II 568.34–569.10. Cf. 582.37–583.2, 17–21.

[18] Z II 588.22–8, 605.38–9, 606.40–1, 607.25; 'ipse et hospes est et epulum' (608.1–2). Cf. Z VIII 87.22–35. Zwingli refers to the body and blood of Christ as not being present before the words of consecration, though in a polemical passage where his own view need not necessarily be expressed. (Z II 569.31–3.)

[19] Z II 606.22–8, 597.28–598.1.

[20] Z II 606.41–607.4; '. . . da, ut factis eum exprimamus, ut in Adam olim obliterata imago hac via speciem suam recipiat. Quod, ut efficacius firmiusque nobis, contingat, da, ut quotquot ex huius filii corporis sanguinisque cibo participaturi sunt, unum solumque spirent et exprimant,

Of the other writings on the eucharist before Hoen's letter the most important is *A Proposal Concerning Images and the Mass* (May 1524). It brings certain new emphases into Zwingli's thinking, in particular the use of 1 Corinthians 10: 16–17. The eucharist is seen as 'an inward and outward union of Christian people', in which we 'testify to all men that we are one body and one brotherhood' and in which we renew our brotherhood. 'Christ wills that his own shall be one, just as he is one with the Father, and for this union he has given us the sacrament . . .'. 'And as he gave himself for us, we also are bound to give ourselves one for the other, as for one's brother, indeed as for one's own member.' This new emphasis on community and mutual commitment goes alongside the old emphasis on the sacrament as 'a sign and assurance of the testament' and follows an acceptance of the fact that without the sacrament we can renew in ourselves the suffering of Christ.[21]

Certain elements emerge clearly, others less so, in the early Zwingli. Fundamental is the relation of the eucharist to Christ. The understanding of the eucharist as a sacrifice was an obscuring or denying of Christ's sacrifice. This is a constant feature of the early writings.[22] Besides the theological reference to Christ there is the historical reference: what did Christ intend with the institution of the eucharist?[23] This leads to a detailed

ac in eo, qui tecum unus est, ipsi unum fiant.' (Z II 607.10–14.) The synaxis is seen as a commemoration of the passion, so that the corporate and commemorative aspects of the meal are stressed. (Z II 592.8–9.)

[21] Z III 124.27–125.15, 26. The importance of 1 Cor. 10.16–17 and the sense of a pledge or covenant in which we pledge ourselves to each other are evident in other writings of the period. (Z III 227.11–228.28, 282.16–32; VIII 208.19–23.) 'Ad hoc enim posita est, ut simul eundem cibum edentes, hoc est fide, quae est in Christo Jesu, in unum corpus coaliti, hac sacra velut initiatione et sacramento in unum exercitum et peculiarem dei populum uniamur.' (Z III 282.29–32.)

[22] Besides those already mentioned it is evident in *A Short Christian Introduction* and *A Reply to Emser*, as well as in *The Second Disputation*. (Z II 660.1–661.7; III 281.10–282.10; II 732.21 ff.) There is the pastoral concern that people imagined that a mass put them right with God, thus in effect encouraging sin, and the practical concern that the mass became a source of greed and wealth and so diverted money from the needs of the poor.

[23] Scripture has authority over the forms of eucharistic service as well as over the formulations of eucharistic doctrine. Both concerns can be found in the same statement. (Z II 808.5–810.20.) Zwingli, however, unlike Grebel, allows liberty to the congregations in what is not clearly prescribed by scripture, and does not regard them as bound by the custom of Christ and the apostles in outward matters like time and dress. (Z II 788.13–793.14.) For the sake of the weak and to avoid division he is prepared to use the old formulations and forms. See, e.g., Z III 773.26–774.19, 812.3–10, and n. 27 below. In this he disagrees with the radicals at the second disputation. (Z II 788.16–789.23.) 'So man aber dieselbigen nit eins mals ab weg thuon mag, so wirt not sin, das man wider dieselbigen das wort gottes styff und handtlichen predige.' He allowed certain vestments for the sake of the weak in faith, but now argues for their abolition, though not at once, 'ja zuo siner zyt, damit nit uffruoren noch einigerley uneinigkeit under den Christen entstande'. (Z II 788.17–19, 32–3, 789.7–11.)

examination of the various new testament texts and to the conclusion: the
eucharist is a memorial and a testament and not a sacrifice; it is to be
received in both kinds; it is to be eaten not carried about or reserved; it is to
be eaten in faith and not with the teeth; and it is food for the soul. The
eucharist brings the assurance of forgiveness and strengthens faith. In a
sense those who are strong in faith do not need the eucharist, at least to
strengthen their faith, but it still has a use, as it has been given so that
Christians may be united with each other, may testify to others that they
are one body, and may live the life of Christ. It is a pledge Christians
make.[24] The manner of Christ's presence is not clear. Transubstantiation is
rejected, but no other view takes its place. Zwingli seems to use many
traditional terms, as for example the body and the blood, in a way or with
an emphasis that differs from the tradition. The body and blood refer to
the death of Christ and that reference is often uppermost, despite appearances. Zwingli uses the prepositions 'in', 'with', and 'under', but they do
not necessarily have the force they will later have in controversy. They can
all be used, apparently without distinction, in contexts where he is arguing
for communion in both kinds.[25] In every case faith is crucial for the
presence of Christ. As faith is the work of the Spirit, there is a clear sense of
the role of the Spirit before the eucharist and in the eucharist. (There is
indeed in *The Second Disputation* the distinction made by Jud, and later to
impress itself on Zwingli in Hoen's letter, between Christ's bodily
presence and the presence of the Spirit, though in Jud it is in the context of
a discussion of images.[26]) John 6: 63, a central text in later controversy, is
important here with its insistence that it is the Spirit who gives life.

The clearest difference between this and the later Zwingli is in the view
that the eucharist strengthens faith. Other differences are less clear cut
because those statements that concern the presence of Christ are in terms
that are—in the light of what he later holds and of what he regards as per-
missible use—capable of more than one interpretation.[27] Christ's presence

[24] *A Proposal Concerning Images and the Mass* is an example of a brief scriptural exposition in
several points of the meaning of the eucharist. (Z III 123.12–127.10.)
[25] See the uses of 'in', 'with', and 'under' in Z II 134.10–13, 606.38–41, 811.16–18; III 79.14–17.
[26] Z II 696.1–12. He speaks here of the schoolmen's objection to adoring the humanity of
Christ and later of Christ's being in heaven, in his manhood. (Z II 697.10–11.)
[27] Zwingli allows that those not strong enough to give up terms that are objectionable may
use them and apply a different meaning to them, so that sacrifice is understood as a
commemoration of Christ's sacrifice, and we offer as we commemorate. Since he allows this as a
temporary expedient, it is at least possible that he uses traditional expressions in a non-
traditional way. Köhler stresses Zwingli's use of terms such as *fronlychnam*, but the way he uses
the word is important, as in 'das der fronlychnam und bluot Christi nüt anders denn ein spys der
glöubigen seel ist . . .'. (Z II 812.7–8.)

seems to be affirmed by the use of the terms 'the body and blood of Christ as a name for the eucharist, by statements such as 'when the bread is eaten and the cup drunk, the body of Christ is eaten and drunk', and by references to enjoying Christ and to 'God flowing into us invisibly and feeding the soul', and the assertion that faith is strengthened.[28] These and other passages are consonant with Köhler's judgement that Zwingli held an Erasmian type view of Christ's presence. But the qualifications that Zwingli uses are coherent with the symbolic view which emerges clearly later, in particular the stress on faith and the association of the body and blood with the death of Christ. The symbolic view is not explicit in the early writings, but it can be held to be implicit in them.[29]

## The Development of the Symbolic View

It is impossible to say how important the letter of Cornelis Hoen in 1524 was in the development of Zwingli's eucharistic theology. Zwingli argued that he already held a symbolic view when he read it and that it enabled him to see that the trope in the clause, 'this is my body', is in the word 'is', and not, for example, in the word 'this'. He affirmed that there was no fundamental change in his view, but that he had kept it hidden until the right moment came to make it known.[30] Whether or not that is the case, there are certainly different notes in Zwingli's eucharistic writings from the end of 1524.

Hoen's letter has throughout a strong emphasis on faith, which it sees as trust in Christ rather than as assent, and on the necessity in baptism and the eucharist for the recipient to have faith. It draws on a variety of biblical examples to argue that 'is' means 'signifies' in the words of institution. It

---

[28] Z II 590.1–6, 592.12–16. The reference in the letter to Wyttenbach 'quicquid hic agitur, divina virtute fieri, modum autem nobis penitus ignotum, quo deus illabatur animae' must be seen in relation to the following sentences with their reference to the food of the soul as being faith in Christ's saving death. (Z VIII 86.23–87.1.) Cf. a similar passage in *The Canon of the Mass* 'quod Christus nos liberavit sua morte et sanguinis effusione, atque eadem in cibum tradidit, quae fide comedimus non dentibus, propter quam deus nobis invisibiliter illabitur ac animum pascit'. (Z II 592.13–16.)

[29] Köhler (I 41, n. 2) draws attention to the way that Zwingli does not use *bedeutet* in his early works where he would have done in his later works. However, in Z II 757.19–33 he is simply taking up the language and imagery of Martin Steinlin in Z II 746.8–26.

Köhler (I 56) regards Erasmus as the primary source of Zwingli's eucharistic teaching: 'Die Grundelemente seiner Abendmahlsanschauung finden sich samt und sonders bei dem grossen Humanisten, die Stufenschichtung, die Betonung des Glaubens, die Realpräsenz in mystischer Form, der ethische Verpflichtungscharakter, das Wiedergedächtnis.' Zwingli agreed with Erasmus, against Augustine, in relating John 6 to spiritual eating. (Z XII 144.38–145.1.) Krodel (pp. 205–20) stresses Zwingli's dependence on and closeness to Erasmus except in his onesided emphasis on the subjective element in Erasmus and the denial of Christ's real presence.

[30] See Additional Note 2, pp. 256–7.

distinguishes in the eucharist between the sign and the thing signified and regards the adoration of the eucharistic bread as parallel to the heathen worship of wood and stones; the bread remains bread. It affirms that Christ withdrew his bodily presence so that the Spirit might come. It speaks of commemoration as more consonant with bodily absence. Of these elements it is the interpreting of 'is' as 'signifies' that is clearly new in Zwingli. The others are in some sense already present, as is much else in the letter.[31]

The impact of Hoen's letter is to be seen in the letter to Matthew Alber in November 1524 where for the first time Zwingli refers to 'is' as meaning 'signifies'. He does this, however, only in the second part of the letter when examining the words of consecration. Important as this element is, it is not all important. It is the end rather than the beginning of his case. Zwingli directs attention first to John 6, which now begins to have a dominant part in his eucharistic teaching, but which was referred to only briefly and used somewhat differently in Hoen's letter. He recognizes that the chapter is not concerned with the eucharist, but for him it disproves certain views of the eucharist, and is his first line of attack. From it he shows that it is the flesh of Christ as slain for us, and not as eaten by us, that is food for the soul. For, as John 3: 6 makes clear, what is born of the flesh is flesh, just as what is born of the Spirit is Spirit. Eating the flesh of Christ therefore cannot give birth to anything but flesh. In fact, however, the phrase 'eating Christ' in John 6 means believing in him. Eating his body means believing that he was slain for us. The passage is concerned not with physical eating, which affects the body, but with spiritual eating or faith.[32]

In the course of demonstrating that the chapter is about faith and not the eucharist, Zwingli reveals certain characteristic notes: the contrast between bodily eating and faith, so that if bodily eating could bless there would be two ways of salvation—bodily eating and faith; the contrast between Christ as God and Christ as man, so that Christ gives life to the world as God and not because he is flesh; and the contrast between the Spirit and flesh in 'It is the Spirit who gives life, the flesh is of no avail' (John 6: 63). John 6: 63 is the text that makes impossible both

---

[31] The letter, published by Zwingli, is in Z IV 512.10–518.13, though there is some dispute about its exact ending. It is worth noting that Zwingli ceases to hold his earlier view that the sacraments confirm faith, a view implied, however, in the opening lines of the letter in association with the idea of a ring. (Z IV 512.10–21.) Carlstadt, whose writings Zwingli reads at this time, opposes such a view.

[32] Z III 336.19–23, 337.2–5, 338.23–30, 339.1, 22–7, 34–6. The centrality of John 6 finds expression in its becoming the invariable gospel at the eucharist. (Z IV 19.30–20.30.) In the medieval church it had been one of the readings for Corpus Christi.

transubstantiation and all views of the eating of the flesh in an essential or bodily way. Zwingli now refers, not to the sacrament, but to Christ's flesh and blood which suffered death on the cross as 'the pledge of our salvation'. In this whole exposition the two fundamental elements are: the flesh is of no avail and eating is believing.[33]

In the second part of the letter Zwingli turns to what he regards as the most difficult point, the so-called words of consecration, which seem to imply that the bread given by Christ was his body slain for us on the cross. Here there is a note of hesitation in what he says. This could be simply tactical modesty, but does more naturally suit the advancing of a new or an untried position.[34] Faith teaches us that salvation comes through believing that Christ died for us, and therefore not through the sacramental eating of bread and wine. Consequently there must be a figure of speech in Christ's words. Zwingli commends Carlstadt's grasp of the nature of faith, but rejects his view that the word 'this' refers to Christ's body rather than the bread. Following Hoen he sees the clue in the word 'is', which is to be understood as 'signifies'. He draws on the biblical examples that Hoen adduces, while using one not in Hoen.[35] After the examples of the seven cows, the vine, and the seed, he points out that Christ follows the words 'Take, eat; this is (or signifies) my body, which is given for you' with the words 'Do this in remembrance of me', thus linking signifying and remembering, and making it clear that he instituted the eucharist that we might remember him. (In this context Zwingli speaks for the first time of the eucharist as a symbol.) Almost in passing, the Lucan form 'This cup is the new covenant in my blood', rather than the words 'This is my blood', is used to interpret the saying 'This is my body' and to support the interpretation of 'is' as 'signifies'. He draws on Tertullian, Augustine, and Origen in support of the term 'signify', referring to Tertullian's use of the term 'represent' and Augustine's use of the term 'figure'. The bread represents his body in that when it is eaten it calls to remembrance that Christ gave his body for us. The term 'figure' is equally concerned with remembering that his body was given and his blood shed for us.[36]

---

[33] Z III 340.14–22, 340.40–341.5, 20–3, 28–31. Hoen refers to the sacrament as a pledge, as of course Zwingli does earlier. (Z IV 512.10–12.)

[34] Z III 342.11–17, 25–36. 'Nam tametsi ea sententia, quam dicturi sumus, vehementer nobis arrideat, nihil tamen definimus, sed nostra in medium proferimus, ut, si domino placuerit, alii quoque sic sentire doceantur, sed a spiritu, qui nos omnia docet. Is enim si vetuerit sic intelligi, frustra verba fundemus.' (342.25–9.)

[35] Z III 342.37–345.21.

[36] Z III 345.22–347.12, 351.28–352.3, esp. 346.9–12, 347.4–6. He uses the word 'symbol' in Z III 345.40, 346.29, 351.16, 26. He makes it clear that the fathers are not the basis of the doctrine. They are used to show that his view is not new. (347.7–11.)

After arguing from Christ's words in his support, Zwingli turns to Paul's words in 1 Corinthians 10: 14–22 and in particular 'The cup of blessing which we bless is it not the communion of the blood of Christ? The bread which we break is it not the communion of the body of Christ?' Communion does not mean sharing in the body and blood of Christ, for the following verse, 'We who are many are one bread and one body', shows that the reference is to the church as the body of Christ. It means that those who believe testify, by eating the bread, that they are members of the same body and bind themselves to each other as by an oath, which is how the term 'sacrament' is to be understood. What is fundamental is not the eating, but faith, so that we become one body, not when we eat the bread and drink the cup, but as soon as we believe in Christ. In effect the bread does not make our unity, but manifests it. In answer therefore to the question what the eating does, Zwingli states, 'Nothing other than make plain to your brother that you are a member of Christ and among those who trust in Christ; and again it binds you to the Christian life so that, if it should happen that you live shamelessly and do not repent, you may be shut out from the other members. Hence excommunication and abstention among the ancients.' He thus uses a passage which his opponents would take to support bodily eating to support his own stress on the corporate, ethical, and to some extent memorial aspects of the eucharist.[37]

In the letter Zwingli does not mention Luther, although he does implicitly attack Luther's views and Alber's position represents Luther's in many ways. His references to Carlstadt are positive and friendly, even when he explicitly rejects some of his views, largely because Carlstadt is right in placing the stress on faith. It is not surprising that Luther regards Zwingli as holding Carlstadt's position. Shortly after his letter to Alber, Zwingli writes on 16 December to Strasburg and responds to questions raised in a letter by Bucer and Capito. He claims that he has held his view for several years, referring shortly afterwards to his opinion that 'is' means 'signifies' or 'is a symbol of', and he asserts as before that it is faith that enables us to understand scripture. John 6: 63 remains the primary text to which

He refers to the first book of Tertullian's *Against Marcion*, to Augustine's exposition of Ps. 3 and John 6 (Tractate 26), and to Origen's exposition of Matt. 26: 26 (Tractate 35). In *A Commentary* he adds to these Augustine's Tractates 27 and 84 and the third book of his *Agreement Among the Evangelists*, Origen's exposition of Matt. 23: 23 (Tractate 20), Hilary's exposition of Matthew, and Jerome's exposition of Zeph. 3. As the controversy develops he quotes an increasingly wide range of references in Augustine. The fathers were used in the early writings in support of understanding the mass not as a sacrifice, but as a memorial of Christ's sacrifice (e.g. Z II 152.7–16, 586.34–7).

[37] Z III 347.13–351.9, esp. 348.6–15, 348.30–349.3. Faith and love of one's neighbour are necessary for worthy participation in the eucharist. (Z III 352.10–353.1.) The memorial aspect involves our remembering and our being reminded.

Zwingli refers, but he adds the new testament statements that we are no longer to know Christ according to the flesh (2 Cor. 5: 6) and that Christ is seated at the right hand of God (Heb. 1: 13). The emphasis on the eucharist is on thanksgiving and the union of Christians. He offers guidance to the Strasburg brethren on how to teach the true doctrine without causing offence. They should begin with 'No one has ever seen God' (John 1: 18) to refute the adoration of the eucharist and then when the time is ripe proceed to John 6: 63 and after that to 1 Corinthians 10.[38] The selection and order of the texts shows something of Zwingli's emphases and priorities at this time.

The much more extended treatment in *A Commentary* does not add significantly to his exposition of the eucharist to Matthew Alber. The title 'eucharist' is the one he naturally uses, because it expresses the fundamental element of our thanksgiving for Christ's death. He does, however, draw on other terms, such as 'the Lord's supper', 'communion', and 'synaxis', pointing to the Greek use of eucharist and synaxis.[39]

The section on the eucharist, which is preceded by an examination of the term 'sacrament', begins with a detailed examination of John 6. Zwingli's concern is to show that it cannot refer to sacramental eating. The reference to food is a reference to faith, the reference to Christ's flesh is to his flesh as slain and not as eaten. Further, since he says that those who eat his flesh abide in him and he in them (John 6: 56), and many people eat the body sacramentally and are not in him or he in them, he cannot be referring to sacramental eating there. Moreover the flesh is of no avail (John 6: 63) and that applies to Christ's flesh, as eaten, though not as slain. It is precisely because the Jews thought that the bodily flesh should be eaten that Christ stated that the flesh is of no avail.[40]

---

[38] Z VIII 274.33–275.3, 23–6, 276.1–16, 277.4–13. In John 6: 63 the part Zwingli refers to is 'The flesh is of no avail'. Among other things the letter of Bucer and Capito refers in some detail to Carlstadt's views. (Z VIII 245–50.) In *Advice in the Ittinger Affair* Zwingli draws attention to Christ's institution of the eucharist, and consequently to its character as a communion of the faithful and as a memorial of Christ. The faithful testify to each other that they believe and are redeemed by Christ. In this sense the eucharist may be compared with the annual gathering to give thanks for the victory God gave the Swiss at the battle of Murten. The ethical dimension is expressed by analogy with the covenant the Swiss make with each other. The corporate dimension is further expressed in the insistence on the place of the people with the priest rather than on the place of the priest alone. (Z III 533.4–537.12.)

[39] Z III 775.20–37, 799.17–21, 802.38–803.2, 807.11–14. Such titles can be used as an argument against the adoration of the sacrament, which is also attacked on the basis of the scholastic view that the humanity of Christ is not to be adored. (Z III 808.14–29.) Whereas Luther's terms express his emphasis on the assurance of pardon, Zwingli's express, among other things, thanksgiving for Christ's death and the commitment to a new life. *A Commentary* shows that Zwingli attacks medieval theology and practice, for example both the ideas involved in Berengar's recantation and the financial abuse associated with such views. (Z III 783.16–784.7, 819.20–3, 30–4.)

[40] Z III 776.23, 777.18–21, 779.28–36, 780.10–11, 782.20–2, 30–2, 791.15–18. For Zwingli's understanding of the term 'sacrament' in *A Commentary* see chapter 9.

'The flesh is of no avail' (John 6: 63) is the key text for Zwingli. It is a wall of bronze which nothing can shake, let alone shatter. It is an unbreakable adamant which stands unshattered when attacked and shatters all weapons used against it. For the godly it is a barrier one cannot leap over, a ruler which makes smooth everything that otherwise is hard and rough. It is important because it requires a different understanding of the eucharist from the traditional one. Of itself, without any of Zwingli's other arguments, it is enough to prove that 'is' must mean 'signifies'.[41] After dealing with John 6 Zwingli turns to the gospel sayings concerning the bread and the cup, and then to 1 Corinthians 10: 16. Here the argument is similar to that in his earlier letter. In the course of his exposition certain elements emerge with new force—in particular the contrast between the spiritual and the bodily, the alternative of salvation in Christ or in the bread, and the use of faith as a principle of interpretation.

The Spirit of God teaches man's spirit, draws it, unites it to himself, and transforms it. To talk of eating the bodily flesh spiritually is for Zwingli a contradiction in terms and in effect asserts that what is body is spirit. To use a phrase such as 'spiritual flesh' is the same as calling fire watery or iron wooden.[42] The traditional understanding of the breads leads to placing one's trust in the bread and not in Christ. That is idolatry, for it is Christ who is the pledge of salvation, and not the eucharist.[43] A true understanding of faith is in fact a vital clue in the interpretation of scripture, not only in the passages involved in the eucharistic controversy. It is a principle frequently used in the controversy. Thus faith, in the sense of trust in Christ alone for salvation, determines the meaning of passages such as John 6 and 'This is my body'.[44]

---

[41] Z III 785.40–786.1, 816.26–30, 791.24–6, 786.1–4, 801.22–8. Zwingli argues against interpreting 'The flesh is of no avail' in the light of 'This is my body' on the basis that John 6 is clear. There is also the witness of faith and the senses. (Z III 792.8–33.) He dismisses any argument from the fact that Christ said only once 'The flesh is of no avail'. Other things were said only once; but in any case heaven and earth will pass away rather than a word of God. (Z VIII 408.9–22.)

[42] Z III 782.6–10, 787.3–13, 809.7–9. In *The Canon of the Mass* the issue is related to man's being made in the image of God. 'Anima nostra spiritus est tua manu ad imaginem tuam factus, unde alio cibo quam spiritali refici non potest.' (Z II 606.16–18.) 'Animi ergo solatium esse reliquum sit; at quomodo potest animam caro, quacunque ratione voces, consolari?' (Z VIII 410.11–12.)

[43] Z III 785.1–8, 808.34–809.1, 819.8–10. Cf. 'Commemorationem adpellavit Christus, non pignus; ipse pignus est . . .'. (Z VIII 410.6.)

[44] Z III 785.1–8, 797.31–798.23. The principle is used in interpreting passages that refer to works. (Z III 790.22–791.9.) The argument from faith is used in a variety of ways. Thus if we eat Christ, in the sense of believing in him, we shall not hunger or thirst again (John 4: 14). Therefore faith does not require bodily eating. (Z VIII 318.24–7.)

Zwingli extends his references to the fathers, quoting Augustine at greatest length but also referring to Tertullian, Origen, Hilary, and Jerome. He recognizes that even Augustine did not always venture to present the truth explicitly because it had fallen into disrepute. He quotes what he calls 'the weightiest of the fathers', not because he wishes 'to support by human authority a thing plain in itself and confirmed by the word of God', but to show that he is not the first to hold his view.[45]

The debate about the eucharist continues both theologically and practically with the abolition of the mass and the introduction of a reformed eucharist at Easter 1525. It is to be celebrated four times a year in future. The new liturgy and practices reflect Zwingli's theology. It is noteworthy that the body is seen as the church, for it is by the unifying work of God's Spirit that we become his body.[46] One of those opposing Zwingli in the abolition of the mass is Joachim am Grüt. Zwingli is clearly impressed by am Grüt, in particular by his arguing that Zwingli has drawn his examples of 'is' as meaning 'signifies' from parables. In *The Eucharist* therefore (August 1525) he presents additional points.

After denying his dependence on Carlstadt and asserting that he delayed expressing his view until the time was ripe, he develops his case in three sections. First, he indicates that Christ called what had been drunk wine and that what he gave could not have been his blood as that had not then been shed.[47] Second, he responds to am Grüt with two points. The first is an argument from Engelhard against the view that in the bread the true body of Christ is eaten. It rests on the fact that in the new testament the body of Christ is used in three senses: for the natural body with which Christ lived and died, for his risen body, and for his mystical body the church. The bread cannot be any of these, for—apart from other problems—the natural body could be eaten only in a bodily way, but Christ has ruled that out by saying that the flesh is of no avail. It cannot be the risen

[45] Z III 809.6–816.8, esp. 810.34–811.3, 816.1–4; *Works* III 247.
[46] Z IV 17.3–5, 22.9–18. Zwingli's stress on the place of the Spirit can be seen in the addition of a reference to the Holy Spirit in the *Gloria*. (Z IV 9.12–13.) Jenny refers to the way the eucharist was seen liturgically as an action *of* the congregation rather than *to* the congregation. He is rightly critical of the suggestion that there is a transubstantiation of the church rather than of the bread. Nevertheless there is in Zwingli a stress on the church as the body of Christ, and the position of the prayer that refers to our being made into the body of Christ through the Spirit may be significant. See *Die Einheit des Abendmahlsgottesdienstes bei den elsässischen und schweizerischen Reformatoren*, (Zurich, 1968), pp. 50, 60–2. Zwingli's understanding of the sacraments, as well as his way of celebrating the eucharist, emphasizes his corporate view of the Christian life.
[47] Z IV 463.11–466.18, 467.31–468.4, 15–17, 471.11–18. The calmness of the disciples is seen as supporting their interpreting Christ's words symbolically. (Z IV 468.24–5.) Zwingli points out that 'really' or 'truly' (*vere*) can be used to refer to the substance or essence of something, but can also be used as hyperbole. (Z IV 473.11–19.)

body, for that is at God's right hand, quite apart from the fact that Christ had not been raised when the disciples ate the bread. However, the reference cannot be to the mystical body, as it is Christ, not the church, who was given for us.[48] The second point is Zwingli's discovering in the passover narrative a clear example, not combined with a parable, of the use of 'is' for 'signifies'. It came to him as from God in a dream and was used with great power in his preaching. The force of the example comes from the fact that the passover foreshadows the death of Christ and that Christ himself is the true passover. He instances some of the many parallels between the two events.[49]

In the third section Zwingli deals with eight objections brought by his opponents. Those concerning sense, fleshly understanding, and God's omnipotence are particularly important. In a discussion of faith as trust he indicates that when he speaks of sense, he refers not just to human sense, but to what is taught by the Spirit of God. The virgin birth and the gospel miracles are not abhorrent to sense, when it is used in this way, because they are clearly recorded in scripture. To the objection that 'flesh' in John 6: 63 refers to fleshly understanding Zwingli argues from the context that Jesus was dealing with what caused the Jews difficulty, that is physical eating, adding that 1 Corinthians 8: 13 disproves the assertion that when 'flesh' is used by itself in scripture it means fleshly understanding. Against the view that if God is omnipotent he can cause the bread to be at once real bread and real flesh, Zwingli denies that something is done simply because God *can* do it. Otherwise it would follow that because God can make a gourd out of an elephant, then an elephant is both a beast and a gourd. The criterion is to be found in what God has done, according to scripture.[50]

In the period following Hoen's letter certain new emphases are found in Zwingli. He continues to attack the sacrifice of the mass, transubstantiation, the adoration of the elements, and communion in one kind. His primary concern now, however, is not the sacrifice of the mass, but the view that the bread and wine are in a bodily sense the body and blood of

[48] Z IV 476.4–478.11.
[49] Z IV 482.32–487.9. In a letter to Jakob Edlibach on 9 Dec. 1525, Zwingli responds to the challenge that in the bible there are clear indications that 'is' means 'signifies', by pointing to the clauses that follow: 'Do this in remembrance of me' and 'I shall not drink again of this fruit of the vine'. (Z VIII 456.1–16.)
[50] Z IV 489.11–502.5, esp. 490.22–491.5, 492.21–31, 494.8–495.9, 496.13–35. Sense need not refer only to believers and it can be placed by Zwingli before faith (Z VIII 410.27–8), although this would not make it independent of faith. On flesh as fleshly understanding and on God's omnipotence, see the letter to Basle on 5 Apr. 1525. (Z VIII 318.18–24, 319.6–15.) Zwingli now refers people for the patristic evidence to Oecolampadius's book on the fathers, which was soon to be published. (Z IV 502.6–9.)

Christ and that they are eaten bodily (or even, were that possible, spiritually). Zwingli's view is based primarily on his exposition of John 6, in particular of John 6: 63. The emphasis in the text now is more on 'the flesh is of no avail' than on 'it is the Spirit who gives life'. The contrast between the bodily and the spiritual is strong, a contrast related to this text and to John 3: 6. Flesh is not seen as fleshly understanding, and embraces all flesh, including Christ's. John 6 requires a symbolic understanding of the words of institution and this understanding in which 'is' means 'signifies' is supported by other examples in scripture, drawn chiefly from Hoen, but in particular by the parallel with the passover. The context of the sayings about the bread and the cup confirms this interpretation, as does 1 Corinthians 10, which, like the sayings about the bread and cup, might seem superficially to support Zwingli's opponents.[51]

Faith is from the beginning a fundamental element in Zwingli's eucharistic theology, although its role varies. Now it becomes an important principle of interpretation, ruling out views that deny faith in Christ, as well as the way of understanding terms such as 'food' and 'eating' in John 6. Zwingli no longer holds that the eucharist strengthens faith, and this raises the question about what it is for. The answer is in terms of thanksgiving for Christ's redemptive death, testifying that we are Christians, binding us to the Christian life and to our fellow Christians. The corporate, ethical, and memorial aspects are stressed. There is indeed a shift in the use of the term 'memorial' which is no longer used primarily against the idea of the mass as a sacrifice. However, the main stress in Zwingli's exposition is on Christ and in particular Christ's death. He therefore contrasts that with any alternative way of salvation, which the bread and wine would be, given certain views of the eucharist.[52] Zwingli's concern remains christological and soteriological.

## The Controversy with Luther

Already in 1525 there was conflict between Zwingli and those holding a Lutheran view of the eucharist, but it was not until early 1527 that he engaged directly with Luther. The eucharistic debate was fiercest in 1527

[51] Zwingli draws attention to the way Paul refers in 1 Cor. 10: 17 to our being partakers of the bread, not partakers of the body, just as Christ also in Matt. 26: 29 refers to the blood as wine or the fruit of the vine. (Z IV 498.21–41, 467.37–469.2.)

Although the later Zwingli's primary concern is with the presence of Christ, yet in *An Exposition of the Faith* there is a major attack on the sacrifice of the mass. (S IV 68.1–73.16.)

[52] The eschatological note is lost in the stress on Christ's death in the use of Paul's words in 1 Cor. 11: 26 in Z IV 18.16–18, 23.3–5.

Saving faith is understood consistently as faith in the Son of God who hung on the cross for us. It has nothing to do with what we determine or with bodily eating. (Z IV 467.25–7.)

and 1528 with major controversial writings from both sides, leading to the Marburg colloquy in 1529. Throughout this period, however, Zwingli was also under challenge from catholics, both in Zurich from men such as am Grüt and Edlibach, and outside from scholars such as Cajetan and Eck. Nevertheless the primary concern is the controversy between Zwingli and Luther and the way Zwingli formulated his theology in response to Luther.[53]

A letter of Bugenhagen in July 1525 marked in effect the beginning of the controversy. In *A Reply to Bugenhagen's Letter* three months later Zwingli indicated that he has had differences with Luther, but has not mentioned him by name. His desire is for peace. He would avoid conflict, but if it must take place it should be based on scripture and reasons sustained by faith and scripture.[54] However, Zwingli sensed the need to present his view of the eucharist, which is attacked on all sides, to a wider audience. To reach ordinary Christians he published in German in February 1526 a clear comprehensive statement, *The Lord's Supper*. It expounded his view in relation to three other views: catholic, Lutheran, and Erasmian.[55]

The main concern in Zwingli's exposition is with the words 'This is my body'. In the first part he seeks to show that, in contrast with the catholic and Lutheran views, the words cannot be taken literally. After affirming that a sacrament is only a sign and that 'the sign and the thing signified cannot be the same thing', he deals with transubstantiation, in which 'the substance of the bread is changed into the substance of the essential flesh of Christ, which lay in the crib and hung on the cross'. This is supported by the argument of catholics such as am Grüt, that God's word is so powerful that everything he says, including 'This is my body', is as he says. Leaving aside the point that it is the priest and not God who says the words, Zwingli asserts the need to understand the word of God correctly and points to biblical sayings which must be figurative, such as 'I am the

---

[53] Zwingli's emphasis is different from Luther's even in *An Exposition of the Articles* in 1523, while in the letter to Matthew Alber in November 1524 he distinguishes his position from the Lutheran view of Alber and the Carlstadtian view of Hermann. The detailed development of the controversy is related by Köhler in *Zwingli and Luther*. Köhler (I 314) points to the closeness between the Lutheran view of the eucharist and the view held by the catholic opposition in Zurich.

[54] Z IV 575.18–576.7. The reply does not present new views, but Zwingli does challenge Bugenhagen's statement that we eat the bread, and, in the bread, the body of Christ as violating Christ's words, 'This is my body'. He argues for his interpretation using trope, affirming that faith is needed in discerning trope and that trope is not present in every instance of a word. (Z IV 567.3–20, 559.17–560.17.)

[55] Z IV 790.13–24. The third view is described as Erasmian by Köhler and as renaissance by Bromiley in their editions of the text.

vine'. In the light of John 6: 63 Christ could not have meant the words 'This is my body' literally. If the words are taken literally, then the flesh must be there and be eaten visibly, bodily, and perceptibly, which the believer knows is not true. Moreover, if they are taken literally, the Lutheran view, consubstantiation, is ruled out, for Christ did not say 'My body is eaten in the bread', but 'This is my body'. Zwingli will not allow as adequate the principle of the simplest and natural meaning of a text, for that principle would, for example, make Christ a vine in John 15. The natural meaning has to be acceptable to the believing heart and consistent with the truth, that is scripture.[56]

In the second part Zwingli argues from scripture and the creed that the words 'This is my body' cannot be taken literally. First, he expounds John 6 and shows from the context that the reference to flesh in John 6: 63 is to Christ's flesh, just as the reference to spirit is to the Holy Spirit.[57] Then he quotes 1 Corinthians 10: 1–4, which says that the people of old had the same spiritual food as we have. As they could not have eaten the literal body and blood of Christ, then neither can we. Rather they believed in the one who was to give his flesh and blood, and we believe in the one has given them.[58] Third, he refers to the three articles of the creed, themselves based on scripture: he ascended into heaven; he is seated at the right hand of God the Father almighty; from thence he will come to judge the living and the dead. In this context Zwingli advances for the first time his argument from the two natures of Christ. According to his divine nature Christ is omnipresent and thus, for example, is always at the right hand of the Father; whereas according to his human nature he is not and thus, for example, ascended into heaven. Some biblical passages refer to his divine nature, such as 'I am with you always' (Matt. 28: 20), others to the human

---

[56] Z IV 793.13–810.7, esp. 794.11–12, 14–17. In Z IV 800.30–810.7. Zwingli supports his case from the papal canons. (Baur (II 333, n. 1) sees the appeal to canon law as in part a response to Eck.) He draws on the literal way in which the body of Christ is pressed by the teeth in Berengar's recantation, but argues that we do not perceive the body to be a body as we perceive the bread to be bread. However, if God speaks the words literally we should perceive the body literally. Zwingli quotes in his support Gratian's insertion—after Berengar's recantation—of Augustine's words, 'Why prepare teeth and stomach? Believe and thou hast eaten.' He does not quote canon law to prove anything to believers, but to show those who accept the papacy that the truth can be obtained from its writings. (Z IV 800.30–801.4, 820.17–22.)

[57] Z IV 810.9–820.12, 823.18–825.27. Zwingli again supports his argument with an appeal to the papal canons and the words of Augustine in them. (Z IV 820.13–823.17.) He also makes the familiar contrast between two ways of salvation, one by eating the flesh of Christ and the other by believing in him. He opposes the first as it makes the atoning death of Christ unnecessary. (Z IV 817.19–27.) It remains axiomatic for Zwingli that physical flesh cannot give life to the soul, only the Holy Spirit can do that. (Z IV 819.5–8.)

[58] Z IV 825.28–827.3. There is a further appeal to Augustine.

nature, such as 'Again, I am leaving the world and going to the Father' (John 16: 28) and 'But you will not always have me' (Matt. 26: 11). If the body is in heaven, it cannot be present in the eucharist. Zwingli allows that because the two natures are the one Christ, things belonging to the one nature are often ascribed to the other. However, although we say 'The Son of God ascended into heaven', the ascension strictly speaking concerns the humanity.[59]

He answers two objections, the first from those who appeal to God's omnipotence in giving us Christ's body. Zwingli states that God's omnipotence is in keeping with his word, and that in accordance with Psalm 110: 1 and Acts 1: 9–11 Christ will not come till he comes to judge and when he comes he will come visibly. Moreover Paul could not have said 'until he come' (1 Cor. 11: 26), if he believed that we eat the body of Christ here.[60] The second objection comes from those who hold an Erasmian view in which the body of Christ can be wherever he wills after the resurrection, so that he sits at the right hand of God and is eaten by us here. Zwingli regards this view as unsupported by scripture, and denies that it is the nature of the resurrection body to be where it wills. In any case Christ wills to be bodily at the right hand of the Father. Moreover it belongs only to Christ's divine nature to be everywhere. In support of this he draws on passages that refer to the disciples' being where Christ is, as clearly applying to his human nature and implying that in the body he is in only one place, otherwise the disciples would be in many places, even in the so-called host. The one place where he is, is in heaven. This view, which speaks of the body as the resurrection body of Christ, is in any case in error as Christ's words make it clear that the body is the body given for us.[61]

The third part is concerned to show from scripture 'the true natural sense', and in doing so deals with figures of speech in the bible. It does this in a familiar way with the metaphorical references to Christ as a vine, a lamb, and a stone, pointing to the frequency with which 'is' means 'signifies'. Zwingli regards it as clear from the case he has made that 'This is my body' cannot be taken literally and argues that it must therefore be taken figuratively or metaphorically. This is supported by the close parallels with the passover in Exodus 12, by the way Christ refers to the fruit of the vine, by fact that the disciples were calm, for they would understand the words in the light of 'The lamb is the passover', heard each year at that

---

[59] Z IV 827.4–830.28.

[60] Z IV 830.29–834.12.

[61] Z IV 834.13–841.8. Zwingli accuses his opponents of the Marcionite heresy that Christ had only an imaginary body. Again he cites a passage from Augustine in canon law which refers to the resurrection body of Christ as in one place.

time, and by the absence of any teaching on the part of the apostles that the bread and wine became the body and blood of Christ. Moreover the other words used by Christ in the institution make the case clear. Since the body is defined as given for us, and as the bread was not given for us, it must be that the bread signifies the body which was given for us. This is borne out by the words in Luke 22: 19 'Do this in remembrance of me', which show why the symbolical bread was instituted. Among the fathers, Jerome, Ambrose, and Augustine, are quoted in support of the symbolic interpretation.[62]

In the fourth part, among other things, Zwingli asserts that the difference between him and Oecolampadius is a difference in words, not in sense, such a difference as one finds at points between the new testament writers.[63] Writing to Billican and Rhegius shortly after this, he emphasizes the unity of those who stand with him over against the divided opposition of catholic, Lutheran, and Erasmian. In this he links with himself not only Oecolampadius and the Strasburg theologians, but also Carlstadt and Schwenckfeld, as those who deny the bodily flesh in opposition to those who affirm it, but who disagree among themselves. Those who think as Zwingli does simply differ in their methods of attack on the fortress, not on the need to take it.[64]

The letters to Billican and Rhegius do not show any new development in Zwingli's theology, although the need to interpret scripture by scripture and for miracles to be seen is stressed. The eucharist is misunderstood by the failure to relate one passage of scripture to others, in particular John 6: 29 and 6: 63, just as Arius misunderstood Christ by failing to relate John 14: 28 to passages such as John 1: 1, 1: 14, and 10: 30. Moreover, if the eucharist is claimed to be a miracle, the miracle must be visible as Christ's miracles were.[65] There is in the letter to Urbanus Rhegius a reference to the sacraments as being given 'so that our senses also might have some comfort'. 'Therefore our eucharist is a visible assembling of the church, in

---

[62] Z IV 793.10–11, 841.10–858.20. Zwingli speaks of the way a widow may refer to a ring left her by her husband as her late husband, meaning that it recalls him. (856.12–19, 858.1–4.)

[63] Z IV 858.22–859.17. Zwingli says 'this signifies my body', Oecolampadius 'this is a figure of my body'. Zwingli also argues for the translation 'thanksgiving' and not 'blessing' in 1 Cor. 10: 16–17 and reiterates his view that 'communion' should be translated as 'community'. (Z IV 859.18–861.2.)

[64] Z IV 902.10–903.22, 928.16–25, 932.12–33. Zwingli's understanding of the eucharist is characteristic. The reference to the *res sacramenti* should be noted: 'Dicimus sacramentum esse, non rem sacramenti, gratiarum actionem semel dati beneficii, commemorationem, collaudationem ac postremo corporis mystici, quod est ecelesia, coniunctionem.' (Z IV 902.10–13.)

[65] Z IV 894.24–898.5, 908.16–909.17. He draws on Bucer's argument in insisting that miracles must be seen. Cf. Z V 594.6–8. See also Hoen's comment. (Z IV 517.24–8.)

which together we eat and drink bread and wine as (*veluti*) symbols, that we may be reminded of those things which Christ has done for us.'[66]

An interesting letter in April 1526 to Crautwald and Schwenckfeld shows that for Zwingli the central issue in the eucharistic controversy is the eating of the bodily flesh of Christ in the bread, as it is a denial of Christ as the source of salvation. He is uneasy with the word 'represent' in 'This bread represents my body' as it could imply the presence of the body and argues therefore in favour of the word 'signify' as less ambiguous. The letter, like others at this time, manifests his confidence in the triumph of his interpretation of the eucharist.[67] For Zwingli it is clear from John 4: 14 that whoever believes in Christ will never thirst again. Anyone therefore who wants his faith to be strengthened by the eucharist must have a weak faith. True faith looks to God alone and does not look anywhere else for help, for nothing creaturely can strengthen faith.[68]

Zwingli did not attend the disputation at Baden in May 1526, although he commented on Eck's theses, using the familiar quotations from scripture. Eck's first thesis was carefully worded and acceptable to some: The true body of Christ and his blood are present in the sacrament of the altar. (Zwingli was later to speak of the true body of Christ as present, but added 'by the contemplation of faith'.) There are three main arguments in Zwingli's eleven-point reply. The first concerns flesh: that Christ could not have given it to us to eat, as it is of no avail (John 6: 63), and that there would be nothing but flesh if we were to eat Christ's bodily flesh (John 3: 6). The second concerns the words of institution: 'This is my body which is given for you' (Luke 22: 19). As this refers to the bread, then a literal interpretation would mean that the bread was crucified for us, which is absurd. The third concerns the ascension. A variety of texts is adduced to show that Christ has left the world, according to his human nature, although he is present, according to his divine nature, and will not return bodily until he comes to judge.[69] On 3 June 1526 Zwingli

[66] Z IV 938.16–23. At the beginning of the letter Zwingli denies that he invented the terms 'esculentus deus, impanatus deus' although he regards them as accurate. (933.1–934.17.) He indicates that the issue is between those who affirm and those who deny the bodily flesh, and characteristically describes the eucharist as a symbol 'of thanksgiving and brotherly love'. (932.12–20.)

[67] Z VIII 568.1–569.9, 570.6. Cf. Z VIII 574.23–6. In his letter to Urbanus Rhegius he speaks of the division as being between those asserting and those denying bodily flesh. (Z IV 932.12–13.) There is only one spiritual eating not two; that is, believing in the Son of God, given for us. There is no scriptural support for a second kind which is a so-called bodily-spiritual eating of Christ's flesh. (Z V 421.17–423.1; VIII 739.19–22.) 'Represent' is, however, used in Z IV 938.31–6.

[68] Z VIII 791.13–793.8. Faith in Christ or in his death is of course in Christ as God and not as man.

[69] Z V 182.1–183.4. The texts referred to are: Matt. 26: 11 and 28: 20; John 16: 28; Mark 13: 21; Acts 1: 11; Acts 7: 55 and Matt. 24: 23; Matt. 26: 64; together with references to the risen

responded to Eck's statement at Baden that the body of Christ is visibly in heaven but invisibly in the sacrament of the altar. As Christ's body was given for us visibly, Zwingli insisted that it must be eaten visibly. To say that he is eaten bodily, but invisibly, is the Marcionite heresy. Moreover Eck cannot take refuge in God's omnipotence, which would enable Christ's body to be visibly at God's right hand, but invisibly eaten in the sacrament, as God does not act against his word.[70]

The last major work before his writings addressed directly to Luther was *An Answer to Strauss's Book* in January 1527. The main point at issue, as in all the Lutheran controversy, is the bodily eating of Christ's body in the eucharist, although Christ's bodily presence is related to it. Zwingli challenges as unscriptural Strauss's view that the body is eaten bodily, but invisibly, as well as that it is present bodily, but invisibly, and that eating the body of Christ bodily strengthens faith. For him the eucharist was not instituted to increase faith, but is a thanksgiving for the death of Christ. If sacramental eating benefited people, then the papacy and a religion of externals would be restored.[71] A new area of discussion is the distinction Zwingli makes between historical words and words of promise, the words of institution coming into the first category and not the second. In this he is rejecting an understanding of the word as effective in the sacrament, an important element in Luther and *The Syngramma*, as well as in Strauss.[72]

Zwingli's four writings against Luther in the period up to the Marburg colloquy can be taken together, as the differences between them are small.[73] They offer a detailed examination of his opponent's case rather

---

Christ, including Mark 16: 6. The same kind of case is made in the letter to the Nuremberg Council in July 1526, in which he lays special weight on three invincible passages of scripture: John 6: 63, Luke 22: 19, and Mark 16: 19. (Z VIII 635.29–640.15.) For his response to Faber, see Z V 50.11–54.15. The bread is not in effect mere bread, but bread of thanksgiving and love—not more than that. (Z V 50.15–16.) In *An Account of the Faith* he refers to the true body of Christ as present by the contemplation of faith. (Z VI ii 806.6–12.)

[70] Z V 221.10–226.2. Not averse to satire, Zwingli rejects the idea that because God can do something, he does do it; otherwise it would follow that because he can make Eck into a mule, therefore he is a mule. Cf. Z V 501.23–6. He also comments on Eck's second thesis concerning the sacrifice of the mass, but this issue does not have the importance it had earlier and there is no significant development in Zwingli's position.

[71] Z V 492.4–10, 547.6–16, 500.11–16. The eucharist expresses the commands to love God and one's neighbour, as—besides thanksgiving—it involves a pledge to one's neighbour. All this implies that one is not dealing with mere bread and wine. (Z V 471.12–21.)

[72] Z V 522.22–529.6. In discussions of the word and its role Zwingli and his opponents talk at cross purposes, as their theological positions and concerns are different.

[73] *A Friendly Exegesis* in February 1527, *A Friendly Answer* in March 1527, *Zwingli's Christian Reply* in June 1527, and *Two Replies to Luther's Book* in August 1528.

than a systematic presentation of his own. His comments on Luther are at points sharp and critical, particularly in the later writings, though never as harsh and dismissive as some of Luther's on him. However, Zwingli is also positive and speaks of Luther's role as 'one of the first champions of the gospel', a David against Goliath, a Hercules who slew the Roman boar.[74] The friendly tone owes much to Bucer and Oecolampadius. They are more concerned with reconciliation and their eucharistic theology is more positively expressed than Zwingli's. They undoubtedly influence some of the ways he formulates his views.[75]

The main issue for Zwingli is that Luther puts 'the chief point of salvation in the bodily eating of the body of Christ', for he sees it as strengthening faith and remitting sins.[76] Zwingli attacks the bodily eating of the body of Christ in effect on two grounds: faith and scripture. It conflicts with the understanding and use of faith and with the testimony of scripture.

Faith is belief or trust in Christ, as Son of God, and not, as Luther makes it, a belief about the body of Christ in the bread. Salvation moreover is promised to faith and not to bread, whereas Luther's view implies that there are two ways of salvation, one the death of Christ and the other the bodily eating. For Zwingli the subject of the eucharist is the death of Christ, not the eating of the body, for the words 'Do this in remembrance of me' refer to giving thanks for Christ's death, his body given for us, and not to the eating of the body.[77] Luther's view would make the death of Christ unnecessary, since the disciples shared in the eucharist before Christ's death.[78] Zwingli appeals to the object of faith and the source of faith. It is God. Saving faith, according to Hebrews 11: 1, is in the invisible and not the visible. It is therefore in God (or in Christ as Son of God) and not in anything created, such as the body of Christ, for saving faith is in Christ as God and not as man. Furthermore such faith does not come from anything created, but from the Holy Spirit, nor is it strengthened by anything created. The bodily presence of Christ cannot of itself produce faith,

---

[74] Z V 613.12–13, 722.3–5, 723.1–2. Cf. Z V 817.13–24. There are, however, some vigorous attacks in the later writings, e.g. Z V 858.18–859.1, 934.17–21. See Additional Note 3, p. 257.

[75] Bucer's concern is expressed in letters such as that of 8 July 1526. (Z VIII 646–50.) For Bucer, see Stephens, *Martin Bucer*, pp. 245–50. In his defence of Bucer Zwingli uses Luther's term 'sacramentarian' against those, like Luther, who seek in the sacraments what they do not have: forgiveness of sins and the strengthening of the mind. He compares them with the people of Israel wrongly attributing to the ark of God the power to save. (Z V 574.11–575.4.)

[76] Z V 572.15–16, 754.10–15. Cf. Z V 793.1–15, 900.8–14, 976.5–977.6. The errors that Zwingli affirms in Luther's position also include the effective power of the words of institution and the giving of the gospel and the body and blood of Christ to the recipient.

[77] Z V 576.1–7, 659.4–661.6, 707.3–708.13.

[78] Z V 572.27–573.2, 706.5–11. Cf. Z VI i 310.21–8; VI ii 99.6–15; S VI i 715.46–716.15.

any more than it did for Simon who received Christ bodily in his home.[79] Faith is from God and for those whom God has chosen. If it could be given or strengthened by our words or by a sacramental act or element, then it would be at our disposal. This would mean the restoration of the papacy and a religion of works. As Zwingli sees it, virtually the only hope the papists have is in keeping alive superstitious views of the bodily eating of the body of Christ.[80] The character of faith, if properly understood, also tells against Luther, because is has no need of bodily food, since 'the one who believes in Christ will not hunger or thirst.'[81]

In the controversy faith is related to the presence of Christ. Sometimes this is done in formulas which seem to bring Zwingli closer to Luther, although they do not in fact depart from his fundamental understanding of faith and the eucharist. When the women visited the tomb they carried Christ with them in their hearts through faith; nevertheless the angel said that he was not there bodily. From this it follows that the body of Christ is not everywhere, although his divinity fills all things. As in the example of the women Zwingli has no difficulty in affirming the spiritual presence of Christ, but that is quite different from his bodily presence. 'If this presence of the body is spiritual' in the sense that 'in our hearts we trust in Christ as having died for us', then Zwingli can assert that there is no difference between him and his opponents. It is such a presence that is necessary, not a natural presence. In such a presence, one can say that the body and blood of Christ are present, but the presence is mental or spiritual. Christ is no more present in the body than Peter is. To say that if the believer eats the body and drinks the blood of Christ, then he has the body and blood present, is not to say any more than that 'the faithful have the body and blood of Christ present in the mind'.[82] This may also be expressed by saying not only that Christ is present with us as believers, as he is God, but also that we are in heaven. However we are there 'in contemplation, faith, hope, and love alone'. Christ may be said to be present in the heart 'essentially according to his divinity' and 'bodily according to contemplation and memory'. The body and blood of Christ cannot be present in the eucharist precisely because the bread and wine are signs of them. (For Zwingli there

---

[79] Z VI ii 206.16–210.4. Cf. Z V 781.21–783.10.

[80] Z V 564.6–8, 575.8–15, 706.12–17, 781.21–27, 819.27–820.15. Zwingli appeals to 1 Cor. 3: 7. (Z VI ii 99.15–100.5.)

[81] Z V 624.26–625.10, 665.13–14.

[82] Z V 583.1–6, 587.16–21, 588.15–589.4. See also the marginal note, 'Also wirt das fleysch Christi imm glouben geessen.' (Z VII ii 210.) The contrast between the earthly life of Christ and the present is that then he was present outside people and visibly, whereas now he is present in the heart and invisibly. (Z V 690.25–6.)

is a sharp distinction between the sign and what it signifies.) The bread and wine do not make them present. What he would say is that those who have found their life in Christ's death, suffered for them, bring him to the supper in their thankful hearts. His body, however, is essentially not in the supper, but at the right hand of God.[83] The presence and action of Christ in the eucharist are qualified by the way Zwingli relates them to faith. On occasion, however, a reference to the Spirit in this context expresses the presence and action of Christ more positively.[84]

Faith is also the fundamental criterion in interpreting scripture. It is a principle that Luther himself used in Matthew 16: 18, where the pope would claim that Peter is the foundation of the church. Zwingli uses this principle against Luther, arguing that the plain sense of a passage is not always the true sense. The true sense is discerned by faith and by a comparison with other relevant passages of scripture. This role of faith as interpreter is witnessed to in the words from Isaiah, 'Unless you believe, you will not understand.' Faith, however, does not simply show where the plain sense is not the true sense, it also shows where it is.[85] In all this faith is not independent of scripture, but joined with it and linked with other principles for interpreting it. Zwingli contrasts such an approach with those who boast of faith and teach contrary to scripture. The two belong together, with faith as the interpreter of scripture. In the eucharistic debate what is crucial is that faith makes it clear that the words 'This is my body' cannot be interpreted literally.[86] Zwingli also uses faith as the ground for rejecting what is absurd. Elsewhere he is accused of rejecting his opponents' views because they conflict with reason or sense, but he insists that it is the reason of faith to which he appeals. It is the same here. Something is absurd only as it is absurd to faith.[87]

[83] Z V 670.6–15, 791.7–10; VI ii 201.5–18, 202.14–19, 203.3–9. Cf. Z VI ii 101.16–22, 142.3–13; XIII 536.14–19. 'Wir erkennend gernn, das Christus' lychnam im nachtmal sye, wie unsere lychnam yetz im himmel sind, das ist, in erkanntnus, wal und fürsichtigkeyt gottes.' (Z VI ii 142.3–6.) See the marginal note, 'Contemplatione est in eucharistia: Trachtlicher anschowung ist Christus lyb im nachtmal, aber nit wäsenlich lyblich'. (Z V 789.) In *A Friendly Exegesis* Zwingli will not allow that God is more present in his essence to those he favours than to others, for in the presence that belongs to his essence or nature he is equally present everywhere. The difference lies not in God's presence, but in his favour, and where God favours one person more than another he deems him worthy of more gifts than the other. (Z V 586.8–26.)

[84] '. . . sed Christus adest in coena spiritu suo, gratia et virtute sua, intus vegetans et pascens fideles, corpus etiam suum adest menti fideli, sed fidei contemplatione, non naturaliter aut corporaliter.' (S VI i 758.33–6.)

[85] Z V 663.9–29, 710.2–10, 731.27–732.11. Cf. Z V 886.9–16. On the use of faith in interpretation, see chapter 2 above. The point at issue was not important enough for the early church to make it an article of faith. (Z V 793.19–21.)    [86] Z V 752.12–15, 773.16–775.3, 21–776.2.

[87] Z V 618 15–17. 'Debuisti enim intelligere, quod absurditatem non a sensu humano, sed a sensu rei, hoc est: fidei et scripturae metimur.' (Z V 665.11–13.)

Besides the appeal to faith there is the appeal to scripture. Zwingli's use of the bible in *A Friendly Exegesis* shows something of what this means. His approach in the debate with Luther is in part dictated by Luther's simple insistence on the words 'This is my body'. He complains that Luther rests his case precisely on the point at issue and seeks to make him argue the case rather than assume it, unless it can be overthrown.[88] The debate causes Zwingli to expound further his use and understanding of scripture and his understanding of Christ.

Zwingli argues that the proper use of scripture requires an understanding of the tropes it uses, the collation of passages of scripture, and analogy. Moreover although scripture must be interpreted by faith, we are to remain within the confines of scripture. Against this background he affirms that if we collate John 6: 63, 16.7-8, 17: 11, Matthew 24: 26-7, Mark 16: 19, Luke 24: 51, and Acts 1: 9-11, we see that there must be a trope in the words spoken at the last supper, for there must be harmony in what is written by the Spirit. The particular tropes he points to are metonomy and catachresis. He then argues by analogy with the passover and from the words of the last supper that the eucharist was given for commemoration and thanksgiving and not for bodily eating.[89]

Of fundamental importance in Zwingli's appeal to scripture is John's gospel—for him the noblest part of the new testament. If you take it away, 'you take the sun from the world'. John has this importance as it provides two fundamental elements in Zwingli's eucharistic theology: John 6: 63 and alloiosis.[90] John 6: 63 is his key text, where Christ cut the knot 'with an axe so sharp and solid that no one can have any hope that these two pieces— body and eating—can come together again'. For Zwingli it is to John 6 that one should turn first in the eucharistic debate. In doing so he continues to defend his interpretation of it over against Luther's view that the flesh refers not to Christ's flesh, but to a fleshly understanding.[91] These discussions are paralleled by discussions of alloiosis or the sharing of properties. The sharp distinction he makes between the humanity and divinity of Christ is central, and helps to explain his differences with Luther over the eucharist. He holds that Luther confuses the two natures. This

[88] Z V 626.29-32, 696.26–697.1.

[89] Z V 729.20–748.11. In Z V 603.5–604.29 he states his view—in response to Luther—that 'is' is not always a trope in scripture, but that such a meaning is not alien to scripture. He then shows by the collation of various passages that the words 'This is my body' cannot have their face meaning, but must include a trope. There are frequent discussions of trope, e.g. in Z V 853.24–921.22, where again it is set in the context of the collation of passages of scripture.

[90] Z V 564.6-16.

[91] Z V 616.9–15. In his exposition he adduces the support of the fathers for his interpretation. (Z V 605.9–612.34.) Cf. Z V 959.14–969.32; VI ii 181.7-205.29.

confusion underlies Luther's holding that the body of Christ is every-where, whereas Christ's body belongs to his humanity and shares the characteristics of his humanity. A reference to this same issue prefaces the examination of alloiosis in *A Friendly Exegesis*.[92]

The proper interpretation of John's gospel requires an understanding of alloiosis, by which, when speaking of one nature in Christ, we use terms that belong to the other. Thus when Christ says, 'My flesh is food indeed' the word 'flesh' properly applies to the human nature, but by interchange it is used here of the divine, for it is as Son of God that he is food for the soul. Zwingli is concerned that the two natures shall keep their integrity.[93] Alloiosis enables this to happen and incidentally buttresses his position in the eucharistic controversy. It is of particular importance in interpreting the references to going away. They must apply to Christ as human, not as divine, for as God he is everywhere. Zwingli insists that they speak of his being absent, not of his being present unseen. (The going is related to the coming of the Spirit to the hearts.) There follow references to the ascension which speak of the ascension of Christ's body and of its being seated at the right hand of God. In the light of the passages he quotes Zwingli can say that Christ has circumscribed his body. The resurrection appearances confirm this, for he never appeared in different places at the same time, and the words about his return show that it will be as circum-scribed and visible as the going away of his body.[94]

That Christ's body is circumscribed continued to be an issue in the controversy. Zwingli rejects Luther's distinctions and clarifications, but at the heart of his rejection is not the philosophical argument, though he uses that, but the scriptural one. He sees Luther's view as denying the humanity which, according to new testament passages such as Philippians 2: 7 and Hebrews 2: 14, 17; 4: 15, Christ shares with us, and the passages that state or imply that his body is in one place, including those that would otherwise mean that we also shall be everywhere.[95] He uses the analogy of the sun, which shines throughout the world without being in each place, to show how Christ can shine everywhere in his divine power while his body is in one place and yet is seen throughout the world by the eye of faith. It is, he adds, sufficient for us that it is in one place. We do not seek to

---

[92] Z V 678.28–679.5. There are substantial discussions in *A Friendly Exegesis*, *Zwingli's Christian Reply*, and *Two Replies to Luther's Book*. In the third of these the section is followed by an excursus on Christ's body. (Z V 679.6–701.18, 922.1–959.12; VI ii 126.1–159.15, 159.16–181.6.)

[93] Z V 680.1–681.4, 682.6–9. Cf. Z V 952.28–953.8.

[94] Z V 683.11–701.18.

[95] e.g. Z VI ii 159.12–167.17, 508.3–10. Cf. Z VI i 469.1–473.10. He continues to insist that he makes his case from scripture. (Z VI ii 170.9–13.)

bring it down, any more than to bring down the sun.[96] The whole thrust of
the argument that the body of Christ can be in only one place at a time and
that that place is at the right hand of God, from which, when he comes, he
will come visibly to judge, is to demonstrate that his body cannot be in the
eucharist. Zwingli has to clarify the phrase 'at the right hand of God' in the
course of the debate, but insists that to hold that the humanity of Christ
must be essentially and bodily where the divinity is, is to deny the whole
new testament witness or to fall into Marcionism. The charge of
Marcionism is in effect a charge that the body of Christ was not a real
human body.[97]

Within the appeal to scripture certain texts or ideas have particular
importance for Zwingli, in particular the words 'which is given for you'
and the view that the soul cannot be fed with flesh. The use of the first can
be taken as an example of the collation and comparison of scripture. He
accuses Luther of emphasizing one passage, 'This is my body', to the
neglect of other passages with which it must be compared and also to the
neglect of the context presented by the words which follow it. In this case
the words were doubtless included by Paul and Luke, writing later, to
make the matter clearer. They make it evident that the body is the body
that hung on the cross and therefore, if the words are to be taken literally,
we must eat him as he was given for us, visibly and passibly. Christ therefore will have to suffer pain, being crushed by the teeth.[98] Passages such as
John 3: 6 and 6: 63 lie behind the strong contrast in Zwingli between mind
and flesh. The flesh cannot penetrate to the mind or give it life. The pious
mind cannot be fed or strengthened by the body. This fundamental
presupposition rules out any eating of the body of Christ which is not
spiritual. Such an eating, however, Zwingli can allow.[99]

The appeal to scripture may include not only the strongly exegetical
approach to the debate, but also a defence of the indirect method of argument which he employs, the appeal being to the example of Christ and his
apostles. In this Zwingli uses a variety of texts, for example that Thomas
refused to believe that Christ had risen from the dead, which he would not
have done if he had believed that he ate the body of Christ in the supper,

[96] Z VI ii 167.18–168.13. Cf. Z VI i 471.9–31.
[97] Z V 918.12–919.26, 941.23–942.7.
[98] Z V 846.10–16, 850.11–853.14, 855.28–34, 904.16–905.21, 620.20–621.7. It could not have
been the resurrection or glorified body, as Christ was not yet raised from the dead.
[99] Z V 622.12–15, 625.7–8; VI i 476.9–22; VI ii 210.9–11. 'Habend sy aber in allein geystlich
geessen, das ist danckbar gewesen, das er den lychnam inn tod ergeben hat, so darff es keines
zangges mer . . .'. (Z VI ii 212.24–6.) In his exegesis of Exod. 21: 28 Zwingli allows that the eating
of the flesh of a cruel animal could make one cruel. Not surprisingly, he does not relate what
natural reason suggests to the eucharist, but allegorizes it. (Z XIII 408.1–22.)

and that James did not mention partaking of the body of Christ when he said that the elders should visit the sick and pray for them and anoint them.[100] In his appeal to scripture, as well as to faith, Zwingli rejects the accusation that he has thought up a position and then sought justification for it in scripture. Rather has he weighed all the relevant passages of scripture, and not just one or two, since the other passages are also God's word. In this way the meaning of scripture has emerged.[101]

The controversy does not change Zwingli's position, though it leads to clarifications. He responds to the charge that for him the bread is mere bread by saying that, viewed materially, it is only bread, but that viewed in terms of its use it is not. It is a token, a pledge, a sign of unity. It is symbolical bread, eucharistic bread. One may understand it by a comparison with the difference in the splendour of a flower in a bride's crown, rather than outside it, or between a king's signet ring and the ring seen in terms of its gold. He has never heard it spoken of as baker's bread, of which Eck accused him. He sees it sacramentally as 'a splendid bread, a glorious bread'.[102]

The use of the term 'sacramental' appears to bring him closer to Luther in the phrase 'sacramental unity', suggested by Bucer. There is, however, no change in substance, for in a sacrament there is always a sharp distinction for Zwingli, though not for Luther, between the sign and what it signifies. The bread and the body of Christ are sacramentally one, but no more so than any sign is one with what it signifies. The body of Christ is sacramentally in the eucharist, but it does not follow 'that the body of Christ is, where the sacrament of his body is'. Essentially his body is at the right hand of God.[103]

The controversy with Luther reaches its climax in the Marburg colloquy. Many factors contribute to the colloquy and the concord, both political and theological, not least the mediating approach of Bucer, Oecolampadius, and Melanchthon. Nothing new in Zwingli's eucharistic theology emerges in the debate, nor is there a real understanding on the part of Luther or Zwingli of the other's fundamental position. The discussion is dominated, like the writings between them, by Luther's insistence

---

[100] Z V 598.1–599.26.

[101] Z V 906.16–907.8.

[102] He speaks of it as 'ein verzeichenlich brot', 'ein war- unnd pflicht- oder eynigungzeychen' (Z V 833.16–834.12), 'ein brot des nachtmals und dancksagung des tods Christi'; 'der bruch und wirde des nachtmals gibt im höhe, dass es nit ist wie ein ander brot' (Z VI i 481.19–482.2); 'Der substantz unnd wäsens halb ist's nützid denn brot und wyn, des sacraments halb es ein herrlich brot, ein eerlich brot . . .'. (Z VI ii 34.22–3.)

[103] Z VI ii 199.21–202.25.

on the words 'This is my body'. They do not change their positions, indeed they cannot, because they reflect their underlying theology and their grasp of the gospel. They do, however, clarify and to some extent develop them in the course of the controversy.

In the end the colloquy produces agreement on fourteen articles. The fifteenth article, on the eucharist, has five points of agreement and only one of disagreement. The point of disagreement is real, but by being placed in a subordinate clause is not emphasized: whether the true body and blood of Christ are bodily in the bread and wine. The agreement on communion in both kinds and the mass as a work are not significant. The reference to 'the institution of Christ' is ambiguous and can be used by Zwingli or Luther. Zwingli understandably interprets it in terms of a memorial and a thanksgiving. The reference to 'a sacrament of the true body and blood of Jesus Christ' may not sound Zwinglian, but is so, given his understanding of sacrament. The reference to the spiritual eating of the body and blood as above all (*vornehmlich*) necessary is a Zwinglian emphasis, in which Zwingli sees the main point of religion as saved. However, it could imply other kinds of eating as necessary. The more obviously Lutheran emphasis in the reference to the sacrament as given by God, like the word, to move weak consciences to faith is made acceptable for Zwingli by the addition of the words 'through the Holy Spirit'. This secures that salvation is utterly dependent on God and in no sense at man's disposal. For Zwingli this was at stake in Luther's understanding of the bodily eating of the body of Christ.[104]

The controversy had in some ways a negative effect on the development of Zwingli's eucharistic theology. It led him to express his views primarily in opposition to Lutheran and catholic views and caused him virtually to identify the Lutheran and catholic positions. That made his reconciliation with Luther more difficult, and meant that any agreement between them would seem to the Swiss to be a return to catholicism. Their catholic opponents were partly instrumental in intensifying this division between them. Yet the controversy was also fruitful. It made Zwingli and Luther clarify their views and led to some accommodation between them. For Zwingli this was helped by the mediating position of Bucer and

---

[104] For the article and Zwingli's comments, see Z VI ii 523.12-27, 551.1-21. His comments include the sentence: 'Fürnehmlich: Principalis est manducatio spiritualis.'

In the controversy with Luther one of Zwingli's major objections to the bodily eating is that it makes the Holy Spirit dispensable, for all that Luther ascribes to bodily eating (whether faith, or unity, or the resurrection of the body) comes from the Spirit. (Z V 625.4-7, 689.13-14, 897.16-18, 899.8-11; VI i 311.8-13, 332.19-333.2, 336.31-337.3, 357.13-359.4, 473.12-19; VI ii 101.22-102.1.)

encouraged by the need to secure the reformed faith. Thus Zwingli made it clear that the bread was not mere bread and began to affirm terms such as 'presence', 'true', and 'sacramental'. The controversy revealed the fundamental differences in Zwingli's and Luther's theology. They had different understandings of faith, a different emphasis in christology, a different view of man, and a different grasp of God's way of dealing with man. There were differences in their approach to, and use of, scripture, Zwingli's being much more comprehensive and more rational, though not rationalistic. Such differences made agreement impossible, quite apart from any personal or political factors that might hold them apart.

## The Later Writings

Zwingli's view of the eucharist is presented more positively in his later writings in 1530 and 1531. This is in part because he states what he believes rather than what he does not believe and in part because he gives priority to the first rather than the second. There is no real change in substance in what he says, except perhaps the role given to the senses, but the writings are statements of faith rather than primarily attacks on his opponents.

In *An Account of the Faith* and *The Letter to the Princes of Germany*, and to some extent in *An Exposition of the Faith*, the eucharist is presented after more general comments on the sacraments. In the first his concern is with the sovereignty and grace of God, which would be denied if God were bound to the sacraments in the sense that he could not act apart from them and must act in them. A similar denial that the sacraments confer grace is made in the second, with the distinction between the sign and what it signifies, but then they are viewed positively in terms of their appeal to the senses.[105] However, when the eucharist is discussed it is first to affirm the presence of Christ rather than to deny it.

Zwingli asserts that the true body of Christ and everything done by him is present by the contemplation of faith before he denies the bodily presence and the bodily eating. This fits his view that something should be defined in terms of those for whom it is instituted, and the eucharist was instituted for believers. In *The Letter to the Princes of Germany* he states that he has never denied that Christ's body is truly, sacramentally, and mysteriously present in the supper. The presence, however, is immediately related to

---

[105] Z VI ii 803.5–806.5; VI iii 252.13–262.7. In *An Exposition of the Faith* the main section on the eucharist precedes that on the sacraments; it begins negatively, although there are earlier and positive references. For Zwingli's view of the sacraments in this period, see chapter 9 above.

faith, a faith which is already present.[106] Zwingli continues to attack the
bodily presence and the bodily eating with the familiar texts of scripture,
arguments from scripture, and quotations from the fathers, arguing that
his opponents deny scripture and the humanity of Christ, if they do not
accept that Christ's body is in heaven and therefore not in the eucharist.[107]
In *An Exposition of the Faith*, where the case begins with Christ's true
humanity, the argument is used more soteriologically than usual, for our
resurrection is made to depend on Christ's being a man as we are. It also
draws on the familiar texts to argue that the body of Christ is in heaven.[108]

As the body is present sacramentally, it can be eaten sacramentally. This
sacramental eating is clearly distinguished from spiritual eating, which is
trusting in the mercy and goodness of God through Christ. In effect we eat
Christ's body spiritually when we trust in the humanity he assumed for
our sake. We eat the body of Christ sacramentally when we 'eat the body
of Christ with the mind and spirit in conjunction with the sacrament'. We
do inwardly what we are representing outwardly. Without faith, however,
we do not eat sacramentally. Moreover the fact that we are to examine
ourselves before coming to the supper implies that we should have faith
before we come.[109]

If we must have faith before we come and if faith does not come from
the sacraments, but from the Spirit, who can act with them or without
them, what is the benefit of the sacraments? Zwingli's answer in this
period is related to the need of the senses. Preaching appeals to the hearing,
whereas the eucharist appeals to sight and touch and taste as well as to the
hearing. 'Then by the symbols themselves, namely the bread and wine,
Christ himself is presented as it were to the eyes, so that in this way not
only the hearing, but also the sight and taste see and perceive Christ,
whom the mind has present within and in whom it rejoices.' Moreover, as

[106] Z VI ii 806.6–17; VI iii 263.3–265.19. 'Cum igitur omnis ista praesentia nihil sit sine fidei
contemplatione, iam fidei est ista esse aut fieri praesentia, non sacramentorum.' (Z VI iii 265.5–
6.) 'Sic in coena Christi corpus tanto praesentius est fidei contemplatione menti, quanto maior
est fides et charitas Christi.' (Z VI iii 281.24–5.)
   Zwingli draws an analogy (not developed) between faith's clear contemplation of Christ's
dying for us on the cross, and Stephen's seeing Christ reigning at the right hand of God. (Z VI iii
263.1–264.11.) Büsser draws attention to positive statements about Zwingli's view of the
eucharist in *The Letter to the Princes of Germany*. (Z VI iii 243.4.)

[107] Z VI ii 806.17–812.18. The main patristic support comes, as usual, from Augustine with
references to the resurrection body's being in one place and to Christ's giving a sign of his body.
Augustine's importance is even more evident in *The Letter to the Princes of Germany*. (Z VI iii
265.21–270.17.)

[108] S IV 51.7–31.

[109] S IV 53.33–55.29. In his letter to Alber, Zwingli cited Augustine to support the separation
of spiritual and sacramental eating. (Z III 351.28–352.1.) And see Additional Note 4, pp. 257–8.

we are tempted by the devil through the senses, the eucharist helps to increase our faith by its engagement of the senses. The sacraments assist the contemplation of faith, which could not happen to the same extent without their use. The mind works best when the senses are not distracted, but work with it, and this can be said to happen in the eucharist, in which 'the whole Christ is as it were sensibly offered even to the senses'. Indeed he refers to the eucharist as a pledge (*pignus*) of Christ's love.[110] Faith, as trust in God, remains a gift of the Spirit. The eucharist can give historical faith, as to believers and unbelievers it bears witness to the birth and death of Christ, but only to believers does it bear witness that Christ died for us.[111]

With the more positive emphasis on the eucharist goes a more positive reference to the bread and wine, for they signify high things. A sign increases in value according to the value of what it signifies, just as the wedding ring given to the queen by her husband is of more value than the gold of which it is made. The bread therefore which was common is now divine and sacred.[112]

In a letter to Bucer in February 1531 Zwingli makes it clear that there is no dispute about Christ's being present in the supper, only about whether he is present bodily and thus offered and eaten in it. He affirms that Christ is eaten spiritually and sacramentally. However, Zwingli is weary of formulas that unite him and Luther, but only outwardly, for the Lutherans do not interpret them symbolically. He now sees them as worse than the papists in their view of Christ's body as present locally in the bread and eaten with the teeth. He is critical of terms such as those used in the Tetrapolitan Confession about Christ truly giving his true body, although he can speak of Christ as truly present and of his true body as present. He is determined to stand by the truth. 'For we do not live to this age, nor to the princes, but to the Lord.'[113] However, it is Bucer who has helped and encouraged him to express himself more positively and some of the fruit

[110] Z VI iii 259.5-265.19; S IV 46.18-21, 57.12-58.5. '. . . iam constat sacramentis non esse gratiam alligatam et secundum hoc nec iustificare nec iustificationem dispensare, sed fidem aut promissionem, quae prius adest, suis quasi fomentis incitare atque testari reliquis de ecclesia membris'. (Z VI iii 265.16-19.) The commentaries also refer to the role of the senses in the sacraments. They were instituted because of weakness and involve the whole person in giving thanks to God. (S VI ii 58.34-44; Z XIV 599.1-3.) See also Z XIV 574.1-14, 596.12-597.2.
[111] S IV 55.9-29.
[112] Z VI iii 271.13-272.3; S IV 56.32-46. The sacraments are sacred, joyful, and venerable things. (Z VI iii 259.5-8.) The bread is symbolic and mystic, and the symbols are not bare. (S VI ii 9.43-45, 10.4-7.) And see Additional Note 5, p. 258.
[113] Z XI 339-343, in particular 340.7-12, 342.5-8, 340.24-341.8, 339.4-10, 340.2-4. '. . . nam nisi adsit, abhorrebimus a coena'. (Z XI 340.8-9.) See Additional Note 6, p. 258.

of this is to be seen in *The Letter to the Princes of Germany*.[114] The positive note emerges in some of the commentaries, in particular *The Death of Christ*, which refers to Christ the eternal high priest feeding the faithful with his body and blood. In an exposition of the Emmaus story the presence of Christ is linked both to God's omnipresence and to the promise to be present when two or three are gathered in his name.[115] However the historical and transcendent elements of the Christian life are expressed in the need for us to lift our eyes to Christ in heaven, something in fact which the Spirit does.[116]

The familiar marks of the eucharist are present. It is thanksgiving for Christ's death for us, a confession of our faith, and a commitment to our brethren, to love them as Christ loved us. It is moreover a corporate act, for as the bread comes from many grains, so the body of the church is joined together from many members. Moreover the fact that the sacrament is an oath stresses this unity, as does the sacramental eating of Christ's body.[117]

There are many influences on Zwingli's eucharistic theology, though it is impossible to say that any of them is determinative. Thus the fundamental importance of John 6: 63 could be traced to Erasmus's *The Enchiridion*, although Erasmus is not the only one who uses it.[118] However, Zwingli ascribed his understanding of the sacrament to Erasmus and certainly many elements in it are characteristic of Erasmus, such as the subjective, corporate, and ethical emphases, with the stress on faith and on commemoration. Köhler draws attention to the fact that so many of the positions

[114] See, e.g. Z XI 89.22–5. Bucer appeals to the fathers in defence of the words 'the true body truly present'. He also shows how he can express something in positive terms, such as 'food for the soul', which Zwingli expresses negatively. (Z XI 298.4–6, 300.10–16.)

[115] S VI ii 9.32–10.40, 58.31–8.

[116] S VI ii 55.25–32, 74.28–33. The reference to the Spirit's lifting our eyes is not in a eucharistic passage. This is an example of how Zwingli has not developed some of the potential in his understanding of the eucharist.

[117] The *res* of the eucharist is said to be giving thanks with faith for Christ delivered to us by God and crucified for our sins. (Z VI iii 254.1–8.) Cf. 256.17–20. (In *A Commentary* he refers to Origen in speaking of the *res* of the sacrament as the faith by which we believe Christ made a sacrifice for us; in *The Providence of God* 'res autem ipsa, quod Christus vere pro nobis est traditus et oblatio factus, quae quidem res nunciatur, praedicatur et creditur ab his scilicet, qui dominicam coenam agunt'. (Z III 812.14–813.2; VI iii 167.19–168.2.)

For confession, see Z VI iii 270.21–271.7. For the love of neighbour, see S IV 46.44–7. For the corporate element, see S IV 57.6–11, 58.6–15.

[118] See, e.g., J. Staedtke 'Voraussetzungen der Schweizer Abendmahlslehre', *Theologische Zeitschrift*, 16 (1960), 19–32. He refers in particular to the Modern Devotion and the Brethren of the Common Life. The Erasmian character of Zwingli's view is argued by Köhler, *Zwingli und Luther* I 49–58, and G. Krodel, 'Die Abendmahlslehre', pp. 205–20.

advanced in the eucharistic controversy have their antecedents in medieval and scholastic discussion, such as the memorial character of the meal, the place of faith, the distinctions between spiritual, sacramental, and bodily eating, the modes of presence of the body, and the body as in only one place, that is heaven. He sees the elements of reformation teaching as in the medieval tradition, the difference being that they come together in new groupings and with other emphases.[119] The Augustinian and Neoplatonist contribution is evident in the whole of Zwingli's theology, and especially in his understanding of the sacraments. It helped to shape his thought and to give him some of the categories he used. Augustine was in some sense a source as well as a support for his position in several crucial areas.[120] The influence of Hoen's letter is often exaggerated and the fact ignored that some elements in it were rejected by Zwingli.

The controversy began with the issue of the sacrifice of the mass, and Zwingli's affirmation that it is a memorial of the sacrifice. After that the crucial question was that of the presence of Christ, in particular Zwingli's opposition to a bodily presence and a bodily eating. The fact that he put the emphasis on the bodily eating shows that the issue was essentially a soteriological one. Precisely because the issue was soteriological it engaged the whole of Zwingli's theology; for if you allow that bodily eating, which is possible for believer and unbeliever alike, is a means of grace, then the entire doctrine of God, Father, Son, and Holy Spirit, is overthrown. The sovereignty and the grace of God in our salvation are denied, and salvation is put at man's disposal in administering and receiving the eucharist. The place of Christ and his death in our salvation is also denied, for another way of salvation is offered; his institution of the sacrament for believers is contradicted; and the human nature he shares with us is called in question. The role of the Spirit in our salvation is also denied, for his taking the place of Christ's bodily presence is rejected, and his initiative in creating faith is overturned. The argument from the nature of faith is at heart a theological argument, for faith is faith in God, not in anything created; it is faith in Christ as dying for us, not as eaten; it is faith that comes from the inward working of the Spirit, not from bodily eating.

Zwingli developed a view of the eucharist which coheres with his theology. It is seen as a thanksgiving for, and memorial of, Christ's death, a confessing of one's faith in that death, and a pledging of oneself in response to Christ's death. Compared with much medieval practice his was a strongly corporate and ethical emphasis. Zwingli had greater difficulty in

[119]  Köhler, I 808–12.
[120]  For Hoffmann's summary of Zwingli's use of the fathers, see Additional Note 7, pp. 258–9.

expressing the initiative of God in the sacrament, in part because of the strong opposition of body and Spirit and the sharp distinction of a sign from what it signifies. He did not develop the positive elements in his theology as far as, for example, Bucer did in his. He could have done this and yet safeguarded the sovereignty of God in terms of God's choosing to use the sacraments and choosing to use them for believers, as well as in terms of the Spirit at work in the believer when he receives. He could equally have developed the few references to Christ or the Holy Spirit as feeding us in the eucharist. This would have enabled him within the constraints of his own theology to speak of the sacraments as presenting, and not simply representing, Christ.

The positive emphasis in the later Zwingli is related to the senses. God can make use of the eucharist in relation to them to strengthen faith. As this was present in the early Zwingli as well, it may be that it is a constant, if sometimes unexpressed, part of his theology. Nevertheless Zwingli could not in any sense speak of the eucharist as necessary for salvation without thereby denying his understanding of God and salvation.

## ADDITIONAL NOTES

1. Zwingli preferred the term 'memorial' to Luther's term 'testament', though it was also used independently by Zwingli, and he was happy to accept it. The former describes the eucharist 'nach dem bruch und verhandlung', the latter 'nach siner natur und eigenschafft'. (Z II 137.32–138.16.) Zwingli's preference is therefore for the more subjective term. Remembering is primarily something that *we do*, hence the statement that if the dead eat and drink the body and blood of Christ they also remember his suffering. (Z II 153.10–13.) There is a characteristic appeal to the fathers in support of the view that the eucharist is a memorial of the sacrifice and not a sacrifice, though he recognizes that some did erroneously call it a sacrifice. (Z II 151.21–153.1.)

Locher stresses the importance of understanding 'memorial' or 'remembrance' in an Augustinian or Platonic way, so that it means 'nicht Rückschau . . . sondern Ver-gegenwärtigung, gültige Gegenwart des Leidens der Herrn'. (*Streit unter Gästen* (Zurich, 1972), pp. 10–11; *Zwingli's Thought*, pp. 314–15.) He sees this making present as the action of God: 'die Kraft jener Vergegenwärtigung des Todes Christi als unseres Heils liegt für ihn jedoch nicht in unserer Seele sondern auf Grund der Ewigkeitswirkung des Opfers des Herrn im Heiligen Geist; das empfangende Organ ist der Glaube, beziehungsweise die bewusste contemplatio desselben', ('Grundzüge', p. 585; *Huldrych Zwingli in neuer Sicht* (Zurich, 1969), p. 260; *Zwingli's Thought*, p. 223.) He points to Oecolampadius's words at Berne in 1528 'Man soll da vermercken was das Wort Erinnern uff ihm hab . . . Wil man ansehen wie der Mensch innerlich erinnert werde und wer das würcke so soll das unserm einigen Meister der da in Himmel ist Christo selbs der sölichs mit synem Geist würcket zuogegeben werden.' ('Die Berner Disputation 1528–Charakter, Verlauf, Bedeutung und theologischer Gehalt', ZWA 14 (1978), 560.) Unfortunately there is no corresponding reference in Zwingli. Nor does he develop this approach in expounding John 14: 26 in St John. (S VI i 752.38–48.)

Bucer brings out part of the meaning of remembrance in 1529 when he says, 'Now if one has and enjoys these through faith, as John 6 teaches, one has and eats them truly, not as one has one's absent wife present with him through remembrance, but in such a way that through this the spirit is fed and renewed to eternal life.' (BW 3. 462.18–22.)

2. Zwingli's account of the differences or changes in his understanding of the eucharist can be seen in Z III 773.26–774.17, 816.4–9; IV 463.11–24, 560.18–561.3; V 738.4–739.9, 907.9–908.4. This issue is discussed among others by Köhler and Bauer. See Köhler, I 61–3, 84–7; 'Zu Zwinglis ältester Abendmahlsfassung', ZKG 45 (1926) 399–408 and 'Zur Abendmahlskontroverse in der Reformationszeit, insbesondere zur Entwicklung der Abendmahlslehre Zwinglis', 47 (1928) 47–56 and Bauer, 'Die Abendmahlslehre Zwinglis bis zum Beginn der Auseinandersetzung mit Luther', Theologische Blätter, 5 (1926) 217–26 and 'Symbolik und Realpräsenz in der Abendmahlsanschauung Zwinglis bis 1525' Zeitschrift für Kirchengeschichte, 46 (1927) 97–105. For some of the issues involved in Zwingli's use of trope, see H. Rückert 'Das Eindringen der Tropuslehre in die schweizerische Auffassung von Abendmahl', ARG 37 (1940) 199–221, S. N. Bosshard, Zwingli, Erasmus Cajetan, Die Eucharistie als Zeichen der Einheit (Wiesbaden, 1978), pp. 53–8; Locher, Die Zwinglische Reformation, p. 300, n. 158.

In 'Zur Abendmahlskontroverse in der Reformationszeit' Köhler outlines five broad views of the eucharist: transubstantiation, consubstantiation, a mystical view, a purely symbolic view, and faith-presence. He sees Zwingli as moving (not later than 15 June 1523, in the letter to Wyttenbach) from the first of these to the third. This mystical view he associates with Erasmus. It involves real presence and objectivity, but avoids definition, so that there is no stress on, but also no denial of, a bodily real presence. The emphasis is on the subjective, e.g. faith, not on the objective. Then, after receiving Hoen's letter in 1524, Zwingli moves to the symbolic view, represented by Hoen and Carlstadt. In this view 'is' means 'signifies'; the real presence is denied; Christ is present in our remembrance; the stress is on Christ's death and our faith. Finally Zwingli moves to faith-presence (Fiduzialpräsenz). This view is represented by Bucer and Calvin. It is a view that Zwingli came to under Bucer's influence, and should not be read back from 1530 (and the attempts at an understanding with Luther's position) to an earlier period. It rejects a bodily and real presence and stresses a spiritual real presence by the contemplation of faith. In contrast with the symbolic view, the emphasis lies on the object and not the subject of faith. Terms such as 'sacrament', 'truly present', and 'substantially', used about the real presence in the first two views are applied to the spiritual real presence.

Against Köhler's theory it must be noted that there is no clear evidence of Zwingli's holding transubstantiation and that the evidence for a mystical Erasmian view is ambiguous. His theory does not give an adequate account of the continuity in Zwingli, not least between his earlier and later views. Pollet (*DTC* 3836), supporting Bauer against Köhler, thinks that Zwingli did not make Erasmus's view his own, at least not as a stage from one position to another. He points to the fact that Zwingli attacked Erasmus's view later without feeling the need to disclaim it. However, he accepts that there are many points where their positions are close. He also doubts whether Zwingli ever really assimilated the doctrine of the real presence.

Like Capito and others, Zwingli may well have doubted transubstantiation long before becoming a reformer. See Baum, *Capito und Butzer*, pp. 13–14.

3. Zwingli, Bucer, Oecolampadius, and others frequently appeal to the early Luther where there is a strong emphasis on the place of faith, without realizing that his position there presupposes a belief also in the real presence. The real presence is vital for Luther's understanding of God's gracious dealings with us in Christ. The sacraments are a means of grace, on which we can rely and in which the whole initiative is with God. They offer us salvation. To dispute the real presence is in effect to dispute salvation. In the course of debate Luther develops and clarifies his position, in particular his understanding of the presence of Christ. Differences in christology underlie Luther's and Zwingli's differences here. Luther's powerful stress on the unity of the person in Christ, together with his view of the sharing of properties, means that the body of Christ can be everywhere. The emphasis in his eucharistic theology is on Christ's being present where he wills to be present, where he has bound himself by his word; hence the importance of 'This is my body'. The prepositions 'in', 'with', and 'under' are used for the relationship of the body and the bread. In the course of debate he uses various analogies, such as the sun or the voice, to illustrate the presence of Christ, and he draws on scholastic, partly Occamist, distinctions of local or circumscriptive, definitive, and repletive, to describe three modes of presence.

4. The appendix to *An Exposition of the Faith* includes positive statements on the presence of Christ such as 'We believe Christ to be truly present in the supper;' indeed we do not believe that it is the Lord's supper unless Christ is present.' They are, however, characteristically qualified. 'Christum credimus vere esse in coena; imo non credimus esse domini coenam nisi Christus adsit. Confirmatur: Ubi duo vel tres fuerint in nomine meo congregati, isthic sum in medio illorum. Quanto magis adest ubi tota ecclesia ei est congregata? Sed quod corpus eius ea dimensione edatur qua isti dicunt, id vero est a veritate et fidei ingenio alienissimum. A veritate, quia ipse dixit: Ego posthac non ero in mundo; et: Caro non prodest quicquam, ad edendum scilicet . . . A fidei autem ingenio abhorret . . . Nam veritas et mens ab huiusmodi manducatione abhorrent, religio vero et fides sanctius observant et amplectuntur Christum quam ut hac ratione cupiant mandere. Adserimus igitur non sic carnaliter et crasse manducari corpus Christi in coena ut

isti perhibent, sed verum Christi corpus credimus in coena sacramentaliter et spiritualiter edi a religiosa, fideli et sancta mente; quomodo et divus Chrysostomus sentit.' (S IV 73.36–74.20.)

5. The analogy with the wedding ring is different from its earlier use by Zwingli and Hoen. For Hoen it is given by a bridegroom to assure his bride lest she should have any doubts. He says, 'Take this, I give myself to you.' She accepts the ring, believes that he is hers, and turns herself from all others to him. Likewise the eucharist is a pledge of Christ's giving himself, and when we receive it we turn from all whom we used to love and give ourselves to Christ alone. (Z IV 512.10–21.) For Zwingli it is the master of the house who, before going on a long journey, gives his wife a splendid ring with his image on it, saying 'Here am I, your husband, for you to keep and delight in in my absence.' With the words, 'This is my body', Christ gave to the church his own image sacramentally and symbolically. It is a symbol of his surrender and testament to awaken in us the remembrance of him and of his goodness. Then Zwingli speaks of the value of the ring and the value of the eucharist. (Z VI iii 278.19–282.7; Works II 122–4.)

6. Zwingli could accept the terms 'true' and 'truly', if rightly understood, but was concerned about the way ordinary people misunderstand them. (Z XI 250.4–11.)

He uses 'truly present' in letters to Capito and Bucer, (Z XI 99.2–6, 119.8–14.) See also the letter of 31 Aug. 1530. (ZWA XIV (1978) 472–7.) Note that Capito, writing in the name of Zwingli, Oecolampadius, and Megander states, 'Nam libenter credemus, a dominis ac fratribus Lutheranis hactenus non animadversum, nos Christum agnoscere in coena vere praesentem, vereque verbo distribuentem in mysterio corpus et sanguinem suum, quae dona credentium anima sola proprie accipiat, et cetera in hanc sententiam, quae missis ad Lutheranos articulis continetur, si fideli examine depensa fuerint.' Bucer's letter included the words: 'Affirmamus . . . Christum re ipsa praesentem vero suo corpore veroque sanguine . . .'. (Z XI 114.18–115.4 and 115, n. 3.) The eighth article of An Account of the Faith states 'the true body of Christ is present by the contemplation of faith'. (Z VI ii 806.7; Jackson 470.)

Melanchthon's comment may be noted. 'Fucum faciunt hominibus per hoc, quod dicunt, vere adesse corpus, et tamen postea addunt, contemplatione fidei, id est, imaginatione. Sic iterum negant praesentiam realem. Nos docemus, quod corpus Christi vere et realiter adsit cum pane, vel in pane.' (CR II 223.29–35.)

7. Hoffmann (Sententiae Patrum', p. 139) summarizes Zwingli's use of the fathers in four points: 'Zwingli führt den patristischen Nachweis für das Abendmahl als Deutemahl einmal von da her, dass die Begriffe, mit denen die Väter vom Abendmahl reden—repraesentare, figura, sacramentum, significatio—nur ein Bedeuten des Leibes and Blutes Christi aussagen, nicht aber eine leibliche Gegenwart. Zum andern weisen die Väter ein Achthaben auf das Fleisch Christi als solches zurück. Sie identifizieren, drittens, Glauben und Essen des Leibes und Blutes Christi und fassen es als die Hauptsache im Abendmahl: viertens

gebrauchen sie das Abendmahl in der Reihe der übrigen Zeremonien als Festver-
sammlung zur Erinnerung and Danksagung an den Tod Christi, Bezeugung des
Glaubens an den Auferstandenen und verpflichtenden Ausdruck demütiger
Bruderliebe.' The fathers were appealed to for the interpretation of John 6, 1 Cor.
10 and 11, and the words of institution, as well as for the christological argument,
in particular the use of alloiosis and the insistence on Christ's body as in one
place. It is above all to Augustine that Zwingli appealed.

# 12. The Church and the Ministry

ZWINGLI 's understanding of the church grew out of controversy with his catholic and anabaptist opponents. With his catholic opponents his initial concern was with the nature of the catholic or universal church and the role of the local church. With the anabaptists he had to wrestle more with the nature and character of the local church. After the initial period, when the controversy was with catholic opponents, the controversy was with both, although the anabaptists were less strong after the mid twenties.

## Christ and the Church

Zwingli's new understanding of Christ and of faith led to a new understanding of the church. This is evident in his first sustained discussion of it in *An Exposition of the Articles*. The articles on the church follow immediately those that speak of Christ, and the church is defined in relation to Christ. Thus the eighth article states: 'From this follows first that all who live in the head are members and children of God; and that is the church or communion of saints, the bride of Christ, the catholic church.'[1]

Zwingli is defining the church in opposition to catholic thinking. After arguing that the church is a communion and not a building, he gives two meanings of the word 'church' in scripture. It is used for the whole communion of all those who are built on faith in Christ and for particular congregations or parishes. In the exposition of the first of these he refers to Peter's confession of Christ in Matthew 16 and argues that Christ is the rock on which the church is built. The church is therefore understood of believers only. It is holy, in so far as it remains in Christ. In this world it comes together through the Spirit of God, and is known only to God. This view is opposed to the view of the church as gathered representatively in the bishops, for, like anyone else, they are members of the church only in so far as they have Christ as their head. The second meaning of 'church', as 'congregation', is seen in passages that refer to the church in a particular place.[2]

---

[1] *Z* II 55.11–14.

[2] *Z* II 55.32–58.33. The reference to the communion of all elect believers in *Z* II 56.29–30 holds together references to the elect and to believers, which at different points are particular emphases in his view of the church. In this discussion Zwingli takes Paul's reference in Gal. 1: 13 to persecuting the church as applying to all believers, as he does the similar reference in 1 Cor. 15: 9, although later he sees this as applying to the church as a mixed community. (*Z* II 57.1–4,

THE CHURCH AND THE MINISTRY

When Zwingli develops his discussion in terms of the catholic church, he argues for the translation of 'catholic' as 'universal' and distinguishes it from the Roman church. It is the church of Christ, that is to say, all Christians united in one faith by the Spirit of God. Although it is gathered together in one body by the Spirit, yet it does not come together visibly on earth. Moreover a person may know himself to be in the church, if he places all his trust in God through Jesus Christ. This is opposed to faith in the creature, that is to say anything other than God.[3] In all this, certain characteristic marks of Zwingli's understanding of the church emerge, above all its indispensable reference to Christ and the Spirit. These are two persistent emphases in Zwingli.[4] Some elements do not emerge, at least explicitly, as they are not central to Zwingli's debate with his catholic opponents, in which a fundamental concern is to distinguish the true church from the institutional or hierarchical church.

But when he declares the church has decreed such, she cannot err, ask what is meant by church? Does one mean the pope at Rome, with his tyrannical power and the pomp of cardinals and bishops greater than that of all emperors and princes? then I say that this church has often gone wrong and erred, as everyone knows . . . But there is another church which the popes do not wish to recognize: this one is no other than all right Christians, collected in the name of the Holy Ghost and by the will of God, which have placed a firm belief and an unhesitating hope in God, her spouse . . . That church cannot err. Cause: she does nothing according to her own will or what she thinks fit, but seeks only what the Spirit of God demands, calls for, and decrees.[5]

571.20–25; III 253.27–9.) The contrast between the church as constituted by bishops and as constituted by believers is made in reference to the canon of scripture. It is believers who have recognized and accepted books of the bible as canonical or uncanonical. (*Z* VI i 402.7–13, 402.33–403.3.)

[3] *Z* II 59.1–64.20. The true unity of the church is not unity through the fathers and their teaching, but unity through the word of God. (*Z* II 61.22–62.13.) Later Zwingli makes greater use of the Augustinian distinction of the visible and invisible church.

[4] e.g. *Z* II 57.33–58.4, 59.16–18, 33–35, 61.15–35. The indispensability of Christ to the church is described by the Pauline picture of the head and the members and the Johannine one of the vine and the branches. The divine origin of the church is also expressed in the reference to it as descending from heaven, adorned by God. (*Z* II 59.2–9.) Cf. *Z* II 57.15–18. The Spirit moreover is not present simply where a council or the representative church is assembled, but only where the word of God is master. (*Z* II 62.21–8.)

[5] *Z* I 537.9–538.8; *Selected Works* 85–6; God does not abandon his church or allow it to err in the essential matters of salvation, although it may err in outward things. (*Z* V 72.8–74.5.)

The references to Christ as head of the church, which precede the discussion of the church, are set in opposition to the pope as head of the church. (*Z* II 54.12–23.) Cf. *Z* II 68.19–26 and *S* VI ii 221.10–19. Christ as true bishop is also set in opposition to human bishops from whose power

The relationship of the church to Christ and also to the Spirit is evident in other writings before *An Exposition of the Articles*. In *The Letter to Erasmus Fabricius* in April 1522 Zwingli draws characteristically on Matthew 16 to say 'the foundation of the church is that rock which gave his name to Peter, the faithful confessor. No one lays other foundation than this, nor can do so.' Furthermore the church, outside which no one can be saved, is the church of 'everyone who confesses the Lord Jesus with his tongue and believes in his heart, that God raised him from the dead . . .'. *The Petition* exhorts the bishops 'to join those also who have this one desire, that the whole concourse of Christians return to their head, which is Christ, and form one body in him, and, having received the Spirit of God, recognize the blessings bestowed upon them by God'.[6] The Spirit moreover is bestowed not on bishops and courtiers only, but on all the people.[7]

The continuing controversy with catholics and the conflict with anabaptists led to a development of Zwingli's earlier ideas, but not to a fundamental change. Zwingli deals with the nature of the church again in *The Canon of the Mass* (1523) and then at greater length in *A Reply to Emser* (1524). (The latter discussion is included in *A Commentary* published the following year.) The church is seen as catholic and local, and is still contrasted with the representative church. The catholic church is those who believe in God through Christ and who are scattered throughout the world. It is known to God alone. It does not come together here on earth, but will do so at the end of the world. Discerned by faith with the eyes of the mind, it is invisible to us, but visible to Christ. The other use of 'church' is of the local or particular church. This church is fed by the word of God and nourished by the body and blood of Christ. It is this church that removes the impenitent and receives back the penitent. Zwingli distinguishes between those who call themselves believers and those who are believers. Although some may use the word 'church' to include the evil, he does not include them, for he regards the evil as unbelievers rather than as believers who lapse.[8]

The treatment in *A Reply to Emser* is longer and shows some new emphases. The mixed character of the church now comes to the fore in

---

he frees men. Christ, and not Zwingli, has removed the people of Zurich from the power of the Bishop of Constance. (Z V 79.3–9.)

[6] Z I 152.8–18, 198.26–32; *Selected Works* 21, 27 (*Works* I 126, 152). Cf. Z I 320.1–8, 323.1–5, 537.17–538.2.

[7] Z I 322.4–12.

[8] Z II 570.19–572.31. Zwingli makes a comparison with those who are Romans, saying that it does not apply to all those who live in Rome, but to those who are Romans in faith and strength of mind.

Zwingli. In expounding the biblical terms for 'church', he affirms that the word was used for the faithful and the unfaithful, although the conduct of some of the latter made it clear that they were not within the church that is without spot or wrinkle. Zwingli draws on the parables of the wheat and tares, the net, and the ten virgins, as well as the examples of Judas, Ananias and Sapphira, and Alexander the coppersmith to show that the word 'church' is used to cover a mixed community.[9]

When he describes the second kind of church, the one without spot or wrinkle, he faces the objection that such a church no more exists than Plato's republic, since all have sinned. His reply is that the holiness and purity is Christ's. Those who rely on Christ are without spot or wrinkle, because he is without them.[10]

It is not clear to men who, or how many, are in Christ's church. The church is not where a few prelates meet together, nor even simply where the word is preached. The church is constituted by the word of God. However, this does not simply mean the written or preached word, for that word does not of itself lead to faith. It is rather the word in conjunction with the Spirit. Thus the church is where people adhere to the word of God and live for Christ. This of course is something which is clear only to God, who cannot be deceived. Again there is the future reference to the day of judgement when the church will come together.[11]

Zwingli speaks thirdly of local churches, such as the church in Corinth. Together these churches are the catholic or universal church. To the local church, as he made clear in *An Exposition of the Articles*, belongs the power of excommunication as well as the judgement of pastors and the discerning of doctrine. The pattern of the Corinthian church is adduced as an example of this (1 Cor. 14).[12]

---

[9] Z III 252.23–254.24. His understanding of the church as mixed is not new. The parable of wheat and tares was used in 1520 in his letter to Myconius on 24 July 1520. (Z VII 341.12–21.)

[10] Z III 254.25–256.23.

[11] Z III 259.32–261.17, 263.5–26. Locher draws attention to the frequent use of John 10, which speaks of the sheep hearing the shepherd's voice. In *A Christian Answer* Zwingli states that it is the word of God that creates the church, not the church that creates the word of God. (Z III 217.35–218.1.) It is not, however, simply the word preached, but the word heard, for the church of Christ is the church 'which hears his word'. (Z III 223.6–7.) The first article at the Berne disputation embodies this conviction. 'Die heylig christenlich kilch, deren eynig houpt Christus, ist uss dem wort gottes geborn, im selben belybt sy und hört nit die stimm eines frömbden [Joh. 10: 5].' (Z VI i 243.10–12.) See Locher, 'Die Stimme des Hirten', *Oskar Farner, Erinnerungen* (Zurich, 1954), pp. 111–115.

Zwingli does not discuss the church triumphant as it was not an issue, except in terms of the intercession of the saints and purgatory with catholics and the sleep of the soul with anabaptists. (Z III 268.27–9.)

[12] Z III 261.18–264.4. Cf. Z III 78.27–32; IV 74.20–76.35, 393.26–396.5; V 420.21–421.16.

These writings come from Zwingli's controversy with catholic opponents, although elements of importance in his dispute with anabaptists emerge in them, in particular the description of the church as mixed and the insistence that the holiness of the church is in Christ and not in its members. The stress on the word and the Spirit, on faith in Christ, on the church as holy and infallible where it relies on Christ, on the catholic church as universal and as visible to God only, coming together only on the last day, on the congregation as the body which exercises discipline, all this is opposed to the hierarchical and institutional Roman view of the church with its opposite or different emphases.[13] The controversy with Rome continued throughout the twenties and led to constant re-expressions of the same basic position.[14]

## Controversy with the Anabaptists

Zwingli's controversy with the anabaptists did not lead to a new view of the church, but it did cause him to sound notes which otherwise might not have been sounded or at least sounded so strongly.

Zwingli's understanding of the visible church as mixed is related to his understanding of salvation and election. It marks his view off from the anabaptists' view of the church and the sacraments. For them the church is pure and only those who believe should belong to it. Baptism should be administered only to those who believe, and therefore not to children. The eucharist should be celebrated only by those who believe and live purely, so that those whose lives are impure should be excommunicated. In this way the church is kept pure.

Against the anabaptists Zwingli appealed to both the old and the new testaments, in which the term 'church' is used of a community made up of believers and unbelievers. The commentaries, with their exposition of the biblical text, naturally give examples of the church as a mixture of believer and unbeliever.[15] The doctrine of the covenant which was developed in the course of controversy with the anabaptists has a strongly corporate dimension. The covenant is that God is our God and we his people. The

---

[13] By contrast Pollet sees *A Reply to Emser* much more in the context of the anabaptist disputes. (*DTC* 3847-53.)

The Roman church is seen as being a local or particular church and therefore as having no jurisdiction over other local churches any more than they have over each other. (*Z* III 48.15-20.)

[14] See, e.g., Z V 46.19-49.6.

[15] *Z* III 252.23-254.24 and *S* VI ii 246.5-14. In using the parable of the wheat and the tares against the anabaptists, Zwingli accepts Christ's command that the tares should be left until harvest. He did not seek to purify the church by secession, unlike the anabaptists, but by the preaching of the word. He did not regard the anabaptist appeal to the Acts of the Apostles as valid, as the

covenant made with the people of Israel was made with all the people, including the children, and through this people the covenant will extend to all peoples.

Zwingli later affirmed that there is one covenant and one people of God in the old and new testaments. From this he argued that children in the new testament belong to the church as much as those in the old testament, and that they should therefore be baptized.[16] For him the anabaptist approach led to division in the church, whereas infant baptism is a source of unity.[17]

Unity is fundamental concern of Zwingli which emerges in one of his early writings, A Solemn Exhortation, where he writes about peace in the context of mercenary service and foreign alliances. In it he speaks of God as willing all men to be descended from one father, for the sake of unity, otherwise he would have filled the whole world with men at one go. God created man in his own image, so that just as the three persons are one God, who cannot be in disharmony with himself, so also the life of men might be peaceful and united. Christ also prayed that his disciples might be one. God's purpose therefore in creation and regeneration is unity. We are to be one body, whose head is Christ.[18] Although this unity is set in the context of the confederation, the argument is not fundamentally national, but biblical and theological. Not surprisingly, this concern for unity was a factor when controversy developed with the anabaptists, who sought to separate from the church. This strongly corporate note in Zwingli, with a stress on union and communion, is also expressed in his view of baptism and the eucharist. They are concerned with our unity with Christ and with each other.[19]

In his exposition of the words 'When he saw many of the Pharisees . . .' (Matt. 3: 7), Zwingli attacked disunity as contrary to the Spirit of God. The

---

apostles withdrew from those who did not profess Christ, not from those who did. (Z VI i 32.1–35.18.)

[16] e.g. Z IV 637.27–638.1, 641.1–3; VI i 155.22–172.5 (esp. 163.8–10, 165.8, 166.3–5, 23–5, 169.22–3, 171.2–7); S VI i 461.40–7.

[17] Z IV 641.19–26.

[18] Z I 167.14–169.4. Moeller relates the stronger sense of the Christian community in Zwingli's view of the church and the sacraments to his being part of an urban community (Imperial Cities and the Reformation (Philadelphia, 1972), pp. 87–90).

[19] In A Christian Answer he quotes again Christ's prayer in John 17 touching the unity that Christ wills us to have with each other and in him. It was indeed for unity that the eucharist was instituted: 'Und sölche einigheit under den Christglöubigen zuo bestäten, hat er ee und er in 'n tod gieng, ein gmächt oder sacrament ufgericht, damit wir Christen uns ewigklich zesammen pflichtind gegen einandren . . .'. (Z III 227.11–228.6.)

Spirit of God does not separate or divide, but binds together and draws into unity. Those who are endowed with the Spirit do not despise sinners or separate from them, but they call them from their evil and join them to themselves.[20] Here Zwingli uses the example of John the Baptist against the anabaptists; later he adduces the example of Christ teaching in the synagogue. Christ taught publicly, whereas the anabaptists separate themselves from the churches and teach in corners or in the woods.[21] The anabaptist approach is based on a fundamental misconception of the church. The true church is known only to God and therefore people cannot be certain (as the anabaptists—or those who join them—think) that they are God's church and truly believing. Moreover Paul teaches in Romans 14 that one should bear with the weak and not separate oneself from them. (The Pauline concern for the weak is a constant element in Zwingli.) In scripture people do not separate themselves from others because of their piety, but they exclude from the church those who are evil.[22]

Zwingli has already stressed the role and authority of the congregation in opposition to the catholic stress on the hierarchy. He continues this emphasis in debate with the anabaptists, though now the stress is on the whole congregation over against the views of one or some of the congregation.

How dare you introduce innovations into the church simply on your own authority and without consulting the church? I speak only of those churches in which the word of God is publicly and faithfully preached. For if every blockhead who had a novel or strange opinion were allowed to gather a sect around him, divisions and sects would become so numerous that the Christian body (*der Christus*) which we now build up with such difficulty would be broken to pieces in every individual congregation. Therefore no innovations ought to be made except with the common consent of the church and not merely of a single person. For the judgement of scripture is not mine or yours, but the church's (1 Cor. 14) . . .[23]

[20] 'Ubi sectae sunt, ibi non est spiritus dei. Nam divinus spiritus non segregat, non dividit, non dissecat; sed colligit, et in unum contrahit . . . Qui ergo spiritu dei praeditus est, non contemnit peccatores, non deserit eos, non separat se ab eis, non abiicit eos, modo spes arrideat resipiscentiae; sed corrigit, emendat, et a vitiis ac sceleribus avocat, ac sibi iungit.' (*S* VI i 211.23–212.9.)

[21] *S* VI i 218.20–24. See also the example of Thomas in *S* VI ii 62.2–4.

[22] *S* VI i 447.36–448.14. Cf. 337.45–338.11. See Additional Note, p. 281.

[23] *Z* IV 254.24–255.3; LCC XXIV 158. 'Ein yede kilch sol in den offnen dingen handlen und urteilen, nit einer oder glych hundert besunder, als wir wol ermessen mögend Math. 18 und 1 Cor. 14 und Philip 3.'

*Later Writings*

Zwingli continued to distinguish his view from that of catholic and anabaptist in his later writings. His view of the church is not fundamentally different from that of his earlier writings, although its emphasis springs rather more from opposition to catholics than from opposition to anabaptists.[24] Pollet asserts that there is a greater stress on the church as the company of the elect rather than as the company of believers, and on the Spirit rather than on Christ.

It is true that Zwingli defines the church more often in terms of the elect in his later writings than in the earlier ones. However, once he develops his doctrine of election, in part in response to the anabaptists, he inevitably defines the church in terms of election as he is thereby able to include those who do not yet believe, but who nevertheless belong to the church, not least infants. In all this he continues to speak of the church almost indiscriminately in terms of the elect or of believers. Thus *An Account of the Faith* begins by defining the church in terms of the elect, though it goes on to speak of those who are members of the church as having faith and therefore knowing that they are members of the church. By contrast *An Exposition of the Faith* speaks of the church in terms of all who believe, though with a later reference to the church as elect. A similar movement between the terms believers and elect can be found in his comment on Matthew 18: 17.[25]

The church continues to be related to Christ and to the Spirit, although there is greater emphasis on the Spirit than in some of the early writings. The church and its members are still seen on occasion in terms of Christ as the rock or foundation on which the church is built and the one in whom Christians believe. The church is also described as nourished by the Spirit and those who believe in Christ are taught or enlightened by the Spirit.[26] Yet neither *An Account of the Faith* nor *An Exposition of the Faith* gives so strong an emphasis as the earlier writings to the church's relation to Christ. However, this may be in part because the visible church is seen in terms of those who profess Christ, possibly leading to a greater stress on

---

[24] Pollet seems to see Zwingli's development rather more in terms of periods. (*DTC* 3842.)

[25] Z VI ii 800.16–26; S IV 58.33–41; VI i 337.25–30, 447.18–31.

[26] This stress on Christ and the Spirit is present in the old testament commentaries, e.g. Z XIII 137.38–138.1 and XIV 391.1–7, and in *St Matthew, S* VI i 337.26–45, 447.18–448.5. From the beginning the church is defined in terms of the Spirit as well as in terms of Christ. It is the Spirit who unites those who believe. (Z II 59.16–20, 59.33–60.4.) If one has faith in Christ one has the Spirit. At the same time it is the Spirit who gives such faith. (Z II 61.25–30.)

the Spirit as characteristic of the true or invisible church.[27] Controversy with the anabaptists gave a greater attention to the visible church, whereas the earlier controversy with catholics gave more attention to the invisible church. On occasion there is strong reference to the Spirit without any corresponding reference to Christ.[28]

The later writings offer a twofold or threefold definition of the church, parallel to the earlier definitions, although the term 'visible church' is not limited to particular congregations. *An Exposition of the Faith* makes a twofold distinction. 'We also believe that there is one holy, catholic, that is, universal church, and that this church is either visible or invisible.' To the invisible church 'belong all who believe the whole world over. It is not called invisible because believers are invisible, but because it is concealed from the eyes of men who they are: for believers are known (*perspecti*) only to God and to themselves.' The invisible church is distinguished from the visible church which 'is not the Roman pontiff and others who bear the mitre, but all who make profession of faith in Christ the whole world over. In this number there are those who are called Christians falsely, seeing they have no inward faith. Within the visible church, therefore, there are some who are not members of the church elect and invisible.' In *An Exposition of the Faith* Zwingli makes clearer than sometimes earlier the close relation between the visible and the invisible church.[29]

*An Account of the Faith* gives a more detailed account of the church. It does not use the terms 'invisible' and 'visible', but in place of 'visible' uses 'sensible'. The church—in the sense of the elect—is 'known to God alone', and only those 'who have firm and unwavering faith know that they are members of this church'. There is also the church that is sensible or perceptible to the senses. It is those 'who have enlisted under Christ, a large number of whom sensibly acknowledge Christ by confession or participation in the sacraments and yet in heart either are averse to him or ignorant of him'. The descriptions of the first-named church, such as 'elect', are applied to this church, because we (unlike God) judge by the confession people make that they are the church of God and therefore that they are elect, just as Peter did in his first epistle.[30] A third use of the term 'church'

---

[27] Z VI ii 800.27-33, 801.9-20, 802.3-5; S IV 58.31-41. True faith in Christ comes of course from the Holy Spirit. (Z VI ii 801.2-5; S IV 60.27-9.)

[28] There is a notable example in the letter to Konrad Sam and Simpert Schenk on 18 Aug. 1530, with its picture of the body animated by the Spirit. (Z XI 68.10-69.10.) Cf. Z XIV 418.21-2.

[29] S IV 58.30-41; LCC XXIV 265-6 (*Works* II 260-1).

[30] Z VI ii 800.16-801.30; Jackson 463-4 (*Works* II 33-4). Cf. S VI i 341.27-32. In *St Matthew* the church is called the church of Christ because of its members who are godly and believing and

is for 'every particular congregation of this universal and perceptible church, as the church of Rome, of Augsburg, of Lyons'.[31] The particular or local church is related to the universal church and there is no sense of division, as Zwingli makes clear in *St Matthew*.[32] The unity of the invisible church is related to the fact that its members share the same Spirit, who makes them certain that they are the true children of God. The Spirit is, however, related to faith, for this church does not err in the fundamental matters of faith. The visible church is said to be one, while it maintains the true confession of Christ.[33]

Controversy with anabaptists led Zwingli to stress the confession of Christ as a feature of the visible church. We cannot tell whether those who confess Christ are in fact believers, any more than the apostles could of Judas, though Christ knows. Those who confess Christ are, however, baptized and become members of the church. On the other side where there is no confession of Christ, there is no church. To that extent confession of Christ is a mark of the church. (Zwingli can even talk of infants as confessing, but this must clearly be in a metaphorical sense.)[34]

Controversy with the anabaptists did not lead Zwingli to deny the part of the congregation in reform, in discipline, or in the discerning of doctrine, though it led to a change of emphasis. A concern for peace and order, combined with his characteristic sense that there is a time and a place for everything, led him to stress the role of the few acting in the name of the many, though with their consent.[35] In opposition to the anabaptists Zwingli affirmed the role of the magistrate in the church, especially in discipline. This is present in *An Exposition of the Articles*, but is developed through the twenties, with particular reference to the role of rulers in the old testament, for example as shepherds, and in the new. It is the magistrate who is able to deal with impenitent sinners.[36]

Consequently the visible church contains within itself many who are insolent and hostile, thinking nothing of it if they are excommunicated a hundred times, seeing they have no faith. Hence there arises the need of government for the punishment of flagrant sinners . . . Seeing, then, that there are shepherds in the church, and amongst these we may number princes, as may be seen from

who are its chief part. (*S* VI i 340.18–33.) In *Questions Concerning the Sacrament of Baptism* Zwingli distinguishes between the spiritual and the sensible church. (*S* III 574.42–5, 577.19–20.)

[31] *Z* VI ii 801.31–802.2. Zwingli allows that there are other uses of the term 'church'. (*Z* VI ii 802.2–3.)

[32] *S* VI i 338.21–3.

[33] *Z* VI ii 802.3–8.

[34] *Z* VI ii 801.9–30, 802.7–803.4. Cf. *S* IV 58.

[35] See pp. 286–95 below.

[36] *Z* II 324.9–11; XIV 517.4–8; *S* VI i 338.26–31.

Jeremiah, it is evident that without civil government (*magistratu*) a church is maimed and impotent. . . . we teach that authority (*magistratum*) is necessary to the completeness of the body of the church.[37]

Controversy with catholics led Zwingli to stress two uses of the church: catholic (or universal) and local. He expounded the catholicity of the church, in terms of the church that is without spot or wrinkle. It is the whole company of believers or—as he later says—of the elect, visible to God but invisible to us. At the same time he argued for the role of each local church in the ordering of its affairs, in independence of other local churches, and for the place of the magistrate in reform and discipline. His view of the church is opposed to that of the church as the hierarchy.

In his controversy with anabaptists Zwingli stressed the universal visible church, as a mixed church, made up of both those who professed belief in Christ and their children. This is opposed to a view of the church as pure and set apart. (With the anabaptists it might be said that he is con-cerned with the church as one and holy, whereas with the catholics it is with the church as one and catholic.) Alongside this he affirmed the place of the local church as a whole community as opposed to the views of its individual members acting independently. Against them equally he asserted the task of the magistrate, especially in discipline.

### Discipline

Excommunication was an issue that Zwingli faced personally as well as pastorally. In a letter to Myconius on 24 July 1520 he writes of going to the pontifical commissary to persuade the pope not to excommunicate Luther. Then he turns to his own position. 'I beseech Christ for this one thing only, that he will enable me to endure all things courageously, and that he break me as a potter's vessel or make me strong, as it pleases him.'[38] The possibility of being excommunicated would cause him, like Luther, to examine the meaning of excommunication. This he naturally did both in terms of scripture and in terms of the way excommunication was prac-tised in the medieval church.

At the first disputation Zwingli advanced two theses: 'That no private person may excommunicate anyone, but only the church, that is, the com-munity of those among whom the person to be excommunicated lives,

---

[37] *S* IV 58.42–59.4; LCC XXIV 266.

[38] *Z* VII 344.15–17; Jackson 148. He has just commented 'non quod excommunicationem contemnam, sed quod putem damnationes istas magis corpori quam animae infligi, si iniquae infligantur.' (*Z* VII 343.34–344.1.)

together with the watchman, that is, the minister.' 'That one may excommunicate only the person, who causes public offence.'[39] The fundamental basis of excommunication is to be found in Christ's words in Matthew 18: 15–18. In the light of verses 7–9 Zwingli gives the reason for removing a member as the concern 'not to infect or ruin the whole body'. He sees the offence moreover as one against the church rather than against the individual. The offence must, however, be a public offence and not a matter such as financial debt. Excommunication was not for any and every sin, but only for sins giving public offence, since Christ commanded Peter to forgive his brother seventy times seven. We should also forgive an excommunicated person if he repents.

Initially the minister should warn the person privately, after that if need be he should take witnesses with him, and only if that and the subsequent warning of the congregation fail to move him to repent should he be excommunicated. Excommunication does not belong to an individual, whether pope or bishop. It belongs to the church, and that means the congregation since there are only two uses of the word 'church' in the bible, the universal and the local. It cannot be the universal church, as it would be impossible for the universal church to come together in one place as Matthew 18 requires, and 'church' is not used in any further sense, so as to refer to bishops. It would be a good and wholesome thing if excommunication were rightly used, whereas, on the contrary, bishops who have used it have been regular in collecting debts, but slow in Christian exhortation.[40]

The example of Paul and the church in Corinth is then used point by point to sustain the case that Zwingli has argued. In particular we may note that Paul and the Corinthians do not act in their own power, but in the power of Christ. Zwingli relates this to the binding on earth and in heaven in Matthew 18. Moreover the handing over to the devil excludes only the body. If the man is penitent his soul will be saved. In the case in Corinth the man was penitent and Paul exhorted the congregation to forgive him. Thus excommunication is concerned with the repentance of the sinner and not only with keeping the church whole. In any case excommunication is a matter for the church with the minister.[41]

[39] Z I 462.6–9.

[40] Z II 277.1–284.13. Note especially Z II 277.14–15, 25–6, 28, 277.34–278.9, 28–29, 279.10–12, 280.8–10, 21–2, 281.24–8, 282.8–9, 284.7–8.

[41] Z II 284.14–286.10, esp. 285.14–23, 286.1–10. 'Dann was mag die offnen sünd bas hynnemmen und besseren denn der bann?' (Z II 287.26–288.1.) Adultery is a particular public sin which Zwingli judges should be dealt with by exhortation and if need be by excommunication, but always in the hope and expectation of the person's repentance and readmission (Z II 287.26–

In expounding the fortieth article Zwingli deals with the power of the magistrate to take life. He quotes Matthew 18 and applies it to the magistrate although he allows that its primary reference is to excommunication. He argues that if the magistrate finds that someone who offends publicly would harm the body of Christ by remaining alive, then the magistrate may take his life. It is better for one member to perish than the whole body. In doing this the magistrate is a servant of God. If he does not do this, he will in effect be allowing thorns to take over the whole field.[42]

Zwingli's view of excommunication is almost completely expressed in *An Exposition of the Articles*, including the understanding of the keys in Matthew 16 in terms of preaching the gospel.[43] Many of the points are made again in *A Commentary*, *The Berne Notes and Speeches*, and *St Matthew*. The understanding of excommunication as a power of Christ and not of men is taken up in *The Berne Notes and Speeches*. A person is excommunicated by us, who has already been rejected by God. If the person repents, it is a sign that divine grace, which let him fall, has again raised him up. For Zwingli therefore those put out are those who were first removed by God, and those received back are those whom God has first favoured. Where excommunication is not the action of God, it is tyrannical and presumptuous, as indeed happens with an ungodly congregation. A characteristic emphasis is that excommunication belongs to the congregation with the minister. Zwingli defends this view against the objection raised that Paul acts alone in 1 Timothy 1: 20, by claiming that the reference is an example of synecdoche, where one person stands in effect for many.[44]

In *St Matthew* Zwingli takes further the relation between God's action and ours, particularly with the reference in Matthew 18: 18 to God's binding what we have bound. This could imply that our action would conflict with God's election of someone, and thus the words of Christ would conflict with Paul's word about God's election as immutable. Zwingli asserts that the judgement of the church does not affect election. Thus a robber may be one of God's elect, but the law commands us to remove the evil from our midst. If God converts him, it is the Lord's work. We are nevertheless to do our work. It is moreover God's will that those who do wrong should be punished as an example to others. Such punishment is within

---

288.14.) Other such sins are mentioned in Z II 282.9–13, 285.26–7. Excommunication is concerned not only with the church, but also with the life of the person excommunicated, although Roger Ley sees the stress as on the former (*Kirchenzucht bei Zwingli* (Zurich, 1948), p. 15).

[42] Z II 334.24–335.19.

[43] e.g., Z II 373.11–390.22; III 723.21–741.2; V 719.2–720.2; IX 76.33–77.13—and frequently elsewhere. This view is the same as Luther's and Bucer's, though Bucer's view changes later. See Stephens, *Martin Bucer*, p. 162.    [44] Z VI i 258.9–260.14.

the providence of God. If the person is elect, he will repent, and therefore he is not Satan's. (The reference is to the handing over to Satan in 1 Corinthians 5: 5, a verse which seems to imply that we can determine a person's destiny by excommunication.) If he does not repent, then he is Satan's. Paul writes of the church's handing someone over to Satan, because the church unlike God judges by the outward acts. However we can also understand the matter by analogy. Thus, just as the church which consists of pious and impious is called the church of Christ, though only the pious and not the impious belong to Christ, so all those excommunicated are said to be handed over to Satan, though only the impious and not the pious are Satan's. Moreover the action is not ours but God's, even though it is ascribed to us, just as salvation is ascribed to faith whereas faith is only a sign of salvation and election. Thus our binding on earth comes from, and is a sign of, the binding in heaven. Likewise someone is not handed over to Satan by virtue of our excommunication, but only if he does not repent.[45]

For Zwingli excommunication is not appropriate for those small sins that all Christians commit, which Christ tells us to forgive, but only for public sins.[46] The latter, however, can be so gross and persistent that the help of the magistrate is needed. It is in expounding in *St Matthew* the two texts 5: 29 and 18: 18, to which he refers in *An Exposition of the Articles*, that Zwingli makes this point. On this occasion he makes the point against the anabaptists, with their opposition to a Christian magistrate, whereas the articles were advanced against his catholic opponents. His concern remains the twofold one of preventing the infection of the whole body by a corrupt member and of leading those excommunicated to salvation.[47] His last major work, *An Exposition of the Faith*, devotes almost half of its brief article on the church to the place of the magistrate in the discipline of the church, asserting that without him the church would be maimed and impotent.[48]

By contrast with Zwingli, Oecolampadius sought a greater independence for the church in its discipline. He challenged the exercise of such

---

[45] *S* VI i 338.32–341.15, esp. 338.37–339.4, 31–5, 340.15–33, 46–7, 341.2–6, 9–11.

[46] *S* VI i 301.30–43, 428.44–429.9.

[47] *S* VI i 228.3–39. 'Duplex enim virga est, priori ferit ecclesia, nempe excommunicatione aut abstentione. Eiicit enim ecclesia emendatione et resipiscentia. Qui vero hanc virgam contemnunt, et scelerati cum iactura totius corporis esse pergunt, iis gladius (gravior scilicet virga) adhibendus est . . .'. *S* VI i 228.23–9. 'Quod si exclusi tam impudenter peccant, ut etiam ceteros offendant, potest magistratus auxilium implorari, ut suo in eos officio fungantur, ut vel compescantur, aut in universum abscindantur, ne caetera membra contagione illius infecta pereant.' (*S* VI i 338.27–30.)

[48] *S* IV 58.30–59.4. The anabaptist position as expressed in the Schleitheim Confession of 1527 is totally different from Zwingli's. The magistrate is ordained by God for those outside the

discipline by the civil authorities, and pointed out that Christ did not say,'Tell it to the magistrate' but 'Tell it to the church'.[49] From the first, however, Zwingli sees a much more co-operative role for the magistrate. With *The Zurich Marriage Ordinance* of 1525 the council appointed a tribunal of six judges, two ministers and four members of the council, to deal with matrimonial and other matters. In the case of adultery the ministers were to excommunicate and the magistrates were to deal with corporal punishment and property.[50] However, in the following year it was the council alone that dealt with adultery. For its part, the council was naturally eager to have power in its own hands.

In keeping with primitive Christian practice Zwingli associated excommunication with the eucharist in *A Commentary*. In *Excommunication from the Eucharist* he made proposals for introducing it then, in connection with the re-ordering of the service. A number of public sins, such as adultery, prostitution, drunkenness, and blasphemy, not to mention graver sins, were considered grounds for what amounted to the greater excommunication (exclusion from social intercourse as well as from communion.)[51]

## The Ministry

Zwingli's fundamental understanding of the minister as the preacher of the word is evident in his own ministry and in his early writings. His understanding of the word of God determined for him, as for Luther, what it is to be a minister of the word. It is first and foremost to be a preacher of the word, as Zwingli makes clear in the sixty-second article, which declares that the scriptures 'know no priests, except those who proclaim the word of God'.[52]

church. Inside the church only excommunication is to be used.

[49] Z XI 129.2–130.9. 'Intolerabilior enim erit Antichristo ipso magistratus, qui eccelesiis authoritatem suam adimit. Magistratus gladium gerit, et recte quidem. At Christus medicinam et pharmacum dedit, quo curemus fratres lapsos. Si ecclesię manserit sua dignitas, adhuc lucrifacere poterit . . . Non dixit Christus: "si non audierit, dic magistratui", sed: "ecclesiae". . . . Unde, mi frater, multa subinde me movent, ut videatur plane officii nostri esse, ecclesias nostras hortari, ut claves recipiendi excludendique a Christo sibi traditas non negligant.' (129.4-130.9.) Zwingli employs the same text in *A Commentary*, but to make the point that Christ did not say 'Tell it the pope'. Indeed he insists in that context that the power of excommunication belongs not to the magistrate, but to the whole church. (Z III 879.24-36.) A concern for independence similar to that of Oecolampadius is to be found in Bucer and Calvin.

[50] Z IV 186.26–187.2.

[51] Z IV 31.1-20. See in particular W. Köhler, *Zürcher Ehegericht und Genfer Konsistorium*, I *Das Zürcher Ehegericht und seine Auswirkung in der deutschen Schweiz zur Zeit Zwinglis* (Leipzig, 1932), and R. Ley, *Kirchenzucht bei Zwingli*.

[52] Z I 465.1-2. Zwingli rejects the traditional sacrificial understanding of the ministry as a denial both of Christ's once for all sacrifice for sins and of his being a priest for ever, to whom no

In expounding the previous article he rejects the medieval idea of character in ordination, as not present in scripture or in the early church. A priest is to be 'an honourable proclaimer of the word of God and a guardian for the salvation of souls . . . If he does not do that, he should be dismissed, then he is no longer a priest.'[53] The exposition of these two articles shows that Zwingli has no narrow concept of the ministry. After a reference to 1 Timothy 5: 17, he allows that the word 'priest' can be used for those who teach in the church, who proclaim the word of God, who interpret Greek and Hebrew, who preach, heal, and visit the sick, and who give help and alms to the poor and visit them, offering as his reason 'that all these things belong to the word of God'.[54] The combination of preaching and pastoral care which is later to feature largely in his view of ministry is present here, indeed is present still earlier. In expounding 1 Timothy 3: 1–2 in *A Friendly Request* he stresses the idea of a bishop as one who watches.[55]

Preaching the word was at the heart of Zwingli's own ministry in Zurich. It was the way in which the word of God was given free scope to do its work. That word can be seen as law and gospel, as it was for Luther.[56] It can be taken in a broader sense to include God's whole will for man. The word is in the profoundest sense Christ himself and for that reason Christian preaching is concerned with him and therefore with the whole of scripture.[57] Zwingli himself preached deliberately and in a particular order

one can succeed. It is replaced by an understanding of ministry as the ministry of the word. (Z III 805.5–8.) 'Id autem nec esse nec facere qum praeter filium dei quisquam possit, impium est de offerante sacerdotio quicquam loqui.' (Z III 806.17–19.)

On Zwingli as preacher, Farner, III 29–187. He suggests (pp. 128–9) increasing concern with political matters and a decreasing concern with ecclesiastical matters in Zwingli's sermons.

A term that gains increasing importance in Zwingli's understanding of the ministry as well as in his practice of the ministry is 'prophet'.

[53] Z II 438.14; 440.16. Zwingli avers that up to the time of Jerome people did not hold to the notion of character, but dismissed someone who was not suited to the office of minister. The ordained ministry is to be understood in terms of office (*Amt*) not dignity, lordship, or character. In making this point he draws a comparison with a mayor who is dismissed if he does not look after peace and justice. Already in *The Clarity and Certainty of the Word of God* Zwingli has asserted the priesthood of all Christians, in denying the sacrificial character of the ordained priesthood. (Z I 376.34–377.6.) Cf. Z III 824.8–16 where he denies that the laying on of hands ('exterior haec consignatio') has anything to do with conferring character.    [54] Z II 440.18–441.12.

[55] Something of the variety of terms Zwingli uses is seen in the same context. '. . . das ist ein uffseher oder pfarrer, kilchher oder lütpriester, die allesammen nach griechischer sprach episcopi, das ist bischoff oder uffseher genennet werden . . .'. (Z I 231.22–232.2.)

[56] 'Thus the pure word of God should be preached without ceasing; for in it we learn what God demands of us and with what grace he comes to our aid.' (Z II 494.10–13.)

[57] In *A Friendly Request* Zwingli points out that the gospel is to be discovered in the springs, that is scripture. He then refers to making known the will and doctrine of God. (Z I 220.3–221.6.) Cf. Z III 13.6–17.

from the books of the new testament, recognizing the importance of the whole range of scripture. However, the preacher and the preaching were only instruments in God's hands. 'This is the seed I have sown. Matthew, Luke, Paul, and Peter have watered it, and God has given it splendid increase . . .'.[58]

The first of Zwingli's two major works on the ministry was *The Shepherd*, a sermon preached by him to the ministers attending the second disputation in October 1523 and published in the following March. It compares the true with the false shepherd. The false shepherd or pastor is in effect the priest who either does not teach or does not teach God's word, but his own ideas; or if he does teach God's word, he does not act to the glory of God and does not challenge those who cause the greatest offence. The false shepherd fails also in his life, for he tears down more by his deeds than he builds by his words. He rules in a worldly way, and he does not care for the poor, but rather seeks his own wealth. He leads people, not to the creator, but to the creature. Such a person is a wolf rather than a shepherd.[59]

In contrast with such a priest who is unreformed in doctrine and in life, Zwingli has portrayed the true shepherd or pastor. He preaches nothing but God's word, which he learns from the bible, in which he needs to be well instructed. His message is a call to repentance and the offer of good news. He preaches it to high and low alike, rebuking those who need to be rebuked, as Christ and the prophets did. He does not stop preaching because there is no success or because he faces opposition. He acts altogether out of love in his care of the sheep. Indeed he is willing to suffer and die as the Good Shepherd himself did. Behind all this lies the fact that he has denied himself and put his trust wholly in God. Christ empowers him in his preaching with his Spirit. His life moreover witnesses to his words, 'for a living example teaches more than a hundred thousand words'.[60]

If *The Shepherd* is a defence of the reformed pastor against the unreformed priest, by contrast *The Ministry* in June 1525 is a defence of the reformed pastor against the anabaptist preacher, a defence of an ordered, educated, and paid ministry. The attack is not on the faith and life of the unreformed priest, with his images, mumbled masses, and clerical luxury.

---

[58] Z I 284.39–285.28.   [59] Z III 59.8–60.4.

[60] This brief sketch draws on some of the points made in Z III 12–45. References are given in the order in which the points appear in the text. (Z III 21.25–26, 22.14–15, 18.13–17, 28.31–29.20, 32.14–22, 26.7–9, 41.19–26, 17.21–3, 18.1–5, 19.30–2, 21.17–19.) The picture of pastors who watch and warn like the prophets of the old testament is developed. The political or social dimension in the pastor's preaching is apparent here. See also pp. 305–308 below. However, the importance of the old testament in Zwingli's understanding of the ministry should not be exaggerated. The new testament has a fundamental role in *The Shepherd*.

The main concern is manifest in the sub-title with its reference to self-appointed troublemakers, not apostles as they wish to appear, who act against God's word, obtruding themselves on faithful ministers and preaching to their people, without need and without the permission of the whole congregation and the ministers.[61]

The fact that anabaptists were coming into parishes without permission and were on their own initiative beginning to preach and rebaptize, thus confusing the truth and leading to disturbance, causes Zwingli to challenge both teaching, when one has not been sent, and rebaptizing. Zwingli seeks to show that such people are not sent by God, and he argues his case in the light of Ephesians 4.[62] From this passage Zwingli affirms that Christ instituted the ministry, appointing some to it and not others, and that it is therefore not for everyone to exercise it. After describing the nature of the various offices of apostle, prophet, evangelist, pastor, and teacher, he states that not all are apostles, prophets, and teachers. (He indicates that the anabaptists do not really fall into any of the categories.) At Jerusalem there were many thousands of believers, but not more than a dozen apostles, whereas here they are all apostles. He gives the example of someone who insisted on entering the pulpit and preaching, but who did not understand part of the passage and who in the end was made by the congregation to give way to the minister. This shows the nature of such claims to have the Spirit.

No godly Christian has ever undertaken such an office without being sent by God or chosen by the churches or apostles. Zwingli uses a host of examples from the old and new testaments, including that of Christ himself, to show that people do not take an office on themselves, but are sent by God. Moreover God does not only call inwardly, but also uses outward signs, either a miracle or a public choice, though the choice may happen in different ways: through the whole church, the apostles, or one of the apostles. As the judgement of excommunication and of teaching belongs to the church, how much more does the choice of the teacher. Here, however,

---

[61] Anabaptist activity was at its height in Zurich in 1525. The letter of Markus Murner (Z VIII 337–340), with its discussion of lay preaching, may have been a particular stimulus to Zwingli in this work dedicated to Toggenburg. (Z IV 370–1.)

[62] Z IV 383.4–8, 389.27–35. In the course of his exposition he challenges the position and practice of the anabaptists: e.g. they appeal to 1 Cor. 14, yet they are not members of the congregation as in 1. Cor. 14, but go into other congregations. Nor are they willing to be controverted, even if they allow people to speak after them. Again, they argue against ministers having houses and yet the new testament's pastoral letters refer to a bishop as having a house. Zwingli does not develop Eph. 4 in terms of a fourfold ministry as Bucer did. In effect the ministries described in Eph. 4 are embraced in the different terms he uses for a minister. Particularly important is the way he regards the understanding of the biblical languages as part of what is involved in being a prophet.

Zwingli significantly associates the prophets and evangelists in the choice. He points out that the teaching of scripture is committed not to the congregation, but to the prophets and those who know the biblical languages. After using various tests to show that the anabaptist preachers are not sent by God, he argues that they do not fulfil what is involved in the different offices enumerated in Ephesians. Thus they do not, like apostles, work among unbelievers, yet—unlike bishops, who remain with those committed to them—they are not chosen by the congregation.

Against the anabaptist use of 1 Corinthians 14, Zwingli points out that people may speak only after the prophets and interpreters and those knowing the biblical languages have spoken. However, someone does not become a bishop as soon as he has spoken in church, for that is to confuse the distinction Paul makes between the different offices in Ephesians 4, 1 Corinthians 12, and Romans 12. Moreover in commenting on 1 Peter 2 Zwingli agrees that we are all dedicated to the priesthood, but that we are not therefore all apostles and bishops.[63]

Although many other matters are raised against the anabaptists, the fundamental matter is the defence of an ordered ministry. A person must not presume to take the ministerial office upon himself, but must be commissioned by God and by the church. (In keeping with the new testament he may be paid.[64]) The conformity of a person's doctrine and life with certain scriptural tests will show whether or not he is called of God. Zwingli also challenges the lack of learning of the anabaptists and their false identification of the unlearned with the simple to whom God makes his revelation in Matthew 11. They claim to be able to interpret scripture precisely because they are not learned. Zwingli asserts that God chose many very learned men, such as Paul, Barnabas, and Luke. However, they had to become as children and not rely on their learning, nor interpret scripture according to the flesh, but according to the Spirit. In this way he calls in question the anabaptist claim to the Spirit.[65] Zwingli uses 1 Corinthians

---

[63] Z IV 390–433, esp. 419.15–17, 420.3–24, 421.19–22, 427.8–17, 428.23–429.21, 430.25–431.1. Zwingli bases the church's judgement of what is said by the prophets on the fact that God dwells in the church. (Z IV 295.25–30.) The assertion that not all are called to be preachers continues in the later writings. (Z IX 113.1–4; S VI i 222.24–25, 607.42–5.)

[64] Zwingli argues for the support of the ministry in expounding the sixty-third article. (Z II 441.18–444.20.) His defence of a paid ministry singularly fits his understanding of the ministry as prophetic. The alternative to receiving a stipend is begging, with all the risk of greed that that involves. Moreover, if ministers have to beg, instead of preaching boldly they will practise flattery. (Z IV 403.30–405.19, 415.2–17.)

[65] Z IV 410.19–412.17, 398.3–10, 416.26–421.22. Zwingli later defends his position against Hubmaier's likening the dependence on those versed in the biblical languages to the former dependence on pope and councils, as creating a new popery. (Z IV 601.1–602 and 601, n. 8.) If languages were to be lost again, the church would be back in its former darkness. (Z IV

to argue for the role of prophets (in the sense of those skilled in the biblical languages) in the interpretation of scripture, and the development of the prophecy in Zurich is related to this.

There is a range of biblical allusion behind Zwingli's view of the minister, expressed in part in the variety of words used to describe the minister. He used terms such as 'watchman', 'bishop', 'shepherd', and 'prophet', but it was the term 'prophet' that became the most characteristic. An understanding of the minister as prophet is present in early writings, such as *An Exposition of the Articles*, even in a certain sense in *The Ox* and *The Labyrinth*. It is however developed in *The Shepherd* and *The Ministry*. In *The Ministry* he points to two elements in the ministry of the prophet: the plucking up, tearing down, and the destroying of whatever is set up against God, and the building and planting of whatever is willed by God, to which Jeremiah refers (in Jer. 1: 9–10), and the expounding of the scriptures to which Paul refers (in 1 Cor. 14: 16–23).[66] The Pauline reference lies behind that study of the scriptures, known as the prophecy, which began in Zurich in June 1525, and which was to have a profound influence there and elsewhere in the reformation.

The term 'prophet' is inclusive rather than exclusive. For although it is only one of the terms used by Paul in Ephesians 4, yet in the end the terms 'prophet', 'evangelist', 'pastor', and 'teacher', all have the same fundamental meaning.[67] For Zwingli these varied ministries belong to a minister like him, who may be described equally as bishop, prophet, or pastor. Because he is a minister of the word of God he is concerned with understanding the word of God in its wholeness and with proclaiming it to the whole life of the people.

There is no fundamental change in Zwingli's view of the ministry in the succeeding years. The combination of preaching and pastoral care and the concern with the individual and with society are constant features, as is the setting of the ministry in the context of the church, rather than the placing of it above the church. (All gifts are for the sake of the body and are to be used for it.[68]) There is a continuing sense of the necessity of the

627.11–14.) See also Z VI i 559, n. 15, for Stumpf's rejection of paid full time ministers in favour of those possessing the German bible and the Holy Spirit.

[66] Z IV 393.26–398.10. The two tasks are related, as the prophet interprets the scriptures so that he may reveal God's will. (Z IV 395.18–20.)

[67] Z IV 394.1–3, 397.32–398.2, 398.12–399.7, 416.5–18, 26–31.

[68] Z VI ii 293.8–20 and S VI ii 121.5–9. In *A Refutation* Zwingli refers in passing to the laying on of hands as one of the three ceremonies given by Christ. Baptism belongs to all in the church, the eucharist to those who examine themselves concerning the certitude of faith (1 Cor. 11:28), and the laying on of hands to the few who superintend the ministry of the word. (Z VI i 182.10–183.4.)

ministry for the church. That necessity is sometimes expressed historically, in terms of the way God has acted in sending preachers so that
people will repent; however, it is always to be understood as a means by
which God chooses to act, not as a means by which he must act or without
which he cannot act.

The work of prophecy or preaching I believe to be most holy, so that above any
other duty it is in the highest degree necessary. For in speaking canonically or
regularly we see that among all nations the outward preaching of apostles and
evangelists or bishops has preceded faith, which we nevertheless say is received by
the Spirit alone. For alas! we see very many who hear the outward preaching of
the gospel, but believe not, because a dearth of the Spirit has occurred.[69]

In his exposition of Luke 1: 76, with its reference to John as prophet,
Zwingli explicitly raises the question whether God, who can do all things
and whose will no one can resist, could not illuminate men's hearts by his
Spirit—in effect without sending a prophet. His answer is that that is not
the way God has chosen to act.[70] In his comment on Christ's choosing
twelve whom he called apostles in Luke 6: 13, he raises the question in the
form what need Christ has of apostles if no one believes unless he draws
him inwardly. The answer is partly in terms of what God wills, and partly
in terms of the way man is made: he is not an angel, but has outward
senses.[71] The work that God does in the heart, he does through
instruments.[72]

On occasion the power in the preaching is ascribed to the preacher, but
it is always God's power, and the ascription of power to others (such as the
apostles) may be understood in terms of ascribing to the members what
belongs to the head.[73] From beginning to end it is the Holy Spirit who is
indispensable in ministry. He must be active in the hearer as in the
preacher, since without his action there is no effective preaching of the
word, 'for we are only ministers. We effect nothing, unless the Lord works
inwardly through his Spirit.' 'But for this the minds are prepared by the

---

[69] Z VI ii 813.7-13; Jackson 478 (*Works* II 56). Cf. *S* VI ii 113.44-114.12. In *The Ministry*
Zwingli has spoken of the necessity of the pastoral office for the unity of the church. (Z IV
429.33-430.7.)

[70] *S* VI i 550.8-22.

[71] 'Homo vero, qui carne circundatus est, admonitione subinde opus habet. Organa enim
habet et sensus exteriores ad haec aptos et commodos. Stulta ergo quaestio est, cur deus sic vel sic
faciat. Sufficere nobis debet voluntas dei, qui est sapientissimus, iustissimus, optimus: quando-
quidem ergo videmus deum uti prophetis, Christum apostolis, debemus credere hoc non temere
fieri. Cum homine humano more agit deus. Exercet hominem eo ordine quo eum creavit.' (*S* VI
i 582.18-28.)

[72] Z XI 476.25-8.

[73] *S* VI i 263.17-22, 266.38-43; VI ii 68.48-69.4. Cf. Z II 440.13-15.

prophets as ministers, and by the Spirit as the leader both of teacher and hearer.'[74]

The word 'prophet' is used with increasing frequency by Zwingli, but the same diversity of ministry is implied whatever term is used. The description in *An Account of the Faith* shows the continuing breadth of his view.

This kind of minister—viz. they who teach, console, terrify, care for, and faithfully watch—we acknowledge among Christ's people. That also we acknowledge which baptises, administers in the Lord's Supper the body and blood . . . visits the sick, and feeds the poor from the resources and in the name of the church; that, finally, which reads, interprets, and teaches so that either they themselves or others are prepared for presiding at some time over the churches.[75]

## ADDITIONAL NOTE

In Z VI i 555.4–556.2, 557.6–20 and in the letter to Michael Wüst in Z VIII 560–1 Zwingli points to separation from other Christians as a sign of self-righteousness and arrogance rather than of goodness. There is a parallel with monasticism rather than with Christ and the apostles. Already in *Baptism, Rebaptism, and Infant Baptism* Zwingli has accused the anabaptists of considering themselves purer than others, indeed as without sin. Their separation is interpreted in the light of 1 John 2: 19 as showing that 'they were not of us'. (Z IV 208.24–209.3.)

In support of his view of the church, and against the separatist view of the radicals, Zwingli appeals to his experience in Zurich. He accepted from the parable of the wheat and tares that the church was mixed, but his expectation was that more and more people would respond to the preaching of the word, and that the church would grow that way and not by division. A secession, which was the way of the anabaptists, would have caused confusion. Moreover, contrary to the anabaptists' view, the council, like Jehoshaphat, favoured the preaching of the word. (Z VI i 35.4–36.5.)

---

[74] S VI i 362.18–20; Z VI ii 813.22–3. Cf. Z I 366.30–3; S VI i 333.20–21, 759.9–11, 760.5–9; VI ii 64.29–30, 69.45–7.

[75] Z VI ii 813.23–814.4; Jackson 479 (*Works* II 57). As the demands in a particular place increase, Zwingli sees a division in which one engages in preaching and another in pastoral oversight. (Z IV 416.18–25.)

# 13. The State

THE relation of church and state in Zwingli is dramatically symbolized in the statue by the Wasserkirche in Zurich, where he stands with the bible in one hand and a sword in the other. Church and state are not two communities, but one and the same community under the sovereign rule of God. Zwingli as reformer therefore was concerned not with the church alone—any more than the magistrate was concerned with the state alone—but with the whole life of the community. However, his role in it as preacher or prophet was different from that of the magistrate. The complex relation between church and state in Zwingli can be understood only in the context of his life, both before and after he became a reformer, and in the context of the city of Zurich and the wider federation, where he engaged in his reforming ministry.[1]

## The Gospel is Social

The different paths by which Zwingli and Luther became reformers were one factor in their different approaches as reformers. Luther's life as a monk and his sense of God's judgement on him were quite different from Zwingli's life as a parish priest and army chaplain and his sense of God's judgement on his people. There was a difference not only in ministry, but also in the political circumstances in which their ministries were exercised. Thus the concern for liberty and justice and the threat to them from mercenary service for a variety of foreign powers, which is such an important factor for Zwingli in Zurich, was not a factor for Luther in Saxony.

There was furthermore a continuity between Zwingli's ministry and message before and after his becoming a reformer. The patriotism, the concern for liberty and justice, the sense of God's judgement on the life of the people, were all present before his full development as a reformer and remained vital elements in the structure of his message and ministry.

His earliest writings, written before he became a reformer, reveal a person with a passionate love of his native land and a longing for liberty.[2]

---

[1] Apart from books and articles dealing with his theology as a whole, with the anabaptists, and with important historical issues such as the secret council and his relations with Philip of Hesse, there is a considerable literature on questions of church and state in Zwingli. Note the works in the Bibliography marked with double asterisk.

[2] 'Liberty is such a blessing . . . But where bribes besiege the hearts of animals, all friendship,

These led to his fierce opposition to the mercenary service which entangled his fellow countrymen in the service of foreign powers—a concern expressed in allegorical form in *The Ox* in 1510 and then in *The Labyrinth*, probably in 1516. The first poem is patriotic rather than religious, whereas the second, coming from a period where the influence of Erasmus had been felt, has a clearly religious element as well, with its concern that we live in love and peace as Christ taught, and its range of biblical references.[3]

Zwingli claimed that he had had a love for his country from childhood and there was certainly a strongly patriotic dimension in his ministry and his understanding of the gospel when he became a reformer.[4] His attack on mercenaries always sprang out of deep patriotism. As a reformer, however, he came to see that it was precisely the gospel that brought in its train the abolition of mercenary service. Moreover this was not a case of the gospel's serving political ends, rather of its having a political expression. Nevertheless Zwingli could also speak of preaching the pure gospel for the good of the confederation.[5] He assured others of the renewing power of the gospel and claimed it in Zurich.[6]

liberty, and faithful alliance is despised.' (*Z* I 21.171–22.178; *Works* I 34.) He comes to see liberty as something favoured by God in the exodus and elsewhere in the bible, and also in the history of his own people. (*Z* I 171.4–15.) Note the reference to liberty in *Isaiah* in note 5 below. There are many references throughout his writings to his love of his country, some made almost in passing. (*Z* V 218.17–219.1; VII 603.7–13.)

[3] *Z* I 59.185–60.242.

[4] There is a striking personal testimony in June 1526: 'Wenn ein andrer üns Eydgnossen geschmützt und geschendt oder verlogen hatt, bin ich dem von kindswesen uf widerstanden, ouch etwan mich darumb in gevar ggeben; denn wer ein Eydgnoschaft schendt, der hatt mich ouch geschendt.' (*Z* V 250.8–11.) Cf. *Z* I 575.21–4. '... our country has more, finer, and braver people than any land on the face of the earth...'. (*Z* I 180.18–21; *Works* I 143.) His country's past is frequently drawn on as a source of inspiration for action in the present and William Tell is likewise portrayed in heroic terms. (*Z* I 170.26–171.7, 185.19–186.1, 187.12–14; III 103.22–104.13, 105.31–106.3; IV 48.15–49.6; *Hauptschriften* II 8.28–9.5.) Blanke notes that Luther would have had a very different attitude to Tell. He also contrasts Luther's passivity in relation to the emperor in 1523 with Zwingli's response to the threat posed by the catholic cantons and Austria in 1524. ('Gedanken zur Frage der Eigenart Zwinglis', *Der Kirchenfreund* 65 (1931), 323–6.)

[5] *Z* I 223.28–30. *A Solemn Exhortation* was written 'out of fear of God and love for an honourable confederation'. (*Z* I 167.1–2.) See also his concern for the unity of the confederation and the common good in the context of the disputation at Berne. (*Z* VI i 227.20–228.3.) Cf. *Z* VI iii 316.13–14. In the dedicatory letter in *Isaiah* two elements in Zwingli's theology need to be seen together: 'Religionem ergo et aequitatem in consilium et auxilium vocemus, si per maiorum manus traditam libertatem custodire satagimus! ... Religio proinde et aequitas nobis, o cives, ante omnia curandae sunt, ut sine quibus ne civitas quidem, nedum *Christiana* civitas, consistere possit.' (*Z* XIV 13.1–3, 39–41.)

[6] *Z* I 393.20–21; III 11.10–13, 112.29–113.4. 'For Zurich more than any other of the Swiss cantons is in peace and quiet, and this all good citizens put down to the credit of the gospel.' (*Z* I 148.32–3; *Selected Works* 16 (*Works* I 121).) 'I do not deny, nay, I assert, that the teachings of Christ

His patriotism was combined with a strong moral concern and a sense of outrage at the injustice and immorality to which mercenary service leads.

The second danger that threatens us from the princes and warfare in their behalf is that ordinary justice and equity will disappear ... Yes, if in war one only injured the disobedient, or war were only waged to make one's own people obey proper demands, we could put up with it. But how do you explain the fact that you take money from a foreign lord to aid him wantonly destroy, damage, and ravage countries innocent of all guilt?[7]

His patriotism and concern for morality and justice received a more explicit Christian motivation as his grasp of the gospel deepened, but it is important to see that they provided part of the mould in which this understanding was expressed. They were already fundamental elements in the man and his ministry before he became fully a reformer. In this context the letter to Zwingli from Myconius in May 1520 is revealing. It shows the grounds for some of the opposition to a consciously social and political ministry and on the other side the belief that such a ministry is inescapable.[8]

The gospel, and therefore the ministry, was not limited to a private sphere, but touched the whole life of the people. Undoubtedly the example of the old testament prophets influenced Zwingli, not least in developing his own prophetic ministry and his exposition of the ministry, but the development was continuous with his earlier practice and insights. In *Those Who Give Cause for Tumult*, when discussing interest and finance, he answers the question what that has to do with the gospel simply with the words 'much in every way'. To the later question what financial transactions, adultery, or drunkenness have to do with the minister, he replies that that is the same as the response of the devils when they said, 'Jesus what have we to do with you?'[9] This conviction is expressed even more

contribute very greatly to the peace of the state, if indeed they are set forth in their purity.' (Z I 308.24-6; *Works* I 267.) 'Wöllend ir nun gottes erkantnus under üch haben, damit ir frydlich und gotsvörchtlich läbind, so stellend allein darnach, das üch das gotswort eygenlich nach sinem natürlichen sinn gepredget, one zwang und gwalt aller menschlichen wyssheit klarlich und verstentlich an tag gelegt werde.' (Z III 112.29-33.)

A similar claim is made in *An Account of the Faith* for the transforming power of God's word in contrast with the corrupting power of the mass. (Z VI ii 817.3-14.) In *The Shepherd* it is the word of God that has put an end to mercenary service in Zurich. (Z III 11.10-13.)

[7] Z I 179.1-15; *Works* I 142. Zwingli regarded this as a human argument and goes on to argue that it does not become Christians to wage war. The greatest danger from mercenary service is that it brings God's wrath on the people. But it has many other dangers. It threatens justice and leads to the perverting of justice through bribes. It brings home wealth and so encourages envy and a luxurious way of life. It tends to the exercise of power by foreign rulers. (Z I 175.5-185.18.) Later writings contain detailed denunciations of the social evils that mercenary service brings, e.g. Z III 103-13.    [8] Z VII 317.15-318.14.

[9] Z III 432.1, 26-30. There is the same strong sense that public justice has to do fundamen-

strikingly in *Preface to the Prophets* in 1529. There he accuses some of preaching the gospel of Christ crucified, but without the cross. They speak sweetly and cleverly of God's work, but, because they are enemies of the cross of Christ, they do not attack greed, the wanton exercise of power by those in authority, the giving of false weight or false judgement, and the monopolies.[10] Zwingli sees the Christian life in the context of society and not only in the context of private life. It is a life like Christ's who 'gave himself up to death on our behalf'. The consequence is that 'we ought to give up ourselves for the good of all men'. 'From early boyhood, then, the young man ought to exercise himself only in righteousness, fidelity and constancy: for with virtues such as these he may serve the Christian community, the common good, the state and individuals.'[11]

Society's ills sprang, in Zwingli's eyes, from the lack of a true faith in God and were in turn its punishment for deserting God. A people, however, which relies on God will be victorious, as Israel was and as their ancestors were. It is only by repentance (in the context this meant rejecting mercenary service) that they will avoid worse suffering. Such repentance may cost money and foreign support, but Zwingli quotes Paul confidently, as he often does, 'If God is for us, who is against us?'[12]

Patriotism, opposition to mercenary service, a concern for social justice, a conviction that national ills were a punishment from God, were not original elements in Zwingli's theology, but were characteristic of many in the sixteenth century.[13] Political groups organizing support for, or opposition to, mercenary service, bishops and priests seeking reform in both church and society, men like Erasmus advocating a life based on the example of Christ, with a particular stress on peace and love, all were part of the total environment in which Zwingli worked, when he ministered in Glarus, Einsiedeln, and Zurich. However, the way the various elements combined with Zwingli's new understanding of the word of God gave his ministry and message their distinctive character.[14]

---

tally with God, who is angered above all by the perverting of justice and who never lets a nation go unpunished for it, in *Z* XIV 540.35–41. Opposition comes from those whose material interests are threatened, but Zwingli points out that there are those whose opposition is not to the preaching of social righteousness but to Christ. (*Z* XI 476.28–37.)

[10] *Z* VI ii 299.21–300.5.      [11] *Z* II 547.16–22; V 442.11–22; LCC XXIV 113.

[12] *Z* I 169.5–170.1, 170.22–171.3, 185.19–188.11.

[13] Examples of the way cities sought to avoid divine judgement are given in Moeller, *Imperial Cities*, pp. 45–7.

[14] The order of the closing words of *A Commentary* shows a characteristic emphasis in Zwingli's thinking: 'Nos enim quicquid diximus, in gloriam dei, ad utilitatem reipublicae Christianae conscientiarumque bonum diximus.' (*Z* III 911.30–1.) Cf. *S* VI i 310.27–9. The role of Zurich as a factor in the development of Zwingli's ministry and theology must also be noted,

## The Role of the Council

The council had an essential role at each stage of the reformation in Zurich. Its role is linked to the historical circumstances of Zurich, but also to Zwingli's understanding of its place in the economy of God. Long before the reformation the council in Zurich acquired a relatively independent role in the affairs of the church, though not in matters of doctrine and worship, which were under the authority of the bishops and the pope. However, Zwingli's conviction that doctrine and worship must be reordered in conformity with the word of God, rather than in obedience to the pope and bishops, increased—at least potentially—the areas in which the council could act. Such an extension of its authority would be welcome to it and in keeping with the growth of its powers.

From the beginning of his reforming ministry in Zurich Zwingli recognized that the council had a part to play. In this he accepted the fact that it had already in the past taken action in church affairs, and that it was the only body with power to act if the authorities in the church would not undertake reform. As a man of action Zwingli could not ignore what was historically possible, any more than, as a man of the bible, he could ignore biblical precedent. Like Erasmus and others before him, Zwingli saw in the Christian prince the one who would reform the church where the leaders of the church had failed. But there is more than simply historical or practical necessity in his approach. Zwingli had a theocratic view of society, in which preacher and prince are both servants of the kingly rule of God. He did not think of church and society as separate entities. They coincided, so that the city was both church and civic community. Within the city the minister and the magistrate have different tasks which they are to exercise in different ways, the one by preaching, the other by ruling, but their tasks are related to each other and both are subservient to the kingship of Christ.[15] Their relationship and their submission to Christ are

because it provided the immediate context for their development. He was invited to Zurich with a reputation as one involved politically and socially.

Walton regards Zwingli's faith in the Christian magistrate and his belief in the *corpus christianum* as reinforced by, but not dependent on, his study of Erasmus. He thinks that through Erasmus Zwingli may also have been influenced by Marsilius of Padua and Occam. He recognizes, however, with Moeller, the importance of the strongly communal character of the urban setting within which Zwingli worked (R. C. Walton, *Zwingli's Theocracy* (Toronto, 1967), pp. 17–29). Köhler posits a more direct influence from Marsilius (*Zwingli*, p. 99).

[15] Article 43 states 'Summa: Dess rych ist aller best unnd vestest, der allein mitt gott herschet, und dess aller bösest unnd unstätest, der uss sinem gmuet.' (Z I 463.10–11.)

There has been considerable debate on the use of the term 'theocracy' in Zwingli. It is used here to express the view that the whole life of the community is under the rule of God and that minister and magistrate seek to establish that rule, and not that the state or magistrate is subservient to the church or minister, nor vice versa. See, e.g., the summary of various positions in Walton, *Zwingli's Theocracy*, pp. xi–xxii.

evident, though in different ways, in the actual unfolding of the reformation and in Zwingli's exposition of the council's role. It is his exposition, rather than his practice, that concerns us: the context in which he argued and the arguments with which he presented his views.

For Zwingli the council's task was to help Christ back into his kingdom.[16] In no sense was it to usurp Christ's rule. It was not autonomous, but subject to the word of God. It was not to prescibe any law not drawn from scripture, and if it did, Zwingli would preach against it with God's word.[17] It summoned the first disputation, but it was not to be judge, as if superior to God's word. In response to Faber's suggestion that it should be judge, Zwingli replied, 'in these matters which pertain to divine wisdom and truth, I will accept no one as judge and witness except the scriptures, the Spirit of God speaking from the scriptures'.[18] Once the matter was clear, the council had the duty to see that the word of God was preached. This in fact it did.[19]

Undoubtedly the council played an increasing part in the reformation of Zurich. It is not our primary concern here to give an account of the varied changes that took place, but rather to understand them historically and theologically. Historical factors certainly encouraged Zwingli to seek the help of the council in Zurich and outside. The growing influence of the anabaptists, with their ability to disrupt the reformation in Zurich and to discourage governments elsewhere from permitting it, caused Zwingli to seek the aid of the council at home and to justify the role of government.[20]

[16] See the words of Schmid at the second disputation. 'So die geistlichen nit darzuo wöllen helffen, dass Christus widerumb gantz und uffgericht werde, wirt not sin, dass die weltlichen das understandint. Ir haben bisshar lieben herren, mengem weltlichen fürsten gholffen widrumb in sin herrschaft umb gelts willen, so helffen nun umb gots willen Christo unserm herren, widerumb in sin herrschaft, das er in üwren gebieten allein werde anbettet, geeret und angeruefft, und in uns Christen allein hersche und regiere . . .'. (Z II 797.31–798.8.) He has already drawn on the example of King Nebuchadnezzar and King Darius. (Z II 794.4–27.) Zwingli explained earlier to Schmid that Shradrach, Meschach, and Abednego, and also Daniel, tolerated images because the king was not a believer, and that Paul did so in Athens because the people were not Christian. (Z II 709.16–27.)

[17] Z II 775.12–16. In response to Simon Stumpf's charge that he is leaving judgement to the council, Zwingli makes it clear that no one, including the council, is to pass judgement on the word of God. The assembly is to learn what scripture says about the mass and to advise how to act without disturbance. (Z II 784.10–26.)

[18] Z I 558.2–5; Selected Works 103. Cf. Z III 317.23–4.                     [19] Z II 330.21–3.

[20] Pollet argues that Zwingli's views change, as do his opponents. Against catholics Zwingli argues for Christian liberty, whereas against anabaptists he defends the right of Christian authorities to intervene. (DTC 3865.) He sees a shift in the centre of gravity in Zwingli from the church to the city, which he regards as taking place in 1525 under the pressure of the anabaptists. In this he rejects Kreutzer's view that Zwingli maintains the autonomy of the church to the end. (DTC 3862–3.) This view has, however, more force than Pollet allows, as a comparison of The Eucharist and some of the later writings shows.

The power of bishops and catholic rulers to prevent or suppress the preaching and practice of the reformed faith abroad led him to seek to establish alliances to secure the proclamation of the gospel in other places.[21] Likewise his theology and his understanding of ministry led him to a closer association of spiritual and temporal leadership, or of church and state. His theology made him see all things as ultimately serving the glory of God and as subservient to his will. His understanding of ministry led him to involve himself in social, moral, and political affairs, and his natural interest and sense of service to God made him not only the prophet declaring God's will, but also the participant in the effecting of that will socially and politically.

The action of the council in reform raises the question of Zwingli's understanding of the church and of the council's relationship to it. Some hold that he began with a view of the church as gathered, but abandoned this at, or after, the second disputation. That is improbable. Zwingli's view of the church in his early writings is often implicit rather than explicit, but it does not appear to be of a church separate from the rest of society. The analogies he drew between his people and Israel suggest a view of the church embracing the whole community. He does speak of the church in terms of believers only, but this is always, for him, the church known only to God. Naturally the emphasis in a reformer is on people coming to faith in Christ, but Zwingli does not seem to see this in terms of the few who are to separate themselves from the others. Indeed throughout the early writings his concern is with the whole life of the community and not simply with the life of individuals or with the gathering of a small group. Moreover his attitude to the council and the assemblies called by the council confirms the view that he sees the church and the community as one. He does

---

Jakob Kreutzer distinguishes between fact and theory: 'Wir sehen, wie einerseits Zwingli seine anfängliche theoretische Unterscheidung zwischen Staat und Kirche dauernd behauptet, zugleich aber auch, wie er die Zürcher theokratische Verschmelzung beider begünstigt, obwohl sie seinem Gemeindeprinzip nicht völlig entspricht.' He relates these two elements to Zwingli's being a religious and a political reformer (*Zwinglis Lehre von der Obrigkeit* (Stuttgart, 1909), pp. 77–8).

[21] One of the guiding elements in Zwingli's thinking is the free preaching of the gospel. His confidence that it will prevail, if preached, does not diminish, as is sometimes alleged. His fundamental concern with alliances is to secure the freedom for people to hear and respond to the gospel. (Z II 331.11–13; VI iii 310.1–8; X 147.6–148.1, 153.20–154.7, 158.2–5; XI 35.2–15.) Cf. Z I 482.8–13. Alliances are not a sign of a lack of confidence in God and his word, for God is seen as often giving his help and protection by using men as his instruments. (Z VI i 200.4–9.) Zwingli's urging of alliances shows his continuing awareness of the threat to the gospel from one source or another. His plan for battle in 1526 has to be set in the same context, as the first words indicate: 'In gottes namen! Amen. Disen radtschlag hatt der autor betracht zuo eer gottes und zuo guotem dem euangelio Christo . . .'. (Z III 551.1–3.)

not envisage a separate gathering of the church to make decisions in church matters, but sees the church making these decisions through its civic assemblies and leaders.

Zwingli describes the assembly that the council summoned at his instigation 'in order to stop great unrest and disunity' as 'a Christian assembly'.[22] He relates this to the fact of their being assembled in Christ's name (Matt. 18: 20). The council summons it and the council acts after it, but the judge in the end is not the council nor the assembly, but scripture.

There is a coherence between the role Zwingli assigns to the council at the beginning of his reforming ministry and the one he assigns at the end, although the emphasis changes. As the bishops (or the pope) would not take the initiative in reform, the council had to. It did this fundamentally in requiring the preaching of the word after the first disputation. That was not an act external to the church, but one that showed that the council might, if properly authorized, act within the church. Furthermore the exposition of the thirty-sixth article discusses 1 Corinthians 6, a passage which the papists used to support their courts. Zwingli argues that it is concerned with bringing disputes before Christians rather than before non-Christian judges, but that since all the princes among whom Christians live are Christian, Christians should seek judgement from them. This is an early example, of which others will follow, where Zwingli ascribes to temporal rulers prerogatives that belong in some sense to the church or its members.[23] The council could also act in removing members from the church for the good of the church.[24] Here are some of the seeds of Zwingli's later statements that closely associate government with the life of the church.

The writings that follow the disputation, *Divine and Human Righteousness* and *An Exposition of the Articles*, display Zwingli's fundamental theological position. There is a basic division of power between magistrate and preacher. The preacher is concerned with divine righteousness, the magistrate with human righteousness. Outward matters belong to human righteousness and Zwingli leaves these to the magistrate. The second disputation fits the already established pattern. It is concerned to ascertain what the scripture says, but it does this so that the magistrate may act in

---

[22] Z I 484.11–14, 495.7–11.

[23] Z II 310.13–28. He also uses terms which most would take to apply to leaders in the church and applies them to princes, as in Heb. 13: 17, a text he was to draw on later. (Z II 313.9–25.)

[24] Z II 324.11–18. In his letter to Strasburg in December 1524, he implies that the council should take the initiative in removing preachers who do not preach the gospel or whose lives deny what they preach, and if they do not do so the church will have to act. (Z VIII 265.25–266.11.)

the light of it.[25] Whoever acts, whether it is the congregation or the council, the fundamental matter is for it to be ruled by the word of God.[26]

Zwingli affirms the role of government in reform, but the role does not change as dramatically in the later Zwingli as is often alleged.[27] Certainly the role is larger and the emphasis is different, but that has to do with historical, rather than theological, changes. Zwingli continues to base it on the same principles as earlier: submission to the word of God, the assent of the church, the need for peace, and the furtherance of the gospel.[28] A comparison of the position presented in *The Eucharist* with that in the letter to Blarer does not show in principle a lessening of the independence or authority of the church.

In *The Eucharist* Zwingli digresses to discuss the role of the council. He responds to the charge levelled by some that the reformers 'allow matters which ought to belong to the whole church to be dealt by the two hundred when the church of the whole city and the neighbourhood is seven thousand, more or less'. Zwingli has made it clear to the council that it is allowed to make decisions in matters that belong to the jurisdiction of the whole church, but only on condition that its deliberations and decisions are made under the leading of the word and 'that it is not in place of the church except in so far as the church itself has by silent consent till now kindly accepted its deliberations and decisions'. Yet he clearly does not regard this as the normal way of acting. The appeal of some people to the Spirit in defence of their senseless passions means that certain matters cannot be entrusted to all the people. Zwingli adds that he is not afraid that God will not direct the church, but he is concerned to avoid contention. He therefore advises entrusting judgement in outward matters to the council, on condition that it orders things in accordance with the word, while he promises to speak if the council scorns the authority of the word. The quiet in the church is in his judgement a sign of its consent, although it has not published a decision on the question at issue. Zwingli implies that the underlying concern is with the furtherance of the gospel, and not just with preserving peace.

[25] Z II 784.8–26.

[26] Z III 131.1–4.

[27] Government plays its part in excommunication, in requiring baptism and church attendance, and in instituting ordinances about marriage and social behaviour. The government's part is not seen as calling in question the authority of the church, as the government is not acting strictly on its own initiative, but in obedience to the word and in response to the church.

[28] The concern for peace is evident in other contexts. Thus he defends Paul's having Timothy circumcised on the grounds that his not being circumcised would have created a disturbance among Jewish Christians, although such an action was against Christian liberty and truth. (Z I 123.11–33, 153.29–154.3.)

He adduces from the Acts a precedent for delegating such authority. In Acts 15 the church of Antioch sent Paul and Barnabas to Jerusalem, although it could rightfully have made the decision itself. It acted in this way, according to Zwingli, to avoid contention which increases with the size of an assembly. He argues that it is clear that the council acts 'in the name of the church and not its own name' because it leaves the churches in the towns and country free in matters such as images and the celebration of the eucharist, as there is no great reason to fear contention there, since those churches are not large. (This reference to the council could imply a certain initiative of the council.) He adds that he always instructs the people beforehand in the matters to be considered by the council, so that whatever is determined by council and ministers has already been determined in the minds of the faithful. It is after this that he goes to the council, so that in the name of the whole church, it will order things to be carried out, and thus everything will be done fittingly.[29]

Essentially in this way of acting the primacy lies with the word, in accordance with which all are to act. This primacy is expressed in the initiative taken by the ministers of the word in their preaching to the people and in their dealings with the council. It is in that context that the council acts, not over the word but under it, not independently, but in the name of the church, and in the endeavour to avoid disruption and strife. It acts moreover only in outward matters. The furtherance of the gospel is of paramount concern. This remains a constant element in Zwingli's attitude to, and use of, the government in Zurich or elsewhere. It is precisely this principle that leads to Zwingli's being accused of opportunism, for each situation must be examined in the light of it. If the pope or the bishops were to act, the government would have no need to act in, for example, the reform of worship or the support of biblical preaching. If the whole congregation were agreed and there were no risk of strife and disorder, there would be no need for a smaller number to act in their name and with their silent consent. (Therefore Zwingli can consistently argue that the whole

---

[29] Z IV 478.10–480.29. Zwingli uses the terms *ecclesiae vice* and *ecclesiae totius nomine*.

Yoder argues for important changes in Zwingli, especially after the first disputation. First, the use of the term 'outward' changes to include (by 1525) the entire visible life of the church, although originally it meant politics and the economy. Second, there was originally the silent assent of the congregation in an assembly, as at the first disputation. Later there was no assembly of the congregation, so that silent assent was inevitable rather than real. Third, the government could be said to have acted in the name of the church at the first disputation, because there was a genuine meeting of the church. Later there was no meeting, and therefore no real delegation by the one to the other. ('The Evolution of the Zwinglian Reformation', *MQR* 43 (1969) 95–122.)

congregation should decide.)[30] In all this he draws on more or less convincing biblical precedents.

The biblical precedents are extended in his letter to Ambrosius Blarer on 4 May 1528. (The letter is notable for its assertion, in opposition to Luther, that the kingdom of God is outward. Zwingli's support for this, on the basis of the actions of Christ and the apostles, leads into a discussion of the role of the magistrate in outward things.[31]) He refers to Hezekiah and Josiah, but he continues to give greater weight to new testament examples, as the anabaptists refused to accept arguments based on the old testament. He is, however, driven to use some of the ingenuity shown in his argument for infant baptism on the basis of the new testament. (The parallel between the kings in Israel and the council in Zurich is clearly closer than that between Paul and Barnabas and in other circumstances Zwingli would have been likely to argue more strongly from the old testament analogy.[32]) Typically he argues, 'If a Christian magistrate may not do any of the outward things that pertain to religion and may not command or forbid, then much less may the apostles or the churches command or forbid, for they are prohibited from ruling.' Since, however, the apostles, did away with circumcision, for example, and the law about strangling and blood, an action which pertains very much to ruling, then the magistrate who is the authority referred to in Romans 13: 1 may act in outward things, if he is a Christian. Nevertheless this may happen only with the consent of the church. In response to those who say that this is something permitted to the apostles with the church but not to the magistrate with the church, Zwingli appeals to the use of the term 'presbyteros' in Acts 15: 6. He argues that this term is used not only of those who preside over the word but also of elders, that is, councillors or senators. These men, venerable in age, prudence, and faith, were to the church in the directing and ordering of affairs what the council or senate is to the city.[33]

---

[30] There are specific examples, like the eucharistic controversy, in which Zwingli affirms the importance of congregations deciding, so that he asserts their need to be informed about the different views. (Z VIII 640.16–641.14.)

[31] Z IX 452.15–455.24. The letter is discussed by H. R. Lavater in 'Regnum Christi etiam externum—Huldrych Zwinglis Brief vom 4. Mai 1528 an Ambrosius Blarer in Konstanz', ZWA 15 (1981) 338–81. Schmid (Zwinglis Lehre, p. 37) contrasts Zwingli's view with that of Aquinas, Luther, and the anabaptists. 'Nach ihm bilden der Staat und die Kirche eine Einheit. Er versteht ihre Beziehung weder wie Thomas von Aquin als ein Übereinander, noch wie Luther und die Täufer also ein Nebeneinander, sondern als ein Ineinander.'

[32] 'Und befundend zum letsten, das unser zit (do wir die ziten gegen anandren verglichtend) vil mer der propheten dann der apostlen ziten mag verglichnet werden und die kilch an ander gstalt dann zumalen habe, nit der ler und predig, sunder der oberkait halb.' (J. Kessler, Sabbata, ed. E. Egli and R. Schoch (St Gallen, 1902), 355.18–21.)

[33] Z IX 455.21–456.8.

In the light of this Zwingli argues that the council of Constance can act in the outward matters of religion, even if some are offended. He admits that the council and the church are not the same, but argues partly on the basis that if one asked the meetings of the guilds (*comitia curiata*) for their judgement, one would need no other agreement of the church, and partly on the basis that sometimes with the agreement of the church a matter can be settled by a few people or even one, as happened in the church at Antioch. Moreover the example of Christ in the temple shows that force may be used.[34] In a discussion of magistrates Zwingli asserts that if we are to obey an unbelieving magistrate when he commands something outward, surely we are to obey a believing one when he does. Then, moving from our obligation to that of the magistrate, he argues that a Christian magistrate has the same obligation to us as Christians, as Josiah had to the Jews. He ought therefore to remove images when the church agrees, just as Josiah did.[35]

The role of the council in acting in the name of the church is not necessary absolutely, but only relatively. Zwingli can therefore in this period speak of decisions as belonging to the whole church, without any theological inconsistency. Undoubtedly, however, he chooses direct action (through the whole church) or indirect action (through the council acting in its name) according to which will best further the cause of the gospel in a given situation.[36]

There is little doubt that circumstances led to the council's becoming more involved in the affairs of the church, as they led to the council's involvement in the first place.[37] Zwingli saw the need to carry the council as well as the people with him, if the whole church was to be reformed, and not simply part of it.[38] As the reformation developed it had to be

---

[34] Z IX 457.24–458.23. The criteria for the action of the council are like those in *The Eucharist*: the word of God, the consent of the church, outward matters. (Z IX 456. 30–5, 457.24–30.)

[35] Z IX 459.13–17, 464.31–465.5. Cf. the reference to Hezekiah and Josiah in 1525 in Z IV 13.13–18.

[36] Pollet speaks of Zwingli's opportunism in his dealings with Esslingen and Walenstadt in 1526 and 1530. (Z V 419–426; Z VI iii 357–65.) For Pollet, Zwingli holds only ideally to the principle of the autonomy of the Christian community. (*DTC* 3879.) Paul Meyer points to Zwingli's advantage in having the decision in Esslingen and Walenstadt made by the congregation (*Zwinglis Soziallehren* (Linz, 1921), pp. 76–7).

[37] See, e.g. W. Köhler, 'Alfred Farner, *Die Lehre von Kirche und Staat bei Zwingli' Zeitschrift der Savigny—Stiftung für Rechtsgeschichte*, 51 (Kanonistische Abteilung 20, 1931), 669–83. Cf. Pollet, *DTC* 3875–6.

[38] The council's acceptance of the authority of scripture in determining what is to be preached and done enables him to let it determine the best way and time for something to happen. This is made explicit at the second disputation and marks him off from the radicals: 'Sy söllend ouch über das wort gottes gantz nit urteilen, nit nun allein sy, ja ouch alle welt nit. Dise zuosamenberueffung ist ouch nit darumb geschehen, dass sy darinn wellind urteilen, sunder ein

clothed in outward forms, and that meant changes in forms of worship and in forms of behaviour. The various changes that took place, including compulsory baptism (1525), compulsory church attendance (1529), and certain social and moral laws, culminating in major legislation in 1530, must be seen in relation to the powers exercised by the council at earlier times and by other civil authorities. They must also be understood in relation to Zwingli's view that the whole of human society is under the rule of God and is to conform at least outwardly to the law of God. As it is the magistrate who can compel (for compulsion belongs to government and not to the preaching of the word), he has an indispensable role in the ordering of a society that corresponds to God's will, or at least to his commands.

The unity of church and society which is often only implicit in the early Zwingli is more explicit in the later Zwingli. Already in *An Exposition of the Articles* in 1523 there is a sense of the wholeness of the community, so that government can remove members from the church for the sake of the body.[39] In *A Commentary* he poses the question how the state (or city) differs from the church. He allows that there is a difference inwardly, for 'the state can be content if you show yourself a faithful citizen, even if you do not trust in Christ'. But the life of the state does not differ at all from the life of the church, for each demands what the other demands. Indeed in this context Zwingli refers to the Christian church as the Christian city or state.[40]

The relation of the two is expressed in *An Exposition of the Faith* in terms of the analogy of soul and body.

In the church of Christ government and prophecy are both necessary, although the latter takes precedence. For just as man is necessarily constituted of both soul and body, the body being the lesser and humbler part, so there can be no church without government, although government supervises and controls those more mundane circumstances which are far removed from the things of the Spirit.[41]

wüssen haben und uss der geschrifft erfaren, ob die mess ein opffer sye oder nit. Dannethyn so werdend sy radtschlagen, mit was fuogen das zuo dem allerkomlichesten on uffruor geschehen mög etc.' (Z II 784.20–6.)

[39] Z II 324.9–13.

[40] Z III 867.13–17, 868.15–22; *Works* III 294–5. Cf. 'Sic principes vestri non turgent fastu, sic prophetae commode, fideliter ac erudite docent, sic plebs tranquilla et doctrinam et imperium capit, ut iam dixisse olim non poeniteat Christianum hominem nihil aliud esse quam fidelem ac bonum civem, urbem Christianam nihil quam ecclesiam Christianam esse.' (Z XIV 424.17–22). G. W. Locher comments, 'Der Satz stellt keine automatische Selbstverständlichkeit fest. Es handelt sich um ein Ideal. Strassburg kommt dem Ziel nahe' ('Zwinglis Politik—Gründe und Ziele', *Theologische Zeitschrift*, 36 (1980) 94).

[41] S IV 60.4–9; LCC XXIV 267–8 (*Works* II 263). This comes in the section on government, not in the section on the church, although at the end of that section he gives the reason for

The role of the magistrate is vital for Zwingli as a protection for the gospel and the church against catholics and anabaptists. Against the first he opposes the power of bishops and princes, thus enabling the gospel to be preached and, where it is preached, sustaining the church in the reformation of its life in accordance with God's word. Against the anabaptists he preserves the integrity of the church when it would be rent by divisiveness. In his controversy with the anabaptists Zwingli affirms, 'Nor is the kingdom of Christ divided when the Christian exercises government, but it is renewed and united.'[42] The fact that church and state both serve the kingly rule of Christ is of fundamental importance. They are mutually involved because of that common service. Zwingli's thinking is fundamentally theocratic, with the emphasis lying sometimes on the Spirit and sometimes on Christ.[43] A theocratic view does not of necessity require the total independence of the church from government, but that government, as well as church, submit itself to the law of God. This concern is expressed in Zwingli's understanding of the prophet and in his exercise of the prophetic role both in his preaching and in his dealings with the council.

## The Task of Government and the Christian's Response

In two early writings Zwingli deals at some length with the task of government. The first, *Divine and Human Righteousness*, is a sermon preached in June and published at the end of July 1523; the second, *An Exposition of the Articles*, was published on 14 July 1523. In them government is set in the context of God's ordering of the world, the Christian's response being one of co-operation by participating and obeying (or, it may be, disobeying). They appeared at a time of considerable tension and, like Zwingli's other writings, were in no sense merely theoretical. Outside Zurich Zwingli was threatened by the federal diet with imprisonment if he entered any of the other cantons, while inside Zurich the controversy over tithes was raging. The work of reformation in the other cantons as well as in Zurich itself could be imperilled by an outbreak of religious or social disorder. Zwingli saw the necessity to present his own positive view of government as given by God, so that the gospel could be properly understood and its preaching safeguarded. He maintained indeed that 'the gospel of Christ is not

needing government. 'Consequently the visible church contains within itself many who are insolent and hostile, thinking nothing of it if they are excommunicated (*eiiciantur*) a hundred times, seeing they have no faith. Hence there arises the need of government for the punishment (*coerceat*) of flagrant sinners . . .'. (*S* IV 58.42–46; LCC XXIV 266 (*Works* II 261).)

[42] Z VI i 141.20–1.
[43] See Additional Note, p. 310.

opposed to government ... but is a support to government', always of course with the qualification 'as far as it acts in a Christian way in accordance with the standard prescribed by God'.[44]

In the sermon he presents the issues in terms of divine and human righteousness. In the way Zwingli uses the terms his position can be distinguished from Luther's on the one side and the radicals' on the other. He develops the distinction between the two kinds of righteousness in controversy with the radicals. Unlike them he sees that government, like human righteousness, is necessary because of man's sinfulness. Basing their views on the Sermon the Mount, the radicals challenge, among other things, the taking of oaths and the paying of tithes and interest. Against them Zwingli argues for the payment of tithes and interest in terms of human righteousness, while criticizing them in terms of divine righteousness.[45] There is within the distinction of divine and human righteousness a contrast characteristic of Zwingli between what is inward and what is outward, the government's concern being with the outward.[46]

Divine righteousness is perfect conformity with the will of God. It is inward and God alone can judge it, for only he knows the hearts of men. If men lived in perfect conformity with God's will, for example in loving their neighbours, there would be no need for human righteousness (or government). However, since we do not love our neighbour, God gives other commands, concerned with our outward actions, and thus with human righteousness, such as those not to steal or to kill. If we obeyed the commands not to steal or to kill then we should be righteous before men, but not necessarily righteous before God, who knows what is in our heart.[47] The two kinds of righteousness are so different that human righteousness does not deserve to be called righteousness in comparison with divine righteousness. Nevertheless it is commanded by God, because we fall short of divine righteousness. However, as the commands of God are not sufficient by themselves to effect even human or outward

---

[44] Z II 473.1–5.

[45] The radicals argue for the abolition of tithes, interest, and private property as contrary to scripture. Zwingli defends them in terms of human righteousness, while challenging them in the light of divine righteousness. The distinction of the two kinds of righteousness is present elsewhere, though the terms are not always used. See, e.g., Z XIII 415.22–31 and S VI i 563.44–564.9, 565.36–566.21, 588.32–42.

[46] The distinction and contrast can be seen in the law: 'Ein teil der gsatzten sehend allein den inneren menschen an, als wie man got, wie man den nächsten sölle lieb haben ... Der ander teil der gesatzten sehen allein den usseren menschen an, und derohalb mag einer usserlich fromm und grecht sin, und ist innerhalb nüt des minder unfromm und vor got verdampt.' (Z II 484.17–24.)

[47] Z II 484.21–485.14.

righteousness, God permits government to punish those who break them. Government, unlike God, cannot know the heart, and is therefore concerned, as Paul makes clear in Romans 13, with the outward and not the inward, with our deeds and not with our thoughts.[48]

The relationship of magistrate and preacher is expressed in the relationship of divine and human righteousness. Human righteousness is the direct and God-given concern of government (indeed the terms 'human righteousness' and 'government' can be used synonomously), whereas divine righteousness is the direct concern of the ministers of the word.[49] Government can secure human righteousness, but it cannot make men righteous before God. It uses compulsion which belongs to human righteousness; whereas compulsion does not belong to divine righteousness, and is not used by ministers of the word.[50] The preaching of the word which leads men to divine righteousness is, however, a service to government, as it helps rulers and subjects by teaching them what is good and what is evil.[51] This is important since government is not autonomous. Its task is to direct everything in accordance with God's will and if that is not possible in accordance with his command.[52] This indicates how close the concern of government comes to the proper concern of the preacher.

Zwingli distinguishes between the two kinds of righteousness and between the preacher and the magistrate, as Luther does between God's spiritual and temporal rule. However, even in his distinguishing of them there are pointers to their closeness, especially in the way human righteousness, and therefore government, must be related to divine righteousness. Government moreover is helped by those who preach God's law, but they are also helped by it. The concern of government with outward things will include outward things such as worship; and its concern

[48] Z II 486.18–487.8, 503.27–33.
[49] Z II 497.23–498.6.
[50] Z II 327.23–30, 337.19–338.18. Cf. Z II 502.27–32.
[51] Z II 504.8–19.
[52] Z II 522.2–6. Rich regards Zwingli as offering a third way, different from those of Luther and Müntzer, the way of radical criticism. He instances the way Zwingli sees divine righteousness as having an outward and not only an inward significance, and as being the standard by which everything is judged, both personal and social. He also points to those whom Zwingli identifies as the true disturbers of the peace. They are the bishops and clergy, and also the princes, the powerful, and the wealthy in society, and not those who rebel against injustice and oppression. Yet in this Zwingli does not make common cause with those who want to do away with what he sees as human justice. (A. Rich 'Zwingli als politischer Pionier', Die Tat, 28 Dezember 1968, and 'Zwingli als sozialpolitischer Denker', ZWA XIII (1969), 67–89.) Dieter Demandt does not see Zwingli's criticism as being so radical, as in his practical policy human righteousness prevails over divine righteousness ('Zur Wirtschaftsethik Huldrych Zwinglis', Beiträge zur Wirtschafts- und Sozialgeschichte des Mittelalters, pp. 306–21). Meyer regards Zwingli's economic views as essentially conservative (Zwinglis Soziallehren, pp. 71-3).

with laws, corresponding with God's will as well as with his commands, will lead it to legislation at least in moral and perhaps also in liturgical matters.

Zwingli's understanding of government is elaborated in *An Exposition of the Articles* and, with certain modifications, remains constant. Like Luther, he holds that there would be no need of government, if all were Christians. 'If all men gave God, what they owe him, we should need no prince or ruler, indeed we should never have left paradise.'[53] But all men are not Christians, and, as he is later to argue against the anabaptists, the church equally has need of government, because 'wherever the members of Christ do not arrive at the measure of the perfection of the head there is need for the sword'.[54]

Government derives from God, and not simply from man and his social needs.[55] It was instituted by him, and its institution was sustained by Christ's own acceptance of the government in his day. (Against the anabaptists Zwingli is later to argue that all government is given by Christ.)[56] In expounding article 35 he uses the words and deeds of Christ to show that he affirmed the authority of government. His words 'Render to the emperor' are interpreted as applying to all rulers and not, as was argued by some, to the emperor alone.[57]

Those exercising rule are not simply ordained by God, they are also servants of God.[58] Indeed they occupy God's place in the world,[59] so that in the old testament they were even called gods.[60] God exercises his rule through them and, it is he who wields the sword they bear in his name.[61] At the same time they have to give an account to God.[62]

[53] Z II 305.26–8. Zwingli does not share the radicals' expectation of establishing God's kingdom in this world. It is only in another world where sin in word or deed is abolished that there will be no need of government. (Z III 871.5–10.)

[54] Z VI i 131.15–16; *Selected Works* 197. The difference in understanding here between Zwingli and the anabaptists is discussed in Z VI i 131, n. 1. Zwingli did not see the church as the anabaptists did, in part because he had a more inclusive view of it. To their picture of Christians as not quarrelling or going to court, but turning the other cheek, he simply commented, 'Would that we had such a church!' (Z III 869.8–9.)

[55] Its institution by God was based primarily on Rom. 13, a text used by all the reformers, buttressed by examples from the old testament. (Z II 311.22, 487.18–25, 651.22–24.) It was, however, primarily against the radicals that Zwingli had to argue that government was of God. In *An Exposition of the Articles* he was concerned initially to argue that temporal rule was not to be exercised by bishops, but that they should be subject to the government. Christ's acceptance of government both in word and deed was important in this context.

[56] Z VI i 131.3–5.

[57] Z II 304.8–9. Cf. *S* VI i 563.15–16. His paying of tax and refusal to act as judge were instances to which frequent reference was made. (Z II 302.18–22, 306.3–11.) 'Render to the emperor . . .' is dealt with in Z II 305.1–16, 498.7–17.

[58] Z II 488.4; *S* VI ii 25.24.

[59] Z II 342.1–4, 492.33–493.3; VI ii 814.8–9; *S* VI i 562.25–9; 565.43–566.1 'dei in terris vicarius'.

[60] Z VI i 140.12–14; XIII 313.29–39, 414.19–24.

[61] Z II 324.9–11; *S* VI ii 25.18–24.

[62] Z II 336.2–5.

Government is seen as one of God's ways of dealing with sin in the world. First, God has given the word through which we can learn our guilt and find salvation. But so that our selfishness may not lead to violence God has also given government.[63] Government restrains us with punishment, in contrast with the word, which does not use compulsion. Government achieves its purposes by having good laws, which are sufficient for some people, and by using punishment as the way of controlling those who do not obey the law.[64] Without government human society would be impossible; it would disintegrate into the life of animals, with power going to the strong.[65]

The task of government is for Zwingli clearly set out in Romans 13: to protect the good and to punish the evil. The stress at many points lies on the wicked, since it is on their account, according to 1 Timothy 1, that government exists and is supported. However, their punishment is in order to protect the good. This means the outwardly good, for no one is good before God. At other points, however, Zwingli places protecting the good before restraining the evil.[66]

In keeping with its divine task, government must see that its laws conform with God's word, so that as article 39 puts it, 'they may protect the oppressed, even if he does not complain'. The underlying assumption is that it is not for a ruler himself to determine what is good or bad. This he will learn from God's law (summed up in loving one's neighbour as oneself), and laws should be in accordance with this. Moreover judgements should conform to this law also.[67] The laws, of course, concern the

[63] Z II 523.9–31. Cf. Z II 337.24–338.8.

[64] 'Duabas autem rebus iusti tuentur, malique cohibentur, aut legibus bonis, aut poenis. Qui intra legis cancellos continentur, altero remedio nihil opus habent: qui carceres legis transiliunt, illis iam gladius imminent et mulcta.' (S VI i 562.14–17.) Where the law is flouted, punishment should be increased, just as punishment for stealing is greater than God commanded in Exodus 22, because stealing did not disappear. (Z II 488.19–489.5.) However in the administration of the law the concern, like God's concern, is for people to change, and if improvement can be hoped for, then judges should show grace. (Z II 334.16–23.)

[65] Z II 487.27–488.8, 490.9–28, 492.33–493.3, 521.20–522.2, 651.22–6. Government is given as a schoolmaster because of the inclination to vice even in those who believe. (Z II 498.16–19.) God has given us two things (his word and government) to control us, so that we do not become more wild and evil than animals. (Z II 523.17–20.) In S VI i 609.28–30 the word and the sword preserve us from a life of beasts and devils. By contrast God gives us laws so that we may live in joy and friendship. (Z II 486.29–30.)

[66] Z II 328.6–329.2; S VI i 332.9–10, 562.14–15. There is a particular concern to care for the poor, the weak, and the oppressed. (Z II 332.17–333.5.)

[67] Z II 323.19–325.2, 329.27–330.5. Cf. Z II 244.24–9, 504.10–19, 524.11–525.20. There should be an intensifying of the punishment for adultery, as there has been for stealing, where there is an increase in the offence. (Z II 488.30–489.5.) An example of a stricter application of the law concerning adultery appears in Zwingli's letter to Zwick on 20 Dec. 1522. (Z VII 643.1–8.)

outward man (what he says and does) and not the inward man, for that is not the sphere of government.[68]

But even laws that conform to God's will need to be carried out according to God's will, and therefore the character of the ruler is as important as the character of the law he is to uphold. This was clear to Zwingli in the first disputation and remained a constant element in his thinking.[69] If true laws are to be made, then the ruler must be one who knows God and believes in him, otherwise he will not understand the law of nature, which is about the love of one's neighbour. Moreover the ruler needs to judge in unexpected situations for which there is no law, as well as decide how far old laws conform to the law of nature. It is therefore a perilous thing to be a judge, but also a beautiful thing if he is a believing and godfearing man, who acts only in accordance with God's word and command.[70]

The necessity for Christians in public office was developed in Zwingli's subsequent writings, in large measure in conflict with anabaptists. An early stage of this is found in *A Commentary*, where he argues that a person can be a true ruler only if he is a Christian. Without the fear of God he will become a tyrant.[71] He will then seek his own good and not the good of his people.[72] Against the anabaptists Zwingli is concerned to argue not only that a ruler needs to be a Christian, but also that a Christian may hold public office or be a ruler.

The anabaptists drew on a cluster of new testament texts to show that Christians do not need government and should not exercise it. Zwingli's response was partly to interpret the texts differently and partly to draw on a different range of texts.[73] Like Luther, he made the distinction between a

---

[68] Z II 334.24–26, 524.11–16, 525.9–10.

[69] Pollet (*DTC* 3879) sees a change of emphasis in the later Zwingli, from an earlier emphasis on the objective (a consideration of divine and human righteousness and their aims) to an emphasis on the subjective (the person of the prophet and the magistrate). From the beginning, however, Zwingli regards the Christian faith and character of the magistrate as vital in the administration of the law and the establishing of righteousness. (Z II 329.10–330.16.)

[70] Z II 329.17–330.16.

[71] Z III 867.7–13, 868.37–869.4. Cf. Z VI i 140.10–14; IX 458.23–24. Zwingli does not use the word 'Christian' in a restricted sense, as is clear from his letter to Ambrosius Blarer on 4 May 1528, where after positive references to Gentile rulers he says that those of them who are godly are Christian, even if they do not know Christ's name. (Z IX 459.5–8.) The ruler needs the Spirit of God, if he is to judge justly, as only God judges justly. (Z XIII 379.31–40.)

[72] Z III 873.12–22.

[73] Zwingli dealt with Matt. 5: 21–2, 20: 26, Luke 22: 26, and Acts 5: 29 in *A Commentary*. He used Exod. 18: 21–2, Rom. 12: 8, 16: 23, Acts 13: 7–13, 1 Tim. 2: 1–2, 6: 1–2, 1 Pet. 2: 13–16, and esp. Rom. 13: 1–7. (Z III 867–88.) As the anabaptists did not regard the old testament testimonies as relevant, Zwingli had to place the emphasis on new testament ones. (On occasion they both used Luke 12: 14, but for different purposes.) In further writings against the anabaptists he tackled other passages, used by them, and drew on others himself.

Christian as a private person and a Christian holding office. Commands not to resist evil and to turn the other cheek apply to the Christian, but not as an office holder. The distinction is used in *An Exposition of the Articles* and developed in the commentaries. In them Zwingli points out that Peter was commanded to forgive up to seventy times seven and yet he killed Ananias and Sapphira, and that Christ himself attacked the Pharisees and did not turn the other cheek before the high priest.[74] Zwingli's positive case is built in part on biblical instances of those who exercised public office, and in part on the fact that Christians cannot do without government and that they are best fitted for a task which is ordained of God. He cites the cases of Erastus, Sergius Paulus, and the instances of those who had slaves, and he expounds Romans 12: 8 to show that God gives some the gift of ruling, which they are to exercise. He points out moreover that if you are going to have rulers it is madness to prefer an ungodly magistrate to a Christian one. As he puts it later, 'the kingdom of Christ is not divided when a Christian exercises the magistracy; it is built up and united'.[75]

Zwingli always saw the ruler as having a close relationship with God's people. Besides the ample old testament precedent for this, Zwingli also used new testament testimony. Examples that might seem to apply to leaders within the church are applied to Christians who were leaders of the whole community.[76] The shepherds of God's people in the old testament included rulers of the people and Zwingli speaks of God's people as being governed by prophets and rulers.[77] Those moreover who are not believers should not rule over God's people, but should rather be put out of the council.[78]

[74] Z II 334.2–23; XIII 396.9–30; S VI i 564.30–565.23. A ruler who kills someone in anger is as guilty of killing as a private person, for in this he is not carrying out the law. (Z II 333.26–334.2.)

[75] Z III 872.34–877.3; VI i 141.20–1. Examples used later include Cornelius and the Ethiopian eunuch. (Z VI i 137.33–138.8.)

[76] e.g. the use of Heb. 13: 17 in Z II 312.9–25 and of Rom. 12: 8 in Z III 872.38–873.6.

[77] Z XIV 517.4–8. Zwingli refers in *A Commentary* to rulers as fathers in the flock. (Z III 873.13–16.) This is developed further later in his writings, as in *An Exposition of the Faith*, where rulers are seen as among the shepherds in the church, without whom the church would be maimed and impotent. (S IV 58.46–59.2.) Zwingli regards it as exceptional when someone combines the office of judge and priest, as in the time of Samuel, the one manifesting the righteousness of God, the other his goodness. Thus it is for the judges and not for the priests to vindicate God's righteousness with the sword. Christ also is priest and king. In his first coming he came as priest and reconciler to save and not to judge, for God wishes to be known first by his goodness. In his second coming he will come as king and judge, and God will exercise his righteousness. (S VI i 532.11–27.)

[78] In expounding 'Shake off the dust' (Matt. 10: 14) he writes, 'Hic sequitur, das man billich uss dem Rat stos, die Gotzwort nit glauben, nüt daruff habent, darwider reden. Dan wie möchtent oder konntent, oder warum soltendt die über das Volck Gotz regieren, die schon den Glauben

As government is ordained by God, Christians are under obligation to obey. 'But that christianity which I advocate is adapted to all cities, obeys the laws and the magistrates of the nation, pays taxes to whom taxes are due, tribute to whom tribute is due, rates to whom rates are due.'[79] In *An Exposition of the Articles* Zwingli argues against the authority of priests and bishops, and their subordination, and that of the pope himself, to temporal government. This is based on Paul's statement in Romans 13: 1 that every soul (which must include the pope) is to be subject to the powers that be. Such obedience is due to evil government no less than to good government, for government that is evil also comes from God. Zwingli quotes Isaiah 3: 4–5 to show that God uses it to punish us for our sins. It is therefore to be endured until God is pleased with us—and therefore removes it.[80] Evil rulers are to be endured where they cannot be removed legitimately, but such endurance is more bearable because God will deliver his people as he delivered Israel from Egypt.[81]

Christian obedience is rooted in the example of Christ, who obeyed the authorities and paid tribute, although he had no need to.[82] Later this obedience is expressed in terms of man's being soul and body, the body being subject to the ruler, the spirit being ruled by the Spirit. We must obey our rulers until we are entirely spiritual, although then, like Christ, we may obey so as not to give offence.[83] Besides the example of Christ, the desire to live peacefully and not to have uproar is also a motive for obedience. Anxiety about disorder arose from the activity of anabaptists and others and persisted throughout Zwingli's ministry.[84] Fundamental, however, is not anxiety about disorder, but the conviction that one must

handt, die Laster straffen, die selb gottlos sind und nit glauben.' (*S* VI i 414.32-6.) Cf. *S* VI i 267.12-17.

[79] At this point in *Archeteles* Zwingli is attacking the necessity for ceremonies and the clerical pattern of Christianity which sees priests living well at the expense of lay people. The quotation continues, 'Under it no one calls any possession his own, all things are held to be in common; everyone is eager to outdo his neighbour in kindnesses, to exercise all gentleness, to share his neighbour's burden, and relieve his need. For he regards all men as brothers . . .'. (*Z* I 308.29-309.5; *Works* I 267.)

[80] *Z* II 311.9-24, 509.28-510.6; III 881.1-4. Zwingli's exposition of Rom. 13: 1 in *Romans* includes quotation both of Christ's word that Pilate would have no authority unless it had been given to him from above, and of Jeremiah's reference to Nebuchadrezzar as God's servant (Jer. 25: 9). (*S* VI i 123.32-7.) On the basis of Romans 13 and new testament passages such as Luke 12: 13-14 Zwingli argues later for the paying of tithes. If the authorities recognize the tithe as a true debt, it must be paid. Those who resist this show that they are using the gospel to make a freedom of the flesh out of the freedom of the Spirit. (*Z* III 391.2-13, 399.24-400.4.)

[81] *Z* III 873.25-37. An example used earlier in terms of papal tyranny. (*Z* II 311.27-312.7.)

[82] *Z* II 306.3-11; III 400.30-401.1.

[83] *S* VI i 331.44-332.4.

[84] *Z* II 509.19-21; III 399.24-28; *S* IV 66.18-67.2.

obey God because government comes from him and is his servant. To disobey it therefore is to disobey God. Yet it is precisely because rulers are the servants of God and because Christian obedience to them is obedience to God, that Christians may also disobey.

Disobedience is an obligation when the authorities set themselves against God whether commanding what is contrary to his will or seeking to control the preaching of the word. They are not lords over the souls and consciences of men. Christians therefore should suffer death rather than obey.[85] The text to which Zwingli constantly appealed in this context was "We must obey God rather than men." God's command takes precedence over other commands.[86]

Another new testament text frequently adduced was 'If your eye causes you to sin, pluck it out, and throw it from you.' The eye referred to bishops or priests, but also to temporal rulers, and could imply either killing or deposing them.[87] In this way it could be used for rulers in removing those resisting the proclamation of the gospel and for citizens removing rulers who did the same. Thus disobedience could lead to resistance and even the overthrow of a ruler if he became a tyrant. Tyranny was seen not only in opposition to the proclamation of the gospel, but also in terms of the exploitation of the people by the ruler for his own ends, with a disregard for his obligation to protect the good and punish the evil. Such rulers permit monopolies, contrary to the law, but to their own advantage. They rob the poor through taxes, raised to meet the cost of their own loose living and the waging of war. They treat their own people not as human beings, but as animals, indeed worse than animals.[88]

---

[85] Z II 320.2-13, 493.25-32, 503.2-9, 514.30-515.3.

[86] Z VII 645.25-9; II 320.5-7, 503.7-9, 651.35-652.3.

[87] Z I 120.31-122.12; II 335.3-8, 344.14-16; VII 645.29; IX 465.11-13; S VI i 336.11-18. On occasion Zwingli explicitly denies that rulers may be killed, but sometimes killing them is certainly implied, as in the early reference to God's sending someone to avenge his people (Z II 510.14-18) and the later exposition of Jer. 15: 14, in which Zwingli offers pagan examples where rulers were killed or should have been killed. But in keeping with his fundamental position he sees this as an act done by someone not on his own initiative, but in response to God. (Z XIV 565.6-25.) Cf. Z VI i 814.17-24. God's initiative is expressed in the reference to the plerophoria of the Spirit in Z IX 465.5-7. The example of Elijah is mostly adduced in terms of his killing the prophets of Baal, though it can refer to the death of Ahab and Jezebel. (Z III 449.24-450.2; IX 465.7-10; S IV 59.47-60.1.)

[88] Z II 331.11-13, 338.19-342.6, III 24.15-23, 883.13-15. Tyrants are as common as fleas in August. The forty-second article states, 'So sy aber untrüwlich und usser der schnuor Christi faren wurdend, mögend sy mit got entsetzt werden.' (Z I 463.8-9.) Zwingli later comments on this article, 'Also verstond wir hie "by der schnuor Christi hin": dem götlichen weg nach. Denn fart der aber nit by der schnuor Cristi hin, so er den sündenden nit strafft sunder uffnet, und den unschädlichen beschwärt.' (Z II 343.13-16.)

Zwingli's attack on tyranny and his call to resistance were related not only to this new testament text but also to old testament examples. God may punish us with unjust rulers, but in his mercy he wishes to liberate us as he liberated Israel from Egypt, by sending them Moses. This example was used initially of liberation from the pope, but later of liberation from temporal rulers as well.[89] Such liberation is not only from foreign rulers, like Pharoah, but also from rulers like Saul, whom God rejected, even though he had earlier chosen him. The initiative is with God rather than with the people, as he has already rejected the king. Indeed the people will be punished if they do not remove such kings, just as God, according to Jeremiah, punished Judah for the atrocities of their king, Manasseh.[90]

The removal of a ruler has to follow a proper procedure. It is not to be achieved by murder or war or an uprising, as God has called us to peace (1 Cor. 7: 15). If he is elected by the people, he should be deposed by them. If he is elected by a small number of princes, a report should be made to them and he should be deposed. But if he is not elected, there is a greater problem. (Zwingli argues that at some point there must have been the people's consent.)[91]

It is the duty of government to let God's word be preached, and in that sense government is of service to the word of God. At the same time, however, government is itself helped by the preaching of the word. Already in *An Exposition of the Articles* Zwingli makes it clear that the gospel helps government in a variety of ways. Scripture overthrows the power wrongly exercised by bishops and priests. (Indeed Christ specifically commanded Peter to put up his sword and if the pope is his successor he should do the same. His task is to preach. His task is not to fight against the Turks, but to preach the gospel, leaving the protection of the country to the princes.) Yet, far from overthrowing the power exercised by the magistrate, scripture actually confirms and prospers it.[92]

    [89] Z II 311.27–312.7; III 468.12–23, 873.32–7, 880.16–19; XIII 327.18–20. Zwingli's concern is initially much more with ecclesiastical rulers in their opposition to the gospel, and that leads him to point out that the leaders of the priests and scribes were much more hostile to Christ than Herod and Pilate. (Z VII 650.16–17.) There is a menacing note in the references to Moses. 'Erlassend ir das volck gottes nit, das es sinem herren nachvolge, so wirt er bald einen senden, der sy mit üwrem undanck hinfueren wirt, und alle, die sich wider inn setzend, nüts minder ertrencken, weder den Pharao.' (Z II 468.19–23.)
    [90] Z II 343.22–344.16. The example of Manasseh is one to which Zwingli frequently returns, on occasion in the context of non-biblical examples. (Z XI 69.41–70.1; XIV 564.38–565.25; S VI i 332.46–333.2, 567.36–44.) Even in writing for the King of France in 1531 Zwingli draws on the example of Saul and David, and states that a Christian should obey a tyrant until the time comes of which Paul speaks when he says, 'If you can become free, use it rather'. (Z VI ii 814.17–22.)
    [91] Z II 342.26–28, 344.17–346.13.
    [92] Z II 303.17–19, 304.8–25, 308.14–309.20. 'Aber der weltlich [Gewalt] hat krafft und

Zwingli points out that it is no use having good laws where people are not minded to obey them. But where the word of God is preached people will be drawn to God and desire to obey the laws. Moreover through the word of God leaders also become wise and discerning. Such a state therefore will be strong and peaceful.[93] In many instances in his later writings Zwingli argues for the indispensable role of the preacher in the life of the community, for 'the laws themselves and the magistrates can be assisted in maintaining public justice by no means more effectually than by prophecy'.[94] The army also needs a courageous Christian preacher, versed in Roman, as well as biblical history. He will teach them to fight honourably, to obey God and their commander, and not to be afraid.[95]

The prophet was an important, not to say indispensable, person for government because Zwingli's vision of society was theocratic, a community under the rule of God. It is the task of government to direct all things in accordance with God's will, and if that is not possible, in accordance with his commands. The preacher or prophet is the one who makes known God's will and his commands.

The prophetic role of the preacher was typical of Zwingli from beginning to end, although the term 'prophet' was not the characteristic one in his earlier writings.[96] The model of the old testament prophets increasingly coloured his presentation of the ministry as prophetic, a model he himself embodied in different ways in Glarus and Einsiedeln, as well as in Zurich. For Zwingli God's word was concerned with the whole life of the community; the prophet therefore was to speak that word to high and low alike. It was a word about people's inward relationship with God, but it was also—and that concerns us here—about man in his outward relationships.

The first extended treatment of this prophetic ministry is in *The Shepherd* (1524). In his description of the pastor or shepherd Zwingli

bevestigung uss der leer und that Christi.' 'Darumb alle oberkeit iro nit entsitzen sol, das die leer Christi inen möge schädlich sin, sunder wirdt sy sehen und empfinden, das ir rych und oberkeit dheinen weg besser, ruewiger, fridsamer, ja richer sin mag, denn so on underlass das wort gottes styff und klar prediget wirt, so verr sy nit tyrannen sind . . .'. (Z II 304.8–9, 18–22.) Cf. Z I 149.31–4; II 308.24–6, 346.15–17, 473.1–5. In *The Canon of the Mass* Zwingli stresses that kings should be placed before the pope and bishops in the intercessions, citing I. Tim. 2: 1–2. (Z II 572.32–573.14.)

[93] Z II 330.26–331.22. Cf. Z II 504.8–19 and III 112.33–113.4.
[94] Z VI ii 813.18–20; Jackson 479 (*Works* II 57).
[95] Z III 580.8–581.2.
[96] He uses terms such as *Wächter* (watchman) or *Hirt* (shepherd, pastor) in his earlier writings, e.g., Z II 313.11–12; III 1–68. On Zwingli's understanding of the prophet, see F. Büsser, 'Der Prophet—Gedanken zu Zwinglis Theologie', ZWA 13 (1969) 7–18. Something of the prophetic role is already present in *The Ox* (1510) and *The Labyrinth* (1516). (Z I 13.24–30, 59.185–60.232.)

appeals primarily to Christ as the Good Shepherd, but he appeals also to the prophets and apostles.[97] It is not only the gospel that one is to preach, for until people are aware of their sin they cannot receive the gospel. Moreover when they have received it, they must then go on to live their lives according to God's will.[98] The pastor, like Christ, must be willing to lay down his life for the sake of the sheep. He will speak against prince, emperor, or pope, not only for an obviously spiritual reason like resisting God's word, but also if they place unjust temporal burdens on the people.[99] The old testament provides striking testimony of such prophetic rebuke to rulers, where Samuel rebukes Saul just at the point where the king returns victorious from battle. Against this background Zwingli attacks an unnamed person (probably the Bishop of Constance) for telling a minister that he should preach the gospel without rebuking anyone, though no doubt the person would allow that a minister might rebuke the peasants. But the truth must be preached to the powerful, and not just to the weak, in such a way that they will recognize their tyranny and will change. Like John the Baptist challenging Herod, the pastor must be fearless in his attack.[100] Following the example of Elijah with Ahab and Jezebel, he must moreover speak against the greatest tyrant even where the matter concerns not the whole people but only a single person.[101] Sparta had its ephors and Rome its tribunes to guard them against their rulers; so God has placed pastors in his people to watch and warn.[102] For such a ministry the shepherd's armour is not to fear, and this comes from his total trust in God as Father and his love for him. It is love that underlies his care for the sheep and his denial of himself, a love that is rooted in undoubting faith.[103]

Such a prophetic ministry is not welcomed by those who are criticized whose response is to ask what their financial dealings or their personal behaviour have to do with the minister. For Zwingli, however, such a

---

[97] Z III 13.6–17. Hermann Escher, like others, sees Zwingli as drawing inspiration more from the old testament than the new, but the importance of the new testament prophets should be recognized ('Zwingli als Staatsman', *ZWA* V (1931), 300).

[98] Z III 18.13–33, 21.25–22.12. Zwingli's understanding of the law as leading to despair and driving us to God's mercy is like Luther's, but his stress on living according to God's will is different.

[99] Z III 26.25–27.1. The sense that the prophet is always in danger is a persistent element, relating to the fact that the prophet has to speak God's word of judgement to kings and rulers. (Z XIII 324.29–38.) Zwingli himself could be vigorous and specific in his denunciations. See, e.g. Farner, III 142–53.

[100] Z III 28.10–29.20, 35.24–36.6.

[101] Z III 34.3–5.

[102] Z III 36.7–22. Cf. *S* VI i 367.25–7.

[103] Z III 39.1–43.5.

response is like the devil in the man whom he possessed saying 'Jesus, what have we to do with you?'[104] The opposition that a prophet undergoes leads some to avoid a critical encounter with evil. *Preface to the Prophets* speaks of those who preach the gospel of Christ crucified, but without the cross, for they refuse to attack greed, usury, war, the mercenary system, monopolies, and companies which harm the common good. They are in fact enemies of the cross of Christ, as they are more eager to be regarded as learned and to be held in esteem than they are concerned for piety.[105]

The social or political dimension to the prophet's preaching is expressed frequently in the old and new testament commentaries. If the prophet does not proclaim the truth, righteousness and public liberty are imperilled.[106] Although the prophets' task is a critical one, it also essentially constructive. 'If faults are committed they will expose them, but not in such a way as to create disorder in temporal affairs. In these matters they always acknowledge the lawful magistrate, no matter how much they may seize on and criticize him when he is at fault.'[107] The prophet and the magistrate are both instruments of God, though the prophet is seen as more necessary or fundamental than the magistrate.[108] If the prophet falls short, the magistrate and people suffer; and yet one prophet who is true can rescue them.[109] Indeed a true prophet could set up a magistrate, if there were no magistrate, though a magistrate could effect nothing, if there were not a true prophet.[110] In the dedicatory letter to *Isaiah* Zwingli affirms that no state can stand, let alone a Christian state, without religion and justice. He sees them as sustained by prophets. It is therefore utterly

[104] Z III 432.26–30. Discussing the prophet in *The Ministry*, Zwingli points to two major elements, drawing on two fundamental texts: Jer. 1: 9–10 and 1 Cor. 14: 26–33. The first refers to the tearing down and destroying of all that is against God and the building and planting of what God wills; the second to expounding the scriptures. (Z IV 393.26–395.25.) A particular form of this second form of prophetic ministry is, Zwingli says, about to begin in Zurich. The prophecy or prophesying began in fact on 30 June 1525. (Z IV 397.33–398.10.)

[105] Z VI ii 299.21–300.5. Here, as in other places, the gospel is seen in a social or political setting.

[106] S VI i 247.6–11. The prophet's concerns will show whether he is true or false: 'Si gloriam dei spectat propheta, si iustitiam, veritatem, pacem et salutem publicam, certum est eum verum esse prophetam et a deo missum. Si alio spectat, falsus est.' (S VI i 247.17–20.)

[107] S IV 67.33–35; LCC XXIV 278 (*Works* II 275). Zwingli writes this to the King of France in a context where he is distinguishing his position from that of anabaptists and papists.

[108] S VI i 367.15–27. The magistrate is concerned with the outward expression of vice, the prophet with what underlies it. (S VI i 433.37–434.2.)

[109] 'Tanto pluris refert prophetam divinis dotibus esse praeditum, ut qui magistratum cum plebe possit pessundare, quam aliorum quemquam. Illo enim desipiente et acrimoniam amittente, quomodo non insulsa et putrida fient omnia? Magistratu vero cum tota plebe errante, quomodo non ambo protinus in viam reducuntur ab uno etiam propheta, cum ille murus aheneus [Jer. 1: 18], cum sal et lux [Matth. 5: 13 ff] fuerit?' (Z XIV 421.4–10.)

[110] S VI i 550.21–5.

characteristic of him to exclaim, 'O happy rulers, cities, and peoples, among whom the Lord speaks freely through his servants the prophets. For thus religion can increase, innocence return, justice reign, without which what we think kingdoms and governments are robbery and violence . . .'.[111]

Zwingli also considered the form of government. In this he takes up the classical discussion of the issue, although he also draws on biblical examples and uses some biblical criteria in the course of his exposition.[112] He recognizes three main kinds (monarchy, aristocracy, and democracy), each of which has a corrupt form. Monarchy or kingship, in which control is exercised by one man, when corrupted becomes tyranny. This happens when 'piety is despised, justice is trampled underfoot, all things are done by force, and the one who stands at the head rules by caprice'. Aristocracy, in which the best possible men rule, when corrupted becomes oligarchy, the rule of the few. In an oligarchy a small number seize power, 'with a view not to the public good but to their own advantage, subjugating the state and using it to accomplish their own ends'. Democracy or a republic, in which the direction of affairs is in the hands of the whole people, when corrupted becomes uproar or sedition. In this 'all restraint is thrown off and obedience is given to the individual will rather than to the authority of the state'.[113]

In his commentary on Isaiah, dedicated to the cities of the Christian Civic Union, whose form of government is an elected and representative aristocracy, he expresses his preference for aristocracy, whereas in *An Exposition of the Faith*, dedicated to the King of France, he expresses no preference.[114] Zwingli's preference is understandable when one considers his own experience of aristocratic government in the Zurich council and in other cities, but also when one considers the greater difficulties involved in deposing tyrants, especially hereditary ones, than oligarchs. In

[111] Z XIV 14.21-4.

[112] Z XIV 6.6-14; S IV 59.6-60.4. Zwingli draws on the classical discussion of the issues, although at one point in *An Exposition of the Faith* he carefully claims that what he is saying derives from scripture. (S IV 60.3-4.) Walton points to the influence of Augustine's understanding of a true republic in his *City of God*. Augustine drew in part on Aristotle. ('The Institutionalization of the Reformation at Zurich', *ZWA* 13 (1972) 500-1.)

[113] S IV 59.6-60.4; LCC XXIV 266-7 (*Works* II 261-62).

[114] This is not simple opportunism, for Zwingli discusses the abuse of monarchy in *An Exposition of the Faith* and the ways in which tyrants should be opposed and deposed, drawing on biblical examples to illustrate the point. Moreover he does not do this for aristocracy and democracy. Nor does he hesitate in *An Account of the Faith*, which is written for the emperor, to speak of the abuse of monarchy and its rejection. (Z VI ii 814.8-24.)

*Isaiah* in 1529 Zwingli writes that there was no monarch who did not degenerate into a tyrant, a view—not surprisingly—which he does not repeat in the two works dedicated to monarchs in 1530 and 1531.[115]

In *Isaiah* Zwingli begins with the question posed by Greek philosophers whether monarchy, aristocracy, or democracy is to be preferred, a question more appropriately tackled in such a preface than in the brief statements of faith, which the other two works are. He rejects a merely theoretical approach. Discussing the rule of a very good and wise prince when one has never been found is like discussing Plato's republic which never existed. The same could apply to aristocracy or democracy. He considers therefore which form of government has been most religious, just, and lasting. This is his concern because no state can stand without religion and justice.[116] His discussion is a defence of aristocracy against monarchy rather than a dispassionate examination of the different forms of government. He does this by showing the disadvantages of monarchy which he presents as inferior to aristocracy, both in theory and in practice. In this he dissents from the classical and medieval preference for monarchy. Although he intends a historical, rather than a theoretical, approach, he nevertheless holds monarchy to be in principle inconsistent with the liberty and good of the people. He uses examples to show that monarchy always turns into tyranny and that it has various disadvantages: a good king is not succeeded by a good one, and one person is more likely to fail, to follow his own will, to lead people astray by his example, and to be corrupted or misled by flattery. All this is contrasted with aristocracy, which involves more people, and which is presented without any fundamental weaknesses. It serves public rather than private good, even if it can turn into oligarchy.[117] The conclusion shows a practical concern for the cities to which he is writing. It seeks to encourage them and to point to the indispensable role of the prophets; for, unlike prelates, they will teach the true worship of God and the proper observance of justice.[118]

[115] *Z* XIV 7.28–30.

[116] *Z* XIV 5.6–7.8, esp. 6.31–7.8.

[117] *Z* XIV 7.8–12.24, esp. 7.17–24, 28–30, 9.12–17, 11.4–6. In passing, he says that he does not want to detract from godly monarchs. Pollet (*DTC* 3893–4) draws attention to Zwingli's political realism in his discussion of the various forms of government. There was a representative element and an accountability to the people in the form of aristocracy which Zwingli experienced in Zurich and presented in his writings.

[118] *Z* XIV 11.35–12.3, 13.37–14.27.

## ADDITIONAL NOTE

J. V. Pollet rightly comments on the important place given to the Spirit in Zwingli, among other things pointing to Zwingli's use of the plerophoria of the Spirit in Z IX 465.5-7. The need to act in response to God in taking the lives of others is present earlier, e.g. in the case of Peter and Ananias and Sapphira in *A Commentary*. (Z III 884.27-31.) However, Zwingli's emphasis on the Spirit needs to be related to the biblical passages to which he refers, as in the dedicatory epistle to *Jeremiah* where he refers to Ps. 51. (Z XIV 419.13-16.) It need not be seen, as Pollet (*DTC* 3882) tends to see it, as fundamentally different from a stress on Christ. Pollet (*DTC* 3899) uses Zwingli's exposition of Jer. 15 in Z XIV 564.38-565.25 to speak of Zwingli's spiritualism, yet Zwingli's reference there, like Jeremiah's, is to the Lord, not to the Spirit. Zwingli is not more spiritualist than Jeremiah, for both hold that the Lord speaks to men. In determining whether or not Zwingli is spiritualist it is necessary to see what criteria he uses for discerning whether the word is from the Lord or not. Nor is it as clear as Pollet suggests (*DTC* 3879) that Zwingli passes from an emphasis on the objective (the two righteousnesses and their aims) to an emphasis on the subjective (concern for the person of the prophet and the magistrate). The latter is also to be found in the early Zwingli, e.g. in the need for a ruler to be a Christian if he is not to be tyrant. (Z III 867.7-13, 868.37-869.4.) Equally the former is to be found in the later Zwingli. (Z XIII 415.22-31.)

# List of Zwingli's Works

ZWINGLI's works are given in the order of the modern critical edition (Z). Those in volumes 1 to 6 are numbered 1 to 167; the old testament writings in volumes 13 and 14 are numbered 1 to 7. Zwingli's letters are published in volumes 7 to 11 and his marginal notes in volume 12. The works not in the modern edition are given in the order of the Schuler-Schulthess edition (S), with the number of the volume (2, 3, 4, or 6) given first. In the modern edition, the date of publication is included in brackets afterwards.

| | |
|---|---|
| 1, 2 | The Ox (1510) |
| 3 | The Account (1512) |
| 4 | The Labyrinth (1516) |
| 5 | The Plague Song (1519) |
| 8 | Choice and Liberty Respecting Food (1522) |
| 9 | The Letter to Erasmus Fabricius (1522) |
| 10 | A Solemn Exhortation (1522) |
| 11 | The Petition (1522) |
| 12 | A Friendly Request (1522) |
| 13 | Archeteles (1522) |
| 14 | The Clarity and Certainty of the Word of God (1522) |
| 15 | A Sermon on the Virgin Mary (1522) |
| 16 | Advice (1522) |
| 17 | The Sixty Seven Articles (1523) |
| 18 | The First Disputation (1523) |
| 19 | A Defence (1523) |
| 20 | An Exposition of the Articles (1523) |
| 21 | Divine and Human Righteousness (1523) |
| 22 | The Education of Youth (1523) |
| 23 | The Canon of the Mass (1523) |
| 26 | An Apology for the Canon of the Mass (1523) |
| 27 | A Short Christian Introduction (1523) |
| 28 | The Second Disputation (1523) |
| 29 | Advice Concerning the Mass and Images (1523) |
| 30 | The Shepherd (1524) |
| 31 | On the Address of the Three Bishops (1524) |
| 34 | A True and Earnest Exhortation to the Confederation (1524) |
| 35 | A Proposal Concerning Images and the Mass (1524) |
| 36 | A Defence against Lies (1524) |
| 37 | A Christian Answer (1524) |

# Bibliography

IN the bibliography general studies of Zwingli's theology are marked with an asterisk, special studies of the eucharist with a dagger, and those of church and state with a double asterisk.

ALTING VON GEUSAU, L. G. M., *Die Lehre von der Kindertaufe bei Calvin, gesehen im Rahmen seiner Sakraments- und Tauftheologie* (Bilthoven–Mainz, 1963).

†BARCLAY, A., *The Protestant Doctrine of the Lord's Supper* (Glasgow, 1927).

†BAUER, K., 'Die Abendmahlslehre Zwinglis bis zum Beginn der Auseinandersetzung mit Luther', *Theologische Blätter*, 5 (1926) 217–26.

†— 'Symbolik und Realpräsenz in der Abendmahlsanschauung Zwinglis bis 1525. Eine Erwiderung', *ZKG* 46 (1927) 97–105.

BAUM, J. W., *Capito und Butzer, Strassburgs Reformatoren* (Elberfeld, 1860).

*BAUR, A., *Zwinglis Theologie. Ihr Werden und ihr System* (2 vols. Halle, 1885 and 1889).

BLANKE, F., 'Zu Zwinglis Entwicklung', *Kirchenblatt für die reformierte Schweiz*, 86 (1930) 197–9.

— 'Zwinglis Beitrag zur reformatorischen Botschaft', *ZWA* 5 (1931) 262–75.

*— 'Gedanken zur Frage der Eigenart Zwinglis', *Der Kirchenfreund. Blätter für evangelische Wahrheit und kirchliches Leben*, 65 (1931) 305–10, 322–7.

†— 'Zwinglis Sakramentsanschauung', *Theologische Blätter*, 10 (1931) 283–90.

†— 'Zum Verständnis der Abendmahlslehre Zwinglis', *Pastoraltheologie. Monatsschrift zur Vertiefung des gesamten pfarramtlichen Wirkens*, 27 (1931) 314–20.

†— 'Antwort', *Theologische Blätter*, 11 (1932) 18.

— 'Zwinglis Urteile über sich selbst', *Die Furche*, 22 (1936) 31–9.

— *Brüder in Christo. Die Geschichte der ältesten Täufergemeinde, Zollikon 1525* (Zurich, 1955), transl. as *Brothers in Christ. The History of the Oldest Anabaptist Congregation, Zollikon, near Zurich, Switzerland* (Pennsylvania, 1961).

†BOSSHARD, S. N., *Zwingli–Erasmus–Cajetan, Die Eucharistie als Zeichen der Einheit* (Wiesbaden, 1978).

**BROCKELMANN, B., *Das Corpus Christianum bei Zwingli* (Breslau, 1938).

BROMILEY, G. W., *Zwingli and Bullinger* (Library of Christian Classics XXIV) (London, 1953).

— *Historical Theology. An Introduction* (Edinburgh, 1978).

BROOKS, P. N., *Thomas Cranmer's Doctrine of the Eucharist* (London, 1965).

BURCKHARDT, A. E., *Das Geistproblem bei Huldrych Zwingli* (Leipzig, 1932).

BÜSCHER, H., 'Von der göttlichen Vorsehung' (Diss. Münster, 1958).

Büsser, F., *Das katholische Zwinglibild* (Zurich, 1968).
— 'Der Prophet–Gedanken zu Zwinglis Theologie', *ZWA* 13 (1969) 7–18.
— 'Das Zwingli-Bild von Emil Egli bis Fritz Blanke', *Neue Zürcher Zeitung*, 3 Jan.
1969, No. 4.
— 'De prophetae officio. Eine Gedenkrede Bullingers auf Zwingli', *Festgabe Leonhard von Muralt*, pp. 245–57 (Zurich, 1970).
— 'Zwingli und Laktanz', *ZWA* 13 (1971) 375–99.
— *Huldrych Zwingli* (Göttingen, 1973).
Cadoux, C. J., 'Zwingli', *Christian Worship*, ed. N. Micklem, pp. 137–53 (Oxford, 1936).
Christ, C., 'Das Schriftverständnis von Zwingli und Erasmus im Jahre 1522', *ZWA* 16 (1983) 111–25.
Clark, F., *Eucharistic Sacrifice and the Reformation* (London, 1960).
Clarke, J. P., 'Zwingli's Doctrine of the Sovereignty of God' (Diss. Bristol, 1974).
Cottrell, J. W., 'Covenant and Baptism in the Theology of Huldreich Zwingli' (Diss. Princeton, 1971).
**Courvoisier, J., 'Zwingli et l'état chrétien réformé', *Alma Mater. Revue universitaire*, 3 (1946) 228–40.
*— *Zwingli. A Reformed Theologian* (London, 1964).
†— 'Réflexions à propos de la doctrine eucharistique de Zwingli et Calvin', *Festgabe Leonhard von Muralt*, pp. 258–65 (Zurich, 1970).
Davies, R. E., *The Problem of Authority in the Continental Reformers* (London, 1946).
**Demandt, D., 'Zur Wirtschaftsethik Huldrych Zwinglis', *Beiträge zur Wirtschafts- und Sozialgeschichte des Mittelalters, Festschrift für Herbert Helbig zum 65. Geburtstag*, pp. 306–21, ed. K. Schulz (Cologne, 1976).
Dix, G., 'Dixit Cranmer et non Timuit', *Church Quarterly Review* 145 (1947) 145–76; 146 (1948) 44–60.
**Dreske, O., *Zwingli und das Naturrecht* (Diss. Halle, 1911).
Ebeling, G., 'Cognitio Dei et hominis', *Geist und Geschichte der Reformation. Festgabe Hanns Rückert zum 65. Geburtstag dargebracht*, pp. 271–322 (Berlin, 1966).
Egli, E., *Analecta Reformatoria, I. Dokumente und Abhandlungen zur Geschichte Zwinglis und seiner Zeit* (Zurich, 1899).
Enno van Gelder, H. A., *The Two Reformations in the Sixteenth Century* (The Hague, 1961).
**Escher, H., 'Zwingli als Staatsmann', *ZWA* 5 (1931) 297–317.
**Farner, A., *Die Lehre von Kirche und Staat bei Zwingli* (Tübingen, 1930).
Farner, O., *Huldrych Zwingli* (4 vols. Zurich, 1943, 1946, 1954, 1960).
Federer, K., 'Zwingli und die Marienverehrung', *Zeitschrift für Schweizerische Kirchengeschichte*, 45 (1951) 13–26.
Finsler, G., *Zwingli-Bibliographie* (Zurich, 1897).
Friedensburg, W., 'Martin Bucer, Von der Wiedervereinigung der Kirchen (1542)' *ARG* 31 (1934) 145–91.
Gäbler, U., *Huldrych Zwingli im 20. Jahrhundert* (Zurich, 1975).

— 'Huldrych Zwinglis "reformatorische Wende"', ZKG 89 (1978) 120–35.

GARSIDE, C., Zwingli and the Arts (New Haven, 1966).

†GERRISH, B. A., 'The Lord's Supper in the Reformed Confessions', Theology Today, 23 (1966) 224–43.

*GESTRICH, C., Zwingli als Theologe. Glaube and Geist beim Zürcher Reformator (Zurich, 1967).

†GOESER, R. J., 'Word and Sacrament: A Study of Luther's Views as Developed in the Controversy with Zwingli and Karlstadt' (Diss. Yale, 1960).

GOETERS, J. F. G., 'Die Vorgeschichte des Täufertums in Zürich', Studien zur Geschichte und Theologie der Reformation. Festschrift für Ernst Bizer, ed. L. Abramowski and J. F. G. Goeters, pp. 239–81 (Neukirchen, 1969).

— 'Zwinglis Werdegang als Erasmianer', Reformation und Humanismus. Robert Stupperich zum 65. Geburtstag, ed. M. Greschat and J. F. G. Goeters, pp. 255–71 (Witten, 1969).

†GOLLWITZER, H., 'Zur Auslegung von Joh. 6 bei Luther and Zwingli', In Memoriam Ernst Lohmeyer, ed. W. Schmauch, pp. 143–68 (Stuttgart, 1951).

GUGGISBERG, K., Das Zwinglibild des Protestantismus im Wandel der Zeiten (Leipzig, 1934).

HAAS, M., Huldrych Zwingli und seine Zeit (Zurich, 1969).

HALL, B., 'Ulrich Zwingli', A History of Christian Doctrine, ed. H. Cunliffe-Jones with B. Drewery, pp. 351–70 (Edinburgh, 1978).

HAUSWIRTH, R., Landgraf Philipp von Hessen und Zwingli (Tübingen, 1968).

HAZLETT, W. I. P., 'Zur Auslegung von Johannes 6 bei Bucer während der Abendmahlskontroverse', Bucer und seine Zeit, Forschungsbeiträge und Bibliographie, ed. M. de Kroon and F. Krüger, pp. 74–87 (Wiesbaden, 1976).

HELLER, C. N., The Latin Works of Huldreich Zwingli, Vol. III (Philadelphia, 1929) (repr. as Commentary on True and False Religion, Durham, NC, 1981).

HILLERBRAND, H. J., 'The "Turning Point" of the Zwinglian Reformation: review and discussion', MQR 39 (1965) 309–12.

HINKE, W. J., The Latin Works of Huldreich Zwingli: Vol. II (Philadelphia, 1922) (repr. as Zwingli. On Providence and Other Essays, Durham, NC, 1983).

†HOFFMANN, G., 'Sententiae Patrum—Das patristische Argument in der Abendmahlskontroverse zwischen Oekolampad, Zwingli, Luther and Melanchthon' (Diss. Heidelberg, 1971).

HOLLENWEGER, W. J., 'Zwingli writes the Gospel into his World's Agenda', MQR 43 (1969) 70–94.

**HUNT, R. N. C., 'Zwinglis Theory of Church and State', Church Quarterly Review, 112 (1931) 20–36.

†HYMA, A., 'Hoen's Letter on the Eucharist and its Influence upon Carlstadt, Bucer and Zwingli', Princeton Theological Review, 24 (1926) 124–31.

JACKSON, S. M., Huldreich Zwingli (New York, 1901).

— The Selected Works of Huldreich Zwingli (Philadelphia, 1901) (repr. 1972).

—— *The Latin Works and the Correspondence of Huldreich Zwingli*, Vol. I *1510–1522* (New York, 1912).

†JENNY, M., *Die Einheit des Abendmahlsgottesdienstes bei den elsässischen und schweizerischen Reformatoren* (Zurich, 1968).

KESSLER, J., *Sabbata*, ed. E. Egli and R. Schoch (St Gallen, 1902).

\*\*KLASSEN, P. J., 'Zwingli and the Zurich Anabaptists', *Gottesreich und Menschenreich. Ernst Staehelin zum 80. Geburtstag*, pp. 197–210 (Basle, 1969).

KNOWLES, D. (and OBOLENSKY, D.), *The Christian Centuries*, Vol. II *The Middle Ages* (London, 1969).

\*KÖHLER, W., 'Zwingli als Theologe', *Ulrich Zwingli. Zum Gedächtnis der Zürcher Reformation, 1519–1919*, pp. 9–74 (Zurich, 1919).

\*—— *Die Geisteswelt Ulrich Zwinglis. Christentum und Antike* (Gotha, 1920).

—— *Huldrych Zwinglis Bibliothek* (Zurich, 1921).

—— 'Aus Zwinglis Bibliothek', *ZWA* 4 (1921) 60.

†—— *Zwingli und Luther. Ihr Streit über das Abendmahl nach seinen politischen und religiösen Beziehungen*, I *Die religiöse und politische Entwicklung bis zum Marburger Religionsgespräch 1529* (Leipzig, 1924); II *Vom Beginn der Marburger Verhandlungen 1529 bis zum Abschluss der Wittenberger Konkordie von 1536* (Gütersloh, 1953).

†—— 'Zu Zwinglis ältester Abendmahlsauffassung', *ZKG* 45 (1926) 399–408.

†—— 'Zur Abendmahlskontroverse in der Reformationszeit, insbesondere zur Entwicklung der Abendmahlslehre Zwinglis' *ZKG* 47 (1928) 47–56.

—— *Das Religionsgespräch zu Marburg 1529. Versuch einer Rekonstruktion* (Leipzig, 1929).

—— 'Zwinglis Glaubensbekenntnis' *ZWA* 5 (1931) 242–61.

—— 'Die Randglossen Zwinglis zum Römerbrief in seiner Abschrift der paulinischen Briefe 1516/17', *Forschungen zur Kirchengeschichte und zur christlichen Kunst. Johannes Ficker als Festgabe zum 70. Geburtstag dargebracht*, pp. 86–106 (Leipzig, 1931).

\*\*Alfred Farner, *Die Lehre von Kirche und Staat bei Zwingli'*, *Zeitschrift der Savigny–Stiftung für Rechtsgeschichte*, 51 (Kanonitische Abteilung 20, 1931). 669–83.

—— *Zürcher Ehegericht und Genfer Konsistorium*, I *Das Zürcher Ehegericht und seine Auswirkung in der deutschen Schweiz zur Zeit Zwinglis* (Leipzig, 1932).

—— 'Die neuere Zwingli-Forschung', *Theologische Rundschau*, NF 4 (1932) 329–69.

—— *Huldrych Zwingli* (Leipzig, 1943).

—— *Dogmengeschichte als Geschichte des christlichen Selbstbewusstseins*, II *Das Zeitalter der Reformation* (Zurich, 1951).

KOHLS, E.-W., *Die Theologie des Erasmus* (Basle, 1966).

—— 'Erasmus und die werdende evangelische Bewegung des 16. Jahrhunderts', *Scrinium Erasmianum* Vol. 1, ed. J. Coppens pp. 203–19 (Leiden, 1969).

Kressner, H., *Schweizer Ursprünge des anglikanischen Staatskirchentums* (Gütersloh, 1953).

**Kreutzer, J., *Zwinglis Lehre von der Obrigkeit* (Stuttgart, 1909).

†Krodel, G., 'Die Abendmahlslehre des Erasmus von Rotterdam und seine Stellung am Anfang des Abendmahlsstreites der Reformation' (Diss. Erlangen, 1955).

**Kügelgen, C. von, *Die Ethik Huldreich Zwinglis* (Leipzig, 1902).

Künzli, E., 'Zwinglis theologische Wertung des Alten Testaments', *Der Kirchenfreund*, 83 (1949) 244–8, 276–84.

—— 'Quellenproblem und mystischer Schriftsinn in Zwinglis Genesis- und Exoduskommentar', *ZWA* 9 (1950–1) 185–207, 253–307.

—— 'Zwingli als Ausleger von Genesis und Exodus' (Diss. Zurich, 1951).

—— 'Zwingli als Ausleger des Alten Testamentes' *Z* XIV 869–99.

—— 'Der Mann bei Zwingli', *ZWA* 11 (1961) 351–71.

Lavater, H. R., 'Regnum Christi etiam externum—Huldrych Zwinglis Brief vom 4. Mai 1528 an Ambrosius Blarer in Konstanz', *ZWA* 15 (1981) 338–81.

Ley, R., *Kirchenzucht bei Zwingli* (Zurich, 1948).

**Locher, G. W., *Die evangelische Stellung der Reformatoren zum öffentlichen Leben* (Zurich, 1950).

*—— *Die Theologie Huldrych Zwinglis im Lichte seiner Christologie*, I *Die Gotteslehre* (Zurich, 1952).

—— 'Die Stimme des Hirten', *Oskar Farner. Erinnerungen*, pp. 111–15 (Zurich, 1954).

**—— 'Von göttlicher und menschlicher Gerechtigkeit', *Reformatio* 10 (1961) 66–80.

**——*Der Eigentumsbegriff als Problem evangelischer Theologie* (Zurich, 1962).

—— 'Die Wandlung des Zwingli-Bildes in der neueren Forschung', *ZWA* 11 (1963) 560–85.

*—— 'Grundzüge der Theologie Huldrych Zwinglis im Vergleich mit derjenigen Martin Luthers und Johannes Calvins', *ZWA* 12 (1967) 470–509, 545–95.

—— 'Zu Zwinglis "Professio fidei". Beobachtungen und Erwägungen zur Pariser Reinschrift der sogenannten Fidei Expositio', *ZWA* 12 (1968) 689–700.

—— 'Geist und Gemeinschaft—Theologie in öffentlicher Verantwortung', *Reformierte Kirchenzeitung*, 110 (1969) 7–9.

*—— *Huldrych Zwingli in neuer Sicht* (Zurich, 1969).

—— 'Zwingli und Erasmus', *ZWA* 13 (1969) 37–61.

†—— 'Die theologische und politische Bedeutung des Abendmahlsstreites im Licht von Zwinglis Briefen', *ZWA* 13 (1971) 281–304.

†—— *Streit unter Gästen* (Zurich, 1972).

—— 'Die Berner Disputation 1528—Charakter, Verlauf, Bedeutung und theologischer Gehalt', *ZWA* 14 (1978) 542–64.

\*—— *Die Zwinglische Reformation im Rahmen der europäischen Kirchengeschichte* (Göttingen, 1979).

\*\*—— 'Zwinglis Politik—Gründe und Ziele', *Theologische Zeitschrift*, 36 (1980) 84–102.

\*—— *Zwingli's Thought* (Leiden, 1981).

MAEDER, K., *Die Via Media in der Schweizerischen Reformation* (Zurich, 1970).

McNEILL, J. T., *The History and Character of Calvinism* (New York, 1954).

\*\*MEYER, P., *Zwinglis Soziallehren* (Linz, 1921).

MEYER, W. E., 'Die Entstehung von Huldrych Zwinglis neutestamentlichen Kommentaren und Predigtnachschriften', *ZWA* 14 (1976) 285–331.

\*\*MOELLER, B., *Reichstadt und Reformation* (Gütersloh, 1962), transl. as *Imperial Cities and the Reformation* (Philadelphia, 1972).

\*\*—— 'Zwinglis Disputationen: Studien zu den Anfängen der Kirchenbildung und des Synodalwesens in Protestantismus I. Teil', *Zeitschrift der Savigny-Stiftung für Rechtsgeschichte*, 87 (Kanonistische Abteilung 56, 1970) 275–324.

\*\*—— 'Kleriker als Bürger', *Festschrift für Hermann Heimpel zum 70. Geburtstag am 19. September 1971*, ii. 195–224 (Göttingen, 1972).

\*\*MURALT, L. VON, 'Zwingli als Sozialpolitiker', *ZWA* 5 (1931) 276–96.

\*—— 'Zwinglis dogmatisches Sondergut', *ZWA* 5 (1932) 321–39, 353–68.

\*\*—— 'Zum Problem der Theokratie bei Zwingli', *Discordia Concors. Festgabe für Edgar Bonjour zu seinem 70. Geburtstag am 21 August 1968* ii. 367–90. (Basle, 1968).

NAGEL, E., *Zwinglis Stellung zur Schrift* (Leipzig, 1896).

†NEUSER, W. H., 'Zwinglis Abendmahlsbrief an Thomas Wyttenbach (1523)', *Wegen en gestalten in het gereformeerd protestantisme*, pp. 35–46 (Amsterdam, 1976).

—— *Die reformatorische Wende bei Zwingli* (Neukirchen, 1977).

†NIESEL, W., 'Zwinglis "spätere" Sakramentsanschauung', *Theologische Blätter* 11 (1932) 12–17.

OBERMAN, H. A., *The Harvest of Medieval Theology* (Michigan, 1967).

—— *Forerunners of the Reformation* (London, 1967).

—— *Masters of the Reformation* (Cambridge, 1981).

OLD, H. O., *The Patristic Roots of Reformed Worship* (Zurich, 1975).

OORTHUYS, G., *De Anthropologie van Zwingli* (Leiden, 1905).

OZMENT, S. E., *The Reformation in the Cities* (New Haven, 1975).

—— *The Age of Reform 1250–1550* (New Haven, 1980).

PAYNE, J. B., *Erasmus. His Theology of the Sacraments* (Richmond, 1969).

PFISTER, R., *Das Problem der Erbsünde bei Zwingli* (Leipzig, 1939).

—— 'Zwingli als Liturg', *Der Grundriss. Schweizerische reformierte Monatschrift*, 5 (1943) 322–9.

—— *Die Seligkeit erwählter Heiden bei Zwingli* (Zurich, 1952).

—— 'Kirche und Glaube auf der Ersten Zürcher Disputation vum 29 Januar 1523', *ZWA* 13 (1973) 553–69.

PIPKIN, H. W., 'The Nature and Development of the Zwinglian Reformation to August, 1524' (Diss. Hartford, 1968).

—— *A Zwingli Bibliography* (Pittsburgh, 1972).

*POLLET, J. V., 'Zwinglianisme' *Dictionnaire de Théologie catholique*, XV 3745–928 (Paris, 1950).

—— 'Recherches sur Zwingli à propos d'ouvrages récentes', *Revue des sciences religieuses*, 28 (1954) 155–74.

—— 'Chronique de théologie historique. Seizième siècle (suite et fin). Réforme suisse', *Revue des sciences religieuses*, 37 (1963) 34–59.

*—— *Huldrych Zwingli et la Réforme en Suisse d'après les recherches récentes* (Paris, 1963).

POTTER, G. R., *Zwingli* (Cambridge, 1976).

REARDON, B. M. G., *Religious Thought in the Reformation* (London, 1981).

*RICH, A., *Die Anfänge der Theologie Huldrych Zwinglis* (Zurich, 1949).

**—— 'Zwingli als politischer Pionier', *Die Tat, 28 Dezember 1968*.

**—— 'Zwingli als sozialpolitischer Denker', *ZWA* 13 (1969) 67–89.

†RICHARDSON, C. C., *Zwingli and Cranmer on the Eucharist* (Evanston, 1949).

RILLIET, J., *Zwingli* (London, 1964).

*RITSCHL, O., *Die reformierte Theologie des 16. und 17. Jahrhunderts in ihrer Entstehung und Entwicklung* (Göttingen, 1926).

**ROGGE, J., *Zwingli und Erasmus. Die Friedensgedanken des jungen Zwingli* (Berlin, 1962).

—— 'Die Initia Zwinglis und Luthers. Eine Einführung in die Probleme', *Luther-Jahrbuch*, 30 (1963) 107–33.

**—— 'Zwingli und Luther in ihren sozialen Handlungsfeldern', *ZWA* 13 (1973) 625–44.

**ROTHER, S., *Die religiösen und geistigen Grundlagen der Politik Huldrych Zwinglis* (Erlangen, 1956).

†RÜCKERT, H., 'Das Eindringen der Tropuslehre in die schweizerische Auffassung vom Abendmahl', *ARG* 37 (1940) 199–221.

RUPP, E. G., 'Word and Spirit in the First Years of the Reformation', *ARG* 49 (1958) 13–26.

—— 'The Swiss Reformers and the Sects. The Reformation in Zürich, Strassburg and Geneva', *The New Cambridge Modern History*, Vol. II *The Reformation 1520–1559*, ed. G. R. Elton, pp. 96–119 (Cambridge, 1968).

—— *Patterns of Reformation* (London, 1969).

† Sasse, H., *This is My Body. Luther's Contention for the Real Presence in the Sacrament of the Altar* (Minneapolis, 1959).

SCHINDLER, A., *Zwingli und die Kirchenväter* (Zurich, 1984).

**SCHMID, H., *Zwinglis Lehre von der göttlichen und menschlichen Gerechtigkeit* (Zurich, 1959).

SCHMID, W., 'Der Autor der sogenannten Protestation und Schutzschrift von 1524/1525', *ZWA* 9 (1950) 139–49.

SCHMIDT-CLAUSING, F., *Zwingli als Liturgiker* (Göttingen, 1952).

— 'Johann Ulrich Surgant, ein Wegweiser des jungen Zwingli', *ZWA* 11 (1961) 287-320.
— 'Zwinglis Stellung zum Konzil', *ZWA* 11 (1962) 479-98.
— 'Das Prophezeigebet', *ZWA* 12 (1964) 10-34.
— *Zwingli* (Berlin, 1965).
— 'Das Corpus Juris Canonici als reformatorisches Mittel Zwinglis', *ZKG* 80 (1969) 14-21.
— *Zwinglis liturgische Formulare* (Frankfurt-on-Main, 1970).
— 'Die liturgietheologische Arbeit Zwinglis am Sintflutgebet des Taufformulars', *ZWA* 13 (1972) 516-43; 13 (1973) 591-615.
†SCHRENK, G., 'Zwinglis Hauptmotive in der Abendmahlslehre und das Neue Testament', *ZWA* 5 (1930) 176-85.
†SCHWEIZER, J., *Reformierte Abendmahlsgestaltung in der Schau Zwinglis* (Basle, 1954).
†SCOTT, C. A., 'Zwingli's Doctrine of the Lord's Supper', *Expositor*, 3 (1901) 161-71.
SEEBERG, E., 'Der Gegensatz zwischen Zwingli, Schwenckfeld und Luther', *Reinhold-Seeberg-Festschrift*, I, *Zur Theorie des Christentums*, pp. 43-80 (Leipzig, 1929).
SEEBERG, R., *Lehrbuch der Dogmengeschichte, IV Bd.*, 1 Abt. *Die Entstehung des protestantischen Lehrbegriffs* (Leipzig, 1933).
SIGWART, C., *Ulrich Zwingli* (Stuttgart, 1855).
SPINKA, M., *Advocates of Reform: From Wyclif to Erasmus* (Library of Christian Classics XIV) (London, 1953).
SPITZ, L. W., *The Religious Renaissance of the German Humanists* (Cambridge, Mass., 1963).
†STAEDTKE, J., 'Voraussetzungen der Schweizer Abendmahlslehre', *Theologische Zeitschrift*, 16 (1960) 19-32.
STAEHELIN, R., *Huldreich Zwingli. Sein Leben und Wirken nach den Quellen dargestellt* (2 vols. Basle, 1895 and 1897).
STAYER, J. M., 'Zwingli before Zürich: Humanist Reformer und Papal Partisan', *ARG* 72 (1981) 55-68.
STEPHENS, W. P., *The Holy Spirit in the Theology of Martin Bucer* (Cambridge, 1970).
— 'Zwingli's Reforming Ministry', *Expository Times*, 93 (1981) 6-10.
STROHL, H., *Bucer, humaniste chrétien* (Paris, 1939).
THOMPSON, B., 'Zwingli Study since 1918', *Church History*, 19 (1950) 116-28.
TIMMS, G. B., 'Dixit Cranmer', *Church Quarterly Review* 143 (1947) 217-34; 144 (1947) 33-51.
USTERI, J. M., 'Darstellung der Tauflehre Zwinglis', *Theologische Studien und Kritiken*, 55. (1882) 205-84.
— *Zwingli und Erasmus* (Zurich, 1885).
— 'Initia Zwinglii' *Theologische Studien und Kritiken*, 58 (1885) 607-72; 59 (1886) 95-159.
VASELLA, O., 'Ulrich Zwingli und Michael Gaismair, der Tiroler Bauernführer', *Zeitschrift für Schweizerische Geschichte*, 24 (1944) 388-413.

**WALTON, R. C., *Zwingli's Theocracy* (Toronto, 1967).

** — 'The Institutionalization of the Reformation at Zurich', *ZWA* 13 (1972) 497–515.

WENDEL, F., *Calvin* (London, 1963).

**WERNLE, P., 'Zwinglis und Calvins Stellung zum Staat', *Verhandlungen des Pfarrvereins (Asketische Gesellschaft) des Kantons Zürich im Jahre 1915* (1916), pp. 60–124.

* — *Der evangelische Glaube nach den Hauptschriften der Reformatoren*, II *Zwingli* (Tübingen, 1919).

WILLIAMS, G. H. (and Mergal, A. M.), *Spiritual and Anabaptist Writers* (Library of Christian Classics XXV) (London, 1957).

— *The Radical Reformation* (Philadelphia, 1962).

WOLF, D. E., 'Luther, Zwingli, Calvin', *Deutsches Pfarrerblatt*, 40 (1936) 602, 618–19, 633–4.

**WOLF, E., 'Die Sozialtheologie Zwinglis', *Festschrift Guido Kisch*, pp. 167–88 (Stuttgart, 1955).

**YODER, J. H., 'The Evolution of the Zwinglian Reformation', *MQR*, 43 (1969) 95–122.

*ZELLER, E., *Das theologische System Zwinglis* (Tübingen, 1853).

# References to Zwingli's Works

The number of each work in the modern edition (Z) is given in brackets. (See pp. 310–13.) The letters (volumes 7 to 11) are given with the year in brackets, and the marginal notes with the volume number in brackets. The commentaries (volumes 13 and 14) and the writings (volumes 2, 3, 4, and 6) in the Schuler-Schulthess edition (S) are given with the number of the volume followed by that of the work in brackets.

The Action or Practice of the Lord's Supper (51) 37, 184, 228, 233, 235, 293
The Account (3) 8, 10
An Account of the Faith (163) 7, 44, 49, 57, 61, 80, 81, 95, 102, 105, 106, 109, 113, 115, 116, 120, 127, 136, 145, 146, 151, 152–3, 174, 181, 186–8, 212–13, 241, 250–1, 258, 267–9, 280–1, 284, 298, 303, 304, 305, 308
Advice (16) 10
Advice in the Ittinger Affair (47) 182, 231
Advice Concerning the Mass and Images (29) 225, 226
An Answer to Strauss's Book (103) 6, 47, 66, 146, 178, 179, 241
An Answer to Valentin Compar (53) 7, 27, 42, 54, 57, 61, 64, 71, 106, 117, 129, 134, 155, 161, 162, 166, 174, 177, 263, 283
An Apology for the Canon of the Mass (26) 35
Archeteles (13) 10, 22, 25, 29, 32–3, 51, 52, 53, 56, 57–8, 60, 61, 62, 63, 85, 98, 156, 170, 174, 218–19, 262, 276, 283–4, 302
Articles of Peace (143) 43

Baptism, Rebaptism, and Infant Baptism (56) 39, 47, 52, 53, 65, 72, 80, 99, 110, 145, 149–50, 159, 161, 178, 185–6, 192, 194, 198, 199–206, 207, 216–17, 266, 278, 281
The Berne Notes and Speeches (112, 113) 42, 56, 58, 61, 78, 110, 118, 127, 146, 155, 178, 242, 249, 261, 263, 272
The Berne Sermons (116) 42, 81, 86, 92–3, 106, 107, 111, 115, 246, 247, 248, 249

The Canon of the Mass (23) 18, 35–6, 67, 122, 137, 154, 175, 187, 194, 219, 224–5, 226, 227, 230, 232, 261, 262, 305
Choice and Liberty Respecting Food (8) 7, 25, 30, 51, 54, 57, 58, 62, 70, 71, 85, 118, 123, 132, 156, 158, 164, 168, 194, 218, 290, 303
A Christian Answer (37) 72, 73, 75–6, 85, 122, 124, 178, 181, 225, 263, 265
The Clarity and Certainty of the Word of God (14) 7, 13, 22, 25, 32, 51–2, 53, 56, 57, 58–61, 66, 73, 82, 104, 121, 124, 132, 133, 134–5, 139–40, 141, 146, 154, 171, 275, 281

# Index of Biblical References

For the Words of Institution, see under Eucharist (page 340)

# Index of Authors

# Index of Subjects

Aaron 92

Abednego 287

Abraham 66, 69, 76, 77, 100, 101, 114, 123, 124, 126, 128, 151, 205, 206–9, 211, 214

Abdala 143

Abel 126

Abelard, Peter 118

Adam 17, 77, 82, 118, 121, 125, 126, 128, 131, 141, 147–52, 155, 159, 210, 213, 224

Adultery 95, 271, 274, 284, 299

Ahab 303, 306

Alber, Matthew 37, 47, 228, 230, 231, 236, 251

Alexander the Coppersmith 213, 263

Alexander the Great 124

Allegory 8, 13–14, 20, 64, 67, 75–9, 247, 283

Alliances 3, 5–6, 8, 41, 43, 44, 174, 265, 283, 288

Alloiosis 48, 73, 112–17, 127, 245, 246, 257, 259

Ambrose (Ambrosiaster) 17–18, 49, 52, 97, 239

Anabaptists (see also Radicals) 44, 57, 59, 64, 70, 71, 72, 73, 75, 98, 99, 100, 101, 123, 126, 132, 133, 137–8, 146, 149, 154, 157, 171, 176, 183, 184, 186, 194, 198–216, 260, 262, 263, 264–6, 267, 268, 269, 270, 273, 276–8, 281, 287, 292, 295, 298, 300, 302, 307

Anagoge 75, 76, 78

Ananias 128, 263, 301, 310

Anselm 49, 118–20, 151, 159

Anthropocentric 3, 11, 24, 26

Antigonus 126

Antioch 291, 293

Apocrypha 56

Apocryphal Gospels 57, 134

Apollos 202

Apostles 21, 36, 54, 57, 67, 72, 94, 101, 130, 135, 157, 171, 174, 175, 187, 196, 199, 203, 204, 210, 214, 216, 219, 224, 225, 247, 269, 277, 278, 280, 281, 292, 306

Aquinas, Thomas 6–7, 9, 35, 48, 49, 87, 97, 98, 102, 147, 149, 153, 292

Aristides 126

Aristophanes 17

Aristotle 6, 49, 54, 94, 308

Arius 32, 60, 66, 239

Articles, The Sixty Seven 33, 45, 51, 134, 155

Ascension 60, 69, 77, 112, 122, 238, 240, 246

Athanasian Creed (see under Creed)

Athanasius 49, 118

Athens 287

Augsburg 150, 269

Augsburg Confession 44

Augsburg, Diet of 3, 43, 44

Augustine 9, 14–15, 17–21, 22–3, 26–8, 30, 32, 49, 53, 55, 67, 73, 75, 77, 81, 82, 86, 90, 97, 115, 122, 124, 125, 126, 131, 137, 139, 140, 141, 145, 147, 149, 153, 168, 181, 182, 187, 188, 203, 205, 207, 210, 214, 227, 229–30, 233, 237, 238, 239, 251, 254, 255, 258, 261, 308

Austria 283

Avignon 31

Baal 303

Baden Disputation 5, 41, 42, 240–1

Baptism 20, 34, 35, 38–9, 40, 48, 52, 71, 72, 73, 74, 99, 101, 106, 110, 118, 122, 123, 125, 126, 145, 149, 151, 180–93, 194–217, 222–3, 237, 279, 290, 294

  and circumcision 65, 71, 99, 101, 186, 196, 197, 203, 205, 206, 208, 209–11, 214, 215, 216

  and the Holy Spirit 195, 200, 201, 202, 214, 217

  infant baptism 38, 48, 65, 72, 99, 100, 147, 149, 186, 194–217, 264, 265, 292

  inward and outward 20, 195, 198, 200–1, 209, 214, 217

God, will of (*cont.*)
  99, 102–3, 106–7, 109, 110, 111, 119,
  120, 125, 140, 141, 144, 147, 154, 163,
  165–8, 173, 261, 275, 279, 288, 294,
  296, 298, 303, 305, 306
  word of 21, 24, 25, 28, 30, 31, 32, 34, 36,
  37, 41, 42, 43, 51, 52, 53–4, 57, 58, 59,
  60, 61, 66, 68, 75, 80, 124, 132, 135,
  146, 154, 155, 168, 169, 199, 261, 263,
  266, 274–6, 279, 284, 285, 286, 287,
  288, 290–1, 293, 295, 299, 300, 301,
  304, 305, 306
  wrath of 31, 33, 90, 119, 120, 123, 147,
  152, 174, 218, 284
Goliath 22, 26, 242
Gomorrah 33
Gospel 5, 10, 11, 19, 20, 21, 23, 24, 25, 26, 30,
  32, 33, 34, 35, 41, 42, 43, 45, 46, 47, 48,
  53, 98, 101, 103, 106, 109, 110, 119,
  121, 124, 125, 126, 136, 155–9, 161,
  173, 174, 175, 202, 218, 242, 249, 272,
  275, 280, 282–5, 288, 290, 291, 293,
  302, 303, 304, 306, 307
Gospel and Law 41, 47, 164–8, 275
Government 33, 35, 40, 41, 44, 48, 71, 164,
  207
  forms of 308–9
Grace 1, 5, 18, 19, 20, 21, 24, 26, 27, 28, 67,
  83, 98, 100, 110, 111, 112, 125, 132,
  133, 141, 142, 148, 152, 154, 155, 157,
  165, 166, 168, 174, 180, 181, 182, 184,
  186, 188, 195, 197, 199, 205, 208, 212,
  214, 216, 217, 224, 250, 252, 254, 272,
  275
Gratian 237
Grebel, Conrad 35, 38, 216, 225
Greek 9, 10, 17, 18, 23, 25, 39, 40, 57, 60, 64,
  137, 275, 277, 278, 279
Gregory of Nazianzus 17, 49, 127
Gregory of Nyssa 17–18, 49, 127
Grüt, Joachim am 42, 233, 236
Guilt 140, 142, 147, 149–52, 204

Haller, Berchtold 22, 54, 88, 138, 210
Haner, John 119
Hätzer, Ludwig 50, 137
Heathen 10, 12, 54, 82, 89, 131, 140, 144,
  152, 228

Heaven 12, 49, 126, 143, 194
Hebrew 30, 39, 40, 57, 60, 64, 67, 73, 137,
  275, 277, 278, 279
Hercules 26, 126, 242
Hermann, Konrad 236
Herod 304, 306
Hezekiah 126, 292, 293
Hilary of Poitiers 21, 49, 230, 233
Hoen, Cornelis 37, 47, 130, 190, 192, 225,
  226, 227–9, 234, 235, 239, 254, 256,
  258
Homer 14, 49
Hubmaier, Balthasar 35, 40, 50, 51, 168,
  194, 207–8, 217, 278
Humanism 2, 3, 5, 7, 8, 9–17, 28, 30, 32, 40,
  41, 44, 49, 59, 74, 93, 109, 126, 144,
  157
Hutten, Ulrich von 11

Idolatry 13, 24, 46, 66, 70, 80, 108, 155, 179,
  223, 232
Image (*see under* God)
Images 5, 7, 34, 35, 36, 37, 42, 46, 62, 67,
  155, 162, 169, 174, 178, 226, 276, 287,
  291, 293
Indulgences 23, 29, 45, 118, 169
Influences 2, 3, 5, 6–21, 26, 49, 108
Intercession of the Saints 23, 31, 33, 37, 42,
  46, 67, 78, 108, 118, 169, 263
Interest 33, 34, 35, 38, 284, 296
Inward-Outward 7, 15–16, 20, 35, 44, 47,
  68, 135–6, 145, 176, 184, 187, 188, 189,
  191, 195, 198, 251, 280, 292, 296–7,
  299, 305, 307
  (*see also under* Man *and* Word)
Irenaeus 49, 118, 151
Isaac 66, 76, 77, 92, 126, 214
Isaiah 67, 68, 126, 188, 244
Israel 31, 75, 88, 100, 211, 242, 265, 285,
  288, 292
Italy 183

Jacob 75, 77, 92, 101, 105, 106, 126, 151
James 66, 248
Jehosophat 281
Jeremiah 188, 270, 279, 302, 304, 310
Jerome 14, 17–19, 21, 49, 55, 56, 73, 74, 97,
  230, 233, 239, 275